W9-ABK-296

WHO SPEAKS for CANADA?

WORDS THAT SHAPE A COUNTRY

DESMOND MORTON
& MORTON WEINFELD

M&S

Copyright © 1998 by Desmond Morton and Morton Weinfeld

All rights reserved. The use of any part of this publication reproduced, transmitted in any form or by any means, electronic, mechanical, photocopying, recording, or otherwise, or stored in a retrieval system, without the prior written consent of the publisher – or, in case of photocopying or other reprographic copying, a licence from the Canadian Copyright Licensing Agency – is an infringement of the copyright law.

Canadian Cataloguing in Publication Data

Who speaks for Canada? : words that shape a country

Includes bibliographical references.
ISBN 0-7710-6502-7

1. Canada – Literary collections.   2. Canada – History.   3. Canadian literature (English).*
I. Morton, Desmond, 1937–   .   II. Weinfeld, Morton.

PS8237.C35W46 1998   C810.8´03271   C98-932081-2
PR9194.52.C3W46 1998

We acknowledge the financial support of the Government of Canada through the Book Publishing Industry Development Program for our publishing activities. We further acknowledge the support of the Canada Council for the Arts and the Ontario Arts Council for our publishing program.

Set in Minion by M&S, Toronto
Printed and bound in Canada

McClelland & Stewart Inc.
The Canadian Publishers
481 University Avenue
Toronto, Ontario
M5G 2E9

1 2 3 4 5   02 01 00 99 98

Acknowledgements

To simplify the lengthy acknowledgements we have cut the information back to the bare bones, thus each listing reads simply author, title of the publication, and the source of the permission to use it here (usually a publisher):

ABELLA, IRVING and TROPER, HAROLD, *None is Too Many*, Key Porter Books; ADAMS, BRYAN and VALLANCE, JIM, "Tears Are Not Enough," Warner-Chappell and United Way of the Lower Main Land, B.C; ATWOOD, MARGARET, *Survival*, McClelland & Stewart; BERGER, THOMAS, *Fragile Freedoms*, Stoddart Publishing; BERTON, PIERRE, *Why We Act Like Canadians*, McClelland & Stewart; BIBB, HENRY and JACKSON, WHITNEY, *Slave Testimony*, Louisiana State University Press; BIRNEY, EARLE, *Turvey*, McClelland & Stewart; BLAIS, MARIE-CLAIRE, *The Manuscripts of Pauline Archange*, John C. Goodwin et Associés; CANADIAN CONFERENCE OF CATHOLIC BISHOPS, *Ethical Reflections on the Economic Crisis*, Canadian Conference of Catholic Bishops; CARRIER, ROCH, *The Hockey Sweater and Other Stories*, Stoddart Publishing; CARROLL, DINK, "Royals win Little World Series for first time in their history," Montreal *Gazette*; BROWN, ROSEMARY, *Being Brown*, Rosemary Brown; CLARK, JOE, "Community of Communities," The Rt. Honourable Joseph Clark; CHONG, DENISE, "Being Canadian," Denise Chong; COHEN, LEONARD, *Selected Poems, 1956-1968*, McClelland & Stewart; CONNORS, TOM, "Sudbury Saturday Night," Crown Vetch Music; CREIGHTON, DONALD, *The Empire of the St.Lawrence*, Estate of Donald Creighton; DAVIES, ROBERTSON, *One Half of Robertson Davies*, Macmillan Canada; DESBIENS, JEAN-PAUL, *Les Insolences du Frère Untel*, Sogides Ltée; DESCHAMPS, YVON, *Tout Deschamps*, Lanctôt Éditeur; DIEFENBAKER, JOHN G., "Unhyphenated Canadian," *Maclean's*; DOUGLAS, TOMMY, *Till Power is Brought to Pooling: Tommy Douglas Speaks*, L.D. Lovick, ed., Oolichan Books; FRYE, NORTHROP, *The Bush Garden*, Stoddart Publishing; GÉLINAS, GRATIEN, *Tit-Coq*, Stoddart Publishing and Production Gratien Gélinas Ltée; GEORGE, DAN, *My Heart Soars*, Hancock House; GRANT, GEORGE, *Lament for a Nation*, Carleton University Press; GUSTAFSON, RALPH, *The Moment is All*, McClelland & Stewart; GZOWSKI, PETER, *The Game of Our Lives*, McClelland & Stewart; HAIG-BROWN, R.,

"British Columbia: Loggers and Lotus-Eaters," Valerie Haig-Brown; HARPER, ELIJAH, *No Ordinary Hero,* Douglas and McIntyre; HEMSWORTH, WADE, "The Blackfly Song," Pear Music; JULIEN, PAULINE, "Les Femmes," Pauline Julien; LAYTON, IRVING, "From Colony to Nation," Westwood Creative Artists; KOGAWA, JOY, "What Do I Remember of the Evacuation," Joy Kogawa; LAURENCE, MARGARET, "Where the World Began," *Maclean's;* LÉVESQUE, RENÉ, *Option Québec,* Sogides Ltée; LEWIS, DAVID, "Corporate Welfare Bums," The New Democratic Party; MACKENZIE, LEWIS, *Peacekeeper,* Douglas & McIntyre; MANNING, PRESTON, "New Canada," Preston Manning; MITCHELL, JONI, "Big Yellow Taxi," S.L. Feldman & Associates; MITCHELL, W.O., *Who Has Seen the Wind,* Macmillan Canada; MOWAT, FARLEY, "Farley Mowat Speaks Out on Vietnam," Farley Mowat Limited; NEATBY, HILDA, *So Little for the Mind,* Stoddart Publishing; NOWLAN, ALDEN, *A Thousand Shall Fall,* Stoddart Publishing; ONDAATJE, MICHAEL, "Burning Hills," Michael Ondaatje; OUELLETTE, FERNAND, "Language, History and Memory," Éditions Hurtubise HMH Ltée; PEDEN, MURRAY, *A Thousand Shall Fall,* Stoddart Publishing; PRATT, E.J., "Towards the Last Spike," University of Toronto Press; RINGUET, "Montreal in the 1950s," Editions Fides; ROGERS, STAN, "Northwest Passage," Fogarty Cove Music; ROY, GABRIELLE, *The Tin Flute,* McClelland & Stewart; RYAN, CLAUDE, "The Canadian Solution," Claude Ryan; SAVARD, FÉLIX, "Les Oies Sauvages," Editions Fides; SCOTT, F.R., "On the War Measures Act," Peter Scott; SCOTT, F.R., *The Collected Poems of F.R. Scott,* McClelland & Stewart; SERVICE, ROBERT, "The Cremation of Sam McGee," M.W. Krasilovsky, Agent; SUZUKI, DAVID, "Ancestors: The Source," Dr. David Suzuki; TRUDEAU, PIERRE, "On Quebec Nationalism and Separation," The Rt. Honourable Pierre Elliott Trudeau.

We also acknowledge the following valuable resource: Michel Le Bel and Jean-Marcel Paquette, *Le Québec par ses textes littéraires, 1534-1976* (Montréal: Fernand Nathan, 1979).

Grateful acknowledgement is given to the copyright holders of material in this book for their permission to reprint. Every effort has been made to secure all permissions required. In case of any error or omission, upon notification a correction will be made in a subsequent printing.

Contents

Part Three: 1921-1960

Part Four: 1960 to the Present

Preface

We have all been shaped by the words that have poured over us since our moment of first awareness – words of love, warning, anger, wisdom, temptation. And some of those words have shaped our understanding of ourselves as people of this country called Canada. Here are voices that express a deep love for the country and its people, and others that are angry because Canada has not lived up to their ideals. Some reflect the special perspective of the cultures, languages, and regions that make up this vast and deliberately diverse country. Some have grown from the experiences of Canadians in peace and war, in cities and countryside, and on the harshly beautiful northern frontier. Indeed, as this project developed, the diversity of Canada became increasingly apparent to us. One expected theme – our alleged complacency and self-satisfaction – faded. On the contrary, Canadians have high, perhaps even impossibly high, aspirations for their country.

This book was conceived by Morton Weinfeld, director of McGill University's Ethnic Studies Program, who then approached Gilles Paquet, a leading economist at the University of Ottawa. Both cheerfully acknowledged the inspiration of Diane Ravitch's *The American Reader*, which captured in words and images the essence of being American. The project was adopted in 1994 by the new McGill Institute for the Study of Canada, whose director, Desmond Morton, joined the team. From the outset, our work was supported by funding and encouragement from the Canadian Department of Citizenship and Immigration, and items have been available since 1995 on its website. Sadly, Professor Paquet found himself hopelessly overburdened with unexpected teaching responsibilities and had to withdraw. We have benefited from his involvement. John Thompson, head of Canadian Studies at Duke University, was another source of ideas, as were Danielle Juteau, a sociologist at the Université de Montréal, and Tina Loo, a historian at Simon Fraser University. The project has also benefited from several patient and highly knowledgeable researchers: Francine McKenzie of the University of Toronto, Sandi Viger of Concordia University, René Guindon of the Université du Québec à Montréal, and Lisa Salhany and Joe O'Shea of McGill University. David Curtis of McGill's Music Library, Sue Adams and Nancy Maclean, librarians at

McMaster University, and Carol Ricketts of McClelland and Stewart provided invaluable help in tracking down copyright and permissions. The book has been reshaped and improved by our editor, Dr. Curtis Fahey. In 1996 we gained the enthusiastic support of Douglas Gibson of McClelland and Stewart. We would also like to thank translators Robert Chodos and Wanda Taylor. In the end, however, the editors alone are responsible for the content of this book.

Who Speaks for Canada? is a compilation of the personal choices of two Canadians of utterly different backgrounds whose common experience is sharing this country for the past half-century and more and spending the last few years of the twentieth century in offices in an old house on Montreal's Peel Street. From our own different experiences, we assembled prose and poetry, fiction and non-fiction that had spoken to each of us, and, if we found that they spoke powerfully to both of us, they survived. There are gaps, sometimes because a few memorable words or lines did not prove to have sufficient context, sometimes because we have not yet found what we were seeking, and mostly because of those twin disabilities of unconscious blindness and "invincible ignorance." Below, you will see how you are invited to repair both of these defects.

Canadians have spoken of their country in more than words. Artists and photographers have left indelible images of a Canada we may remember, and particularly of a land which we are too young to have known. Once again, our selection of illustrations for this book was a highly personal process, guided by our own interests, temperaments, and memories.

But why not your choices? Why not indeed? Canadians speak in many voices, and listen with many ears. *Who Speaks for Canada?* is an unfinished project until you participate. From all the billions of words Canadians have addressed to other Canadians, we have collected only an imperfect sample. Now it is your turn to help entertain, enlighten, and inspire. Contributions from our readers, accepted by a broadly representative editorial committee, will be electronically published on the website of the McGill Institute for the Study of Canada as a second – online – volume. If the response is sufficient, we are as confident as the publisher that a second volume of a more traditional sort will soon appear, even better than the first. All we ask is that contributions, limited to a maximum of a thousand words, accompanied by a brief explanatory note on its source and significance, and publication permission from the copyright owner, be sent by mail to WHOSPEAKS, McGill Institute for the Study of Canada, 3463 Peel Street, Montreal, Quebec, H3A 1W7, or electronically to whospeaks@leacock.lan.mcgill.ca.

To return to the book at hand, a couple of editorial notes are in order. First, except for those pieces that have been translated from French to English, the selections have been reprinted exactly as they appeared in their original form; we have corrected the odd typographical error, but we have not changed the punctuation, grammar, or style. Secondly, the arrangement of most of the selections in the different parts of the book is based on the date of their original publication; for example, a piece published in 1928 appears in Part Three. In some cases, however, an article's historical nature warranted its being placed in the section of the book covering a certain period. So, for instance, Joy Kogawa's essay "What Do I Remember of the Evacuation" is found in Part Three, covering the era of the Second World War, rather than in Part Four, devoted to the years from 1960 to the present, which is when the article was published.

Introduction

I

DESMOND MORTON

A great Canadian historian, Maurice Careless, has argued that Canadians are people with what he calls "limited identities." Canadians live with a number of loyalties. We are French Canadians or Alberta Canadians or Maritime Canadians. Native Canadians are divided among more than six hundred First Nations. If we came from elsewhere – and who hasn't? – we have our hyphens: even those who defiantly reject them are called "unhyphenated-Canadians."

One feature of hyphenated Canadianism is that each of us tends to start the history of Canada from the moment of his or her arrival. The idea that we should respect the traditions and values that made Canada sufficiently attractive to draw immigrants begins to fade soon after the citizenship test. Each wave of newcomers feels entitled to remake the country. Don't complain: this is older than maple syrup. While we don't exactly know how the first settlers from Asia behaved, we do know what Jacques Cartier did in 1534, or Champlain in 1608: they took over the land on behalf of the King of France, as though millions of aborigi-

nal people were shadows in the forest. According to the official version, Ontario's history began in 1784, when refugees from the American colonies became United Empire Loyalists. What about the French living near modern-day Windsor, or the First Nations just about anywhere? They were ignored. Post-1815 British immigrants found Upper Canada too American by far and helped crush an uprising in 1837 that could have made Upper Canada an American state. And successive waves of immigrants have tried, like their predecessors, to make Canada more comfortable for them.

There is another common thread to our history. We are here, on the whole, because we, or our forebears, wanted to get rich or, to be more realistic, to escape poverty. This is crudely materialistic, but let's face facts. Why else did our first inhabitants cross the land bridge from Asia? Why did more recent arrivals brave the terrible voyage from Europe to a country which offered few of the balmy attractions of the South Seas or the Caribbean? They came to make money – from the fishery, the fur trade, forests, or any other portable product from wheat to whisky. Their dream was to go home wealthy and some Canadians still do. To get rich, men and women trekked inland, hunting for fresh supplies of fur, better trade routes, deeper forests, and more good land. They endured hardships, took risks, and sacrificed their present for a future. Newcomers to Canada still do. And, on the whole, most Canadians have prospered. We can deplore poverty as cruelly unnecessary because a majority of people in Canada live comfortably.

Next, we must admit that Canada has been populated by losers. After 1760, French Canadians were left behind when their leaders scooted back to France. The Loyalists lost the American War of Independence. From Britain after 1815 came refugees from the post-1815 depression or the Irish famine. In the 1890s came people who fled tsarist pogroms and central European poverty. Canada has been a refuge for broken economic and national dreams – Poles, Czechs, Ukrainians, Vietnamese boat people. Is this a disaster? Losers have to go somewhere and, when they reflect on their condition, the experience may make them just a little more tolerant and reasonable than their neighbours. And though it would be uncharacteristic for Canadians to admit it, this nation of losers has been a winner for most of its people.

Canadians have some things in common. We support medicare and grumble about Toronto. We tend to mumble in both official languages. Marketers know that English and French Canadians resemble each other more than they resemble any other North Americans. Canada exists because our ancestors rejected the Manifest Destiny that nineteenth-century Americans saw in their tea leaves. We rejected the American way, from the *ancien régime* to Ronald Reagan. We expanded westward before the Americans even saw any use for land north of the 49th parallel. We have institutions, from Parliament to universal health insurance, that most of us instinctively cherish, even without understanding them very well. Of course, some Canadians in each generation wonder whether we made a colossal error in *not* becoming Americans. Until recently, Canada was the largest single source of U.S. immigrants – people who individually tried to remedy that collective error. Critics believe that the 1989 Free Trade Agreement will resume Americanization; others insist that it lowers the costs of remaining Canadian.

My Canadian roots are scattered through that history. Among the four families that bred my parents, the longest settled was my mother's ancestor, Nathaniel Frink. A native-born New Yorker, he accompanied Benedict Arnold (a notorious traitor in American history) to Saint John, New Brunswick, and stayed behind when his boss allegedly burned his well-insured warehouse and decamped to England. Ironically, the Frink family fortunes would come to depend on the insurance business. My maternal grandmother met her husband because of insurance. She was born Constance Vail Howard at Sutton on Lake Simcoe, Ontario, and her parents were part of a small colony of impoverished middle-class families living on remittances and bequests from England. Among her playmates was young Stephen Leacock, whose father, Peter, added zest to local life when he ran away with a governess. Connie took her own fate in hand, and went to Toronto to train as a nurse. She hated it, and learned instead to be a "typewriter" in an insurance office. Through brains and character she absorbed enough about the business to be transferred to New York and to find herself, in due course, the first female corporate secretary of an insurance company. When handsome young Harry Frink came to New York to learn the trade, he became her pupil, she became his wife, and her life was thence bound by domesticity, maternity, and cruel frustration.

My paternal grandmother was Edrol Otter, named by her father, Will, from the initials of the winning crew in Canada's first national rowing championships in 1867. Will Otter was equally a champion in lacrosse and gymnastics. Edrol's grandfather, Alfred Otter, second son of the bishop of Chichester, had come to the Huron Tract of Upper Canada in 1841 to join the landed gentry, and discovered, to his surprise, that farming was hard work. He promptly compounded his troubles by marrying the gorgeous but penniless Anna de la Hooke. Finally, he retreated to a clerk's stool at the Canada Company, where he was eventually fired for conspiring to get his boss's job. Will Otter, Alfred's eldest son, would restore the family's fortunes. He began, like his father, as a clerk for the Canada Company, and died a Canadian general, a knight of the Order of the Bath, and a modestly wealthy man. His daughter Edrol married Edward Morton, heir

to a very Canadian fortune. Edward's father, Benjamin, used his opportunities in a small savings and loan company to buy up suburban land in Scarborough and sell it as Toronto grew. Edward wanted to be a soldier, but his father insisted that he take over the family business, Like many a dutiful son, he rode it down to ruin. At Will Otter's expense, Edward and Edrol's sons went to the Royal Military College in Kingston and became soldiers. Then, on a ship to England in 1929, my father and my mother met and, after a long courtship, my mother abandoned university and dreams of a law degree for the adventures and poverty of a soldier's wife in Calgary, Ottawa, Winnipeg, Tokyo, and a host of smaller places.

Being a soldier's son was an enormous asset for someone who has spent a lifetime engaged with the history, politics, and social reality of Canada. Imagine the benefits of being born in Calgary and schooled in half the provinces of Confederation. I have lived in towns and cities from the Foothills to the Bay of Fundy and, if I have yet to spend more than a couple of months in British Columbia, custom dictates that good Canadians are allowed to go there only if they have been good for a very long time.

Of course, no one can manage to cover more than a small fraction of Canada's diversity. One big block is missing: *le fait québécois*. My father, who had fought alongside the Règiment de Chaudière in Normandy in 1944, believed in Quebec and the French fact as the foundation of Canada's survival. So did his brother, who arranged that I come home from

Japan in 1954 to attend the Collège militaire royal de Saint-Jean. It takes a bit of time to learn some of the things you should know, and even longer to discover the things you don't know. Three years at CMR were only the start of a lifetime (unfinished at the time of writing) of trying to understand and interpret the relationship of French and English in Canada. This book is an instalment in trying to communicate what I have learned.

A typical but key misunderstanding among Canadians underlies Quebec's place in Confederation. Many in Quebec, English- and French-speaking, opposed the federation of Britain's North American colonies because it undermined the balance Canada East and Canada West had achieved by the 1850s. Defeated, the opponents looked again at the constitutions born out of the British North America Act, and a new understanding emerged. Close study of the debates in 1864 and 1865, along with a rereading of Alpheus Todd and other constitutional experts, suggested that Confederation really was a solemn compact, not merely among provinces, but between French and English. That interpretation, little known and generally disparaged outside Quebec, became the basis of understanding Canada's federalism in Quebec law schools and political science departments. Then, in 1982, Canada's new Constitution Act removed any claim that Quebec, as a partner, had a veto in most possible constitutional amendments. Unknown to most Canadians, though not to their prime minister, a cherished

Quebec interpretation of Canadian federalism had died. Would anyone wonder why Quebeckers, federalists and sovereignists alike, would refuse to ratify the 1982 Constitution, or why a deep sense of betrayal persists? Indeed, it may be stronger among those who have seen Canada as their country than among the minority of Quebeckers who unequivocally seek independence.

First Nations peoples are present in this anthology, speaking with eloquence, and sometimes with practicality, about the land and their place in it. But more than most of us, native peoples respect the voices of silence. To those of us trained to fill the air with talk, silence is irritating, then exasperating, even unnerving, and, finally, calming and profoundly informing. There are perhaps two hundred thousand words in this book, some in French, more in English. And there is space for silence too.

Like journalists, historians seem to emphasize bad news. Someone has to do it. *Who Speaks for Canada?* has much that is critical, even dismissive, of Canada. Yet I would not be honest if I did not conclude with my conviction that Canada has the strength to pull through. We can be divided in our identities, uncertain in our allegiances, because we are blessed by unaggressive neighbours. It takes a little time to find that most Canadians, French- and English-speaking, First Nations and newcomers, take a quiet pride in this country and are committed to it. Canadians have a democratic political system; if our leaders fail us, or merely grow wearisome, they are replaced. There are national traditions of civility, tolerance, and cooperation which, however imperfectly, set standards for civil conduct.

Canadians have more in common than our climate. We know that we are partners in a vast, beautiful, and sometimes demanding land. We have a future of hope and opportunity if we can muster the good sense to live quietly and wisely with our good fortune.

II

MORTON WEINFELD

I am the son of Polish Jewish immigrants who came to Canada – to Montreal – in 1948 after having survived the horrors of the Holocaust. My parents spoke Polish to each other, and English to me. Ours was a traditional Jewish home, though not strictly Orthodox. I was educated through the end of high school in the Jewish day-school system, which was unusual for that period. My parents never "made it" financially. Though my father had been a successful lawyer in pre-war Poland, he worked as a bookkeeper and office manager in Montreal, for Jewish communal organizations, at modest pay. We lived in apartments and were never able to buy a house. We got our first car when I was seventeen. From my family and their experiences I learned the dangers of intolerance and the importance of fair treatment for all minorities. I also learned to value the enrichment that can come from ethnocultural and spiritual heritage. And I came to appreciate, and love, Canada, in all its diversity.

The Jewish/anglophone community in Montreal in the 1960s was the decisive feature of my external environment as I was growing up. Sociologists dating back to Karl Mannheim have recognized the importance of "generation" in explaining behaviour. My generation in Montreal came of age as French nationalism in Quebec emerged onto the streets, on ballots, in classrooms, and later in boardrooms. While I was certainly part of a third solitude in Montreal, I felt then – as I do today – a visceral admiration for the efforts of French Quebeckers to retain their identity in a continental sea of English. That struggle resonated with my understanding of a similar Jewish experience, a concern for survival – "*la survivance*" – whether as a Diaspora minority or in the struggling state of Israel. I learned to speak French not in school but working in a hardware store in east-end Montreal.

Parallel to this background was the emergence of the "ethnic revival" of the 1960s and 1970s: Black Power, Red Power, even renewed interest in Jewish and other European identities. The advent of feminism, the student movement, and the counter-culture of drugs, sex, and music provided a socio-cultural counterpoint to the particularistic concerns of group and national identities. The reflexive anti-Americanism that was embraced both by Canadian nationalists and by left-wing Americans involved in the civil-rights movement and the anti-war protests of the Vietnam era was pervasive. All these winds blew hot and heavy through the corridors of McGill University in the late 1960s, where I did my undergraduate degree. Canadian identity was certainly defined in large part by being non-American – or anti-American.

From this foundation I developed a sense of multiple, and non-conflicting, identities – a trademark of Canadian life. Rather than "zero-sum," in a strangely postmodern way such identities can become – when not overly politicized – self-reinforcing. Identities should be used not as a club with which to bash other Canadians but as components of a treasured heritage which can be shared by all. My experience is that when Canadians ask someone, "Where are you from?" they are usually genuinely curious and intend no malice.

In fact, we Canadians of my generation were a privileged, perhaps spoiled, group. Without a Vietnam War and a draft, we were spared the agonizing American choices of service or draft evasion. We were also spared the American urban riots and American racism, which helped nourish a sense of moral superiority. We were smug. We had medicare, the CBC, and few guns to speak of.

Indeed, our generation was also privileged economically. Unlike our parents, who had known privation either in Canada during the Great Depression or in the old country, we baby boomers rode the coat-tails of the post-war expansion. At the time, I sensed that Canada was one of the greatest countries in which to live – and this well before the recent United Nations studies that have tended to confirm that impression. We made sure that we had a maple leaf sewn on our backpacks as we trekked through Europe; we were not ugly Americans.

But what of the ample evidence of anti-Semitism lasting into the post-war period, and the forced relocation of Japanese Canadians during the war? What of the ongoing personal and systemic discrimination directed at First Nations and visible minorities in Canada? Is there really all that much to celebrate in Canada? My answer is a modestly qualified yes. As I make the case for Canada, I reflect both my personal history as well as my professional assessments, rooted in the study of ethnicity and race in Canada and elsewhere.

A sociologist studying the raw socio-economic data of my father's life would have found in his story clear proof of anti-Semitism. Looking at the raw data, she would see a Jewish lawyer working as a poorly paid white-collar worker. Surely this is a result of anti-Semitism, as well as of the anti-immigrant bias which undervalued his Polish law degree? And, as we know from studies like Irving Abella and Harold Troper's *None is Too Many* and John Porter's *The Vertical Mosaic*, anti-Semitism and ethnic prejudice and inequality *were* pervasive in the Canada of the late 1940s. So, case closed.

But the truth is more nuanced. While anti-Semitism no doubt percolated in the boardrooms of elite corporations, some government offices, and, yes, the academy, my father to my knowledge never encountered any as he made his occupational choices. Neither did my mother, who also worked as a bookkeeper for a company owned by another Jewish immigrant. They loved Canada, even though they lived in a world that was insulated from the English and the French communities around them. In this, of course, they emulated the pattern followed by most immigrants to Canada. Theirs was not simply a Jewish world, but one even more circumscribed – comprising mainly Holocaust survivors of Polish origin. Yet they did not feel excluded from anything.

My father's decision to find work rather than try to retrain as a lawyer was based on circumstantial needs of the moment, a dilemma faced by many immigrants. My parents appreciated Canada's freedoms in a way that many immigrants do, and many Canadian-born do not. His was a relative judgment, rooted in other places and times, but it guided his thinking and shaped mine as well. I still evaluate Canada within an implicit or explicit comparative framework. My parents were delighted that, by and large, Canadians were not visited by secret police knocking at their doors at midnight. They recognized that Canada was a land of plenty; my father used to pause and gaze at the well-stocked front window of Dunn's Delicatessen on Montreal's St. Catherine Street,

thereby reaffirming that conviction. Most important, my parents, especially my mother, had a sense that Canada, unlike the Eastern Europe they had left, was a place where their son would be able to advance professionally with very few discriminatory barriers. And they were right.

Societies can be judged best not by their sins but by the nature of their atonement or redress. The abuse of power in Richard Nixon's 1972 campaign was followed by his forced resignation. Similarly, in Germany, the unspeakable horror of the Holocaust was followed by a major program of restitution, of material support for the young state of Israel, and of painful reckoning with the past.

Before reviewing Canada's record in this sense, we should note first that Canada has had to accommodate a rare fourfold pattern of diversity. The French-English divide reflects European-style historic *national and linguistic* antagonisms. The tensions between whites and our First Nations reflect the divide between *aboriginal* communities and European colonists. The *racial* gap is reflected in the merging distinctions between all visible minorities and whites. And, finally, Canada is an *immigrant* society, where tensions of integration exist between successive waves of newcomers and the established host population. Perhaps only South Africa has historically matched Canada in this range of diversity; and Canada's approach has been far preferable to that of South Africa under apartheid.

Much has changed in the second half of the twentieth century. Canada's forced relocation and dispossession of the Japanese during the Second World War was followed, much later, by an official apology and compensation, and soon after 1945 Japanese-Canadian incomes climbed well above the Canadian average. Previously victimized European immigrant groups, including Jews, now take their full place in Canadian society. The increasing proportion of non-European and non-white immigrants in the post-war period, and the inequalities they face, have posed new challenges to Canadian tolerance and social harmony, and also to the image of a racism-free society. While these groups are no longer systematically excluded from our shores as in the past, the record in Canada is mixed. Some groups are making social progress, others are encountering greater resistance.

Two challenges are more daunting. The people of Quebec have yet to determine their proper place in the country. The generations-long discrimination against French Canada by both business elites as well as by the federal government has given way to a determination to enhance the force of the French fact in Ottawa. Canadian federalism has had the suppleness to allow all provinces, but Quebec in particular, to expand their powers in the post-war period. Clearly, the process has not been completed; indeed, it may never be. But it is to the credit of all Canadians, both English and French, that the unfolding of the national and constitutional debate has taken place in relative civility and within a democratic framework, to which all sides seem attached. It is not clear whether other democratic societies would be similarly able to tolerate a situation where the leader of the "loyal" national parliamentary opposition – Lucien Bouchard – was head of a party dedicated to the secession of one unit and a possibly destabilizing rupture of the country. Canada's historic talent for accommodation and compromise is being tested anew. But both English Canadians and Québécois might recall that the French in Canada were and remain *"fondateurs et batisseurs du Canada."* It is the French fact, and Quebec, which help make Canada a distinct society.

The second challenge is the dismal condition of the First Nations in Canada. Here the failures remain greatest, and possible solutions – such as the settlement of outstanding land claims and the granting of self-government – are fraught with theoretical and practical impediments. Though the Canadian process of Indian conquest was not as bloody as the Indian wars in the United Sates, the current social and political conditions of our First Nations are, if anything, worse than those south of the border. Our debt to aboriginal Canadians is greatest, and it remains unpaid. We are diminished as a result.

Despite our unfinished agenda, the rest of the world, for reasons that some Canadians may find strange, continues to look to Canada as a model of a tolerant, harmonious society made up of diverse elements. This is true in policy-making fields dealing with immigration and intergroup relations. Multiculturalism may be our best-known export.

I recall a meeting with officials of the city of Moscow in 1990. They were facing unprecedented migration of minorities into the city and were frightened about the possibility of increased intergroup tensions. Naturally, they thought that Canada had lessons to impart! The same was true when a Japanese social scientist led a delegation to study Canadian multiculturalism one summer. One reason for the visit was the slow increase in the tiny number of non-Japanese, mainly other Asians, in the country. The Japanese, too, wanted to be well prepared to avoid strife by learning from the Canadian experience.

We are seen as a helpful middle power, with a bent for peacekeeping. It may be that others esteem Canada more than we do ourselves. We are so insecure that we believe in our self-worth only when the tributes flow from others, such as the United Nations or the American social critic Ralph Nader in his laudatory book *Canada Firsts*. Perhaps that is not so terrible.

Canada for too long has projected an identity based only on its vast size, seemingly limitless resources, rugged mountains, and beautiful lakes. It is said that in Auschwitz "Canada" was the nickname for the guard detail that collected the new inmates' possessions, as well as for the storehouse where these were kept. The name symbolized wealth and opportunity. "The land is strong" was conceived as a campaign slogan by the Trudeau Liberals in 1972. And the Rockies are indeed inspiring. But the people are strong too. This book, for its part, is about Canada's founders, leaders, crusaders, reformers, artists, and so-called ordinary people who together have tried to make Canada a better place and to define the essence of this unique country.

The strength of Canada is apparent to the world community. It should also be apparent to Canadians, whatever their background, language, region, class, or gender. This volume presents the people who are the foundation of that strength, in their own words and as seen in photos and works of art. There is no reason for excessive triumphalism, for we still have work to do. But, as we move into the next century, let us pause for a moment of quiet satisfaction.

Part One
To Confederation

Pierre Boucher (1622–1717)

LIFE IN NEW FRANCE

What was life like in the tiny colony of New France a couple of generations after Samuel de Champlain established his *Habitation* under the shadow of Quebec's Cap Diamant? This is how it looked to Pierre Boucher, a native of Mortagne in Perche who arrived in New France in 1635 and rapidly emerged as one of the colony's toughest and most efficient leaders.

Governor of Trois-Rivières, judge, and seigneurial founder of Boucherville, Boucher was a redoubtable character who was immensely proud of what his fellow settlers had achieved and, at the same time, enraged that their lives and achievements should be menaced still by the Iroquois. His account is taken from his *Histoire véritable et naturelle des moeurs et productions du pays de la Nouvelle-France*, published in 1664.

During my stay in France, various questions on the subject of New France were put to me by worthy people. I think I shall oblige the curious reader by mentioning them here and by making a chapter of them and of my answers to them, which will give a good deal of information and knowledge to those who have an affection for this country and would like to come to it.

I will begin with a very frequent one, which was whether vines grow well here. I have said already that there are plenty of wild vines and that some from France have been tried and have done pretty well. But why do you not plant vineyards? To this I answer that eating is more necessary than drinking, and therefore the raising of wheat has to be attended to, before the planting of vineyards; one can do better without wine than without bread. It has been as much as we could do to clear land and raise wheat, without doing any thing else.

Are there any horses in the country? I answer no.

Are there not prairies of which hay can be made? Do not oats grow there? Perfectly well, and there are beautiful prairies; but hay making is rather dangerous, particularly near the settlements at Three-Rivers and Montreal, and will continue to be dangerous so long as the Iroquois make war on us, for the mowers and hay makers are always in danger of being killed by them. For this reason we make but little hay, although we have fine large prairies on which there grows very good grass for making it. But there is still another thing that prevents us from having horses, and that is that it would cost a good deal to bring them from France; there are few people here who could afford the outlay, and besides it is feared that the Iroquois would kill them when they come, as they do our cattle, which would be very vexatious to whoever had been to the expense of bringing them out. And besides, we are always in hopes that our good King will come to the assistance of this country and will cause those rascally Iroquois to be destroyed.

Are there many settlers? To this question I cannot give any positive answer, except that I have been told that there are about eight hundred at Quebec: as for the other settlements there are not so many there.

Have the settlers many children? Yes, and they grow up well formed, tall and robust, the girls as well as the boys; they are, generally speaking, intelligent enough, but rather idle, that is to say it is difficult to get them to attend to their studies.

What is the ordinary beverage? Wine in the best houses, beer in some others; there is another beverage called *bouillon*, that is in common use in all the houses: the poorer people drink water which is very good and very common in this country.

What are the houses built of? Some are built entirely of stone, and covered with boards or planks of pine; others are built of wooden frame-work or uprights, with masonry between; others are built wholly of wood; but all the houses are covered, as I have said, with boards.

Is the heat very great in summer? It is about the same as in our province of *Dunis*.

Is the cold great in winter? There are some days when it is very severe, but it does not prevent one from doing what one has to do; one puts on more clothes than usual, one covers one's hands with a kind of glove, called

mittens in this country, and good fires are made in the houses, for wood costs nothing except for cutting it and bringing it on vehicles called sledges; these slide upon the snow, and one ox can draw in this way as much as two could with a cart in summer. And, as I have already said, the air is very calm on most days, and little rain falls in winter. What I find most inconvenient here is that cattle must be fed in the stable for more than four months, on account of the ground being covered with snow during that time, but if the snow puts us to that inconvenience it renders us on the other hand, a great service by facilitating the drawing from the forests of all the wood we have need of for buildings on land and vessels on the water, and for other purposes. We draw all this wood from the forests, by means of the sledges I have spoken of, with great ease, and much more conveniently and at much less cost than we could in summer by means of carts.

The air here is extremely healthy at all times; but particularly in winter; sickness is seldom seen in this country; it is but little subject to drizzling rains or fogs; the air here is extremely thin and keen. At the entrance to the gulf and river, drizzling rains are frequent, by reason of the proximity of the Ocean; very few storms are seen here.

Our neighbours, the English, laid out a great deal of money at the outset on the settlements they made; they threw great numbers of people into them; so that now there are computed to be in them fifty thousand men capable of bearing arms; it is a wonder to see their country now; one finds all sorts of things there, the same as in Europe, and for half the price. They build numbers of ships, of all sorts and sizes; they work iron mines; they have beautiful cities; they have stagecoaches and mails from one to the other; they have carriages like those in France; those who laid out money there, are now getting good returns from it; that country is not different from this; what has been done there could be done here.

Source: Edward Louis Montizambe, *Canada in the 17th Century; From the French of Pierre Boucher* (Montreal, 1883), 69-74.

Isaac Brock (1769–1812)

THE WAR OF 1812

General Isaac Brock was a hero of the War of 1812. He lost his life in the battle of Queenston Heights against invading American troops on October 13, 1812.

Earlier that year, on July 12, American Brigadier General William Hull, with 2500 men, had crossed the Detroit River into the Canadian village of Sandwich. Though war had not yet been declared, he issued a proclamation that, with florid rhetoric, urged Canadians to acquiesce in the pending American invasion and pledged that in so doing they would "be emancipated from tyranny and oppression, and restored to the dignified station of freemen." More ominous were his remarks concerning Indian fighters on the side of Great Britain. Perceiving Indians as "savages" who would butcher women and children, Hull warned that any white man found fighting alongside an Indian would be shot (as would the Indian) by the Americans, rather than taken prisoner.

On July 22 General Brock issued a counter-proclamation. It was equally passionate and rhetorical. As opposed to the American appeal based on liberty, Brock reminded Canadians about the prosperity and security they enjoyed under British rule. He argued that far preferable to rule by a "foreign master" – the Americans – was "participation in the name, character, and freedom of Britons!" Among the arguments marshalled by Brock against the American invasion was that a U.S. victory would lead to the eventual re-annexation of Canada by France, which at the time was ruled by Napoleon, that "despot who rules the nations of continental Europe with a rod of iron." Even more interesting was Brock's defence of the rights of native peoples. With regard to Hull's threat of taking no prisoners among Indians and whites found fighting together, Brock declared: "But they are men, and have equal rights with all other men to defend themselves and their property when invaded."

The unprovoked declaration of war by the United States of America against the United Kingdom of Great Britain and Ireland, and its dependencies, has been followed by the actual invasion of this province, in a remote frontier of the western district, by a detachment of the armed force of the United States.

The officer commanding that detachment has thought proper to invite his majesty's subjects, not merely to a quiet and unresisting submission, but insults them with a call to seek voluntarily the protection of his government.

Without condescending to repeat the illiberal epithets bestowed in this appeal of the American commander to the people of Upper Canada, on the administration of his majesty, every inhabitant of the province is desired to seek the confutation of such indecent slander in the review of his own particular circumstances. Where is the Canadian subject who can truly affirm to himself that he has been injured by the government, in his person, his property, or his liberty? Where is to be found, in any part of the world, a growth so rapid in prosperity and wealth, as this colony exhibits? Settled, not thirty years, by a band of veterans, exiled from their former possessions on account of their loyalty, not a descendant of these brave people is to be found, who, under the fostering liberality of their sovereign, has not acquired a property and means of enjoyment superior to what were possessed by their ancestors.

This unequalled prosperity would not have been attained by the utmost liberality of the government, or the persevering industry of the people, had not the maritime power of the mother country secured to its colonists a safe access to every market, where the produce of their labour was in request.

The unavoidable and immediate consequences of a separation from Great Britain must be the loss of this inestimable advantage; and what is offered you in exchange? To become a territory of the United States, and share with them that exclusion from the ocean which the policy of their government enforces; you are not even flattered with a participation of their boasted independence; and it is but too obvious that, once estranged from the powerful protection of the United Kingdom, you must be reannexed to the dominion of France, from which the provinces of Canada were wrested by the arms of Great Britain, at a vast expense of blood and treasure, from no other motive than to relieve her ungrateful children from the oppression of a cruel neighbour. This restitution of Canada to the empire of France, was the stipulated reward for the aid afforded to the revolted colonies, now the United States; the debt is still due, and there can be no doubt but the pledge has been renewed as a consideration for commercial advantages, or rather for an expected relaxation in the tyranny of France over the commercial world. Are you prepared, inhabitants of Canada, to become willing subjects, or rather slaves, to the despot who rules the nations of continental Europe with a rod of iron? If not, arise in a body, exert your energies, co-operate cordially with the king's regular forces to repel the invader, and do not give cause to your children, when groaning under the oppression of a foreign master, to reproach you with having so easily parted with the richest inheritance of this earth – a participation in the name, character, and freedom of Britons!

The same spirit of justice, which will make every reasonable allowance for the unsuccessful efforts of zeal and loyalty, will not fail to punish the defalcation of principle. Every Canadian freeholder is, by deliberate choice, bound by the most solemn oaths to defend the monarchy, as well as his own property; to shrink from that engagement is a treason not to be forgiven. Let no man suppose that if, in this expected struggle, his majesty's arms should be compelled to yield to an overwhelming force, the province will be eventually abandoned; the endeared relations of its first settlers, the intrinsic value of its commerce, and the pretensions of its powerful rival to repossess the Canadas, are pledges that no peace will be established between the United States and Great Britain and Ireland, of which the resolution of these provinces does not make the most prominent condition.

Be not dismayed at the unjustifiable threat of the commander of the enemy's forces to refuse quarter, should an Indian appear in the ranks. The brave bands of aborigines which inhabit this colony were, like his majesty's other subjects, punished for their zeal and fidelity, by the loss of their possessions in the late colonies, and rewarded by his majesty with lands of superior value in this province. The faith of the British government has never yet been violated – the Indians feel that the soil they inherit is to them and their posterity protected from the base arts so frequently devised to over-reach their simplicity. By what new principle are they to be prohibited from defending their property? If their warfare, from being different to that of the white people, be more terrific to the enemy, let him retrace his steps – they seek him not – and cannot expect to find women and children in an invading army. But they are men, and have equal rights with all other men to defend themselves and their property when invaded, more especially when they find in the enemy's camp a ferocious and mortal foe, using the same warfare which the American commander affects to reprobate.

This inconsistent and unjustifiable threat of refusing quarter, for such a cause as being found in arms with a brother sufferer, in defence of invaded rights, must be exercised with the certain assurance of retaliation, not only in the limited operations of war in this part of the king's dominions, but in every quarter of the globe; for the national character of Britain is not less distinguished for humanity than strict retributive justice, which will consider the execution of this inhuman threat as deliberate murder, for which every subject of the offending power must make expiation.

Source: Ferdinand Brock Tupper, *The Life and Correspondence of Major-General Sir Isaac Brock* (London, 1848), 188–91.

Laura Secord (1775–1868)

"WITH FORCED COURAGE"

Laura Secord is one of Canada's most famous heroes. When the Americans invaded Upper Canada in the War of 1812, she and her husband, James, lived in the Niagara peninsula. On a steamy, hot June 23, 1813, while her husband lay helpless in bed, Laura walked twenty miles through the American lines to warn a detachment of British troops that it was about to be attacked. Her trek was an amazing feat. Described by Lieutenant James Fitzgibbon (1780–1863) as "a person of slight and delicate frame," Secord, though terrified at the prospect of being captured by American troops or Indians, struggled across rotten logs, huge stumps, a couple of miles of swamp, and countless streams. She must have been caked with mud, soaking wet, and utterly exhausted when Fitzgibbon's Indian allies found her.

Forty-five years later, Laura Secord, now an almost penniless widow, told her tale to the visiting Prince of Wales. Fitzgibbon backed her claim; he noted that, because of her valiant deed, he had evaded capture and further, with his Indian allies, had taken 550 Americans prisoner. The Prince of Wales sent Secord £100 (perhaps $25,000 in present-day terms). It was all she ever received as a reward. By the time she died, her legend was growing. In 1913 Senator Frank O'Connor decided to use her name for a new brand of chocolates, with a miniature painting of an old lady as a trademark. Neither she nor the much younger portrait now used bore any resemblance to the real Laura Secord. Yet the real person had done all she could for Canada.

Dear sir, – I will tell you the story in a few words.

After going to St. David's and the recovery of Mr. Secord, we returned again to Queenston, where my courage again was much tried. It was there I gained the secret plan laid to capture Captain Fitzgibbon and his party. I was determined, if possible, to save them. I had much difficulty in getting through the American guards. They were ten miles out in the country. When I came to a field belonging to a Mr. De Cou, in the neighbourhood of the Beaver Dams, I then had walked nineteen miles. By that time daylight had left me. I yet had a swift stream of water (Twelve-mile Creek) to cross over on an old fallen tree, and to climb a high hill, which fatigued me very much.

Before I arrived at the encampment of the Indians, as I approached they all arose with one of their war yells, which, indeed, awed me. You may imagine what my feelings were to behold so many savages. With forced courage I went to one of the chiefs, told him I had great news for his commander, and that he must take me to him or they would all be lost. He did not understand me, but said, "Woman! What does woman want here?" The scene by moonlight to some might have been grand, but to a weak woman certainly terrifying. With difficulty I got one of the chiefs to go with me to their commander. With the intelligence I gave him he formed his plans and saved his country. I have ever found the brave and noble Colonel Fitzgibbon a friend to me. May he prosper in the world to come as he has done in this.

Source: Sarah Anne Curzon, *Laura Secord, the Heroine of 1812: A Drama and Other Poems* (Toronto, 1887), v.

Ezekiel Hart (1770–1843)

RELIGIOUS FREEDOM IN CANADA

The struggle for religious equality in Canadian civic and political life was waged, and eventually won, in the early nineteenth century in Lower Canada (Quebec). In 1807 a Jew named Ezekiel Hart was elected to the Legislative Assembly as representative from Trois-Rivières. A vicious public debate ensued first over his election and then over the fact that he took his oath of office by substituting the word "Jewish" for "Christian" at the appropriate part of the text. His oath was deemed invalid, and he was prevented by a vote of the Assembly from taking his seat.

Hart ran again and was once more elected by the voters of Trois-Rivières. Yet, when he arrived to claim his seat in 1809, he was rebuffed. Again the Assembly voted to deny him his seat, this time more explicitly because he was a Jew. Hart did not run a third time. The Jewish community began to fight to have the phrase "on the true oath of a Christian" removed from the oath of office.

Its efforts eventually bore fruit. An act was passed in 1831, and given royal assent in 1832, which gave to Jews equal rights with non-Jews with regard to the holding of public office. This bill – the first such measure in the British Empire – had strong bipartisan support in the Assembly. Among those voting for it was Louis-Joseph Papineau (1786–1871), leader of the Parti Patriote (formerly the Parti Canadien, which had opposed Hart's entry earlier in the century).

An Act to declare persons professing the Jewish Religion entitled to all the rights and privileges of the other subjects of His Majesty in this Province.

31st March, 1831 – Presented for His Majesty's Assent and reserved "for the signification of His Majesty's pleasure thereon."

12th April 1832 – Assented to by His Majesty in His Council.

5th June, 1832 – The Royal Assent signified by the proclamation of His Excellency the Governor in Chief.

Whereas doubts have arisen whether persons professing the Jewish Religion are by law entitled to many of the privileges enjoyed by the other subjects of His Majesty within this Province: Be it therefore declared and enacted by the King's Most Excellent Majesty, by and with the advice and consent of the Legislative Council and Assembly of the Province of Lower Canada, constituted and assembled by virtue of and under the authority of an Act passed in the Parliament of Great Britain, intituled, "An Act to repeal certain parts of an Act passed in the fourteenth year of His Majesty's Reign, intituled, "*An Act for making more effectual provision for the Government of the Province of Quebec, in North America*," and to make further provision for the Government of the said Province of Quebec in North America;" And it is hereby declared and enacted by the authority aforesaid, that all persons professing the Jewish Religion being natural born British subjects inhabiting and residing in this Province, are entitled and shall be deemed, adjudged and taken to be entitled to the full rights and privileges of the other subjects of His Majesty, his Heirs or Successors, to all intents, constructions and purposes whatsoever, and capable of taking, having or enjoying any office or place of trust whatsoever, within this Province.

Source: Provincial Statutes of Lower Canada, vol. 14 (1831-34).

William Lyon Mackenzie (1795–1861)

"Independence!"

William Lyon Mackenzie is a difficult revolutionary hero to admire. Born in Scotland, he came to Upper Canada in 1820 and by 1824 was publisher of the *Colonial Advocate*. His opinions, for the most part, were reactionary, not progressive. He favoured agriculture over industry, mistreated his own employees, and proved hopeless as Toronto's first mayor. He was erratic and so undependable that he shattered the Reform movement.

Still, Canadians bored with their history find Mackenzie a spark of life, with his flaming red wig, his fervid allegations of Tory corruption, his splendid rhetoric of revolution. The words he spun into print on a hand press on a cold December morning in 1837, with their utter self-confidence, drew hundreds of followers through the sleet and rain to Montgomery's tavern at the northern edge of Toronto, where the Upper Canadian Rebellion was born. If there was *opera bouffe* in the events that followed, there would be tragedy for those who were caught and for those, like Mackenzie himself, who fled for their lives and freedom.

In the end, Mackenzie, pardoned for his role in the Rebellion, returned in 1849, as disillusioned with the United States as he had been with Canada. His grandson, William Lyon Mackenzie King, would cherish his memory and utterly ignore his political example. In so doing he became Canada's most durable, most boring, and perhaps its ablest prime minister.

The nations are fallen, and thou still art young,
Thy sun is but rising when others have set;
And tho' Slavery's cloud o'er thy morning hath hung,
The full tide of Freedom shall beam round thee yet.

BRAVE CANADIANS! God has put into the bold and honest hearts of our brethren in Lower Canada to revolt – not against "lawful" but against "unlawful authority." The law says we shall not be taxed without our consent by the voices of the men of our choice, but a wicked and tyrannical government has trampled upon that law – robbed the exchequer – divided the plunder – and declared that, regardless of justice they will continue to roll their splendid carriages, and riot in their palaces, at our expense – that we are poor spiritless ignorant peasants, who were born to toil for our betters. But the peasants are beginning to open their eyes and to feel their strength – too long have they been hoodwinked by Baal's priests – by hired and tampered with preachers, wolves in sheep's clothing, who take the wages of sin, and do the work of iniquity, "each one looking to his gain in his quarter."

CANADIANS! Do you love Freedom? I know you do. Do you hate oppression? Who dare deny it? Do you wish perpetual peace, and a government founded upon the eternal heaven-born principle of the Lord Jesus Christ – a government bound to enforce the law to do to each other as you would be done by? Then buckle on your armour, and put down the villains who oppress and enslave our country – put them down in the name of that God who goes forth with the armies of his people, and whose bible shows us that it is by the same human means whereby you put to death thieves and murderers, and imprison and banish wicked individuals, that you must put down, in the strength of the Almighty, those governments which, like these bad individuals, trample on the law, and destroy its usefulness. You give a bounty for wolves' scalps. Why? because wolves harass you. The bounty you must pay for freedom (blessed word) is to give the strength of your arms to put down tyranny at Toronto. One short hour will deliver our country from the oppressor; and freedom in religion, peace and tranquillity, equal laws and an improved country will be the prize. We contend, that in all laws made, or to be made, every person shall be bound alike – neither should any tenure, estate, charter, degree, birth or place, confer any exemption from the ordinary course of legal proceedings and responsibilities whereunto others are subjected.

CANADIANS! God has shown that he is with our brethren, for he has given them the encouragement of success. Captains, Colonels, Volunteers, Artillerymen, Privates, the base, the vile hirelings of our unlawful oppressors have already bit the dust in hundreds in Lower Canada; and altho' the Roman Catholic and Episcopal Bishops and Archdeacons, are bribed by large sums of money to instruct their flocks that they should be obedient to a government which defies the law, and is therefore unlawful, and ought to be put down, yet God has opened the eyes of the people to the wickedness of these reverend sinners, so that they hold them in derision, just as God's prophet Elijah did the priests of Baal of old and their sacrifices. Is there any one afraid to go to fight for freedom, let him remember, that

God sees with equal eye, as Lord of all,
A Hero perish, or a Sparrow fall:

That power that protected ourselves and our forefathers in the deserts of Canada – that preserved from the Cholera those whom He would – that brought us safely to this continent through the dangers of the Atlantic waves – aye, and who has watched over us from infancy to manhood, will be in the midst of us in the day of our struggle for our liberties, and for Governors of our free choice, who would

not dare to trample on the laws they had sworn to maintain. In the present struggle, we may be sure, that if we do not rise and put down Head[*] and his lawless myrmidons, they will gather all the rogues and villains in the Country together – arm them – and then deliver our farms, our families, and our country to their brutality – to that it has come, we must put them down, or they will utterly destroy this country. If we move now, as one man, to crush the tyrant's power, to establish free institutions founded on God's law, we will prosper, for He who commands the winds and waves will be with us – but if we are cowardly and mean-spirited, a woeful and a dark day is surely before us.

CANADIANS! The struggle will be of short duration in Lower Canada, for the people are united as one man. Out of Montreal and Quebec, they are as 100 to 1 – here we reformers are as 10 to 1 – and if we rise with one consent to overthrow despotism, we will make quick work of it.

Mark all those who join our enemies – act as spies for them – fight for them – or aid them – these men's properties shall pay the expense of the struggle – they are traitors to Canadian Freedom, and as such we will deal with them.

CANADIANS! It is the design of the Friends of Liberty to give several hundred acres to every Volunteer – to root up the unlawful Canada Company, and give FREE DEEDS to all settlers who live on their lands – to give free gifts of the Clergy Reserve lots, to good citizens who have settled on them – and the like to

---

[*] Sir Francis Bond Head (1793-1875), lieutenant governor of Upper Canada from 1835 to 1838.

While trade in fish, furs, and any other profitable product drew European visitors to North America, claiming the land and settling it was also motivated by a desire to bring post-Reformation Catholicism to the native people of the continent. As a ship waits by the shore, and chapels stand on the foreshore, a symbolic France in Bourbon majesty explains the mysteries of the faith to an awestruck convert, already mantled in the lilies of France. Before Frère Luc (1614-85) entered the Recollet order, he was a court painter to King Louis XIV. He came to Quebec in 1670 with five other Recollets and there completed his painting of France Carrying Faith to the Indians of New France. (The Ursuline Convent, Quebec)

William Berczy (d. 1813), a native of Saxony, came to Canada in 1790 as leader of a party of German immigrants. A talented portraitist, he lived first at York (Toronto) in Upper Canada and later in Quebec, where a successful local merchant, John Woolsey, commissioned him to paint his family. (National Gallery of Canada)

Théophile Hamel (1817-70) was only twenty in 1837 when he painted his self-portrait. A student of Antoine Plamondon, Hamel would go on to become the most commercially successful Quebec artist of his age. In the year of the Patriote rising in Lower Canada and Mackenzie's rebellion in Upper Canada, Hamel appears distant from the world of politics. (National Gallery of Canada)

Joseph Légaré (1795-1855) was a Quebec City glazier and self-taught painter who founded Canada's first art gallery, taught Antoine Plamondon, and struggled, in his paintings, to recreate the past. His Portrait of Josephté Ourné *was among the most memorable of his paintings of native subjects.* (National Gallery of Canada)

Henry James Warre (1819-98), a British officer stationed in Canada, travelled to Oregon in the far northwest in 1845 to help determine the border between American and British territory. He left this watercolour of an Indian chief's tomb on the Cowelitz River. Like people of other civilizations, some natives believed that the dead needed their possessions in the next life, and a chief's canoe became his coffin and his blankets became his shroud. (National Archives of Canada, C 26342)

An ice cone is a natural consequence of a waterfall in winter: as the flying spray freezes, a small mountain of ice forms in front of the base. The Montmorency Falls, just north of Quebec City, were a sight worth seeing by officers of the British garrison in their well-horsed carioles. Robert Todd (d. 1866) came from England in 1835 and moved to Toronto in 1854. He depicted the scene in a stylized, decorative form in 1845. (National Gallery of Canada)

Paul Kane (1810-71) was born in Ireland, came to Upper Canada as a boy in 1821, and returned to Europe in 1841 to learn technique. An exhibit by George Caitlin inspired him to paint the native people of North America, and he persuaded the Hudson's Bay Company to help him go west in 1846. He returned to Toronto in 1848 with 700 sketches and turned them into paintings, among them Big Snake, Chief of the Blackfoot Indians, Recounting His War Exploits to Five Subordinate Chiefs, completed in 1856. (National Gallery of Canada)

Cornelius Krieghoff (1815-72) was born in Amsterdam of German parents, came to the United States, and was enticed to Canada to practise his art. A genre painter, Krieghoff produced hundreds of paintings, many of them depicting the ordinary people of French Canada enjoying themselves. The White Horse Inn by Moonlight, painted in 1851, is typical. While popular and still selling for enormous prices, Krieghoff's work has been condemned for showing French Canadians and their homes in an unflattering light. (National Gallery of Canada)

When Robert Whale (d. 1887) painted his General View of Hamilton *in 1852, he was only a year out from England. Some people already described the town at the end of Lake Ontario as "the ambitious city." Hamilton would be terminus for the Great Western Railway, a home for iron foundries and steel mills, and a bustling rival of Toronto, farther east along the lake. Countless other young communities also dreamed of greatness as they laid waste their forest hinterland.* (National Gallery of Canada)

Crossing the oceans to Canada could often be a terrifying experience. An Atlantic voyage by sail could range from ten days to a couple of months. Ocean storms, sweeping over the horizon in minutes, could engulf a ship, ripping sails and toppling masts. Halifax painter John O'Brien (1831-91) specialized in naval scenes. This painting of 1856 shows three fully crewed Royal Navy frigates running before the wind in angry seas. It would have had plenty of meaning for nineteenth-century Canadians. (National Gallery of Canada)

William Raphael's painting Behind Bonsecours Market, *completed in 1861, is another well-known nineteenth-century image of Canada. A Prussian-born, German-trained painter, Raphael (1833-1914) came to Canada in 1860 and soon established his reputation as a portraitist and a nature painter (especially wild storms). His skill is reflected in the careful rendering of Montreal townspeople and the ships on the St. Lawrence.* (National Gallery of Canada)

Not everyone recognized the Quebec Conference of 1864 as an "international convention," nor do even historians remember that its senior presiding officer was Sir Étienne-Pascal Taché of Canada East, a former Patriote flanked by the senior representatives of five British North American colonies: on his right, Charles Tupper (Nova Scotia), John Hamilton Gray (Prince Edward Island), and John A. Macdonald (Canada West); and on his left, Samuel Tilley (New Brunswick) and George-Étienne Cartier. Newfoundland's delegates, F.B.T. Carter and Ambrose Shea, had already shifted themselves from the centre. Here, on October 27, 1864, are the "white men in tail coats" who put Confederation together. (National Archives of Canada, c 6350)

The Laurentians, a chain of low mountains running down the backbone of Quebec and Ontario west of the St. Lawrence, have provided a century of recreation, beauty, and escape to the people of Canada's most populated region. Long before resorts and cottages covered the lake shores and hillsides, John Fraser (1838-98) recorded in Laurentian Splendour *part of a natural heritage most Canadians take for granted.* (National Gallery of Canada)

Flanked by Hector Langevin and George-Étienne Cartier, John A. Macdonald rises to address the Fathers of Confederation at the Quebec Conference. Painted in 1887 by Prince Edward Island artist Robert Harris, this must be one of the best known of Canada's historic paintings. The original hung in the Canadian Parliament and was lost in the fire of 1916. Other versions survived and a copy by Rex Wood was presented to the government in 1967 by an insurance company. As usual, such group photographs were based on individual portraits of various vintages. (Ontario Legislative Assembly)

After destroying General George Custer and much of the U.S. 7th Cavalry at the Battle of the Little Big Horn in 1876, Sitting Bull and members of the Sioux nation crossed into Canada. While few Americans or Canadians had respect for native lands, American soldiers hesitated to invade Queen Victoria's dominion, and Superintendent James Walsh of the tiny North-West Mounted Police was able to defend Canada's sovereignty at no cost. Whatever the reality of Canada's aboriginal policy, many Canadians believed that the Sioux had preferred our law and order to the seemingly lawless violence of the American frontier. (National Archives of Canada, c 66055)

settlers on Church of England Glebe Lots, so that the yeomanry may feel independent, and be able to improve the country, instead of sending the fruit of their labour to foreign lands. The 57 Rectories will be at once given to the people, and all public lands used for Education, Internal Improvements, and the public good. £100,000 drawn from us in payment of the salaries of bad men in office, will be reduced to one quarter, or much less, and the remainder will go to improve bad roads and to "make crooked paths straight;" law will be ten times more cheap and easy – the bickerings of priests will cease with the funds that keeps them up – and men of wealth and property from other lands will soon raise our farms to four times their present value. We have given Head and his employers a trial of 45 years – five years longer than the Israelites were detained in the wilderness. The promised land is now before us – up then and take it – but set not the torch to one house in Toronto, unless we are fired at from the houses, in which case self-preservation will teach us to put down those who would murder us when up in the defence of the laws. There are some rich men now, as there were in Christ's time, who would go with us in prosperity, but who will skulk in the rear, because of their large possessions – mark them! They are those who in after years will seek to corrupt our people, and change free institutions into an aristocracy of wealth, to grind the poor, and make laws to fetter their energies.

MARK MY WORDS CANADIANS!

The struggle is begun – it might end in freedom – but timidity, cowardice, or tampering on our part, will only delay its close. We cannot be reconciled to Britain – we have humbled ourselves to the Pharaoh of England, to the Ministers, and great people, and they will neither rule us justly nor let us go – we are determined never to rest until independence is ours – the prize is a splendid one. A country larger than France or England, natural resources equal to our most boundless wishes – a government of equal laws – religion pure and undefiled – perpetual peace – education to all – millions of acres of lands for revenue – freedom from British tribute – free trade with all the world – but stop – I never could enumerate all the blessings attendant on independence!

Up then, brave Canadians! Get ready your rifles, and make short work of it; a connection with England would involve us in all her wars, undertaken for her own advantage, never for ours; with governors from England, we will have bribery at elections, corruption, villainy and perpetual discord in every township, but Independence would give us the means of enjoying many blessings. Our enemies in Toronto are in terror and dismay – they know their wickedness and dread our vengeance. Fourteen armed men were sent out at the dead hour of night, by the traitor Gurnett,[*] to drag to a felon's cell, the sons of our worthy and noble minded brother departed, Joseph Sheppard,[**]

---

[*]George Gurnett (c. 1792-1861), journalist and politician; mayor of Toronto 1837-38, 1848-51.
[**]Joseph Shepard (1765-1837), farmer and Reform activist.

on a simple and frivolous charge of trespass, brought by a tory fool; and though it ended in smoke, it shewed too evidently Head's feelings. Is there to be an end of these things? Aye, and now's the day and the hour! Woe be to those who oppose us, for "In God is our trust."

Source: David Flint, *William Lyon Mackenzie: Rebel Against Authority* (Toronto: Oxford University Press, 1971), 138-9.

Louis-Joseph Papineau (1786—1871)

"FELLOW CITIZENS!"

Louis-Joseph Papineau lawyer, orator, and politician, was leader first of the Parti Canadien and then of its successor, the Parti Patriote. In this role he challenged the power of English-Canadian commercial interests, sought to extend the powers of the Legislative Assembly, and championed the culture and heritage of French Canada. He was also one of the leaders of the Rebellions of 1837–38.

Following the defeat of the Rebellions, Papineau left for the United States and later for France. He returned to Quebec in 1844 after an amnesty came into effect. Elected again to the Assembly, he remained in public life until 1854 and during this period came to advocate annexation to the United States. His stature as an intellectual and orator has been confirmed through the common saying in Quebec used to describe someone of exceptional intelligence: "Il a la tête à Papineau" ("He has the head of Papineau").

Papineau's role in the Rebellions of 1837–38 remains controversial. He delivered a major address, partly reproduced here, on October 23, 1837 to a rally at Saint-Charles, following which the Patriotes mobilized against the British. It was after their defeat at Saint-Charles that Papineau fled to the United States. This early call for self-government in French Canada was developed within the context of democratic reform and suffused with the spirit of liberalism.

When a people, even after expressing their views through all the avenues recognized by constitutional procedure, through people's assemblies and through their representatives in Parliament after mature deliberation, are constantly exposed to systematic resistance; when their governors, instead of redressing the various ills that they have themselves produced through their bad government, solemnly record and declare their reprehensible determination to undermine and reverse the foundations of civil liberty, it becomes the people's imperative duty to devote themselves seriously to considering their unfortunate position and the dangers that surround them, and through a well-designed organization to make the necessary arrangements to preserve intact their rights as citizens and their dignity as free human beings.

The wise and immortal writers of the American Declaration of Independence recorded in this document the principles on which the Rights of Man are solely based, and demanded the advantageous establishment of the institutions and form of government that alone can permanently ensure the prosperity and social well-being of the inhabitants of this continent, whose education and customs, linked to the circumstances of colonization, demand a system of government that depends entirely on the people and is directly responsible to the people.

In common with the various nations of North and South America that have adopted the principles incorporated in this Declaration, we regard the doctrines that it contains as sacred and evident: that God did not create any artificial distinctions between man and man; that government is only a simple human institution, formed by those who must be subject to its actions, good or bad, and devoted to the benefit of all those who consent to come or remain under its protection and control; and that therefore the form of government can be changed when it no longer achieves the ends for which it was established; that public authorities and men in power are only the executors of the legitimately expressed wishes of the community, honoured when they possess the confidence of the public and respected when they enjoy public esteem; and that they must be removed from power when they no longer give satisfaction to the people, the only legitimate source of all power.

In conformity with the treaties and capitulations drawn up with our ancestors and guaranteed by the imperial Parliament, the people of this province have for many years unceasingly submitted respectful petitions complaining of the intolerable abuses that poison their days and paralyse their industry. In response to our humble requests, instead of adjustments being granted, aggression has followed aggression, until finally it appears that we can no longer cling to the British Empire for our happiness and prosperity, our liberties and the honour of the people and the crown of England. The only aim has been to enrich a useless horde of officials who, not content with enjoying salaries that are hugely disproportionate to the duties of their position and to the resources of the country, have banded together in a faction driven purely by private interest to resist all reforms and defend all the iniquities of a government that is the enemy of the rights and liberties of this colony.

Source: *L.J. Papineau: Textes choisis et présentés par Fernand Ouellet*, 2nd ed. (Quebec City: Les presses de l'université Laval, 1970), 80-1.

Chevalier de Lorimier (1803–39)

A PATRIOTE'S LAST THOUGHTS, 1839

There were two insurrections in Lower Canada, in 1837 and 1838. The first, in the late fall of 1837, began with the defeat of a British force at Saint-Denis and ended soon after with the defeat of Patriote forces on both sides of the St. Lawrence. However harsh Lord Durham's judgment of the French Canadians, his treatment of the captured Patriote leaders was mild: he sent several of them into exile in Bermuda and the rest were freed. Some of them were active in a second uprising a year later. So were lodges of *Chasseurs* and Hunters from across the American border. By then, Durham had resigned and his successors believed that rebellion must be crushed in blood, as it had been in Upper Canada.

Among those condemned to die was François-Marie-Thomas-Chevalier de Lorimier. Son of a noble family that had remained in Quebec after the Conquest of 1759–60, he was thirty-four years old when he died, a notary and the father of three children. He had been an active leader in the public assemblies that led to the 1837 and 1838 uprisings, and the judge at his court martial held him especially guilty. With only hours remaining in his life, Lorimier, though heartbroken at the prospect of the poverty and misery his young family would face, remained an unrepentant patriot, ready to die as he had lived, for the freedom and independence of Lower Canada.

Montreal Prison
February 14, 1839
11 PM

The public, and especially my friends, are perhaps waiting for a sincere declaration of my feelings: at the fateful hour when we must leave this earth, opinions are always regarded and received with greater impartiality. At this moment, the Christian strips himself of the veil that has obscured many of his actions, allowing himself to be exposed to the light of day; interest and passions expire with his mortal remains. For myself, in these hours before I give up my spirit to its creator, I wish to make known what I feel and what I think. I have decided to do this only because I fear that my feelings will be represented in a false light: we know that the dead do not speak, and the same political design that has made me pay for my political actions on the gallows could well lead to tales being told about me. I both wish and have the time to prevent such fabrications, and I do so in a true and solemn manner at my final hour – not on the gallows, surrounded by a witless crowd with an insatiable blood-lust, but quietly and reflectively in prison. I die without remorse. I wished only the well-being of my country in insurrection and independence. My views and my actions were sincere and were not stained with any of the crimes that dishonour humanity and are only too common in the ferment of unbridled passions. For seventeen or eighteen years, I have taken part in every popular initiative, always with conviction and sincerity. I have devoted my efforts to the independence of my compatriots; we have suffered misfortune to this day. Death has already destroyed a number of my collaborators. Many groan in irons, and even more in exile with their property destroyed and their families abandoned without resources to the rigours of a Canadian winter. Despite so many misfortunes, there is still courage and hope for the future in my heart: my friends and my children will see better days; they will be free. It is an unerring premonition; my untroubled conscience assures me of it. This is what fills me with joy, when all around me is desolation and pain. The wounds of my country will heal after the troubles of anarchy and bloody revolution. The peaceful *Canadien* will see happiness and liberty on the St. Lawrence. Everything converges towards that end, even the executions; the blood and tears spilled on the altar of liberty today are watering the roots of the tree on which will fly the flag marked with the two stars of the Canadas. I leave children whose only inheritance is the memory of my troubles. Poor orphans, it is you whom I pity. The blow of my death struck by the bloody and arbitrary hand of martial law is a blow against you. You will never know the sweetness and pleasure of embracing your father on happy days, on feast days! When you reach the age at which reason allows you to reflect, you will see your father who paid with the noose for actions that rendered other more fortunate men immortal. Your father's crime has been failure. If success had accompanied his efforts, his actions would be mentioned honourably. "It is crime that is shameful, not the gallows." The sorry path that remains for me to follow from an obscure prison to the gallows has been trodden by men with greater merit than my own. Poor children, you will have only a tender and forsaken mother to sustain you. If my death and my sacrifices reduce you to indigence, ask at times in my name; I was never insensitive to the sorrows of adversity. As for you, my compatriots, my people, my execution and the execution of my gallows companions will be useful to you. May they show you what you can expect of the English government. I have only a few hours left to live, and I wanted to divide this precious time between my religious duties and the duties I owe my compatriots. For them I die, on the gallows, the infamous death of the murderer. For them I separate myself from my young children and my wife who have no other means of support. For them I die crying, *Vive la liberté! Vive l'indépendance!*

Source: Michel Le Bel and Jean-Marcel Paquette, *Le Québec par ses textes littéraires, 1534-1976* (Montreal: Fernand Nathan, 1979), 65-6.

Antoine Gérin-Lajoie (1824–82)

"Un Canadien Errant"

In the 1830s, Louis-Joseph Papineau and his Patriote movement paralyzed the administration of Lower Canada in their struggle to win political control. When events reached a crisis in 1837, Papineau fled and his followers around Montreal rose in revolt. Although the Patriotes defeated British troops at Saint-Denis, the Rebellion was soon crushed. So was a similar revolt in Upper Canada. The new British governor, Lord Durham, had harsh views about the French Canadians, but he was mild in his treatment of captured rebels. In 1838, however, Durham was called home. A second rebellion broke out and this time many captured rebels from both parts of the Canadas were executed or "transported" to the harsh penal colonies in Australia. Others, like Papineau, lived in exile in the United States. It is the fate of the exiles that forms the subject of "Un Canadien Errant" ("The Canadian Exile").

Antoine Gérin-Lajoie was born near Trois-Rivières. Trained as a lawyer, he became editor of a Conservative paper, *La Minerve,* and later served as a translator for the Canadian Legislative Assembly and as assistant librarian in Canada's Library of Parliament. He was president of the Institut Canadien, an association of intellectuals, and secretary of the nationalist Societé Saint-Jean-Baptiste. To him, if not to Lord Durham, *les Canadiens* were a distinct nationality. Generations of Canadiens – and Canadians too – would find part of their identity in "Un Canadien Errant," written while Gérin-Lajoie was a student in Montreal in 1842. In time, most of the exiles returned, often to positions of power and influence in the young Dominion of Canada.

Once a Canadian lad,
   Banished far from his home,
Wandered, alone and sad,
   Through foreign lands unknown.

Down by a rushing stream,
   Thoughtful and sad one day,
He watched the water pass
   And to it he did say:

If my land you should see,
   That's held in bondage yet,
Say to my friends for me,
   I'll never them forget.

Oh, those delightful days!
   Those days of hope are o'er,
And my poor land, alas,
   I'll never see it more.

Than exile nothing is worse,
　　From parents I've been torn,
And through my tears I curse
　　The moment I was born.

Forever set apart
　　From friends I loved to greet,
Alas, no more my heart,
　　My heart for grief can beat.

Oh, my dear Canada!
　　Upon my dying day,
My tired head I'll turn
　　To thee so far away.

Source: N. Brian Davis, ed., *The Poetry of the Canadian People, 1729-1920: Two Hundred Years of Hard Work* (Toronto: NC Press, 1976), 234-5.

Lord Durham (1792–1840)

"Two Nations Warring in the Bosom of a Single State"

The outbreak of rebellions in the Canadas in 1837 was acutely embarrassing to Lord Melbourne's government in London. Melbourne's solution was to send the troublesome, independent Lord Durham to Canada to report on the problems and solve them. "Radical Jack" had a brilliant mind, poor health, and many enemies.

What Durham found was not at all what his European liberal mind expected. The struggle was not about democracy but about nationalism, a phenomenon he found as hard to tolerate as his descendants at the end of the twentieth century do. His harsh comments about French Canadians made him one of Quebec's best-known villains. It also set a young patriot, François-Xavier Garneau (1809–66), to work to rebut Durham's claims that French Canadians were an uncivilized people without a history.

In a Dispatch which I addressed to Your Majesty's Principal Secretary of State for the Colonies on the 9th of August last, I detailed, with great minuteness, the impressions which had been produced on my mind by the state of things which existed in Lower Canada: I acknowledged that the experience derived from my residence in the Province had completely changed my view of the relative influence of the causes which had assigned for the existing disorders. I had not, indeed, been brought to believe that the institutions of Lower Canada were less defective than I had originally presumed them to be. From the peculiar circumstances in which I was placed, I was enabled to make such effectual observations as convinced me that there had existed in the constitution of the Province, in the balance of political powers, in the spirit and practice of administration in every department of the Government, defects that were quite sufficient to account for a great degree of mismanagement and dissatisfaction. The same observation had also impressed on me the conviction that, for the peculiar and disastrous dissensions of this Province, there existed a far deeper and far more efficient cause, – a cause which penetrated beneath its political institutions into its social state, – a cause which no reform of constitution or laws, that should leave the elements of society unaltered, could remove; but which must be removed, ere any success could be expected in any attempt to remedy the many evils of this unhappy Province. I expected to find a contest between a government and a people: I found two nations warring the bosom of a single state: I found a struggle, not of principles but of races; and I perceived that it would be idle to attempt any amelioration of laws or institutions until we could first succeed in terminating the deadly animosity that now separate the inhabitants of Lower Canada into the hostile divisions of French and English.

It would be vain for me to expect that any description I can give will impress on Your Majesty such a view of the animosity of these races as my personal experience in Lower Canada has forced on me. Our happy immunity from any feelings of national hostility renders it difficult for us to comprehend the intensity of the hatred which the difference of language, of laws, and of manners creates between those who inhabit the same village, and are citizens of the same state. We are ready to believe that the real motive of the quarrel is something else; and that the difference of race has slightly and occasionally aggravated dissensions, which we attribute to some more usual cause. Experience of a state of society, so unhappily divided as that of Lower Canada, leads to an exactly contrary opinion. The national feud forces itself on the very senses, irresistibly and palpably, as the origin or the essence of every dispute which divides the community; we discover that dissensions, which appear to have another origin, are but forms of this constant and all-pervading quarrel; and that every contest is one of French and English in the outset, or becomes so ere it has run its course.

* * *

No common education has served to remove and soften the differences of origin and language. The associations of youth, the sports of childhood, and the studies by which the character of manhood is modified, are distinct and totally different. In Montreal and Quebec there are English schools and French schools; the children in these are accustomed to fight nation against nation, and the quarrels that arise among boys in the streets usually exhibit a division into English on one side and French on the other.

As they are taught apart, so are their studies different. The literature with which each is the most conversant is that of the peculiar language of each; and all the ideas which men derive from books come to each of them from perfectly different sources. The difference of language in this respect produces effects quite apart from those which it has on the mere intercourse of the two races. Those who have reflected on the powerful influence of language on thought will perceive in how different a manner people who speak in different languages are apt to think; and those who are familiar with the literature of France know that the same opinion will be expressed by an English and French writer of the present day, not merely in different words, but in a style so different as to mark utterly different habits of thought. This difference is very striking in Lower Canada; it exists not merely in the books of most influence and repute, which are of course those of the great writers of France and England, and by which the minds of the respective races are formed, but it observable in the writings which now issue from the Colonial press. The articles in the newspapers of each race are written in a style as widely different as those of France and England at present; and the arguments which convince the one are calculated to appear utterly unintelligible to the other.

The difference of language produces misconceptions yet more fatal even than those which it occasions with respect to opinions; it aggravates the national animosities by representing all the events of the day in utterly different lights. The political misrepresentation of facts is one of the incidents of a free press in every free country; but in which nations in which all speak the same language, those who receive a misrepresentation from one side have generally some means of learning the truth from the other. In Lower Canada, however, where the French and English papers represent adverse opinions, and where no large portion of the community can read both languages with ease, those who receive the misrepresentations are rarely able to avail themselves of the means of correction. It is difficult to conceive the perversity with which misrepresentations are habitually made, and the gross delusions which find currency among the people; they thus live in a world of misconceptions, in which each party is set against the other not only by diversity of feelings and opinions, but by an actual belief in an utterly different set of facts.

Source: Reginald Coupland, ed., *The Durham Report: An Abridged Version with Introduction and Notes* (Oxford, U.K.: Clarendon Press, 1945; rep. 1946), 14-15, 28-9.

Louis-Hippolyte LaFontaine (1807–64)

THE DEFENCE OF FRENCH

After the Rebellions of 1837–38, the British government acted on Lord's Durham's advice that it should waste no time in assimilating French-speaking Canadians into the dominant language and culture of North America. The two Canadas were united in a single colony, the English-speaking minority was given official equality, and English was the only language of the new legislature. Defeated and demoralized, many French Canadians felt doomed. But not the man who had emerged as their leader.

Louis-Hippolyte LaFontaine had played an ambiguous role while Louis-Joseph Papineau was leader of the Parti Canadien. Though a follower of Papineau, he opposed the call to arms in 1837. Afterwards, he made common cause with the English-speaking Reformers of Upper Canada. Shrewder than Papineau and many of his contemporaries, LaFontaine was one of the first to see the potential of an English-French partnership to restore and safeguard French-Canadian rights. Though he accepted the new political order, he assured his fellow French Canadians that he would be inflexible in protecting their language and culture. The law and the government might ban French: he would speak it. And when he rose on September 13, 1842 to deliver his maiden speech in the Parliament of the United Canadas, LaFontaine's career was made. So was Canada's future.

It is asked of me that I give my first speech in this house in a language other than my mother tongue. I am not confident of my proficiency in speaking English. But I must inform the honourable members that, even if I knew English as intimately as I know French, I would still give my first speech in the language of my French Canadian compatriots, if only to protest the cruel injustice of the Act of Union in trying to proscribe the mother tongue of half the population of Canada. I owe it to my compatriots, and I owe it to myself.

The goal of the Act of Union, as its author saw it, was to crush the French population; but he was wrong, because the means used are not up to the task of producing this result. The masses of population in Upper Canada and in Lower Canada have common interests, and in the end they will sympathize with each other.

Yes, without our active cooperation, without our participation in the structures of power, the government will not be able to act to reestablish the peace and confidence that are essential to the success of any administration. We have been placed by the Act of Union in an exceptional situation, a minority situation, in the distribution of political power. If we have to succumb, we will at least succumb in such a way that we will earn respect. I do not shrink from the responsibility I have assumed, for the governor general has chosen me as the one through whom he wishes to make his liberal and just views known to my compatriots. But in the state of subjection in which Lord Sydenham sought to hold the French population, in the presence of acts that were attempted towards this end, as a *Canadien* I have had but one duty to fulfil. This is to maintain the honourable character that has always distinguished my compatriots and that our most implacable enemies have been forced to acknowledge. I will never besmirch this character!

So that the house may appreciate the particular position I am in, allow me to note that before the Union of the two provinces, each one lived under a separate legislature. Is the complete absence of French names in the cabinet not a circumstance that carries an injustice, even a premeditated insult? But, people will say, "You didn't want to accept a job." That is not a reason. My friends and I, it is true, did not want to accept jobs without guarantees; but since you found some French names to sit on the Special Council, and even to help the Court Martial, could you not equally find some to sit in the cabinet? Not that such a choice would have the appearance of not entirely disdaining the origin of half the population. No, the honourable members of the cabinet were not able to, even if they had wanted to, under Lord Sydenham's administration. They were there only to resist. Lord Sydenham imposed silence on them. And they submitted in a servile manner. Do you think that it would be to follow in their footsteps that I would agree to join the Council? Above all, I prefer my independence, the dictates of my conscience. When I am called to give my answer to Her Majesty's representative, I would be deficient both towards my compatriots and towards myself. My career did not begin today. I have no need to be ashamed of the past; I do not wish to be ashamed of the present or the future.

Source: Michel Le Bel and Jean-Marcel Paquette, *Le Québec par ses textes littéraires, 1534-1976* (Montreal: Fernand Nathan, 1979), 79-80.

Joseph Howe (1804–73)

RESPONSIBLE GOVERNMENT

Joseph Howe was Nova Scotia's greatest nineteenth-century politician though he had some close competitors. He began as a defender of the status quo, but his natural combativeness and sense of justice soon made him a fierce critic of the British colonial administration. To him, the essence of "responsible government" was that officials must be answerable to (and appointed by) the politicians who had the support of a majority of the electorate, not to an appointed governor and his friends. If that meant "patronage" – rewarding political friends, not enemies – so be it. How else could the majority's will be carried out in a community where most real decisions were about who would benefit from the paid appointments and the public works that governments created?

In the first of these passages, Howe blasts the wealthy Tories who held power through the governor's influence (and a fair amount of voter allegiance, too). In the second, he explains his view of patronage to an Upper Canadian Reformer, Francis Hincks. Finally, in the third selection, Howe explains to Nova Scotia voters what is at stake in the crucial election of 1847. They answered with a majority of seven seats – not overwhelming but enough. Howe would be the father of responsible government in Nova Scotia, the first colony to achieve it in British North America.

Later, Howe would tire of Nova Scotia's limited possibilities, though he remained too proud of his province to allow it to join Confederation without a bitter fight. In the end, his own appetite for office and influence changed his mind and he ended his days as Ottawa's lieutenant governor in Halifax.

In [Halifax County], as elsewhere, I perceive that the Tory party are chiefly made up of a few of the very rich, operating upon the fears, or the interests, or the ignorance of the poor. The liberal party here, as elsewhere, embraces the sturdy independence and agricultural wealth of the country. It is often said by our opponents that they own Nova Scotia, and that the liberals are almost intruders upon the soil, and unfit to interfere in public affairs. But is this arrogant boast founded in fact? In the whole island of Cape Breton scarcely one hundred Tories can be found, and these chiefly cluster around the villages, and live by the professions or the offices which the people are taxed to support. Who cultivate and own the soil of Cape Breton? Who owns the vessels? who catch the fish? who carry on the trade? The liberals, and the only member from the island who supports the present Government is compelled to acknowledge that his constituents differ with him in opinion. Turning to Guysborough we find that the man who came in at the head of the poll is a liberal, and that the farmers of St. Mary's, who did not vote for him before, have come forward to tender him their independent support because of his opposition to the present Government. The county of Sydney, which contains the finest upland in the Province, is all our own; there are not a dozen Tories in it. And in Pictou we have the vast majority of those who read and speak English, including a large proportion of the most skilful and extensive proprietors; the most enterprising shipowners and wealthy merchants. Do the fifteen hundred good men and true in Colchester own no property? Yes, in that county, as in Kings and Hants, those who are with us own a vast proportion of the broad acres – the real estate; the sure foundation of independent feeling and liberal sentiment. The traders, and attorneys, and officials, or a majority of them, may be against us, but the sturdy yeomanry, the real aristocracy are with us. The same may be said of Digby, Yarmouth, and Shelburne, where but one Tory has been able to find a seat; and yet in the face of these acknowledged facts, we are told that the liberals have no stake in Nova Scotia, and that the preponderance of wealth, moral feeling, and intelligence are on the other side. Why, even in the capital, with all their boasted resources, what is the true state of the case? The Tories have some very wealthy men, a good many that have accumulated property, but what then? Within the last twenty years, slowly and steadily, industrious and intelligent men, professing liberal opinions, have raised themselves to independence and many of them to affluence. The Tories have more wealth in few hands; ours is spread over the mass, and is scarcely less in amount than theirs; while in productive power, in general industry and frugality, we possess elements which, in a very short time will make all the boasted hoards of the Tories kick the beam. Can the government of this country go on, and a body like this be excluded from all influence when they own three-fourths of the territory and pay three-fourths of the taxes?

* * *

The true principles upon which patronage should be dispensed I take to be these: the Sovereign is bound to bestow all offices for the general good without reference to party; but as no single mind can decide in all cases what is for the general good, and as a majority of the people's Representatives are assumed to reflect the wishes, and best understand the true interest of the people, the Crown selects advisers from that majority, and takes their advice in the distribution of patronage. So long as these men really reflect the national sentiment and feeling, it would be most unwise to patronize those who oppose them, and give offices to those who have mistaken the real interests of the country or failed to carry with them the sympathies and confidence of the people. To give force and efficacy to the national will – harmony and vigour to the national councils, public confidence should govern political appointments, and, in order that there may be the necessary firmness and stability in Government, those who conduct it should have their hands strengthened by the Sovereign or the Governor they serve, down to the moment when they are to be dismissed, for some good reason, justifying a reconstruction or an appeal to the constituency, or in obedience to the declared wishes of Parliament.

* * *

You possess, at this moment, the power to surround his Excellency the Lieutenant Governor with Councillors in whom you repose confidence, and to reward the men whom you believe have faithfully served you, by confiding to them the emoluments of office, and the administration of public affairs. Two parties appeal to you for your suffrage – the Liberals, *who won for you this high privilege,* and the Tories who withheld it from you as long as they could, and who would, if they had the power, withdraw it from you now. Decide between them ... That you will decide justly, wisely, and deliver your verdict with emphasis and decision, I confidently believe ...

For my own part, I do not hesitate to say, that, having toiled for nineteen years, to improve your institutions, having devoted the flower of my life to sedentary labour, and active exertion, having written reams, and spoken volumes, that the humblest order of my countrymen, in the most remote sections of the Province, should comprehend the nature of this great controversy, and learn to estimate the value of the new Constitution; if

you falter now – if, with the enemy before you, with the fruits of victory within your grasp, the highest privileges of British subjects, to be secured or cast away, by a single act, in a single day, [if] you show yourselves indifferent or undisciplined, I shall cease to labour, because I shall cease to hope. My private pursuits, my books, my family, will sufficiently employ, and diversify, what remains of life; but I will not waste it in unavailing opposition in the face of a solemn decision of the people, that the principles and services of my friends are valueless, and that all our labour has been in vain.

Source: William Annand, ed., *The Speeches and Public Letters of the Hon. Joseph Howe,* 2 vols. (Boston, 1858), vol. 1: 430-1, vol. 2: 326, 377-8.

Henry Walton Bibb (1815-54) and Jackson Whitney (fl. 1859)

Slave Testimony

After the U.S. Congress in 1850 passed the Fugitive Slave Act, which forced "free" states to return escaped slaves, a network of abolitionists, unable to eliminate the South's "peculiar institution," organized the "underground railway" to assist fugitives to reach safety in Canada. As a result, a trickle of blacks settled in Canadian cities and on the rich farmland near Chatham, close to the Detroit frontier.

Once in Canada, fugitive slaves found that daily life included the experience of prejudice and injustice, but they also had much to be thankful for. The following letters reveal, in plain terms, what slavery forced blacks to endure and how escaped slaves residing in Canada viewed their new home.

[from Henry Bibb to William Gatewood]

Detroit, March 23d, 1844

William Gatewood

Dear Sir: – I am happy to inform you that you are not mistaken in the man whom you sold as property, and received pay for as such. But I thank God that I am not property now, but am regarded as a man like yourself, and although I live far north, I am enjoying a comfortable living by my own industry. If you should ever chance to be traveling this way, and will call on me, I will use you better than you did me while you held me as a slave. Think not that I have any malice against you, for the cruel treatment which you inflicted on me while I was in your power. As it was the custom of your country, to treat your fellow men as you did me and my little family, I can freely forgive you.

I wish to be remembered in love to my aged mother, and friends; please tell her that if we should never meet again in this life, my prayer shall be to God that we may meet in Heaven, where parting shall be no more.

You wish to be remembered to King and Jack. I am pleased, sir, to inform you that they are both here, well, and doing well. They are both living in Canada West. They are now the owners of better farms than the men who once owned them.

You may perhaps think hard of us for running away from slavery, but as to myself, I have but one apology to make for it, which is this: I have only to regret that I did not start at an earlier period. I might have been free long before I was. But you had it in your power to have kept me there much longer than you did. I think it is very probable that I should have been a toiling slave on your plantation today, if you had treated me differently.

To be compelled to stand by and see you whip and slash my wife without mercy, when I could afford her no protection, not even by offering myself to suffer the lash in her place, was more than I felt it to be the duty of a slave husband to endure, while the way was open to Canada. My infant child was also frequently flogged by Mrs. Gatewood, for crying, until its skin was bruised literally purple. This kind of treatment was what drove me from home and family, to seek a better home for them. But I am willing to forget the past. I should be pleased to hear from you again, on the reception of this, and should also be very happy to correspond with you often, if it should be agreeable to yourself. I subscribe myself a friend to the oppressed, and Liberty forever.

HENRY BIBB

[from Jackson Whitney to William Riley]

'FUGITIVE'S HOME,' Sandwich, C.W.,

March 18, 1859

Mr. Wm. Riley, Springfield, Ky. – Sir: I take this opportunity to dictate a few lines to you, supposing you might be curious to know my whereabouts. I am happy to inform you that I am in Canada, in good health, and have been here several days. Perhaps, by this time, you have concluded that robbing a woman of her husband, and children of their father does no pay, at least in your case; and I thought, while lying in jail by your direction, that if you had no remorse of conscience that would make you feel for a poor, broken-hearted man, and his worse-than-murdered wife and child, and could not be made to feel for others as you would have them feel for you, and could not by any entreaty or permission be induced to do as you promised you would, which was to let me go with my family for $800 – but contended for $1,000, when you had promised to take the same you gave for me (which was $660.) at the time you bought me, and let me go with my dear wife and children but instead would render me miserable, and lie to me, and to your neighbors (how if words mean anything, what I say is so.) and when you was at Louisville trying to sell me! then I thought it was time for me to make my feet feel for Canada, and let your conscience feel in your pocket. – Now you cannot say but that I did all that was honorable and right while I was with you, although I was a slave. I pretended all the time that I thought you, or some one else had a better right to me than I had to myself, which you know is rather hard thinking. – You know, too, that you proved a traitor to me in the time of need, and when in the most bitter distress that the human soul is capable of experiencing; and could you have carried out your purposes there would have been no relief. But I rejoice to say that an unseen, kind spirit appeared for the oppressed, and bade me take up my bed and walk – the result of which is that I am victorious and you are defeated.

I am comfortably situated in Canada, working for George Harris, one of the persons that act a part in "Uncle Tom's Cabin." He was a slave a few years ago in Kentucky, and now owns a farm so level that there is not hills enough on it to hide a dog, yet so large that I got lost in it the other day. He says that I may be the means of helping poor fugitives and doing them as much good as he does, in time.

This country is not what it has been represented to me and others to be. In place of its being cold and barren, it has beautiful, comfortable climate, and fertile soil. It is much more desirable in those respects than any part of Kentucky that I ever saw. There is only one thing to prevent me being entirely happy here, and that is the want of my dear wife and children, and you to see us enjoying ourselves together here. I wish you could realize the contrast between Freedom and Slavery; but it is not likely that we shall ever meet again on this earth. But if you want to go to the next world and meet a God of love, mercy, and justice, in peace; who says, "Inasmuch as you did it to the least of them my little ones, you did it unto me" – making the professions that you do, pretending to be a follower of Christ, and tormenting me and my little ones as you have done – had better repair the breaches you have made among us in this world, by sending my wife and children to me; thus preparing to meet your God in peace; for, if God don't punish you for inflicting such distress on the poorest of His poor, then there is no use of *having any* God, or *talking* about one. But in this letter, I have said enough to cause you to do all that is necessary for you to do, providing you are any part of the man you pretend to be. So I will close by saying that, if you see proper to reply to my letter, either condemning or justifying the course you have taken with me, I will again write you.

I hope you will consider candidly and see if the case does not justify every word I have said, and ten times as much. You must not consider that it is a slave talking to "massa" now, but one as free as yourself.

I subscribe myself one of the *abused* of America, but one of the *justified* and *honored* of Canada.

JACKSON WHITNEY

Source: John W. Blassingame, *Slave Testimony: Two Centuries of Letters, Speeches, Interviews and Autobiographies* (Baton Rouge, La.: Louisiana State University Press, 1972), 48-9, 114-15.

George Brown (1818–80)

THE CANADIAN ABOLITIONIST MOVEMENT

George Brown was a prominent journalist and politician of nineteenth-century Canada. Born in Scotland, he emigrated to Canada in 1837 and founded the Toronto *Globe* in 1844. A major figure in the Reform movement that gradually evolved into the Liberal Party, Brown championed the causes of responsible government and representation by population, and in the 1860s he was a leading promoter of Confederation.

Apart from his role as a father of Confederation, George Brown is perhaps best known as one of Canada's most prominent opponents of American slavery. He expressed his views on this subject in issue after issue of the *Globe*. For example, in February 1851, the Anti-Slavery Society of Canada was launched in Toronto. The event gave rise to heated debates in Ontario newspapers, with the *Globe* aligned against papers such as the *Colonist* and *Patriot* which opposed the anti-slavery movement. The following editorial is typical of the kind of moral and rational case which Brown made in his attack on the institution of slavery and in his call to Canadians to join in the abolitionist cause.

The *Colonist* and the *Patriot* have opened their columns to correspondents, who attack the recent movement in this city in favour of the oppressed sons of Africa. They have not uttered a word editorially on the subject, so far as we have observed, – but in the absence of any disavowal of the sentiments of their correspondents, they must be held either to approve, or to be indifferent to this great question, which calls forth the warmest aspirations of the human heart. This cause seems to us to stand on ground so high and unchallengeable, that we regret to see any of our [contemporaries] indifferent about it, or giving their countenance to such attempts to palliate the enormous evil of slavery, and to censure those, who without any other moving principle but that of good will to a suffering race, and detestation of oppression, would aid in eradicating that great evil from the face of the earth. The *Patriot's* man, who has usurped the name of "Common Sense," is smitten with the notion of *checking* those engaged in the Anti-Slavery cause in this city, whom he describes as "a knot of injudicious and comparatively uninfluential persons." He confesses that slavery is attended with "innumerable evils," and then talks of the Abolitionists as carrying out "a crochet," because they wish to destroy a system of "innumerable evils." This may be "common sense" with the abettors of slavery, but it will be pronounced the most wretched folly in any other region. The meeting lately held in the City Hall was a most respectable one, and contained a large proportion of the intelligence and philanthropy of Toronto. It was a meeting of the inhabitants of Toronto, called by public advertisement, and not a whisper of opposition was heard from any one.

If "Common Sense" and the correspondents of the *Colonist* will call another meeting, and try to pass resolutions condemning the "Abolitionists of Vermont and Massachusetts," and in excuse or extenuation of the enormous evil of Slavery they will find how the public of Toronto would frown down the attempt to degrade their rising city in the estimation of the civilized world. Now, we should be curious to know, who would take the chair, and who would move the resolutions, – and curious would these resolutions be.

The first would undoubtedly be, that all men "are born free and equal." The next, Governor Macduffies' declaration, that Slavery is the "corner-stone of the free institutions of the United States." The third, that a three penny tea tax was a good ground for rebellion – but that the holding of slaves in bondage from generation to generation was all right, if the slaves were only held by gallant men who rebelled against the said tea-tax. – And so on would the resolutions proceed. Let these writers come out and show themselves. They would run no risk of being "flogged, shot, or hung," as it is hinted the Abolitionists might be in the slave States. Not one hair of their heads, they well know, would be touched. "Abolition fanatics" here, disown all such means, and only approach their neighbours on the other side, in the language of appeal and remonstrance. And if they have not the right to do so, the world must be in a sad state indeed. – Governments interfere in the affairs of each other, when they conceive their own peace is endangered; and much more a kindred people living in the same land, have an undoubted claim to raise their voice in condemnation of a system which is maintained in violation of the first rights of justice and humanity. The South consists of Slave-breeding and Slave-buying States. The first prepare for the market thousands of victims, many of them the children or grandchildren of the sellers, who are regularly transferred to the more southern States, and, torn from their mothers and other relatives, they are sent far away from the land of their birth into hopeless bondage, among the swamps of the Mississippi, there to linger out their wretched existence, as long as their spirits can bear up under such a fate, or their bodies endure the hardships to which they are compelled to submit.

The poor victims who contrive to escape are hunted in the Northern States, and driven into Canada for shelter. We hear their groans and sympathise with their sufferings, but must not cry aloud against the unutterable atrocities of the system lest, forsooth, we should give offence to the "high mettled race" of the South. We feel exceedingly easy on that score, conscious that we are in the discharge of our duty, both to the slaveholders, and to their "chattels." Nothing was said at the Toronto meeting to incite the slaves to resistance, altho' that often repeated and often refuted calumny on abolitionists is as usual brought up. The *right*, absolute and unchallengeable, to take their freedom by force of arms we hold in the most unqualified manner, – for if resistance be lawful at all, it must be to throw off the shackles of personal slavery, on the part of men who were stolen from Africa, or their fathers before them. But the time to move is their own matter, and sorry would we be to see them rise without strong hopes of success, which present times do not warrant. If the time for action should arrive, most fervently would we cry out – *God speed the right*. We have wished success to the noble Hungarians, against the oppressions of Austria, – to the Romans, and to all Italy, when struggling for liberty, – and why

should we be deaf to the groans of those who labour under a bondage ten times more severe than the oppressed of continental Europe. Because the shouts for European freedom at New York, and the poeans of the fourth of July are drowned in the clanking of the chains in Washington and New Orleans, is the rising spirit of our free Canada to be drilled and broken down to suit the mock liberty of the model Republic? If they have no sympathy for their own oppressed children, they should feel indebted to those whose hearts are large enough to take in the oppressed of every land and of every colour. One letter is chiefly devoted to Rev. Mr. Roaf's simile of interfering to save a wife from being beaten by her husband. We think it an excellent illustration and the *wise saw* about all such interference being dangerous, savours strongly of that selfishness and cowardice which is totally indifferent to the welfare of our neighbours. Lives have been lost by the unlimited exercise of that maxim. We do not find our [contemporaries] rebuking the constant reference in certain American papers to Canadian affairs. The New York *Herald*, so late as last Friday, talks with great coolness of adding Cuba, and perhaps Canada, to the United States in course of the present year. The anti-slavery movement has no such hostile object, it is entirely pacific in its character, and contemplates only such a change as would be beneficial and honorable to the United States, and which is the only true mode of perpetuating the union.

Source: *Globe*, March 6, 1851, 2.

D'Arcy McGee (1825–68)

"A Canadian Nationality"

Thomas D'Arcy McGee was the image-maker of Confederation. An Irish nationalist who had fled his homeland for the United States, he had soon seen enough of the American republic. Moving to Montreal, he was elected to the Legislative Assembly as a liberal and served in the rapidly changing governments of the pre-Confederation period. A short and notably ugly man, McGee captivated friends and audiences with his wit and eloquence. If styles in language have changed radically over a century, some flashes of his brilliance survive.

In this speech, delivered at Quebec City in 1862, McGee hardly needed to remind his audience of the terrible civil war then raging to the south. To survive, he argued, Canada needed more men to defend her – the population of the United Canadas was about the same as the southern Confederacy – and a unifying national spirit of Canadianism. Irish Canadians, divided though they were by the traditional divisions of Catholic and Protestant, must remember that it was in the Canadas that both had found freedom, tolerance, and opportunity. Who owed more to Canada than they did?

McGee would pay with his life for his devotion to Canada and his rejection of his old nationalism. An Irish assassin killed him at his Ottawa doorstep on April 7, 1868.

It is upon this subject of the public spirit which can alone make Canada safe and secure, rich and renowned, which can alone attract population and augment capital, that I desire to say the few words with which I must endeavour to fulfil your expectations. I feel that it is a serious subject for a popular festival; but these are serious times, and they bring upon their wings most serious reflections. That shot fired at Fort Sumter, on April 12, 1861, had a message for the North as well as for the South, and here in Quebec, if anywhere, by the light which history lends us, we should find those who can rightly read that eventful message. Here, from this rock for which the immortals have contended, here, from this rock over which Richelieu's wisdom and Chatham's genius, and the memory of heroic men, the glory of three great nations has hung its halo, we should look forth upon a continent convulsed, and ask of a ruler, "Watchman, what of the night?" That shot fired at Fort Sumter was the signal gun of a new epoch for North America, which told the people of Canada, more plainly than human speech can ever express it, to sleep no more, except on their arms – unless in their sleep they desire to be overtaken and subjugated. For one, I can safely say that if I know myself I have not a particle of prejudice against the United States; on the contrary, I am bound to declare that many things in the constitution and the people I sincerely esteem and admire. What I contend for with myself, and what I would impress upon others, is, that the lesson of the last few months furnished by America to the world should not be thrown away upon the inhabitants of Canada. I do not believe that it is our destiny to be engulphed into a Republican union, renovated and inflamed with the wine of victory, of which she now drinks so freely; it seems to me we have theatre enough under our feet to act another and a worthier part. We can hardly join the Americans on our own terms, and we never ought to join them on theirs. A Canadian nationality – not French-Canadian, nor British-Canadian, nor Irish-Canadian: patriotism rejects the prefix – is, in my opinion, what we should look forward to, that is what we ought to labour for, that is what we ought to be prepared to defend to the death. Heirs of one-seventh of the continent, inheritors of a long ancestral story – and no part of it dearer to us than the glorious tale of this last century – warned not by cold chronicles only, but by living scenes passing before our eyes, of the dangers of an unmixed democracy, we are here to vindicate our capacity, by the test of a new political creation. What we most immediately want to carry on that work is men – more men – and still more men. The ladies, I dare say, will not object to that doctrine. We may not want more lawyers and doctors – but we want more men, in town and country. We want the signs of youth and growth in our young and growing country. One of our maxims should be – "Early marriages, and death to old bachelors." I have

long entertained a project of a special tax upon that most undesirable class of the population, and our friend the Finance Minister may perhaps have something of the kind among the agreeable surprises of his next budget.

Seriously, what I chiefly wanted to say in coming here is this, that if we would make Canada safe and secure, rich and renowned, we must all liberalize – locally, sectionally, religiously, nationally. There is room enough in this country for one great free people; but there is not room enough, under the same flag and the same laws, for two or three angry, suspicious, obstructive "nationalities." Dear, most justly dear to every land beneath the sun are the children born in her bosom and nursed upon her breast; but when the man of another country, wherever born, speaking whatever speech, holding whatever creed, seeks out a country to serve and honour and cleave to, in weal or in woe – when he heaves up the anchor of his heart from its old moorings, and lays at the feet of the mistress of his choice, his new country, all the hopes of his ripe manhood, he establishes by such devotion a claim to consideration not second even to that of the children of the soil. He is their brother delivered by a new birth from the dark-wombed Atlantic ship that ushers him into existence in the new world; he stands by his own election among the children of the household; and narrow and unwise is that species of public spirit which, in the perverted name of patriotism, would refuse him all he asks – "a fair field and no favour." I am not about to talk politics, though these are grand politics; I reserve all else for what is usually called "another place" – and, I may add, for another time. But I am so thoroughly convinced and assured that we are gliding along the currents of a new epoch, that if I break silence at all, in the presence of my fellow-subjects, I cannot choose but speak of the immense issues which devolve upon us, at this moment, in this country. Though we are alike opposed to all invidious national distinctions on this soil, we are not opposed, I hope, to giving full credit to all the elements which at the present day compose our population. In this respect it is a source of gratification to learn that among your invited guests to-night there are twelve or thirteen members of the House to which I have the honour to belong – gentlemen from both sides of the House – who drew their native breath in our own dearly beloved ancestral island. It takes three-quarters of the world in these days to hold an Irish family, and it is pleasant to know that some of the elder sons of the family are considered by their discriminating fellow-citizens worthy to be entrusted with the liberties and fortunes of their adopted countries. We have here men of Irish birth who have led, and who still lead, the Parliament of Canada, and who are determined to lead it in a spirit of genuine liberality.

We Irishmen, Protestant and Catholic, born and bred in a land of religious controversy, should never forget that we now live and act in a land of the fullest religious and civil liberty. All we have to do is, each for himself, to keep down dissensions which can only weaken, impoverish, and keep back the country; each for himself do all he can to increase its wealth, its strength, and its reputation; each for himself – you and you, gentlemen, and all of us – to welcome every talent, to hail every invention, to cherish every gem of art, to foster every gleam of authorship, to honour every acquirement and every natural gift, to lift ourselves to the level of our destinies, to rise above all low limitations and narrow circumscriptions, to cultivate that true catholicity of spirit which embraces all creeds, all classes, and all races, in order to make of our boundless province, so rich in known and unknown resources, a great new Northern nation.

Source: Lawrence J. Burpee, ed., *Canadian Eloquence* (Toronto: Mission Book, 1910), 79-83.

Alexander Muir (1830—1906)

"THE MAPLE LEAF FOREVER"

For years, English-speaking Canadians regarded "The Maple Leaf Forever" as virtually a national anthem. Its author, Alexander Muir, was born in Scotland, came to Canada as a child, and graduated from Queen's University in Kingston in 1851. He composed the song when he was a schoolteacher at Leslieville, in the east end of Toronto, in 1866, when enthusiasm for the new nation about to be created ran high. Patriotic audiences were delighted to remember General James Wolfe, whose army had captured Quebec in 1759, or Canadian victories over the Americans at Queenston Heights and Lundy's Lane in the War of 1812. Later, Muir was a Toronto public school principal and it was in that city that his song enjoyed its greatest popularity.

Muir's Canada, with its emphasis on triumphs over the French and its attachment to England, Scotland, Ireland, and Queen Victoria, had no room for the French-speaking partners who had made Confederation possible, nor did it offer much of a place for the other peoples who would enrich Canada. Cherished as it might be by some Canadians, the song proved less durable than the maple leaf itself. While modern representations of the maple leaf commonly show it in its brilliant but dying colour, red, it was generally portrayed in the nineteenth century in a living green.

In days of yore, from Britain's shore,
　Wolfe, the dauntless hero, came,
And planted firm Britannia's flag
　On Canada's fair domain.
Here may it wave, our boast and pride,
　And, joined in love together,
The Thistle, Shamrock, Rose entwine
　The Maple Leaf forever!

CHORUS –
The Maple Leaf, our emblem dear,
　The Maple Leaf for ever;
God save our Queen, and Heaven bless
　The Maple Leaf for ever!
At Queenston's Heights and Lundy's Lane,

Our brave fathers, side by side,
For freedom, homes, and loved ones dear,
　Firmly stood and nobly died.
And those dear rights which they maintained,
　We swear to yield them never!
Our watchword evermore shall be,
　The Maple Leaf forever!

CHORUS – The Maple Leaf, &c.

Our fair Dominion now extends
　From Cape Race to Nootka Sound;
May peace forever be our lot,
　And plenteous store abound;

And may those ties of love be ours
 Which discord cannot sever,
And flourish green o'er freedom's home,
 The Maple Leaf forever!

CHORUS – The Maple Leaf, &c.

On merry England's far-famed land,
 May kind Heaven sweetly smile,
God bless old Scotland evermore,

And Ireland's emerald Isle!
Then swell the song both loud and long
 Till rocks and forests quiver,
God save our Queen, and Heaven bless
 The Maple Leaf forever!

CHORUS – The Maple Leaf, &c.

Source: Daniel Clark, ed., *Selections from Scottish Canadian Poets* . . . (Toronto, n.d.), 294-5.

George-Étienne Cartier (1814–73)

"I AM ALSO A FRENCH CANADIAN"

Sir George-Étienne Cartier's father named his son in honour of King George III, who in his mind had saved Quebec from falling under the control of revolutionary France at the close of the eighteenth century and the beginning of the nineteenth. For his own part, the young Cartier helped drive Queen Victoria's redcoats from Saint-Denis in 1837. Later, he would be a key leader of the Confederation movement and would receive his baronetcy from the Queen whose troops he had helped to defeat.

Speaking to fellow Montrealers on October 20, 1866, just before leaving for London, Cartier speaks of his pride as a *Canadien* and his optimism for the "new nation" he was about to create. Cartier had done much more. As lawyer for the Grand Trunk Railway, he had helped develop British North America's greatest public work. He had led the long, patient struggle to end Lower Canada's seigniorial system and to provide it with its unique Civil Code. Bitterly attacked for sacrificing Lower Canada's advantages under the Act of Union of 1840, Cartier insisted that he had acted like a wise conservative, abandoning what was indefensible but giving French Canadians the fullest possible protection for their "cultural nationality." Was he wrong?

I too am a French Canadian, like many of those I see around me. I love my race, and of course I have a very natural predilection for it; but as a politician and as a citizen, I love others as well. And I am happy to see, in this meeting of fellow citizens of all classes, races and religions, that my compatriots have recognized these feelings in me: I have already had the opportunity to declare in Parliament that the Protestant minority in Lower Canada has nothing to fear from the provincial legislature under Confederation. I have given my word and, I repeat, nothing will be done of such a nature as to harm the principles and rights of this minority. I take as my witnesses all the Protestant companions who are listening to me. I have given my word and I will keep it; it is the word of a man of honour. I see here beside me distinguished soldiers whose motto is, *"Mourir pour la patrie"* – "Die for one's country." The statesman's motto should be, *"Tiens ta parole jusqu'à la mort"* – "Keep your word until death."

Having told you that the Protestants of Lower Canada will have all possible guarantees, I must add that the Catholic minority of Upper Canada will have the same guarantees, and I give you my solemn word on this as well. The Catholic minority in Upper Canada will be protected equally with the Protestant minority in Lower Canada. Any fears on this score are empty and false. Don't dwell on this subject and, I say it again, all will be well. If I have gone on a little long, I owed it to myself and to you, for I needed to provide you with the means of giving some justification for the honour that you have accorded me.

My friends, a glorious era lies before us: we are entering Confederation. Let it not frighten you! After all, it is nothing but the realization of a plan designed by the first European to set foot in Canada: Jacques Cartier. Would Lower Canada want to limit the influence of the French race to the narrow confines of our province? When Jacques Cartier, in 1534, after landing in Newfoundland, discovered part of Canada and New Brunswick, he guaranteed its possession by France. François I, who claimed his share of America by virtue of Adam's will, sent Jacques Cartier out again, and the navigator extended his discoveries. What Jacques Cartier called Acadia comprises New Brunswick and Nova Scotia.

Thus, the lands that Jacques Cartier identified or discovered, at least in part, will soon be ruled by the same government. With Confederation, we will realize a vision of this great man: the coming together of all the provinces he discovered. If he rose from the grave today, he would undoubtedly look with satisfaction on this great country, enlightened by civilization and soon to enjoy an era of prosperity and happiness brought on by Confederation.

French Canadians have no need to be afraid of the English. After all, they are not so frightening. (Laughter) Instead, let us admire their energy and perseverance; let us imitate them. To be excellent French Canadians we need to have, along with the qualities of our race, the best qualities of the English Canadians. (Applause) We are partly descended from the Normans, and the blood of this heroic race is infused in the veins of the English as well, since the days of William the Conqueror.

Before closing, I would like to say a word about the British institutions under which we are governed. This is the only form of government in the world that, while making use of the democratic element, has been able to keep it within reasonable limits. The democratic element has a fortunate effect in the political sphere when it is balanced by another force. We have this advantage over our neighbours the Americans, who have extreme democracy. It is the same in politics as it is in the physical world. The centripetal force has to be greater than the centrifugal force.

Jacques Cartier brought with him monarchical principles that I love and cherish. He is my namesake: I would like to walk in the footsteps of this illustrious man and I do not want to detract from his great plans. If, when three more centuries have passed, history remembers my name as someone who did something for his country, and if it says that one day I deviated from the virtue of my ancestors, it will hold my memory in abhorrence, and I do not wish it to be so! (Prolonged applause)

Source: Joseph Tassé, ed., *Discours de Sir George Cartier, Baronnet* (Montreal, 1893), 514-15.

George Brown (1818–80)

"Confederation Day"

George Brown's role as a father of Confederation took shape in the 1860s when he came to the conclusion that a federation of the British North American colonies was the best means to reform the existing Union of the Canadas, established in 1840. He launched a coalition with his political rivals, the Conservatives of John A. Macdonald, to create a new federal union, and he played a key part in the nation-building conferences at Charlottetown and Quebec.

The following selection from the *Globe* of July 1, 1867 reflects the sense of optimism which was found among both English- and French-speaking Canadians and in all of the four provinces in the early days of Confederation.

The Union of the Provinces of Canada, Nova Scotia and New Brunswick, under the new Constitution, takes effect to-day. We heartily congratulate our readers on the event, and fervently pray that all the blessings anticipated from the measure, by its promoters, may be fully realized.

So far as the people of Upper Canada are concerned, the inauguration of the new Constitution may well be heartily rejoiced over as the brightest day in their calendar. The Constitution of 1867 will be famous in the historical annals of Upper Canada, not only because it brought two flourishing Maritime States into alliance with the Canadas, and opened up new markets for our products, and a direct railway route to the Atlantic through British territory, but because it relieved the inhabitants of Western Canada from a system of injustice and demoralization under which they had suffered for a long series of years.

The unanimity and cordiality with which all sections of the people of Canada accept the new Constitution, gives the happiest omen of its successful operation. And, assuredly, if the people of the United Provinces are true to themselves and exercise a persistent and careful control over all public proceedings, there is not a shadow of doubt as to success. The only danger that threatens us is, lest the same men who have so long misgoverned us, should continue to misgovern us still, and the same reckless prodigality exhibited in past years should be continued in the future; but this we do not fear. We firmly believe, that from this day, Canada enters on a new and happier career, and that a time of great prosperity and advancement is before us.

Susanna Moodie (1803–85)

"Canadian Hunters' Song"

Susanna Moodie, her sister, Catherine Parr Traill (1802–99), and her brother, Samuel Strickland (1804–67), were typical of the impecunious English gentry who set out to make their fortunes as pioneers in the Upper Canadian wilderness. Susanna's snobbish contempt for the crudity of many of her fellow pioneers around Peterborough was reciprocated by the hostility of her neighbours. Later, when her husband, W.D. Moodie, was appointed sheriff of Hastings County after the Rebellion of 1837, she could enjoy a more comfortable life. She also mellowed in her view of frontier folk. One of the colony's earliest writers, she contributed to the *Literary Garland*, one of the rare early magazines to pay its authors. Among Susanna Moodie's best-known books were *Roughing It in the Bush* (1852) and *Life in the Clearings* (1853).

The "Canadian Hunters' Song" will win no prizes for subtlety or elegance of rhyme or diction but it does provide a glimpse into a time when success in the hunt postponed hunger in a pioneer homestead.

The Northern Lights are flashing
  On the rapids' restless flow;
But o'er the wild waves dashing
  Swift darts the light canoe,
  The merry hunters come,
    "What cheer? What cheer?"

"We've slain the deer!"
  "Hurrah! you're welcome home!"

The blithesome horn is sounding,
  And the woodman's loud halloo;
And joyous steps are bounding

To meet the birch canoe.
"Hurrah! the hunters come!"
And the woods ring out
To their noisy shout,
As they drag the dun deer home!

The hearth is brightly burning,
The rustic board is spread;
To greet their sire returning
The children leave their bed.

With laugh and shout they come,
That merry band,
To grasp his hand
And bid him welcome home!

Source: William D. Lighthall, ed., *Canadian Poems and Plays: Selections of Native Verse, Reflecting the Seasons, Legends and Life of the Dominion* (London: Walter Scott, n.d.), 114.

Part Two

1867—1920

John A. Macdonald (1815–91)

A NATION-BUILDER

Canada's first prime minister, Sir John A. Macdonald was born in Scotland and raised in Upper Canada. A lawyer in Kingston before entering politics, he was an instinctive conservative who supported the monarchy, mistrusted the prejudices and mood swings of the masses, and opposed the idea of Confederation until it seemed almost inevitable. Yet few Upper Canadians had an earlier or clearer sense of the political possibilities of the French-English partnership in the United Canadas created in 1840. Writing in 1856 to William Chamberlin, a prominent English Montrealer, he offered some shrewd, frank, and deeply felt advice about the role of the French-speaking population in Canada:

No man in his senses can suppose that this country can for a century to come be governed by a totally unfrenchified government – If a Lower Canadian Britisher desires to conquer, he must "stoop to conquer" – He must make friends with the French – without sacrificing the status of his race or lineage he must respect their nationality – Treat them as a nation and they will act as a free people generally do – generously. Call them a faction, and they become factious – Supposing the numerical preponderance of British in Canada becomes much greater than it is, I think the French could give more trouble than they are said now to do – At present they divide as we do, they are split up into several factions – & are governed more [or] less by defined principles of action – As they become smaller & feebler, so they will be more united – from a sense of self-preservation – they will act as one man & hold the balance of power ... So long as the French have 20 votes they will be a power & must be conciliated – I doubt much however if the French will lose their numerical majority in [Lower Canada] in a hurry ...

Source: John A Macdonald to Chamberlin, January 21, 1856, in National Archives of Canada, Brown-Chamberlin Papers, cited in Michael Bliss, *Canadian History in Documents, 1793-1966* (Toronto: Ryerson Press, 1966), 97.

As prime minister, Macdonald made an early attempt to settle bitter outstanding quarrels with the United States and to launch a transcontinental railway to fulfil the Confederation dream of a country stretching from the Atlantic to the Pacific. Concessions to the Americans cost him support, and, when his desperate appeals for election donations from the Pacific Railway syndicate became public knowledge, the resulting scandal brought humiliation and defeat in the

election of 1873. However, Macdonald's political fortunes turned as Canada was caught in the great worldwide depression of the 1870s. In power, the Liberals under Alexander Mackenzie (1822–92) clung to the principle of free trade; in opposition, Macdonald was able to choose his own ground. By 1878, the Conservatives could mobilize Canadian manufacturers and their workers in a campaign for high tariffs to protect Canadian-made products and jobs. Macdonald's argument was simple though controversial: what country would ever prosper by selling only raw materials and unfinished products?

We must, by every reasonable means, employ our people, not in one branch of industry, not merely as farmers, as tillers of the soil, but we must bring out every kind of industry, we must develop the minds of the people and their energies. Every man is not fitted to be a farmer, to till the soil; one man has a constructive genius, another is an artist, another has an aptitude for trade, another is a skilful mechanic – all these men are to be found in a nation, and if Canada has only one branch of industry to offer them, if these men cannot find an opportunity in their own country to develop the skill and genius with which God has gifted them, they will go to a country where their abilities can be employed, as they have gone from Canada to the United States.

Source: House of Commons *Debates*, December 10, 1880, 28-31, cited in Bliss, *Canadian History in Documents*, 157.

In 1889 Sir John A. Macdonald faced one of those disputes that periodically explode in Canadian politics, setting Catholics against Protestants, French against English. In Quebec, Premier Honoré Mercier (1840–94) proposed to settle an old dispute about the ownership of former Jesuit property by referring the issue to the Pope. Militant Protestants were outraged. How dare Mercier invite a foreign potentate to meddle in a loyal dominion of the British Empire? Led by one of the most popular and eloquent Conservatives of the day, Toronto lawyer D'Alton McCarthy (1836–98), a mass movement demanded that Ottawa disallow Mercier's Jesuit Estates Bill.

Macdonald understood what was really at stake: bigotry. He knew that Mercier had cleverly designed his legislation to split Catholics and Protestants. When he rose in the House on March 28, 1889 to address the issue, Macdonald teased both sides for their attempt to create bitter divisions but the conclusion of his speech was deadly serious. Canada's first prime minister knew that the country could survive only in a spirit of compromise and understanding. Disallowance of the controversial legislation would light the fire that could destroy Canada.

No Government can be formed in Canada either by myself or by the hon. member who moves this resolution (Mr. O'Brien) or by my hon. friend who sits opposite (Mr. Laurier) having in mind the disallowance of such a measure. What would be the consequence of a disallowance? Agitation, a quarrel – a racial and a religious war would be aroused. The best interests of the country would be prejudiced, our credit would be ruined abroad, and our social relations destroyed at home. I cannot sufficiently picture, in my faint language, the misery and the wretchedness which would have been heaped upon Canada if this question, having been agitated as it has been, and could be, had culminated in a series of disallowances of this Act.

Source: House of Commons *Debates*, 28 March 1889, 908.

In 1891 the Old Chieftain, as supporters called him, gave his final months to winning what would turn out to be his party's last victory for twenty years. Many believed that his government was already doomed. A deepening depression mocked the promise of the National Policy of high tariffs. In 1885 the Canadian Pacific had linked Vancouver and Montreal, but the vast prairie region had been parched with drought since 1886. Many Canadians passed judgment on Confederation with their feet; they emigrated to the United States. Others demanded "unrestricted reciprocity," virtual free trade with the United States. Some even wanted "continental union," amalgamation with the neighbouring republic. To outflank his critics, Macdonald secretly sought a trade deal with Washington, only to be rebuffed.

What was left? Through his career, Macdonald had often bridled at British arrogance, and he had done much to expand Canada's control of its own affairs, but as he addressed the packed election rallies in the bitter winter of 1891, the old man's emotions were genuine too. He delivered a speech that countless Canadian schoolchildren would have to memorize and declaim. It worked. The Conservatives won and free trade was dead for another ninety-eight years. It was Sir John A.'s last effort for Canada: on June 6, 1891 he was dead. The following is Macdonald's famous "A British Subject I Was Born" speech of 1891.

I have pointed out to you a few of the material objections to this scheme of Unrestricted Reciprocity, but they are not the only objections, nor in my opinion the most vital. For a century and a half this country has grown and flourished under the protecting aegis of the British Crown. The gallant race who first bore to our shores the blessings of civilization passed by an easy transition from French to English rule, and now form one of the most law-abiding portions of the community. These pioneers were speedily recruited by the advent of a loyal band of British subjects, who gave up everything that men most prize, and were content to begin life anew in the wilderness rather than forgo allegiance to their Sovereign. To the descendants of these men, and of the multitude of Englishmen, Irishmen, and Scotchmen who emigrated to Canada, that they might build up new homes without ceasing to be British subjects – to you Canadians I appeal, and I ask you what have you to gain by surrendering that which your fathers held most dear? Under the broad folds of the Union Jack we enjoy the most ample liberty, to govern ourselves as we please, and at the same time we participate in the advantages which flow from association with the mightiest Empire the world has ever seen. Not only are we free to manage our domestic concerns, but, practically, we possess the privilege of making our own treaties with foreign countries, and, in our relations with the outside world, we enjoy the prestige inspired by a consciousness of the fact that behind us towers the majesty of England. The question you will shortly be called upon to determine resolves itself into this: shall we endanger our possession of the great heritage bequeathed to us by our fathers, and submit ourselves to direct taxation for the privilege of having our tariff fixed at Washington, with a prospect of ultimately becoming a portion of the American Union? I commend these issues to your determination, and to the judgment of the whole people of Canada, with an unclouded confidence that you will proclaim to the world your resolve to show yourselves not unworthy of the proud distinction that you enjoy, of being numbered among the most dutiful and loyal subjects of our beloved Queen.

As for myself, my course is clear. A British subject I was born – a British subject I will die. With my utmost effort, with my latest breath, will I oppose the "veiled treason" which attempts by sordid means and mercenary proffers to lure our people from their allegiance. During my long public service of nearly half a century I have been true to my country and its best interests, and I appeal with equal confidence to the men who have trusted me in the past, and to the young hope of the country, with whom rests its destinies for the future, to give me their united and strenuous aid in this, my last effort, for the unity of the Empire and the preservation of our commercial and political freedom.

Source: Lawrence J. Burpee, *Canadian Eloquence* (Toronto: Mission Book, 1910), 66, 69.

Edward Blake (1833–1912)

SPEECH AT AURORA, 1874

Easily one of the most brilliant Canadians of his age, Edward Blake enlightened his times with his liberalism and sense of justice. Then, as quickly, he would bend to the necessities of political office and electoral prejudice. In 1871 he used Ontario outrage against Louis Riel to defeat a provincial government; fifteen years later, as Opposition leader, he defended Riel's cause in Parliament. When his successor endorsed unrestricted reciprocity with the United States before the 1891 election, Blake was silent, only to denounce his party soon after its defeat. When he left for British politics in 1892 to fight for the cause of Irish Home Rule, few Liberals mourned his departure.

One of Blake's most memorable speeches was at Aurora, north of Toronto, on October 3, 1874, before a rally of Liberal farmers. His party had just won national power in 1873 and Blake, as a minister without portfolio, had no business being controversial. Instead, young Canadian nationalists from Toronto came to listen and then cheered themselves hoarse. Rather than offer political bromides, Blake challenged the government to assert Canada's independence in the world and to establish a national identity for its people. Until then, by their own choice, Canadians remained "four million Britons who are not free."

Let me turn to another question which has been adverted to on several occasions, as one looming in the not very distant future. I refer to the relations of Canada to the Empire. Upon this topic I took, three or four years ago, an opportunity of speaking, and ventured to suggest that an effort should be made to reorganize the Empire upon a Federal basis. I repeat what I then said, that the time may be at hand when the people of Canada shall be called on to discuss the question. Matters cannot drift much longer as they have drifted hitherto. The Treaty of Washington produced a very profound impression throughout this country. It produced a feeling that at no distant period the people of Canada would desire that they should have some greater share of control than they now have in the management of foreign affairs; that our Government should not present the anomaly which it now presents – a Government the freest, perhaps the most democratic in the world with reference to local and domestic matters in which you rule yourselves as fully as any people in the world, while in your foreign affairs, your relations with other countries, whether peaceful or warlike, commercial, financial, or otherwise, you may have no more voice than the people of Japan. This, however, is a state of things of which you have no right to complain, because so long as you do not choose to undertake the responsibilities and burdens which attach to some share of control in these affairs, you cannot fairly claim the rights and privileges of free-born Britons in such matters. But how long is this talk in the newspapers and elsewhere – this talk which I find in very high places, of the desirability, aye, of the necessity of fostering a national spirit among the people of Canada, to be mere talk? It is impossible to foster a national spirit unless you have national interests to attend to, or among people who do not choose to undertake the responsibilities and to devote themselves to the duties to which national attributes belong. We have been invited by Mr. Gladstone and other English statesmen – notably by Mr. Gladstone, in the House of Commons, very shortly before his Government fell, to come forward. Mr. Gladstone, speaking as Prime Minister of England, expressed the hope he cherished that the Colonies would some day come forward, and express their readiness and desire to accept their full share in the privileges and in the responsibilities of Britons. It is for us to determine – not now, not this year, not perhaps during this Parliamentary term, but yet at no distant day – what our line shall be. For my own part I believe that while it was not unnatural, not unreasonable, pending that process of development which has been going on in our new and sparsely settled country, that we should have been quite willing – we so few in numbers, so busied in our local concerns, so engaged in subduing the earth and setting up the country – to leave the cares and privileges to which I have referred in the hands of the parent State; the time will come when that national spirit, which has been spoken of, will be truly felt amongst us, when we shall realize that we are four millions of Britons who are not free, when we shall be ready to take up that freedom, and to ask what the late Prime Minister of England assured us we should not be denied – our share of national rights. To-morrow, by the policy of England, in which you have no voice or control, this country might be plunged into all the horrors of a war. It is but the other day that, without your knowledge or consent, the navigation of the St. Lawrence was ceded forever to the United States. That is a state of things of which you may have no right to complain, as long as you choose to say, "We prefer to avoid the cares, the expenses and charges, and we are unequal in point of ability to discharge the duties which appertain to us as free-born Britons;" but while you say this, you may not yet assume the lofty air, or speak in the high-pitched tones which belong to a people wholly free. The future of Canada, I believe, depends very largely upon the cultivation of a national spirit. We are engaged in a very difficult task – the task of welding together seven Provinces, which have been accustomed to regard themselves as isolated from each other, which are fully of petty jealousies, their Provincial questions, their local interests. How are we to accomplish our work? How are we to effect a real union between these Provinces? Can we do it by giving a sop now to one, now to another, after the manner of the late Government? By giving British Columbia the extravagant terms which have been referred to[*]; by giving New Brunswick $150,000 a year for an export duty which cannot be made out as worth more than $65,000 a year? Do you hope to create or to preserve harmony and good feeling upon such a false and sordid and mercenary basis as that? Not so! That even were we disposed, as I hope we shall never be disposed, to offer to join them [the United States], [they will display] a great reluctance to take us. But I believe we have a future of our own here. My opinion coincides with those to which I have been referring in the United States. I believe that that country is even larger than it ought to be in order to be well governed, and that an extension of its territory would be very unfortunate in the interests of civilization. "Cribbed, cabined and confined" as we ourselves are to the South, by the unfortunate acts of English diplomats in the past, giving up to the United States territory which, if we had it to-day, would make our future absolutely assured, but still retaining as we do the great North-West, I believe we can show that there is room and verge enough in North America for the maintenance of two distinct governments, and that there is nothing to be said in favour, but, on the contrary, everything to be said against the notion of annexation. These are the material

reasons, independent altogether of the very strong and justly adverse feeling arising from our affection for and our association with England, and the well settled conviction which I believe exists among the people of this country that a Constitutional Monarchy is preferable to a Republican Government. The Monarchical Government of England is a truer application of real Republican principles than that of the United States, and I have no hesitation in saying that the Government of Canada is far in advance, in the application of real Republican principles, of the Government of either England or the United States. (Cheers.) But, with the very great advantages which we enjoy over that portion of our fellow-subjects living in England, by reason of our having come into a new country, having settled it for ourselves, and adapted our institutions to modern notions, by reason of our not being cumbered by the constitution of a legislative chamber on the hereditary principle, by reason of our not being cumbered with an aristocracy, or with the unfortunate principle of primogeniture and the aggregation of the land in very few hands, by reason of our not being cumbered with the difficulties which must always exist where a community is composed of classes differing from one another in worldly circumstances so widely as the classes in England differ, where you can go into one street of the city of London and find the extreme of wealth, and a mile or two away

---

[*] The terms governing British Columbia's entry into Confederation in 1871.

the very extreme of poverty; living, as we do, in a country where these difficulties do not exist, where we early freed ourselves from the incubus of a State Church, where we early provided for the educational needs of our people, under these happy circumstances, with these great privileges, there are corresponding responsibilities.

Source: Speech by the Hon. Edward Blake (MP for the South Riding of Bruce) at Aurora. Delivered October 3rd, 1874 on the occasion of a meeting of the Reform Party of North York (Montreal, 1875), 10-15.

Adolphe-Basile Routhier (1839–1920), Calixa Lavallée (1842–91), and Robert Stanley Weir (1858–1926)

"O Canada"

Canadians have had notorious difficulty in agreeing on national symbols. The adoption of the flag in 1964 took almost a year of bitter parliamentary debate and followed a long series of attempts to find a nationally acceptable design. Yet Canadians seem to have accepted "O Canada" long before Parliament endorsed it as our national anthem in 1967 (it was *officially* adopted only in 1980 under the National Anthem Act).

The song was prepared for the Société Saint-Jean-Baptiste in June 1880. The words were by Judge Adolphe-Basile Routhier, and the music by Calixa Lavallée, who published the piece as "Chant National." Popular in Quebec, it was not known in English-speaking Canada until 1901, when it was sung in Toronto during a visit by the future King George V. English words were later supplied by Robert Stanley Weir, a Montreal lawyer, author, and later judge. Parliament took a hand in 1967, amending the text in two places to make Weir's version less repetitive and more inconclusive. Nevertheless, some critics have since complained that someone should have found a more inclusive replacement for "all thy sons command."

O Canada, terre de nos aïeux,
Ton front est ceint de fleurons glorieux.
Car ton bras sait porter l'épée,
Il sait porter la croix!
Ton histoire est une épopée

O Canada! Our home and native land!
True patriot love in all thy sons command.
With glowing hearts we see thee rise,
The True North strong and free!
From far and wide, O Canada,

Des plus brillants exploits.	We stand on guard for thee,
Et ta valeur, de foi trempée,	God keep our land glorious and free!
Protégera nos foyers et nos droits,	O Canada, we stand on guard for thee.
Protégera nos foyers et nos droits.	O Canada, we stand on guard for thee!

Thomas-Jean-Jacques Loranger (1823-85)

THE COMPACT THEORY

Is Canada's federal system the result of an agreement by a few dozen politicians in frock coats, or does it stem from a solemn compact or treaty among the provinces of British North America? Thomas Loranger knew his answer. In 1884 the Quebec City lawyer set out a carefully argued interpretation of Confederation that most Quebeckers still accept. Citing the great Canadian constitutional expert of his day, Alpheus Todd (1821–84), Loranger insisted that Canada, far from creating provinces, had been created by them, and that this solemn treaty could not be changed without their consent. Nor could Ottawa seize powers not conceded to it.

Apart from constitutional lawyers and historians, few Canadians outside Quebec have ever heard of Loranger or his "compact theory" of Confederation; to most Québécois, however, the theory explains how federalism should work, and, if its principles are violated, Canada is broken as much as the Confederation treaty. Sovereignists use Loranger's ideas to justify breaking with Canada; many federalists insist that Loranger's Canada can still work, particularly if Quebec is brought back into the constitutional consensus of which it was not a part at the time of the patriation of the British North America Act in 1982. Either way, Loranger's interpretation of the BNA Act is part of the "dialogue of the deaf" in our Confederation.

SUMMARY OF THE PROPOSITIONS
SET FORTH IN THIS LETTER.

A summary of these propositions may be stated as follows: –

1. The confederation of the British Provinces was the result of a compact entered into by the provinces and the Imperial Parliament, which, in enacting the British North America Act, simply ratified it.

2. The provinces entered into the federal Union, with their corporate identity, former constitutions, and all their legislative powers, part of which they ceded to the Federal Parliament, to exercise them in their common interest and for purposes of general utility,

keeping the rest which they left to be exercised by their legislatures, acting in their provincial sphere, according to their former constitutions, under certain modifications of form, established by the federal compact.

3. Far from having been conferred upon them by the federal government, the powers of the provinces not ceded to that government are the residue of their old powers, and far from having been created by it, the federal government was the result of their association and of their compact, and was created from them.

4. The Parliament has no legislative powers beyond those which were conferred upon it by the provinces, and which are recognized by section 91 of the British North America Act, which conferred upon it, only the powers therein mentioned or those of a similar nature, *ejusdem generis.*

5. In addition to the powers conferred upon the legislatures by section 91 and section 92, their legislative jurisdiction extends to all matters of a local or private nature, and all omitted cases fall within provincial jurisdiction, if they touch the local or private interests of one or some of the provinces only: on the other hand, if they interest all the provinces, they belong to Parliament.

6. In case it be doubtful whether any special matter touches all, or one, or a few provinces only, that is to say, if it be of general or local interest, such doubt must be decided in favor of the provinces, which preserved all their powers not ascribed to Parliament.

7. In the reciprocal sphere of their authority thus recognized, there exists no superiority in favor of Parliament over the provinces, but, subject to Imperial sovereignty, these provinces are quasi-sovereign within their respective spheres, and there is absolute equality between them.

8. The British North America Act, was not, as the constitutional acts which preceded it, a law made by the Sovereign authority of England imposing a constitution upon its colonies.

a. It contained a simple ratification by the Mother Country of the agreement entered into by the provinces, which in confirming its provisions rendered them obligatory by giving them the authority of an Imperial act.

b. Without attacking British sovereignty and without, in any way, hindering its exercise with respect to the Dominion, the appreciation of the relations between the federal government and the provinces, created by this agreement, thus made an Imperial statute, the distribution of the respective duties of the two bodies, and the interpretation of the statute, must be made as if the provinces had originally the right of their own private authority to enter into this agreement, and as if they had been sovereign powers.

c. The Imperial Government, which alone had the right to contest this fiction, renounced the same by retroactively legalizing their acts by its ratification.

This eighth and last proposition, which is the justification of those which precede it, and the foundation alone of my work, I will prove in a future letter, as well from the act itself, its comparison with the resolutions of the conference, and the discussion before the Colonial and Imperial Parliaments, as from a narration of the events respecting Confederation which took place both in Canada and in England.

Source: T.J.J. Loranger, *Letters upon the Interpretation of the Federal Constitution Known as the British North America Act (1867), First Letter* (Quebec City, 1884), ch. 8.

Wilfrid Laurier (1841–1919)

THE PLUMED KNIGHT

Few expected Wilfrid Laurier to become prime minister of Canada. A McGill University graduate and country lawyer at Arthabaskaville, Quebec, he entered Parliament in 1874 and served briefly as postmaster general. Charming and eloquent, he was also sickly, shy, and seemingly destined for an early grave. Still, when more renowned leaders refused the burden of leading the Liberals in opposition, the frail Laurier seemed a good interim choice. He would give an Ontario-dominated party a profile in Quebec. But could a French-speaking Catholic be made acceptable to Ontarians and especially to the fanatically Protestant and pro-British voters of Toronto? After all, only a year before, he had proclaimed that if he had been living on the banks of the Saskatchewan River, he, too, would have shouldered a musket with the Metis rebels. On December 10, 1886 Toronto Liberals held their breath and listened as the pale, handsome Quebecker reminded the throng that rebels had fought and won the freedoms that made England great:

[G]entlemen, the spirit of liberty is not the result of culture. It may be found in the lowest man. And let a man be ever so low, he had the right to justice whenever justice is denied to him. And remember this – remember this – these half-savage people who rebelled in the North-West did not rebel against the authority of Her Majesty the Queen. They did not rebel through any sense of disloyalty to the British Crown or dislike of British institutions. They rebelled without any plan or order of proceedings. The reason they rebelled is simple enough, and the reason is this: that the meanest worm that crawls upon the earth, when trampled upon, will endeavour to recoil and strike back, and I say that the guilt of the rebellion does not rest with these men so much as with those who provoked them.

Later, in the same speech, Laurier gave his Toronto audience one of the most powerful images of the Canadian partnership ever uttered:

Below the Island of Montreal, the water that comes from the north, from the Ottawa, united with the waters that come from the western lakes, but uniting, they do not mix. There they run parallel, separate, distinguishable, and yet are one stream, flowing within the same banks, the mighty St. Lawrence, and rolling on toward the sea, bearing the commerce of a nation upon its bosom – a perfect image of our nation. We may not assimilate, we may not blend, but for all that we are still the component parts of the same country.

Source: *Globe*, December 11, 1886.

As a politician aspiring to lead all of Canada, Laurier had to reassure his fellow French Canadians that he had not forgotten their concerns as a minority. At the Club National in Montreal, he spoke of the partnership of the two main Canadian races as a "unity in diversity":

[T]he day is coming when this country will have to take its place among the nations of the earth. But I do not want to see my country's independence attained through the hostility of one race to the others. I do not want my country's independence to be conceived in the blood of civil war. I want my country's independence to be reached through the normal and regular progress of all the elements of its population towards the realization of a common aspiration.

We of French origin have the sentiment of our own individuality. We want to hand down to our children the language we received from our forefathers. But, while cherishing this feeling in our hearts, we do not admit that it is incompatible with our title of Canadians. We are citizens of Canada and intend to fulfil all the duties which that title involves.

. . . the moments we invite to our table men of another race . . . we affirm that we acknowledge them as our fellow-countrymen as they acknowledge we are theirs. Their country is our country. Their political views are our political views. What they want, we want. That they want and we want is that the rights of the minorities should be respected, that the constitutional guarantees be safeguarded, the provinces sovereign in their authority, and Canada united in its diversity.

Source: Ulric Barthe, *Wilfrid Laurier on the Platform, 1871-1890* (Quebec City, 1890), 613-14.

Laurier lost his first election, in 1891, to Macdonald's passionate appeal to Canadian nationalism. It appeared that he would lose again in 1896, because fellow Liberals in Manitoba had destroyed the educational rights of the province's Catholic and French minority, the Conservative government was committed to remedying this injustice, and Quebec's powerful Catholic hierarchy supported its efforts. What could Laurier do? He could remind Quebeckers that education was a provincial matter and that federal interference in Manitoba might be a precedent for future meddling in Quebec. He could recall a famous fable of La Fontaine: when the wind and the sun challenged each other to see which could persuade a man to remove his splendid new cloak, it was the sun that prevailed. Manitoba's minorities would gain more from Laurier's sunny ways than from Conservative bluster. In the long parliamentary debate on the Manitoba schools question, Laurier proclaimed a higher loyalty than denominational allegiance:

Not many weeks ago I was told from high quarters in the church to which I belong that unless I supported the School Bill which was then being prepared by the Government, and which we have now before us, I would incur the hostility of a great and powerful body. Sir, this is too grave a phase of this question for me to pass it by in silence . . . I am here the acknowledged leader of a great party composed of Roman Catholics and Protestants as well . . . in which Protestants are in the majority, as Protestants must be in the majority in every part of Canada. Am I to be told, I, occupying such a position, that I am to be dictated the course I am to take in this House, by reasons that can appeal to the consciences of my fellow Catholic members, but which do not appeal as well to the consciences of my Protestant colleagues? No. So long as I have a seat in this House, so long as I occupy the position I do now, whenever it shall become my duty to take a stand upon any question whatever, that stand I will take not upon grounds of Roman Catholicism, not upon grounds of Protestantism, but upon grounds than can appeal to the consciences of all men, irrespective of their particular faith, upon grounds which can be occupied by all men who love justice, freedom and toleration.

Source: House of Commons *Debates*, March 3, 1896, vol. 1, 2758-9.

Despite the odds, Laurier won in 1896 and again in 1900. In 1904, he campaigned once more for re-election. Times were good. Discovery of gold in Yukon in 1896 brought prosperity to the west. Better weather and the filling up of American free land turned the stream of immigrants northward to what Canadians called "The Last Best West." In a series of speeches and interviews, Sir Wilfrid shaped and reshaped a slogan that would accompany Canadians throughout the century:

I tell you nothing but what you know when I tell you that the nineteenth century has been the century of the United States development. The past hundred years has been filled with the pages of their history. Let me tell you, my fellow countrymen, that the twentieth century shall be the century of Canada and of Canadian development. For the next seventy-five years, nay for the next hundred years, Canada shall be the star towards which all men who love progress and freedom shall come.

To those, sir, who have life before them, let my prayer be this: Remember from this day forth, never to look simply at the horizon as it may be limited by the limits of the Province, but look abroad over all the continent . . . and let your motto be: "Canada first, Canada last, and Canada always."

Source: Speech at Massey Hall, Toronto, October 14, 1904, printed in the *Globe*, October 15, 1904.

Laurier won in 1904 and again in 1908, but the issues that had bedevilled him throughout his political career remained. Was Laurier too imperial for Quebec, too nationalist for Canadian imperialists? In the 1911 election, Conservatives denounced him for favouring a new reciprocity agreement with the United States while Quebec nationalists denounced Canada's tiny new navy as an imperial commitment. A nation built on compromise and moderation suddenly seemed to be in the hands of extremists. Laurier could only plead his consistency:

I am branded in Quebec as a traitor to the French, and in Ontario as a traitor to the English. In Quebec I am branded as a Jingo, and in Ontario as a Separatist. In Quebec, I am attacked as an Imperialist, and in Ontario as an anti-Imperialist. I am neither. I am a Canadian. Canada has been the inspiration of my life. I have had before me as a pillar of fire by night and a pillar of cloud by day a policy of true Canadianism, of moderation, of conciliation. I have followed it consistently since 1896, and I now appeal with confidence to the whole Canadian people to uphold me in this policy of sound Canadianism which makes for the greatness of our country and of the Empire.

Source: O.D. Skelton, *The Life and Times of Sir Wilfrid Laurier*, 2 vols. (Toronto, 1921), 2: 380.

Clifford Sifton (1861–1929)

"The Quality Standard"

Clifford Sifton was a prominent Liberal politician who served in the Manitoba legislature and in the federal government of Wilfrid Laurier at the turn of the nineteenth century. In 1896 he became federal minster of the interior, and in that position he aggressively supported immigration into the Canadian west. Sifton and his government recognized the need to enlarge the thinly scattered western population base so as to resist American encroachments.

The best-known feature of this policy was Sifton's decision to include, among those he recruited for western settlement, immigrants of eastern and central European origin. In the passage reprinted here, we note his often-quoted description of "quality" as referring to "a stalwart peasant in a sheep-skin coat." In its day, and given the strongly Anglo-centric nature of the Canadian establishment, this position was dramatic and progressive.

But it had a different context as well. For Sifton, part of the attraction of these peasants was their non-urban character and their perceived aptitude for the back-breaking work of farming the Canadian prairies. Moreover, they would be unlikely to be excessively liberal, or pro-union, or touched with socialist or Communist sympathies, all traits that were anathema to Sifton and the elite and that were to be found among other European immigrants.

When I speak of quality I have in mind, I think, something that is quite different from what is in the mind of the average writer or speaker upon the question of Immigration. I think a stalwart peasant in a sheep-skin coat, born on the soil, whose forefathers have been farmers for ten generations, with a stout wife and a half-dozen children, is good quality. A Trades Union artisan who will not work more than eight hours a day and will not work that long if he can help it, will not work on a farm at all and has to be fed by the public when work is slack is, in my judgment, quantity and very bad quality. I am indifferent as to whether or not he is British born. It matters not what his nationality is: such men are not wanted in Canada, and the more of them we get the more trouble we shall have.

For some years after the changes in policy which followed my retirement from office, Canada received wholesale arrivals of all kinds of immigrants. As above stated, there was no selection. Particularly from the continent it is quite clear that we received a considerable portion of the off-scourings and dregs of society. They formed colonies in Ottawa, Montreal, Toronto, Winnipeg and other places and some of them and their children have been furnishing work for the police ever since.

The situation at Hamburg is practically the same now as it was then, except that there is a larger proportion of ne'er-do-wells and scalawags who desire to get away from Europe. The peasants can be brought there and they wish to emigrate, but it is imperative that an effective method be adopted for making a selection. We want the peasants and agriculturists; we do not want the wasters and criminals.

Source: *Maclean's Magazine*, vol. 35, April 1, 1922, 16, 22.

Richard Hardisty (1871–1942)

"THE LAST SUN DANCE"

Richard Hardisty was the son of Richard Hardisty, chief factor of the Hudson's Bay Company for the Edmonton district, and Elizabeth McDougall, daughter of a well-known missionary in the northwest. His parents claimed that he was the first white child born in the territory of Rupert's Land (modern-day northern and western Canada).

Many cultures have rituals to test the fitness of their young to enter adulthood. In our society one such ritual is a university or college education. Among the Cree, it was the ability of young men to endure physical agony. Hardisty's memory of a Cree Sun Dance, held on the banks of the North Saskatchewan River in present-day Edmonton, reminds us that much of what we know about the lives and civilizations of the First Nations has been passed down to us by non-natives. To them, the Cree Sun Dance was a "savage and gruesome pagan ritual."

I shall never forget my boyhood impressions of an Indian festival of which I was an eye-witness when the Last Sun Dance was held on the river-flats in the heart of the area now known as the City of Edmonton. Prior to the time of which I shall speak civilization had been slowly but surely creeping into the west, yet at that time with the exception of the employees of the Hudson's Bay Company, there were not more than ten white men between Fort Garry and the Rocky Mountains, and they were mostly missionaries. Civilization had already affected the Indians, sometimes disastrously, for thousands had died of smallpox and scarlet fever, and contacts with Hudson's Bay officers and missionaries had already modified some of the tribal rites and customs. The Sun Dance, which but a few years earlier had been a savage and gruesome pagan rite, was becoming a more peaceful and social gathering.

Up to the early eighteen-seventies there had been a practically constant state of war between the Crees and the Blackfeet . . . At last the tribes met in a great peace conference near where Wetaskiwin now stands . . .

A few years later a great gathering of Cree Indians at Fort Edmonton staged the last Sun Dance, and though I was but a youngster at the time, the picture is still clear in my mind's eye after all these years. For more than a week the Indians had been coming in, and the river flats below the Fort were dotted with tepees of buffalo hide. The encampment was about three quarters of a mile east of the Fort . . . After sunset, camp fires glowed, the banks of the river, covered with pine and spruce, making an intensely dark background below the skyline, made the camp fires bright and dotted the plain with brilliant light. The beating of drums, the howling of dogs joined the voices of those keeping time to the drum beat. This religious gathering had been for ages an annual event at which were featured the making of sacrifices and the enduring of self-inflicted torture. The conjuror rehearsed his medicine hymns – looked to his medicine bag – fixed his rattles and bells and retouched his ghastly costume. The warriors burnished their war dress. The women made ready their finery, though all they had, such as beaded leggings, a leather girdle – decorated with brass tacks – would be contained in a small bag made of calfskin.

The selection of the tree to be used as the "Idol Pole" was carried out with great ceremony. This "Idol Pole" was set up in the centre of the enclosure. For walls, small poles were set in the ground, sloping inward, and covered with leafy branches, making a good shelter from rain or sun. The walls formed a large circle with the pole standing about thirty feet high in the centre. One opening was left as an entrance, but this was closed with a buffalo robe during the ceremony. The "Idol Pole" was decorated with different coloured clays and streamers of red and blue tape or braid. Long pieces of shaganapie, reaching from the top of the centre pole to the circumference of the lodge, carried small bells, dried bones, and in former days the scalps taken in their last battle. Strong lines made from buffalo hide swung loose to the ground from the very top of the centre pole.

The enclosure would hold, seated on the ground, about a hundred braves. No women or children were permitted to enter during the ceremony. They, however, sat outside encircling the enclosure and taking part in the pow-wow, raising shrill but musical voices to the high heavens, keeping time to the rhythm of the drum beats. This all took time – it took preparation and rehearsal. The festival lasted for six days with but one performance a day and that at noon, by the sun.

In former days any of the warriors who desired to call upon the Sun God to favour him against his enemies in war and to supply his needs to maintain himself and family, took part in the ceremony, by sacrifice and self-inflicted torture. At this time, however, the Sun was invoked to witness only the cruel ordeals of youths who desired to become warriors and be recognized as men. In this last Sun Dance, twelve young men qualified as braves daily. The warriors, led by the chiefs and headmen, gathered in full war paint, naked but for a breech cloth – brass rings hanging loose on their ankles; dozens of brass rings on their wrists and forearms – strings of bear claws and elk teeth round their necks. They move towards the temple, led by conjurors and medicine men, the medicine men chanting, in doleful notes and in unknown tongues, petitionary and sacrificial hymns, their faces and bodies painted in alternate streaks of white and yellow – their ornaments around neck, waist, and ankles are human bones. The drums beat and the medicine men dance, going forward. The chief walks quietly behind, but the warriors, sounding the tribal war whoop, go through all kinds of contortions. They enter the enclosure and sit on the ground, their bodies moving and swaying, their voices raised to the beat of the drums.

The medicine men, now opposite each other, dance back and forth, chanting their incantation to the Sun to bless the gathering, working themselves and the warriors up to a frenzy of excitement. In the meantime, the women and youngsters have taken their place on the outside, and their voices blend with the warriors' and the drums beat louder.

About fifteen minutes before noon six young men, clean, their copper skins glistening in the sun – they are naked but for the breech cloth, no ornament, no paint – enter and dance the war dance, facing outward from the centre pole. They look fearlessly into the eyes of the

warriors as they circle several times. Proud they are, for they have become experts in the use of bow and arrow, in tracking game, in trapping, in wood and prairie lore and all the many activities of the hunter and provider. Now they are to go through the test of courage and endurance to become warriors – taking their place in councils of the tribe – winning the privilege of seeking the hand of some girl – their eyes having no doubt already caught the eye of one girl.

The drums continue, the women's and children's voices grow shriller and shriller, war whoops fill the air. Three of the boys stop before one medicine man, standing erect, their chests thrown out. Three others face the medicine man on the opposite side. The medicine man produces two short pieces of red willow, prepared for the occasion, looking somewhat like the skewers butchers use to fasten the roast of beef. The stick is about four inches long with one end pointed – the point hardened by fire and then scraped. Now the medicine man gathers as much of the flesh on the youth's chest as he can between his thumb and forefinger, forcing the stick through the flesh. The second stick is placed in the same manner on the opposite side, an equal distance from the centre of the youth's body. A loop of deer hide, about the width and length of a boot lace, is then fastened to each of the sticks. The youths face about, when all are skewered, and to the loops are attached one of the rawhide ropes hanging from the centre pole – the loops when tied are about six inches from the youth's chest, directly in the centre of his body. The drums beat, the medicine man cavorts, the war whoop rings out, there is a frenzy of movement and sound. The young men, their legs extended, their bodies thrown back, their weight carried by that portion of their flesh punctured by the stick, sway back and forth, blood streaming down their bodies from their wounds, sweat pouring from them. They leap and tumble, but utter no sound. The agony must continue until the flesh is torn through and they are free.

As each frees himself, he rushes from the enclosure, into the midst of his family – mother, cousins and aunts – each prepared to minister to his suffering torn flesh. The wound is covered with the fine brown powder taken from dried toadstools, which to my own knowledge will stop bleeding, and is soothing and healing. It has taken less than fifteen minutes for the six to complete their ordeal; immediately six others take their place.

At the same time, daily, for six days, the test is carried out, not one of the forty-eight young men failing to qualify as warriors. It is a great disgrace to the young man should he fail to pass the test, for in that event he is compelled to help the women-folk around the camp gathering wood, making fires, cleaning game, drawing water – not for such as he are the pleasures of the hunt or the thrill of war. The young girls avoid him.

At the conclusion of the trials for the day, the visiting, feasting, and drinking begins and continues day and night. The older women have kept the pots boiling; buffalo, moose, bear fat, beaver tail, deer tongues, ducks, geese, partridges, saskatoons and cranberries fill the pots. Tea – tea on the boil day and night. Drums beat, boys and girls shout and romp, young boys with bows and arrows aim at targets of interwoven willow hoops, which are thrown and shot at while rolling and seldom missed.

Continual movement, family to family, lodge to lodge, eating and drinking everywhere, young braves singing and dancing. To increase the potency of the boiled tea, blackstrap and other tobaccos, saskatoons, and cranberries are added. These cocktails, with the added excitement of the drum beats and noise, bring out actions very similar to present-day cocktail parties – the difference only the surroundings – instead of chesterfields or bed, the bare ground, the same ideas, however, lying down wherever sleep overtakes them – waking – eating – drinking.

Source: Edith Fowke, *Folklore of Canada* (Toronto: McClelland and Stewart, 1976; rev. ed., 1982), 18-22.

Pauline Johnson (1861–1913)

"THE SONG MY PADDLE SINGS"

Born at Brantford, Ontario, the daughter of G.H.M Johnson, grand chief of the Six Nations and his English wife, Emily Pauline Johnson, or Tekahionwake, grew up with little formal education but a passion for verse. In 1892 Toronto's Young Liberals included her on their program for a public concert, and the audience was overwhelmed by her poem on the Northwest Rebellion of 1885 as seen from the Indian side.

Within a week, another concert was organized at which she would be the sole performer. For the occasion, she wrote "The Song My Paddle Sings." In mid-rendition, her mind froze but, conquering her terror, she began reciting another poem. Her career as one of Canada's best-known public performers was launched and the poem that had almost cost her that career became a national favourite, reprinted in countless textbooks and anthologies of her day.

Sick and exhausted from years of travelling, Johnson died in Vancouver in 1913. The first volume of her collected poems, *White Wampum,* was published in 1928.

West wind blow from your prairie nest?
Blow from the mountains, blow from the
    west.
The sail is idle, the sailor too;
O! wind of the west, we wait for you.
Blow, blow!
I have wooed you so,
But never a favour you bestow.
You rock your cradle the hills between,
But scorn to notice my white lateen.

I stow the sail, unship the mast:
I wooed you long but my wooing's past;
My paddle will lull you into rest.
O! drowsy wind of the drowsy west,
Sleep, sleep,
By your mountain steep,
Or down where the prairie grasses sweep!

Now fold in slumber your laggard wings,
For soft is the song my paddle sings.

August is laughing across the sky,
Laughing while paddle, canoe and I,
Drift, drift,
Where the hills uplift
On either side of the current swift.

The river rolls in its rocky bed
My paddle is plying its way ahead;
Dip, dip,
While the waters flip
In foam as over their breast we slip.

And oh, the river runs swifter now;
The eddies circle about my bow.
Swirl, swirl!

How the ripples curl
In many a dangerous pool awhirl!

And forward far the rapids roar,
Fretting their margin for evermore.
Dash, dash,
With a mighty crash,
They seethe, and boil, and bound, and
    splash.

Be strong, O paddle! be brave, canoe!
The reckless waves you must plunge into.
Reel, reel.
On your trembling keel,
But never a fear my craft will feel.

We've raced the rapid, we're far ahead!
The river slips through its silent bed.
Sway, sway,
As the bubbles spray
And fall in tinkling tunes away.

And up on the hills against the sky,
A fir tree rocking its lullaby,
Swings, swings,
Its emerald wings,
Swelling the song that my paddle sings.

Source: E. Pauline Johnson, *Flint and Feather* (Toronto and London: Musson, 1928), 63.

Émile Nelligan (1879–1941)

"Le Vaisseau d'Or" ("The Ship of Gold")

No Quebec writer embodied the romantic vision of the poet more than Émile Nelligan. Born in Montreal to an Irish father and a French-Canadian mother, he grew up insisting on the French side of his heritage. Well educated, his brilliance recognized early, he wrote and recited his poems to rapt audiences, who were entranced by his pale face, his shock of black hair, and his passion. Nelligan, in turn, was entranced by the poetry of Lamartine, Hugo, Baudelaire, Verlaine, and Arthur Rimbaud, and by the darker works of Edgar Allan Poe.

Nelligan's own darkness turned to insanity and in August 1899 he was committed to an asylum; for the rest of his life, he remained institutionalized. Yet his name survived as a tragic symbol of poetic genius. "Le Vaisseau d'Or" has been described as unforgettable by his biographer, Paul Wyscynski. The translation given here was done by another major Canadian poet, A.J.M. Smith (1902–80).

There was a gallant vessel wrought of gold,
Whose tops'ls raked the skies in seas
  unknown;
Carved on the prow a naked Venus shone,
With wind-tossed locks, in the immoderate
  Sun.

But ah! one night she struck the famous reef
In treacherous Ocean where the Siren sings.
Ghastly, a slanting hulk, she twists and
  swings
Down the profound Abyss, her changeless
  shroud.

She was a golden ship whose glassy hull
Betrayed the treasure-trove for which the
  three
Foul Captains, Hate, Disgust, and Frenzy
  strove.

What rests at last after the hasty plunge?
What of my heart's lost fate, poor derelict?
– Foundered, alas! in the black gulf of
  Dream!

Source: J.R. Colombo, ed., *The Poets of Canada*
(Edmonton: Hurtig, 1978), 86.

Ce fut un grand Vaisseau taillé dans l'or
  massif:
Ses mâts touchaient l'azur, sur des mers
  inconnues;
La Cyprine d'amour, cheveux épars, chairs
  nues,
S'étalait à sa proue, au soleil excessif.

Mais il vint une nuit frapper le grand écueil
Dans l'Océan trompeur où chantait la
  Sirène,
Et le naufrage horrible inclina sa carène
Aux profondeurs du Gouffre, immuable
  cercueil.

Ce fut un Vaisseau d'Or, dont les flancs
  diaphanes
Révélaient des trésors que les marins
  profanes,
Dégoût, Haine et Névrose, entre eux ont
  disputés.

Que reste-t-il de lui dans la tempête brève?
Qu'est devenu mon coeur, navire déserté?
Hélas! Il a sombré dans l'abime du Rêve!

Source: Louis Mailhot and Pierre Nepveu, eds., *La Poésie
québécoise* (Montreal: Typo poésie, 1990).

Cavendish Boyle (1849—1916)

"ODE TO NEWFOUNDLAND"

Born in England, Sir Cavendish Boyle served as governor of Newfoundland from 1901 to 1904. Known as the "Poet Governor," he composed "Ode to Newfoundland" when he took up his post as governor of the colony. The work was set to music by his friend Sir C. Hubert Parry (who composed the music for Blake's "Jerusalem") and was first performed at St. John's on January 21, 1902. It served Newfoundlanders as an anthem when they formed a dominion within the British Commonwealth, and it remains today the province's unofficial anthem.

When sun rays crown thy pine-clad hills,
    And Summer spreads her hand,
When silvern voices tune thy rills,
    We love thee, smiling land.

    We love thee, we love thee,
    We love thee, smiling land.

When blinding storm-gusts fret thy shore,
    And wild waves lash thy strand;
Through spindrift, swirl and tempest roar
    We love thee, wind-swept land.

    We love thee, we love thee,
    We love thee, wind-swept land.

When spreads thy cloak of shimmering white
    At winter's stern command;

Through shortened day and star-lit night
    We love thee, frozen land.

    We love thee, we love thee,
    We love thee, frozen land.

As loved our fathers so we love,
    Where once they stood, we stand;
Their prayer we raise to Heaven above,
    God guard thee, Newfoundland.

    God guard thee, God guard thee,
    God guard thee, Newfoundland.

Source: J.R. Colombo, ed., *The Poets of Canada* (Edmonton: Hurtig, 1978), 56-7.

Robert W. Service (1874–1958)

"The Cremation of Sam McGee"

Though the identification of Robert Service with the Canadian north is ineradicable, he lived mostly in France, driving an ambulance in the First World War, working briefly as a film actor in Hollywood, and retiring early to the Riviera. All his life he denied that he was more than a versifier, but his lines have been read and recited by countless people who imagine that these poems portray what it was really like in the Klondike.

Chance took a vagabond Service to Vancouver in 1894 and, after the gold rush was over, to Whitehorse and later Dawson City as a clerk in the Canadian Bank of Commerce. In 1904–06 he wrote "The Cremation of Sam McGee," which was published in a collection entitled *Songs of the Sourdough* in the United States in 1907. The Dawson City cabin of "the Canadian Kipling" and the "Poet of the Yukon," as Service was known, is now a museum.

Now Sam McGee was from Tennessee,
    where the cotton blooms and blows.
Why he left his home in the South to roam
    'round the Pole, God only knows.
He was always cold, but the land of gold
    seemed to hold him like a spell;
Though he'd often say in his homely way
    that 'he'd sooner live in hell.'

On a Christmas Day we were mushing our
    way over the Dawson trail.
Talk of your cold! through the parka's fold it
    stabbed like a driven nail.
If our eyes we'd close, then the lashes froze
    till sometimes we couldn't see,
It wasn't much fun, but the only one to
    whimper was Sam McGee.

And that very night, as we lay packed tight
    in our robes beneath the snow

And the dogs were fed, and the stars o'er-
    head were dancing heel and toe.
He turned to me, and 'Cap', says he, 'I'll cash
    in this trip, I guess;
And if I do, I'm asking that you won't refuse
    my last request.'

Well, he seemed so low that I couldn't say
    no; then he says with a sort of moan:
'It's the cursed cold, and it's got right hold
    till I'm chilled clean through to the bone.
Yet 'tain't being dead – it's my awful dread of
    the icy grave that pains;
So I want you to swear that, foul or fair,
    you'll cremate my last remains.'

A pal's last need is a thing to heed, so I swore
    I would not fail;
And we started on at the streak of dawn; but
    God! he looked ghastly pale.

He crouched on the sleigh, and he raved all
    day of his home in Tennessee;
And before nightfall a corpse was all that
    was left of Sam McGee.

There wasn't a breath in that land of death,
    and I hurried, horror-driven,
With a corpse half hid that I couldn't get rid,
    because of a promise given;
It was lashed to the sleigh, and it seemed to
    say: 'You may tax your brawn and brains,
But you promised true, and it's up to you to
    cremate those last remains.'

Now a promise made is a debt unpaid, and
    the trail has its own stern code.
In the days to come, though my lips were
    dumb, in my heart how I cursed that
    load.
In the long, long night, by the lone firelight,
    while the huskies, round in a ring,
Howled out their woes to the homeless
    snows – O God! how I loathed the thing.

And every day that quiet clay seemed to
    heavy and heavier grow;
And on I went, though the dogs were spent
    and the grub was getting low;
The trail was bad, and I felt half mad, but I
    swore I would not give in;
And I'd often sing to the hateful thing, and
    it hearkened with a grin.

Till I came to the marge of Lake Lebarge,
    and a derelict there lay;

It was jammed in the ice, but I saw in a trice
    it was called the 'Alice May'.
And I looked at it, and I thought a bit, and I
    looked at my frozen chum;
Then 'Here', said I, with a sudden cry, 'is my
    cre-ma-tor-eum.'

Some planks I tore from the cabin floor, and
    I lit the boiler fire;
Some coal I found that was lying around,
    and I heaped the fuel higher;
The flames just soared, and the furnace
    roared – such a blaze you seldom see;
And I burrowed a hole in the glowing coal,
    and I stuffed in Sam McGee.

Then I made a hike, for I didn't like to hear
    him sizzle so;
And the heavens scowled, and the huskies
    howled, and the wind began to blow.
It was icy cold, but the hot sweat rolled
    down my cheeks, and I don't know why;
And the greasy smoke in an inky cloak went
    streaking down the sky.

I do not know how long in the snow I wres-
    tled with grisly fear;
But the stars came out and they danced
    about ere again I ventured near;
I was sick with dread, but I bravely said: 'I'll
    just take a peep inside.
I guess he's cooked, and it's time I looked';
    . . . then the door I opened wide.

And there sat Sam, looking cool and calm,
    in the heart of the furnace roar;

And he wore a smile you could see a mile,
    and he said: 'Please close that door.
It's fine in here, but I greatly fear you'll let in
    the cold and storm –
Since I left Plumtree, down in Tennessee, it's
    the first time I've been warm.'

There are strange things done in the midnight
*   sun*
By the men who moil for gold;

The Arctic trails have their secret tales
*   That would make your blood run cold;*
The Northern Lights have seen queer sights,
*   But the queerest they ever did see*
Was that night on the marge of Lake Lebarge
*   I cremated Sam McGee.*

Source: Margaret Atwood, ed., *The New Oxford Book of Canadian Verse in English* (Toronto: Oxford University Press, 1983), 62-4.

Ernest Thompson Seton (1860–1946)

"WILD ANIMALS I HAVE KNOWN"

Born in England, raised in and around Toronto, and later a settler in Manitoba, Ernest Thompson Seton became one of North America's best-known naturalists. His animal stories were immensely popular and also contributed significantly to the creation of a genre. His views and experiences in organizing adolescents to imitate his idea of Indian values and practices influenced Baden-Powell (1857–1941) in his establishment of the Boy Scouts, although Seton himself hated the militarism and hierarchy of the Scout movement.

Some of Seton's style and viewpoint is reflected in this story about his dog Bingo during his time in Manitoba. Seton believed that animals had near-human emotions and reasoning but, unlike other storytellers of his time, he struggled to avoid both anthropomorphism and any attempt to impute religious morality to animals.

It is wonderful and beautiful how a man and his dog will stick to one another, through thick and thin. Butler tells of an undivided Indian tribe, in the Far North which was all but exterminated by an internecine feud over a dog that belonged to one man and was killed by his neighbor; and among ourselves we have lawsuits, fights, and deadly feuds, all pointing the same old moral, "Love me, love my dog."

One of our neighbors had a very fine hound that he thought the best and dearest dog in the world. I loved him, so I loved his dog, and when one day poor Tan crawled home terribly mangled and died by the door, I joined my threats of vengeance with those of his master and thenceforth lost no opportunity of tracing the miscreant, both by offering rewards and by collecting scraps of evidence. At length it was clear that one of three men to the southward had had a hand in the cruel affair. The scent was warming up, and soon we should have been in a position to exact rigorous justice at least, from the wretch who had murdered poor old Tan.

Then something took place which at once changed my mind and led me to believe that the mangling of the old hound was not by any means an unpardonable crime, but indeed on second thoughts was rather commendable than otherwise.

Gordon Wright's farm lay to the south of us, and while there one day, Gordon, Jr., knowing that I was tracking the murderer, took me aside and looking about furtively, he whispered, tragic tones:

"It was Bing done it."

And the matter dropped right there. For I confess that from that moment I did all in my power to baffle the justice I had previously striven so hard to further.

I had given Bingo away long before, but the feeling of ownership did not die; and of this indissoluble fellowship of dog and man he was soon to take part in another important illustration.

Old Gordon and Oliver were close neighbors and friends; they joined in a contract to cut wood, and worked together harmoniously till late on in winter. Then Oliver's old horse died, and he, determining to profit as far as possible, dragged it out on the plain and laid poison baits for wolves around it. Alas, for poor Bingo! He would lead a wolfish life, though again and again it brought him into wolfish misfortunes.

He was as fond of dead horse as any of his wild kindred. That very night, with Wright's own dog Curley, he visited the carcass. It seemed as though Bing had busied himself chiefly keeping off the wolves, but Curley feasted immoderately. The tracks in the snow told the story of the banquet; the interruption as the poison began to work, and of the dreadful spasms of pain during the erratic course back home where Curley, failing in convulsions at Gordon's feet, died in the greatest agony.

"Love me, love my dog," no explanations or apology were acceptable; it was useless to urge that it was accidental, the long-standing feud between Bingo and Oliver was now remembered as an important side-light. The wood-contract was thrown up, all friendly relations ceased, and to this day there is no county big enough to hold the rival factions which were called at once into existence and to arms by Curley's dying yell.

It was months before Bingo really recovered from the poison. We believed indeed that he never again would be the sturdy old-time Bingo. But when the spring came he began to gain strength, and bettering as the grass grew, he was within a few weeks once more in full health and vigor to be a pride to his friends and a nuisance to his neighbors.

* * *

Changes took me far away from Manitoba, and on my return in 1886 Bingo was still a member of Wright's household. I thought he would have forgotten me after two years absence, but not so. One day early in the winter, after having been lost for forty-eight hours, he crawled home to Wright's with a wolf-trap and a heavy log fast to one foot, and the foot frozen to stony hardness. No one had been able to approach to help him, he was so savage, when I, the stranger now, stooped down and laid hold of he trap with one hand and his leg with the other. Instantly he seized my wrist in his teeth.

Without stirring I said, "Bing, don't you know me?"

He had not broken the skin and at once released his hold and offered no further resistance, although he whined a good deal during the removal of the trap. He still acknowledged me his master in spite of his change of residence and my long absence, and notwithstanding my surrender of ownership I still felt that he was my dog.

Bing was carried into the house much against his will and his frozen foot thawed out. During the rest of the winter he went lame and two of his toes eventually dropped off. But before the return of warm weather his health and strength were fully restored, and to a casual glance he bore no mark of his dreadful experience in the steel trap.

* * *

During that same winter I caught many wolves and foxes who did not have Bingo's good luck in escaping the traps, which I kept out right into the spring, for bounties are good even when fur is not.

Kennedy's Plain was always a good trapping ground because it was unfrequented by man and yet lay between the heavy woods and the settlement. I had been fortunate with the fur here, and late in April rode in on one of my regular rounds.

The wolf-traps are made of heavy steel and have two springs, each of one hundred pounds power. They are set in fours around a buried bait, and after being strongly fastened to concealed logs are carefully covered in cotton and in fine sand so as to be quite invisible.

A prairie wolf was caught in one of these. I killed him with a club and throwing him aside proceeded to reset the trap as I had done so many hundred times before. All was quickly done. I threw the trap-wrench over toward the pony, and seeing some fine sand near by, I reached out for a handful of it to add a good finish to the setting.

Oh, unlucky thought! Oh, mad heedlessness born of long immunity! That fine sand was *on the next wolf-trap* and in an instant I was a prisoner. Although not wounded, for the traps have no teeth, and my thick trapping gloves deadened the snap, I was firmly caught across the hand above the knuckles. Not greatly alarmed at this, I tried to reach the trap-wrench with my right foot. Stretching out at full length, face downward, I worked myself toward it, making my imprisoned arm as long and straight as possible. I could not see and reach at the same time, but counted on my toe telling me when I touched the little iron key to my fetters. My first effort was a failure; strain as I might at the chain my toe struck no metal. I swung slowly around my anchor, but still failed. Then a painfully taken observation showed I was much too far to the west. I set about working around, tapping blindly with my toe to discover the key. Thus wildly groping with my right foot I forgot about the other till there was a sharp "clank" and the iron jaws of trap No. 3 closed tight on my left foot.

The terrors of the situation did not, at first, impress me, but I soon found that all my struggles were in vain. I could not get free from either trap or move the traps together, and there I lay stretched out and firmly staked to the ground.

What would become of me now? There was not much danger of freezing for the cold weather was over, but Kennedy's Plain was never visited excepting by the winter wood-cutters. No one knew where I had gone, and unless I could manage to free myself there was no prospect ahead but to be devoured by wolves, or else die of cold and starvation.

As I lay there the red sun went down over the spruce swamp west of the plain, and a shorelark on a gopher mound a few yards off twittered his evening song, just as one had done the night before at our shanty door, and though the numb pains were creeping up my arm, and a deadly chill possessed me, I noticed how long his little ear-tufts were. Then my thoughts went to the comfortable supper-table at Wright's shanty, and I thought, now they are frying the pork for supper, or just sitting down.

My pony still stood as I left him with his bridle on the ground patiently waiting to take me home. He did not understand the long delay, and when I called, he ceased nibbling the grass and looked at me in dumb, helpless inquiry. If he would only go home the empty saddle might tell the tale and bring help. But his very faithfulness kept him waiting hour after hour while I was perishing of cold and hunger.

Then I remembered how old Girou the trapper had been lost, and in the following spring his comrades found his skeleton held by the leg in a bear-trap. I wondered which part of my clothing would show my identity. Then a new thought came to me. This is how a wolf feels when he is trapped. Oh! what misery have I been responsible for! Now I'm to pay for it.

Night came slowly on. A prairie wolf howled, the pony pricked up his ears and walking nearer to me, stood with his head down. Then another prairie wolf howled and another, and I could make out that they were gathering in the neighborhood. There I lay prone and helpless, wondering if it would not be strictly just that they should come and tear me to pieces. I heard them calling for a long time before I realized that dim, shadowy forms were sneaking near. The horse saw them first, and his terrified snort drove them back at first, but they came nearer next time and sat around me on the prairie. Soon one bolder than the others crawled up and tugged at the body of his dead relative. I shouted and he retreated growling. The pony ran to a distance in terror. Presently the wolf returned, and after two or three of these retreats and returns, the body was dragged off and devoured by the rest in a few minutes.

After this they gathered nearer and sat on their haunches to look at me, and the boldest one smelt the rifle and scratched dirt on it. He retreated when I kicked at him with my free foot and shouted, but growing bolder as I grew weaker he came and snarled right in my face. At this several others snarled and came up closer, and I realized that I was to be devoured by the foe that I most despised, when suddenly out of the gloom with a guttural roar sprang a great black wolf. The prairie wolves scattered like chaff except the bold one, which seized by the black new-comer was in a few moments a draggled corpse, and then, oh horrors! this mighty brute bounded at me and – Bingo – noble Bingo, rubbed his shaggy, panting sides against me and licked my cold face.

"Bingo – Bing – old – boy – Fetch me the trap-wrench!"

Away he went and returned dragging the rifle, for he knew only that I wanted something.

"No – Bing – the trap-wrench." This time it was my sash, but at last he brought the wrench and wagged his tail in joy that it was right. Reaching out with my free hand, after much difficulty I unscrewed the pillar-nut. The trap fell apart and my hand was released, and a minute later I was free. Bing brought the pony up, and after slowly walking to restore the circulation I was able to mount. Then slowly at

first but soon at a gallop, with Bingo as herald careering and barking ahead, we set out for home, there to learn that the night before, though never taken on the trapping rounds, the brave dog had acted strangely, whimpering and watching the timber-trail; and at last when night came on, in spite of attempts to detain him he had set out in the gloom and guided by a knowledge that is beyond us had reached the spot in time to avenge me as well as set me free.

Stanch old Bing – he was a strange dog. Though his heart was with me, he passed me next day with scarcely a look, but responded with alacrity when little Gordon called him to a gopher-hunt. And it was so to the end; and to the end also he lived the wolfish life that he loved, and never failed to seek the winter-killed horses and found one again with a poisoned bait, and wolfishly bolted that; then feeling the pang, set out, not for Wright's but to find me, and reached the door of my shanty where I should have been. Next day on returning I found him dead in the snow with his head on the sill of the door – the door of his puppyhood's days; my dog to the last in his heart of hearts – it was my help he sought, and vainly sought, in the hour of his bitter extremity.

Source: Ernest Thompson Seton, *Wild Animals I Have Known* (1898; repr. Toronto: McClelland and Stewart, 1991), 135-46.

Stephen Leacock (1869–1944)

"THE GREAT ELECTION IN MISSINABA COUNTY"

Stephen Leacock was both a professor of economics at Montreal's McGill University and one of Canada's best-known humorists. In this passage, the last of his *Sunshine Sketches of a Little Town*, he turned his wit to the rituals of politics in the small Ontario town of Mariposa. In the Canada Leacock was describing, most people were either Liberals or Conservatives, and most government employees, from judges to letter carriers, were chosen among supporters of the winning party, with those who backed the losers often being removed for "offensive partisanship." Then, as now, people could be a little cynical about elections but most Canadians took their political responsibilities seriously. For the duration of a campaign, congregations were split, rival newspapers saw no need to take notice of their opponents, and taverns rang with angry debate.

So did Leacock. Anyone reading *Sunshine Sketches* will know that he is describing the 1911 federal general election, when Canadians rejected a free-trade agreement with the United States and Sir Wilfrid Laurier's Liberal government that had endorsed it. Leacock was then a strong Conservative and was gratified by the election results. A few years later, when both Canada and the United States were involved in the First World War, the two economies were more closely linked than Leacock could have imagined in 1911.

D on't ask me what election it was, whether Dominion or Provincial or Imperial or Universal, for I scarcely know.

It must, of course, have been going on in other parts of the country as well, but I saw it all from Missinaba County which, with the town of Mariposa, was, of course, the storm centre and focus point of the whole turmoil.

I only know that it was a huge election and that on it turned issues of the most tremendous importance, such as whether or not Mariposa should become part of the United States, and whether the flag that had waved over the school house at Tecumseh Township for ten centuries should be trampled under the hoof of an alien invader, and whether Britons should be slaves, and whether Canadians should be Britons, and whether the farming class would prove themselves Canadians, and tremendous questions of that kind.

And there was such a roar and a tumult to it, and such a waving of flags and beating of drums and flaring of torchlights that such parts of the election as may have been going on elsewhere than in Missinaba county must have been quite unimportant and didn't really matter.

Now that it is all over, we can look back at it without heat or passion. We can see – it's plain enough now – that in the great election Canada saved the British Empire, and that Missinaba saved Canada and that the vote of the Third Concession of Tecumseh Township saved Missinaba County, and that those of us who carried the third concession – well, there's no need to push it further. We prefer to be modest about it. If we still speak of it, it is only quietly and simply and not more than three or four times a day.

But you can't understand the election at all, and the conventions and the campaigns and the nominations and the balloting, unless you first appreciate the peculiar complexion of politics in Mariposa.

Let me begin at the beginning. Everybody in Mariposa is either a Liberal or a Conservative or else is both. Some of the people are or have been Liberals or Conservatives all their lives and are called dyed-in-the-wool Grits or old-time Tories and things of that sort. These people get from long training such a swift penetrating insight into national issues that they can decide the most complicated question in four seconds: in fact just as soon as they grab the city papers out of the morning mail, they know the whole solution of any problem you can put to them. There are other people whose aim is to be broad-minded and judicious and who vote Liberal or Conservative according to their judgment of the questions of the day. If their judgment of these questions tells them that there is something in it for them in voting Liberal, then they do so. But if not, they refuse to be the slaves of a party or the henchmen of any political leader. So that

anybody looking for henches has got to keep away from them.

But the one thing that nobody is allowed to do in Mariposa is to have no politics. Of course there are always some people whose circumstances compel them to say that they have no politics. But that is easily understood. Take the case of Trelawney, the postmaster. Long ago he was a letter carrier under the old Mackenzie Government, and later he was a letter sorter under the old Macdonald Government, and after that a letter stamper under the old Tupper Government, and so on. Trelawney always says that he has no politics, but the truth is that he has too many.

So, too, with the clergy in Mariposa. They have no politics – absolutely none. Yet Dean Drone round election time always announces as his text such a verse as: "Lo! is there not one righteous man in Israel?" or: "What ho! is it not time for a change?" And that is a signal for all the Liberal business men to get up and leave their pews.

Similarly over at the Presbyterian Church, the minister says that his sacred calling will not allow him to take part in politics and that his sacred calling prevents him from breathing even a word of harshness against his fellow man, but that when it comes to the elevation of the ungodly into high places in the commonwealth (this means, of course, the nomination of the Conservative candidate) then he's not going to allow his sacred calling to prevent him from saying just what he thinks of it. And by that time, having pretty well cleared the church of Conservatives, he proceeds to show from the scriptures that the ancient Hebrews were Liberals to a man, except those who were drowned in the flood or who perished, more or less deservedly, in the desert.

There are, I say, some people who are allowed to claim to have no politics – the office holders, and the clergy and the school teachers and the hotel keepers. But beyond them, anybody in Mariposa who says that he has no politics is looked upon as crooked, and people wonder what it is that he is "out after."

In fact, the whole town and county is a hive of politics, and people who have only witnessed gatherings such as the House of Commons at Westminster and the Senate at Washington and never seen a Conservative Convention at Tecumseh Corners or a Liberal Rally at the Concession school house, don't know what politics means.

Source: Stephen Leacock, *Sunshine Sketches of a Little Town* (Toronto: McClelland and Stewart, 1960), 124-6.

Henri Bourassa (1868–1952)

THE LANGUAGE QUESTION

Henri Bourassa was born and lived most of his life in Montreal. A descendant of the leader of the 1837 Rebellion in Lower Canada, Louis-Joseph Papineau, Bourassa was a man of deep intellect and high principle. Raised as an admirer of Wilfrid Laurier, he was elected to Parliament in 1896 but broke with his leader in 1899 over Canada's contribution to Britain's war in South Africa. Canada, Bourassa insisted, owed Britain no more than friendship: certainly it was not Canada's role to contribute to imperial wars. Later, he founded the Montreal newspaper *Le Devoir*, making it the most powerful voice of his *nationaliste* movement. During the First World War, he initially supported the struggle in the hope of bringing English and French together. When that did not happen, he opposed Canada's growing contribution and fought the imposition of conscription in 1917.

Long before it was fashionable, Bourassa was a Canadian nationalist. His Canada was a country of two founding nations, French and English, with two cultures and two languages. Often he met the same enemies both in his crusade against imperialism and in his defence of Canada's bilingual and bicultural character. English-speaking Canadians whose first loyalty was to the Empire also believed that, except perhaps for Quebec, Canada must remain a British country with a single language. How else would immigrants from Europe inherit a clear, confident national culture? Bourassa, for his part, believed as passionately as anyone in the identity of language, culture, and nationality. Like many other French Canadians, he insisted that Confederation was a compact between two peoples, with absolute equality for the two nations at its core. **If English-speaking Canadians feared for the survival of their culture, they should defend it by controlling immigration, not by victimizing their French-speaking neighbours.**

In old age, Bourassa became disillusioned with his dream of a Canada where both nations were equal partners, and increasingly he defended Quebec's distinct role as defender of a unique French-speaking, Catholic, and North American culture. Some sovereignists have claimed him as an ancestor of their movement, though he never favoured an independent Quebec.

The day a race ceases to express its thought and its sentiments in its language, in that language which has grown with it and which took form with its ethnic temperament, it is lost as a race. The preservation of its language is absolutely necessary to the preservation of the race, of its genius, its character and its temperament.

One day, in a private meeting, an eminent French Canadian expressed regret that his compatriots had lost so many years in fighting for the preservation of their language; for, he said, it was indeed difficult to suppose that they would always succeed. They would finish by adopting the language of the majority – and so why not accept it from now on – or they would remain isolated, like the Hebrews in the land of Egypt; they would be deprived of the many advantages which they could enjoy if they fused with the other races, through language, through morals and through customs of common life. Moreover, he added, in preserving their own qualities and acquiring those of the Anglo-Saxon, they would be exercising a preponderant influence.

Certainly, with all nationalist pride abstracted, this parochial opinion, is perhaps tenable. But Gentlemen, does not our pride and instinct warn us that the day we lose our language we lose precisely this very peculiar character, these special faculties which can make us a desirable element in the construction of the Canadian nation and the development of the American nation? The day we lose our language we will perhaps be mediocre Englishmen, passable Scotsmen or bad Irishmen, but we will no longer be truly Canadian.

Remember that concise phrase which you applauded a short time ago, that phrase pronounced by the eminent delegate of the French Academy, Mr. Lamy: "Each language draws out, reveals and consecrates the genius of a race." In effect, it is language which gives the spiritual works of a race that indelible stamp which gives it all its value, just as the art of a race has no real value unless the works which it inspires reflect the particular genius of the race . . .

What is the exact significance of the terms of 1867? We have no need to discuss this tonight. All that is useful to remind those who have forgotten and to impress it more on their minds, is that in whatever concerns the Federal laws and administration, the principle of absolute equality of the two languages is

All-male crowds pack downtown Toronto to celebrate another election victory by Ontario's durable Liberal premier, Oliver Mowat, in 1879. Even the pro-Conservative Evening Telegram *has to admit the victory, while a magic lantern projects Mowat's face on a screen across the street. Mowat taught Canadians two key political lessons: voters like many small reforms more than dramatic change, and, when all else fails, provincial premiers can attack the federal government. Mowat held Ontario by small majorities from 1874 to 1896.*
(Metropolitan Toronto Library Board)

If Robert Harris's painting of the Fathers of Confederation is his best-known contribution to the Canadian memory, his portrayal of A Meeting of the School Trustees *probably has inspired more thought. In 1885, when Harris (1849-1919) painted the young teacher facing her sceptical employers, most children started and finished their education in one-room schools with a single teacher, financed by small communities with no spare cash. Was education important or merely a costly distraction?*
(National Gallery of Canada)

Louis Riel addresses the jury in a crowded, stifling, Regina courtroom while a bearded Judge Hugh Richardson wonders at his decision to ignore the Metis leader's counsel and accept Riel's passionate desire to speak. In one of the most dramatic moments in Canadian judicial history, Riel's eloquent explanation won the jury's hearts and a plea for mercy but he destroyed his lawyer's best hope of saving his life, a plea of insanity. For the crime of treason – "levying war against Her Majesty" – a profound sense of injustice was no defence in 1885. (National Archives of Canada, C 1879)

On November 7, 1885, at Craigellachie, British Columbia, Donald A. Smith, president of the Bank of Montreal, drives in the last spike, linking sections of the Canadian Pacific Railway from the east and west. Behind him stand the railway's chief engineer, William Van Horne, and the white-bearded Sandford Fleming, the brilliant surveyor who made the key decisions on the route. Among the officials and workers, there is no sign of the Chinese labourers who had helped build much of the line from the Pacific. The work, boasted Van Horne, was "well done throughout" and by 1900 would begin to provide its owners with a profit. (National Archives of Canada, C 3693)

Reproduced in countless oleographs and even in needlepoint, Mortgaging the Homestead *depicted a tragedy many farmers would experience and many more feared. Was it the result of bad luck, mismanagement, or extravagance? Would the old people who had laboured to build the farm spend a penniless and shameful old age in the poorhouse? George Agnew Reid (1860-1947), a western Ontario farm boy who had studied in Paris, knew what tugged at Canadian hearts.* (National Gallery of Canada)

Ozias Leduc's Boy with a Piece of Bread, *painted in 1892, was one of his many scenes of simple everyday life. Deeply religious, Leduc (1864-1955) was well known as the decorator of many churches in eastern Canada and the United States, as well as the teacher of the great modernist artist and author of* Refus Global, *Paul-Émile Borduas.* (National Gallery of Canada)

Polly, recorded by an Ottawa photographer in 1895, was a resident of the Ottawa Home for Friendless Women, a cheerless place where unmarried mothers, elderly abandoned wives, and spinsters lived out their days doing laundry for the city's wealthier households and depending on their generosity. (National Archives of Canada, PA 27436)

Digging out after a snow slide at the Chilkoot Pass in the spring of 1898. The endless line of men humping their packs up the steep pass remains one of the most vivid images of the Yukon gold rush. At the top of the pass, members of the North-West Mounted Police insisted that each prospector had enough supplies for the winter – and no personal weapons – before being allowed to proceed. The contrast between a regulated Yukon and the criminal violence of Skagway, Alaska, has always appealed to Canadians. (J.G. McJury, National Archives of Canada, c 26413)

A joyful Toronto celebrates the British capture of Pretoria, the Boer capital, in the South African War, packing Yonge Street and forcing even cyclists to lift their "wheels" from the ground. Overwhelmingly British in ancestry and devoutly loyal to the Empire, these Torontonians of 1900 could never have imagined how rich and diverse their city would become in the twentieth century. (City of Toronto Archives, James Collection, 524)

Boys carry out a traditional ritual for choosing ends for a hockey game on December 29, 1908, in Sarnia, Ontario. On open ice, with a chill wind, the end really could make a difference. Clothing, equipment, rules, and coaching have all changed since then, but hockey remains part of Canadian culture, and many youngsters still learn skills and dream dreams with pick-up teams on stray pieces of ice. (National Archives of Canada, Boyd Collection, PA 60732)

All in their best clothes and on their best behaviour, Edna Boyd's friends wait to be photographed by John Boyd, her father, in 1903. Mrs. Boyd, the maid, and a couple of aunts look on. Canadian ensigns and Union Jacks decorate the white linen tablecloth. Modern birthday parties are very seldom like this. (National Archives of Canada, Boyd Collection, PA 60631)

The Grenadiers' Chapter of the Imperial Order, Daughters of the Empire, gather for their annual ball at the Temple Building, Toronto, on November 16, 1910. The IODE might claim to unite Fine Old Ontario Families, or FOOFs, but its founder, Mrs. Edith Boulton Nordheimer, had mixed the bloodlines of one of Toronto's oldest families with Samuel Nordheimer, a Bavarian Jew who had come to Canada as a piano tutor and who died as one of the city's wealthiest manufacturers. (Col. R. A. Mason Collection)

recognized in full; and this suffices. In effect, if the law recognizes the principle, common sense as much as justice argues that this principle should receive the sanction of all means suitable to assure its application. Otherwise, to claim that under the jurisdiction of the constitution of 1867, the rights of the French language existed only for Quebec, is to say that the pact of 1867 was a delusion, that the Cartiers, the Macdonalds, the Browns, the Howes, all the authors of this magnificent constitution came to an understanding to deceive the people of Lower Canada.

As for me, I do not believe it; I believe that the true interpretation of the constitutional law which rules us is that which its principal author, Sir John A. Macdonald, gave twenty four years later in the memorable words, which were quoted the other day by the speaker of the Senate and of which I limit myself to recalling the substance. It is that since 1867 there is no longer in Canada a conquered race or a conquering race, a dominant race or a dominated race but on the contrary there exists, under the jurisdiction of the law itself, a perfect equality in all that concerns the political rights, the social rights and the moral rights of the two races, and particularly in that which concerns the public and private usage of the two languages.

If French and English constitute the double vocabulary of the entire Canadian people, how is it that there are to be found provincialists so narrow-minded as to affirm that any one of the Legislatures of the Dominion of Canada can deprive the French speaking citizens in any province of the means of giving their children a perfect knowledge and control of their language, and of sending them to all the schools where their funds are accepted just as much as the funds of those who speak English?

If the two languages are official, in the very terms of the constitution, these languages have the right to co-exist wherever the Canadian people has its public life: in Church, in school, in Parliaments, before the courts, and in all public services.

If they have the right to exist, each one of them has the right to demand from the state, whether federal, provincial or municipal, which are all only parts of the entire state, that is of power derived from all the races and all the individuals who compose the Canadian nation – each one of these two languages has the right to demand from the state, under whatever form it exists, with whatever authority and under the jurisdiction of whatever law it exercises its power, the complete and absolute recognition of the co-existence and equality of the two languages . . .

Now, if Canada, is to remain separate from the United States, it is high time that our Anglo-Canadian compatriots opened their eyes and ears, and above all broadened their outlook, to understand that a real danger threatens the unity of the Canadian people and the preservation of its political existence. This danger is the slow but sure penetration of Americanism into all phases of our national, political and social life.

Here is something which will perhaps astonish you; but in reality Quebec, the old city of Champlain, so French, is more Canadian and more British than Montreal. Montreal is more Canadian and more British than Toronto. Toronto is more Canadian and more British than Winnipeg. Why? Because at Quebec, thanks to the preponderance of the French language, you are better protected from the American invasion than in Montreal. Toronto, the "loyal" city par excellence is, not only in the eyes of travellers but also attentive observers, half-conquered by American ideas, by American mentality, by American morals, by American pronunciation, by the American fashion of seeing, feeling and acting in every day life; and this danger is far more formidable than any commercial treaty or any attack on the constitution because it is the moral and inner conquest of individuals who compose the nation.

As a consequence of the community of language, there is much more immediate contact between Canada and the United States than between Canada and England. Moreover communications between the Maritime provinces and Quebec, and New England, between Ontario and the state of New York, between Manitoba and Minnesota, between British Columbia and Oregon or Washington are more frequent and more intimate than those between the different provinces of the Canadian confederation. If we do not put all our energy into working together, if we do not make every effort that men of good will in both races can make, American thought will not only have separated us from England but will have broken up the Canadian confederation, before

Ontario and Manitoba will have repulsed the invasion of the habitants of "medieval" Quebec.

All these battles which we French Canadians have had to wage for twenty years in the field of teaching, against what have we been waging them? Against English thought, against English tradition? No, the principle of the "national" school, the opposition to the separate or bilingual school in Ontario and the Maritime provinces, in Manitoba as in the new provinces of the North West – where must one go to find its source? To the American ideal, which fashions all intellects, all wills in the same mould, by the same intellectual make-up, whereas public education in England is based on the principle of individual liberty, of the education of individuals and groups according to their aspirations and to their abilities.

If the projects of those who wish to Anglicize us should succeed we can make a prediction which will surely come true; that is, if they succeed in Anglicizing French Canadians, they will not make Englishmen out of them, but Americans.

It is useless to have the slightest illusion on this subject. We have been separated from Europe for a hundred and fifty years. We love England with an intellectual love, and if I am allowed to add my personal thought, I will add that I love England with an admiring love. But it is not only by admiration and reason that the temperament of a race is formed. We have been saying for a long time: men govern themselves by instinct much more than by laws or intellect. And the day when the French Canadian people will have learnt, by a series of successive humiliations, that their rights are only respected where they are strongest but are violated wherever they are a minority; the day when they will have definitely established that in the single province of Quebec they can speak their language but in Manitoba, in Saskatchewan, in Alberta and even in Ontario their rights are not recognized or are reduced to those of Italians, Galiciens or Doukobours, that day they will become American for they will see no further advantage to remaining British.

And yet, the surest barrier that one can build to the slow but sure conquest of the English provinces – in the West above all – by the American idea would be to plant in each of these provinces groups of French Canadians as powerful as possible, to grant them schools of their own, to give them priests of their language so that they might found their own parishes and bring into being many little Quebecs. Thus, there would be everywhere men from whom the American ideal, the cult of the golden calf, the profits of commerce and of industry would not be the principal objective. Thus there would be, in all parts of Canada, people still backward, *stupid* enough – pardon the expression, gentlemen – to keep to an ideal higher than that of fortune and success; of people who would continue to do outside of Quebec that which they have done for a hundred and fifty years in Quebec: to maintain British institutions intact, while claiming always, there as here, the right to express freely their thoughts on all the aspects of the general policy of Canada and the Empire . . .

I repeat, those who are searching for the destruction of the French language are the worst violators of the Canadian constitution; those who put shackles on the propagation of the language from one end of Canada to the other are, some without knowing it, others perhaps knowing it, the surest agents of destruction of British institutions and the unity of Canadian confederation, and the most efficient instruments which the Americans could employ to absorb the Canadian confederation gradually.

Source: Joseph Levitt, *Henri Bourassa on Imperialism and Bi-culturalism, 1900-1918* (Toronto: Copp Clark, 1970), 134-8.

Sundar Singh (fl. 1912)

"THE SIKHS IN CANADA"

Racism was long part of life in Canada. In the late nineteenth and early twentieth centuries, people were commonly categorized by so-called racial origins and then ranked, with one's own group naturally coming at or near the top. Motives ranged from arrogance to fear of competition in a world of scarce resources. In British Columbia, for example, whites feared that their

control of the province's resources could easily be lost if people from the big Asian countries were admitted as immigrants. On the other hand, employers welcomed low-paid and obedient workers from China and India.

While a distant Ottawa heard employers more than workers and their middle-class allies, restrictions on Asian immigrants were imposed, including a heavy head tax on Chinese immigrants. The same objective was served by a "gentleman's agreement" arranged with Japan by the then deputy minister of labour, William Lyon Mackenzie King, and by a regulation requiring immigrants from India to come without stopovers in other Pacific ports. The continuous-journey regulation was particularly resented by the Sikhs, who regarded themselves as loyal subjects of the British Empire and were certainly among its most gallant defenders. One of their Canadian leaders, Dr. Sundar Singh, brought their message to the Empire Club of Canada in Toronto on January 25, 1912. Members applauded but they did not press to change the law.

Two years later, in the summer of 1914, Sikhs chartered a steamer, the *Komagata Maru,* filled it with 376 would-be immigrants, and sailed direct from Calcutta to Vancouver, in defiance of the continuous-journey regulation. The government and courts refused to admit more than a few of the immigrants. After two months of waiting, officials attempted to force the ship to go back to India, but they were pelted with coal and driven off. Finally, on July 23, under the guns of the Canadian cruiser *Rainbow,* the *Komagata Maru* left port for Calcutta. In India, veterans of the voyage rioted and Indian nationalism found a new cause.

I understand that your Club is called the Empire Club, and that it is interested in the discussion of Imperial affairs. The subject which I am to discuss today is of great importance to the Empire.

I am to speak to you about the Sikhs, who are a part of this Empire, and I would like to speak of their customs and religion. The religion of the Sikhs was founded by a great teacher called Nana who was born in the Punjaub in the northwest provinces of India about the same time as Martin Luther. He taught the people that the highest ideal of worship that could be attained was the service of their fellow-beings.

He travelled north, south, east, and west; he went to Europe, and to Persia, and taught the people the same doctrines as the prophets who were born in the fifteenth century – Knox in Scotland, Luther in eastern Europe. In the same way, in India, these doctrines were being taught to the Hindoo people. Its believers were persecuted and their children were burnt alive, but in spite of this persecution it grew and became a strong power, and after Nana, there followed nine teachers.

In his own religion it was the same as in other religions; like those who went preaching that Mahomet was the only way to God, so did he, and after his death his son united his followers into a strong body, and the religion they preached and practised reached over the Punjaub.

* * *

But it is not about their religion that I wish to speak now, but about the local problems as they affect Canada. Some few years ago a few troops of the Sikhs passed through Canada on their way to the jubilee of the late Queen Victoria, and the gentlemen who were in charge of them spoke very highly of them. These Sikhs went back home and they spoke of the vast prairies where they saw wheat growing the same as we grow wheat. The consequence was that a score of them came out in 1905 – about forty of them came in that year and the next, and this went on till in 1909 there was quite a strong body of them, about 4,000 in all, engaged in agriculture; they were farmers in India, and of course they naturally took to farming when they came to this country.

They are British subjects: they have fought for the Empire; many of these men have war medals; but, in spite of this fact, they are not allowed to have their families with them when they come to this country; in spite of their being British subjects, they are not allowed to have their wives here. People talk about these Oriental races, and the phrase is understood to include not only the Chinese and the Japanese, but the Sikhs as well, which is absurd. Letters giving inaccurate statements are appearing in the press all the time. I do not know why all this objection should be directed against the Sikhs – against that people, more than against any other Oriental people.

These people are here legally; they have satisfied every process of law; they have been here over five years; they have been good to their employers – Colonel Davidson employs 350 of them in his mills in New Westminster – their work is equal to that of other labourers; their quarters are better, and they are making more wages now; they have fitted into the situation here; they have made good. (Applause.)

In spite of this, there are these letters going through the papers, and there are attacks upon these men; yet, although they are British subjects, nobody stands up for them. We appeal to you of the Empire Club, for we are only 4,000 in number, to help us in this matter, and to see that justice is done to these subjects of our King.

We are subjects of the same Empire; we have fought, we have sacrificed. We have fought for the Empire and we bear her medals; we have an interest in this country: we have bought about $2,000,000 of property in British Columbia; we have our church and pay our pastor, and we mean to stay in this country. I understand that there is a society called the Home Reformation Society and that it says that it is better for a man to have a wife and family. To others you advance money to come here, and yet to us, British subjects, you refuse to let down the bars. All we are asking of you is justice and fair play, because the Sikhs have believed in fair play, and have believed all the time that they will get justice; that ultimately they will get justice from the British people. (Applause.)

Many people have been telling me that it is useless my trying to bring this question before the Canadian people, but I am firmly persuaded that, if the question, is properly brought before right-minded Canadians, that they will say that the same rights should be given to the Sikh people as are given to any other British subjects.

Some people have spread the false statement that the Sikhs are polygamous; they are monogamous in India, and are not more polygamous than you are. They are strictly monogamous by their religion, and it is useless to spread these false stories. There are officers in India – perhaps some have come from Canada – and they can take their families to India to our people; are the laws made so invidious that it cannot work both ways! That law was meant to shut out the Japanese, yet, in the year 1908, 5,000 came from Honolulu, and they let them in. We do know that we are British subjects and we ask for our rights; if you can allow the alien to come over here, surely a British subject ought to have the same rights as an alien.

The position cannot hold good; it is inevitable that it cannot hold good. These Sikhs are the pick of their villages, they are not out here like the Japanese and Chinese. The Japanese has to show only 50 cents when he arrives, but the Sikh has to show $200, and, if he cannot, he is sent away. Of course you can understand what the reflex action of this treatment might be in the present state of India. These people who are here, are here legally; if they were new people coming in, it would be a different matter; but as such they have rights, and I think those rights ought to be respected. (Applause.)

It is only a matter of justice. If this Empire is to be and continue to be a great Empire, as it is sure to be, then it must be founded on righteousness and justice; your laws cannot be one thing for one set and a different thing for the rest of us.

These Sikhs are quite alone; they do the roughest labour; they do not come into competition with other labour, and yet this is the treatment they receive. They are plainly told: "We do not want you to bring your wives in." You cannot expect people to be moral, if you debar them from bringing in their wives and children. They can travel in Japan, they can travel in Europe; they can travel anywhere under the British flag, except here.

Just at present there are two Sikh women confined on board a boat at Vancouver; they came on the 22nd. One is the wife of a merchant, the other is the wife of a missionary. These men have been settled in this country for five years, and are well spoken of. They went back some time ago to bring out their wives and children. They asked the steamship company to sell them tickets, and the company told them that they would be refused admission. They came to Hong Kong, and the steamship company refused to sell them tickets; they waited ever since last March and last month the C. P. R. sold them tickets. On the 22nd, they arrived here, and the men were allowed to land, but the ladies are still confined as if they were criminals.

Now, if these men were allowed to land, why not their wives; why should they not be allowed to land, too? That is what they do not understand, and, although they are well versed in the occult sciences and mystical philosophy, why this should be so, they cannot see. (Applause.)

We have the promise of Queen Victoria that all British subjects, no matter what race or creed they belong to, shall be treated alike. These promises have been confirmed by King Edward, and by His Majesty King George the Fifth. When he was in India, he granted their full rights to the Hindoo people. The Indian people are loyal British subjects. They are as loyal as anybody else. Why should there be such a difference in the treatment of these loyal people?

We appeal to you, gentlemen, to say that in any country, under any conditions, the treatment that the Sikhs are receiving is not fair. We appeal to your good sense and to your humanity to see that justice is done, that this thing is not continued, for it has been going on for quite a long time. You may well imagine the feeling of these two men, who are suffering as I have described, for no fault at all, except that they are Sikhs.

Source: Empire Club of Canada, *Addresses Delivered to the Members during the Session of 1911-12* (Toronto, 1913), 112-16.

Sam Hughes (1853–1921)

"Where Duty Leads"

As Canada's First Contingent waited to sail to a war which would cost many of them their lives, Colonel Sam Hughes, the minister of militia, visited their ships, leaving behind stacks of a message he had composed for the occasion. While Hughes was unusual in expecting and praying for a war in his lifetime, his message was a flamboyant version of the patriotic prose that captivated most Canadians in the fall of 1914. Later, after experiencing war at first hand, the "Old Originals" of 1914 remembered the message with bitterness.

A former athlete, schoolteacher, railway promoter, and newspaper editor, Hughes was an intellectual curiosity: though he was a fervent imperialist and a pillar of the anti-Catholic Orange Lodge, he was also a strong supporter of women's rights. Elected to Parliament by Ontario's Victoria County in 1892, Hughes volunteered for the Boer War in 1899 and was sent home when British generals found his denunciations of them, published in Cape Town newspapers, offensive. As minister, Hughes almost doubled pre-war defence spending, banned liquor from camps, and predicted the war with Germany. Undoubtedly Hughes's energy helped transform vacant land near Quebec City into a camp for 33,000 men but the feat was necessary only because the minister had scrapped the pre-war mobilization plan.

FELLOW SOLDIERS: –

Six weeks ago, when the call came to Arms, inspired by that love of freedom from tyranny dominant in the British race; actuated by the knowledge that, under British Constitutional Responsible Government, you enjoyed the utmost of human liberty, you loyally and promptly responded in overwhelming numbers to that call.

Twenty-two thousand men were accepted by the Motherland. Today upwards of thirty-three thousand are en route to do duty on the historic fields of France, Belgium, and Germany for the preservation of the British Empire and the rights and liberties of humanity.

Lust of power; the subjugation of inoffensive and law abiding neighbors; autocratic aggrandizement, have caused this war. In its cause the Allies are guiltless.

Belgium and Holland have long excited Prussian ambition for ownership. Austria has desired extension towards the Euxine and Aegean seas – Insane lust of conquest bringing ruin, rapine and misery in the train.

It has long been predicted that when the Kiel Canal would be completed, Germany would begin the long dreaded war. The Kiel Canal was completed early in July. War was begun before the end of that month. Germany was found absolutely ready and waiting. Great Britain, Belgium and France were unprepared. Three weeks elapsed before the regular armies of the latter countries could take the field.

Soldiers! The world regards you as a marvel. Within six weeks you were at your homes, peaceful Canadian citizens. Since then your training camp has been secured; three and a half miles of rifle ranges – twice as long as any other in the world – were constructed; fences were removed; water of the purest quality was laid in miles of pipes; drainage was perfected; electric light was installed; crops were harvested; roads and bridges were built; Ordnance and Army Service Corps buildings were erected; railway sidings were laid down; woods were cleared; sanitation was perfected so that illness was practically unknown, and thirty-three thousand men were assembled from points some of them upwards of four thousand miles apart. You have been perfected in rifle shooting and today are as fine a body – Officers and Men – as ever faced a foe. The same spirit as accomplished that great work is what you will display on the war fields of Europe. There will be no faltering, no temporizing – The work must be done. The task before us six weeks ago seemed Herculean – but it has been successfully accomplished. So following the same indomitable spirit, you will triumph over the common enemy of humanity.

That you will render a splendid account of yourselves for King and Country is certain. You come of the right breed – English, Scotch, Irish, French, Welch, German and American – your courage and steadfastness are proverbial. In South Africa, your presence was a guarantee of success. So in this most righteous struggle on the part of Britain. When side by side with soldiers from the Motherland stand the freemen from the Dominions beyond the seas; when

Australians, New Zealanders, South Africans, Hindu, Newfoundlanders and Canadians tread the soil of Europe, then will the Prussian autocracy realize the gigantic power of liberty.

And amid it all you will never forget that you war not on the innocent and lovely people of Germany. Your aim is the overthrow of tyranny and aggrandizement.

Every man among you is a free will volunteer. Not one has been invited. No more typical army of free men ever marched to meet an enemy.

Soldiers! Behind you are loved ones, home, country, with all the traditions of Liberty, and loyalty; love of King and constitution. You bid adieu to those near and dear to you.

You sing;

I go then sweet lass to win honour and fame,
    And if I should chance to come gloriously
        hame
I'll bring a heart to thee with love running
        o'er
    And then I'll leave thee and the Home-
        land no more.

That you will so bear yourselves, individually and collectively wherever duty may call you, as to win the respect of the foe in the field; the admiration and regard of the good citizens of all lands in which your lot may be cast; and the love and regard of those near and dear at home, is the conviction of all Canadians.

And when with years and honour crowned,
    You sit some homeward hearth around
And hear no more the stirring sound
    That spoke the trumpet's warning
You'll sing and give one Hip Hurrah
    And pledge the memory of the day
When to do and dare you all were there
    And met the foe in the morning.

Some may not return – and pray God they be few – For such, not only will their memory ever be cherished by loved ones near and dear, and by a grateful country; but throughout the ages freemen of all lands will revere and honour the heroes who sacrificed themselves in preserving unimpaired the Priceless Gem of Liberty. But the soldier going down in the cause of freedom never dies – Immortality is his. What recks he whether his resting place may be bedecked with the golden lilies of France or amid the vine clad hills of the Rhine. The principles for which you strive are Eternal.

May success ever attend you, and when you return rest assured a crowning triumph will await you.

SAM HUGHES,
Colonel.
Minister of Militia and Defence for Canada.

Source: A.F. Duguid, *Official History of the Canadian Forces in the Great War, 1914-1919*, General Series 1 (Ottawa: King's Printer, 1938), 122-3.

Nellie McClung (1873–1951)

"The Land of the Second Chance"

Nellie McClung was a prominent reformer and author as well as one of the early pioneers in the struggle to acquire the vote and other rights for women. In addition to her crusading zeal as a suffragist, she was also deeply involved in the Women's Christian Temperance Union. She believed that alcoholism played a major role in the inequalities faced by women, besides being ungodly. While no radical by contemporary standards, and a strong supporter of traditional family values, she helped lay the groundwork for later advances by the Canadian women's movement.

McClung had a vision of a Canadian future that knew no limits. But she also felt strongly that Canada would have to find human resources to match the bounty of nature if it was to progress. This selection was written and first published in 1915 while Europe was being ravaged by the First World War. She sensed that Canadians were not constrained by Europe's legacy of intolerance and that survivors of the Great War might start again in Canada, the "land of the second chance."

Every nation has its characteristic quality of mind; we recognize Scotch thrift, English persistency and Irish quickwittedness wherever we see it; we know something, too, of the emotional, vivacious nature of the French, and the resourcefulness of the American; but what about the Canadian – what will be our distinguishing feature in the years to come? The cartoons are kind to us – thus far – and in representing Canada, draw a sturdy young fellow, strong and well set, full of muscle and vim, and we like to think that the representation is a good one, for we are a young nation, coming into our vigor, and with our future in our own hands. We have an area of one-third of the whole British Empire, and one-fifth of that of Asia. Canada is as large as thirty United Kingdoms and eighteen Germanys. Canada is almost as large as Europe. It is bounded by three oceans and has thirteen thousand miles of coast line, that is, half the circumference of the earth.

Canada's land area, exclusive of forest and swamp lands, is 1,401,000,000 acres; 440,000,000 acres of this is fit for cultivation, but only 36,000,000 acres, or 2.6 per cent of the whole, is cultivated, so it would seem that there are still a few acres left for anyone who may happen to want it. We need not be afraid of crowding. We have a great big blank book here with leather binding and gold edges, and now our care should be that we write in it worthily. We have no precedents to guide us, and that is a glorious thing, for precedents, like other guides, are disposed to grow tyrannical, and refuse to let us do anything on our own initiative. Life grows wearisome in the countries where precedents and conventionalities rule, and nothing can happen unless it has happened before. Here we do not worry about precedents – we make our own!

Main Street, in Winnipeg, now one of the finest business streets in the world, followed the trail made by the Red River carts, and, no doubt, if the driver of the first cart knew that in his footsteps would follow electric cars and asphalt paving, he would have driven straighter. But he did not know, and we do not blame him for that. But we know, for in our short day we have seen the prairies blossom into cities, and we know that on the paths which we are marking out many feet will follow, and the responsibility is laid on us to lay them broad and straight and safe so that many feet may be saved from falling.

We are too young a nation yet to have any distinguishing characteristic and, of course, it would not be exactly modest for us to attribute virtues to ourselves, but there can be [no] harm in saying what we would like our character to be. Among the people of the world in the years to come, we will ask no greater heritage for our country than to be known as the land of the Fair Deal, where every race, color and creed will be given exactly the same chance; where no person can "exert influence" to bring about his personal ends; where no man or woman's past can ever rise up to defeat them; where no crime goes unpunished; where every debt is paid; where no prejudice is allowed to masquerade as a reason; where honest toil will insure an honest living; where the man who works receives the reward of his labor.

It would seem reasonable, too, that such a condition might be brought about in a new country, and in a country as big as ours, where there is room for everyone and to spare. Look out upon our rolling prairies, carpeted with wild flowers, and clotted over with poplar groves, where wild birds sing and chatter, and it does not seem too ideal or visionary that these broad sunlit spaces may be the homes of countless thousands of happy and contented people. The great wide uncultivated prairie seems to open its welcoming arms to the land-hungry, homeless dwellers of the cities, saying: "Come and try me. Forget the past, if it makes you sad. Come to me, for I am the Land of the Second Chance. I am the Land of Beginning Again. I will not ask who your ancestors were. I want you – nothing matters now but just you and me, and we will make good together." This is the invitation of the prairie to the discouraged and weary ones of the older lands, whose dreams have failed, whose plans have gone wrong, and who are ready to fall out of the race. The blue skies and green slopes beckon to them to come out and begin again. The prairie, with its peace and silence, calls to the troubled nations of Middle Europe, whose people are caught in the cruel tangle of war. When it is all over and the smoke has cleared away, and they who are left look around at the blackened ruins and desolated farms and the shallow graves of their beloved dead, they will come away from the scenes of such bitter memories. Then it is that this far country will make its appeal to them, and they will come to us in large numbers, come with their sad hearts and their sad traditions. What will we have for them? We have the fertility of soil; we have the natural resources; we have coal; we have gas; we have wheat land and pasture land and fruit land. Nature has done her share with a prodigality that shames our little human narrowness. Now if we had men to match our mountains, if we had men to match our plains, if our thoughts were as clear as our sunlight, we would be able to stand up high enough to see over the rim of things.

Source: Nellie McClung, *In Times like These* (Toronto: University of Toronto Press, 1972), 96-8.

John McCrae (1872–1918)

"IN FLANDERS FIELDS"

In April 1915 Canada's ill-trained army faced its first real battle of the First World War. Led by a massive bombardment and clouds of poison gas, the Germans were determined to capture the old Flemish city of Ypres. At a cost of six thousand men – half its infantry – the Canadian line held. One of those caught up in the battle was a doctor and former artillery officer from Guelph and Montreal, John McCrae. For days, the wounded bodies of Canadians and Germans passed under his hands, savagely tortured by wounds no romantic vision of warfare ever contemplated. Soon after, McCrae wrote his short poem "In Flanders Fields," revised it, and mailed it to the English magazine *Punch*. It immediately achieved fame. Sometimes cited as a pacifist message, McCrae's poem was in fact an appeal from the dead to avenge them. Its spirit reflected the mood that led half a million Canadians to volunteer for the struggle, most of them after the terrible battle at Ypres had shattered the easy patriotic illusions about war.

McCrae died of pneumonia in France before the end of the war. After the armistice, McCrae's poem helped to make the red Flanders poppy a symbol of remembrance for the most terrible war western civilization could remember. Probably no Canadian poem is better known to the world.

In Flanders fields the poppies blow
Between the crosses, row on row,
   That mark our place; and in the sky
   The larks, still bravely singing, fly
Scarce heard amid the guns below.

We are the Dead. Short days ago
We lived, felt dawn, saw sunset glow,
   Loved and were loved, and now we lie
   In Flanders fields.

Take up our quarrel with the foe:
To you from failing hands we throw
   The torch; be yours to hold it high.
   If ye break faith with us who die
We shall not sleep, though poppies grow
   In Flanders fields.

Source: Margaret Atwood, ed., *The New Oxford Book of Canadian Verse in English* (Toronto: Oxford University Press, 1982), 61.

Anonymous

A PARODY OF "IN FLANDERS FIELDS"

This parody of John McCrae's poem appeared in *The Worker*, a Communist newspaper, in 1923. Most of the interim arrangements to help veterans "re-establish" themselves had run out in 1921, just as Canada entered its first serious post-war depression. As revenues collapsed, governments and private employers cut back on patriotism and "returned men" found themselves out of work with none of the benefits Canadians would adopt a generation later. Yet *The Worker*'s appeal to unemployed war veterans was in vain. Few veterans found the Communists an option; instead, returned soldiers more often saw them as unpatriotic.

In city parks the papers blow
   Between the benches row on row,
That mark our places; and in the street
   The sparrows dodge the hurrying feet
That seem to mock us as we go.

No work! And yet, short days ago
   We fought your battles with the foe
And won it, too, and now we loaf
   In city parks.

You promised it would not be so
   When we returned. By that word know
Here is the fate that you must meet
   If you break faith with us, grim death
Will grip you, too, though poppies grow
   In Flander's fields!

Source: N. Brian Davis, ed., *The Poetry of the Canadian People, 1900-1950* (Toronto: NC Press, 1978), 138.

J.-A.-E. Cloutier (fl. 1919)

"THE DEVIL AT THE DANCE"

Part of country life in both French- and English-speaking Canada is a memory of dancing and merry-making in long-ago times. This is a living tradition as well. The violin, specially tuned and played with short strokes, is known as the fiddle and the reputation of a fine fiddler or a brilliant dancer carries up and down the rural roads and valleys. So it was, this story tells us, when the devil himself came to dance on Twelfth Night, a festival at the end of the Christmas season.

Contes, or fables, were part of French-Canadian folklore and this one, sometimes called "Rose LaTulippe" or "Le Diable à la danse," is one of the best known. It was collected by J.-A.-E. Cloutier of Cap Sainte-Ignace in 1919. Respect for the Catholic Church and belief in the saving grace of faith – both found in this story – were typical of most Quebec folklore of the period.

They were very good people in the home of François C. . . , not proud, religious, charitable to the poor, not haughty. They owned little. Besides, straight as the king's sword. And when they were selling they gave generous measure, always a good trait. They never spoke ill of anyone; and they never missed the First Friday of the month. Why, to tell all, they were first-class people.

It isn't often that they had a dance in this house. But the reason, this year, was that young François, their son, had just returned from a great trip to a distant country with Captain Basile Droy. They had to have a feast for his arrival.

Always at François C. . .'s home there'd be a great party the day after Twelfth Night. After supper a great many guests came, a lot of young people especially. They followed the great Dédé from the top of the island who was a fine fiddler and singer. It disturbed Mother

Catherine when she saw many come who weren't invited, but she was too good natured to make a fuss. After all, they were all childhood friends of young François.

Toward nine o'clock the great musician took out his fiddle from its fine varnished case. He began to pass the rosin over the bow. Then *zing, zing,* he started to chord. Ho, then, some hymn tunes, some songs: "Nouvelle agréable," "Ça bergers," "En roulant ma boule." After that it was some simple jigs, and then reels. Why, one could never miss the chance to hear such fine music!

Young François, with Germain Chiasson, little Blanche's suitor, and José Moreau, who was nicknamed "Golden Throat" because of his fine talk, went to call his father into the study to speak to him in private. There he asked permission to dance some rigadoons. There's nothing wrong with that, is there? Father François had to be begged because of the priest's sermons, and also the unexpected guests, some of whom smelled of liquor. He went to consult his wife. Why, it was too bad to refuse this to young François who'd just returned from such a long voyage. So he gave permission.

As soon as he agreed, they cleared the middle of the room. Everyone settled around the kitchen. Old François opened the dance with his wife Catherine, in a simple jig with not a few flourishes, I'm telling you. Of fine steps there were many. I tell you that for old people of their age, it wasn't easy to match them. It was Pierre, his son, who came to relieve them with his wife, Manda Berton. They were two fine dancers also, but they didn't beat Father François and his wife, oh, no!

The great Dédé played like one possessed, tapping his heel, which there was nothing so fine to hear. He wasn't controllable, this lad, when he had a little shot. They organized reels, *casse-reels*, cotillions, *spendys*, "*salut-des-dames*" . . . The great Dédé seemed set for twenty-four hours. Between dances he stopped just long enough to take a little shot, then hurrying back, played all kinds of things – dances, songs, hymns, even laments. It went like real wildfire!

At eleven o'clock there was a little lull to catch breath. Suddenly they heard some small bells, then the sound of a sleigh which slid over the ice. *Crunch*! it said.

After a little while there's a knock on the door. "Come in," says Pierre. The door opens, then they see a tall handsome man with curly hair and a fine black beard cut to a point. He had lively black eyes which seemed to throw

sparks. He had a fine beaver cloak, with a fine sealskin cape. He also had very fine moccasins of caribou, decorated with beads in thirty-six colours, and porcupine quills, also dyed all kinds of colours. He looked like a real gentleman, indeed! Then, just imagine! A fine sleigh gleaming like a mirror, with fine buffalo skins, a fine glossy black horse, with a white harness that had cost five or six gold coins. He looked unbelievably vigorous, this horse. He was all covered with hoar frost. All the horse dealers went around him to have a good look, but no one recognized him. He must have come from a distance. They offered to unharness him for the gentleman, but he refused, saying it wasn't worth the trouble, that he'd just put the fur robe on his back. He wouldn't be long. When passing he'd seen that people were enjoying themselves and he came in to dance a couple of dances.

They offered to take his wraps. He took off his cloak and cap but he wouldn't remove his kid gloves. The young people thought that was to show off, like city gentlemen, who did that, it seemed. At all events, I tell you that he certainly looked nice, that unexpected guest, and I assure you that the young women were strutting around and eyeing him. They wanted to know who would have the honour of dancing with this fine cavalier. But as he was a great gentleman who knew how things were done, he went to ask the daughter of the house, Mamselle Blanche, who was not to be overlooked, you know. She was a fine-looking girl who had manners and a good bearing; she was a little shy at first; it took away some of her confidence. Imagine it, then, to dance with this gentleman before everyone, it was embarrassing. Also, when he asked her like this: "Mademoiselle, will you do me the honour to dance with me?" she replied, blushing and trembling a little: "With pleasure, sir, but excuse me, I don't know how to dance very well." The little hypocrite, she knew very well that she was one of the best dancers on the island.

He wasn't only a beautifully dressed gentleman, this guest, my children; he was also a very fine dancer indeed, I assure you. Father François couldn't believe it and he was all dumbfounded: "My, my, what a fine dancer he is," he didn't tire of repeating to himself. He didn't know where he got all these steps. "He invents them, he invents them," he repeated endlessly.

He had begun by dancing a simple jig that lasted a good half hour. The fellow seemed infallible. After little Blanche, all the best dancers at the party were rising in turn to face him, but he was coping with them all. He didn't seem tired as he came to make his first bow to his partner.

Several young men tried to replace him, but they lost the step quickly and he signed to them by waving with his arms to return to their place. After that he jigged two or three fine flourishes which were really something to see.

One would say that there was a game between the fiddler and him, to see which would outlast the other. Dédé was starting to feel weak, he was finding the game a little hard. He was sweating heavily. He was much too proud to slow up. He seemed rather to catch fire little by little, one would say that he was getting inspired. I'm telling you, the dust was flying under his feet, and he was tapping his heels always without losing a beat.

But suddenly *crack*, a broken string! Oh, the wretch, he had done it on purpose. Luckily, he had some spare strings. Meanwhile, while he restrung, it gave him time to catch his breath a little. The guest of honour took advantage of it to organize a spendy, with the participation of course of the handsome stranger who during that time was flirting with all the girls.

At last the fiddle was restrung. Dédé, replenished with a good shot of rum, seemed as fresh as at the beginning of the party.

"Gentlemen, pray take your place for a spendy," cried José Moreau in his fine singing voice, and they form up with more enthusiasm than ever. All this commotion finally ended by waking Pierre's little boy who was two years old. As Manda, who was doing the honours of the house, was too busy to take care of him, Grandmother Catherine had taken him on her knee, and then to amuse him she sat with him right in the door of the bedroom where the little one could enjoy the whirling of the dancers. But each time the fine strange dancer passed before the child, he uttered cries of fright, and, gripping the old woman around the neck, he cried: "Bur ... bur ... burning, sir, burn ... burning!" "I say, how strange he is this evening," Catherine said to herself. As these fits were repeated each time the dancer passed before the child, the old woman began to find this funny; then, suddenly she noticed that the stranger's black eyes pierced the child with looks full of hatred.

He was dancing at this time with a young girl who wore a fine golden cross on her neck. As he passed below her, Grandmother Catherine heard him ask the girl if she would exchange this cross for a fine locket decorated with diamonds and containing his portrait. She rose, ran into the bedroom where a small jug of holy water stood at the head of the bed. She dipped her trembling old fingers in it and, still holding the child in her arms, she came through the door, making a sign of the cross over the dancer. It was magical and frightening. The Devil – for it was he in person – leaped to the ceiling, uttering a hellish cry. He wanted to spring toward the door but he saw over it a temperance cross mounted on a holly bough. Mad with rage, Satan threw himself through the stone wall, leaving behind him a great hole in the dark stone. Then they heard a fearful uproar outside. The Devil and his horse disappeared into the night; a trail of flames flashed under the horse's feet.

Everyone came out appalled, and saw that the ice was completely melted where the infernal horse had touched. It hardly needs saying that the party broke up then.

Next day a bricklayer came to fill up the hole where the Devil had passed, but he never succeeded. Each stone that he tried to put in seemed possessed by an unknown force, and nothing would make it stay in place. They had the house blessed again, but the opening still remains, as if God wished to give a continual warning.

The old stone house stands today. Facing the hole in the room there is always a chest of drawers where they set holy candles, and outside the wall you see all year round a cord of stove wood piled.

But since then they never dance in the stone house of François C. . . .

Source: Edith Fowke, *Folklore of Canada* (Toronto: McClelland and Stewart, 1976; rev. ed., 1982), 59-62.

Duncan Campbell Scott (1862—1947)

"ON THE WAY TO THE MISSION"

There was a time when being a poet and a bureaucrat was not wholly contradictory. Indeed, a government job was a respectable source of income for someone who earned little or nothing from writing. The most prominent of these bureaucrat-poets was Duncan Campbell Scott, who combined a distinguished poetic career with his responsibilities as deputy superintendent of Indian affairs. His long service in government spanned the period from 1879 to 1932. He was a friend and supporter of Archibald Lampman (1861–99), composer Murray Adaskin (1906–), and painters Homer Watson (1855–1936), Clarence Gagnon (1881–1942), and Lawren Harris (1885–1970).

For Scott and other enlightened members of his generation, there was nobility in Indian values and traditions and, as in this poem, "On the Way to the Mission," evil white men were the villains in the sad history of native impoverishment and depopulation. Nonetheless, if a shrinking native population was to survive the twentieth century, he felt that their route lay through cultural and economic assimilation.

Since what is liberal today is reactionary tomorrow, Scott's ideas are now freely and enthusiastically denounced. But, in his own day, Scott spoke for the majority of Canadians and, in his admiration for native values, he still does.

They dogged him all one afternoon,
Through the bright snow,
Two whitemen servants of greed;
He knew that they were there,
But he turned not his head;
He was an Indian trapper;
He planted his snow-shoes firmly,
He dragged the long toboggan
Without rest.

The three figures drifted
Like shadows in the mind of a seer;
The snow-shoes were whisperers
On the threshold of awe;
The toboggan made the sound of wings,
A wood-pigeon sloping to her nest.

The Indian's face was calm.
He strode with the sorrow of fore-knowledge,
Be his eyes were jewels of content
Set in circles of peace.
They would have shot him;
But momently in the deep forest,
They saw something flit by his side:
Their hearts stopped with fear.
Then the moon rose.

They would have left him to the spirit,
But they saw the long toboggan
Rounded well with furs,
With many a silver fox-skin,
With the pelts of mink and of otter.
They were the servants of greed;
When the moon grew brighter
And the spruces were dark with sleep,
They shot him.
When he fell on a shield of moonlight
One of his arms clung to his burden;
The snow was not melted:
The spirit passed away.

Then the servants of greed
Tore off the cover to count their gains;
They shuddered away into the shadows,
Hearing each the loud heart of the other.
Silence was born.

There in the tender moonlight,
    As sweet as they were in life,
Glimmered the ivory features,
    Of the Indian's wife.

In the manner of Montagnais women
    Her hair was rolled with braid;
Under her waxen fingers
    A crucifix was laid.

He was drawing her down to the Mission,
    To bury her there in spring,

When the bloodroot comes and the wind-
    flower
    To silver everything.

Source: Jack David and Robert Lecker, eds., *Canadian Poetry*, vol. 1 (Toronto: General Publishing, 1982), 111-12.

J.S. Woodsworth (1874–1942)

"THE BUSINESS MAN'S PSYCHOLOGY"

Born outside Toronto, James Shaver Woodsworth was educated as a Methodist minister but then redirected his life to social service. His pacifism during the First World War drove him out of the Methodist Church. In 1921 he won a parliamentary seat for Winnipeg and in 1932 he became the first leader of the Co-operative Commonwealth Federation (CCF), Canada's first successful social-democratic party. At the outbreak of the Second World War in 1939, Woodsworth's pacifism forced him to vote against his party on the issue of Canadian participation in the conflict and to abandon its leadership.

Woodsworth was a man of unbending principle. A tireless educator, he believed that socialism would be destroyed if it did not capture the hearts of its supporters and, ultimately, of a majority of the voters. It was a doctrine that demanded more patience than most of his colleagues could muster. At the same time, Woodsworth was no friend of class warfare and the brutal tactics of the far left. As the following selection, written in 1918 or 1919 when he was working as a longshoreman in Vancouver, suggests, Woodsworth understood those he had grown up with and, unlike many of his followers, he saw his task in intensely realistic terms.

A good deal of nonsense is often solemnly uttered by Socialist speakers and other working class advocates with regard to the "capitalist bunch." They are classified as bourgeois and petty bourgeois. They are often depicted as a set of self-conscious hypocrites ... Now, as a matter of fact, most of these descriptions are second-hand, being borrowed from translations of European writers ... Our "middle class" occupies a very different position from what is known in Europe as the "middle class."

In the background of the majority of the successful business men of Canada there is an old Eastern homestead. The successful business man may lunch at a high-class club or occupy a box at the theatre or spend his vacations in Europe, but as a boy he "did the chores," swam in the village millpond, cut his name in the desks of the little red school-house, and generally lived the all-round democratic life of a farmer's boy . . . The labor problem was confined to the hired man and the hired girl . . . Flitting recollections of such a life pass before the half-shut eyes of the big business manager as he rests in his comfortable leather chair after a heavy day at the office. In the nearer background of his consciousness is the life of the small town in which he experienced his early business struggles. Here he married and set up his first home. Here his children had measles and croup and he knew what it was to be on friendly terms with all sorts of neighbors. In his business he called most of his employees by their first names and knew more or less of their personal affairs. There were few poor in the town, and they were generally shiftless and addicted to drink. If a man didn't make things go, it was more or less his own fault. Organized labor was unknown and Socialism was unheard of.

Since our successful business man moved to the city and entered upon larger commercial and financial enterprises, the life has been very different. The greatest change lies in his isolation from the common life about him. His offices in the fine new warehouses are open only to employees of the highest rank. He throws the responsibility for details upon managers and foremen . . . At noon he lunches at an exclusive club with men of his own group and way of thinking. He drives or is driven in his own car, so that he does not even rub shoulders with the strap-hangers in the street cars. His home is in the best residential district . . . His isolation is complete, his class-consciousness assured.

He is kind-hearted . . . His early childhood and the village life gave him personal sympathy. But he has had no personal experiences of the desperate struggles of modern industrial life, and no enlightenment with regard to modern methods of social service. He will send a Christmas basket to a poor family at Christmas but he will fight valiantly against organized labor. Again the key to his action lies in his own personal experiences with their limitations. He thinks he knows the problems of labor because he knew his father's hired man . . . He fails to realize that just as his mahogany-furnished office and beautiful residence differ widely from the old barn in which he forked hay or his little bedroom with the rag carpet, so an absolutely new world has grown up about him.

But is he not a leader in the new commercial and industrial life? Undoubtedly; but he has seen life not as a series of human relationships, but merely from the standpoint of dividends. He thinks himself just. He would not commit a vulgar theft. He would not insult his neighbor's wife. He does not realize that he is the beneficiary of a system that is degrading womanhood and crushing out manhood. Can he be made to understand?

Source: Frank Underhill, *James Shaver Woodsworth: Untypical Canadian: An Estimate of His Life and Ideas* (Toronto: Ontario Woodsworth Memorial Foundation, 1944), 28-30.

Part Three

1921—1960

William Lyon Mackenzie King (1874–1950)

KEEPING CANADA UNITED

It was not by accident that William Lyon Mackenzie King, Canada's tenth prime minister, proved to be its most enduring leader. A grandson of the fiery Upper Canadian rebel of 1837, King felt himself to be a social reformer but primarily he was a conciliator. Having proved himself in the field of industrial relations, he brought the same cautious skills to politics. Those who associate leadership with courageous actions and dramatic rhetoric will read the King record in vain. His goal was to unite a badly divided country, and if that meant reconciling the factions in his own Liberal Party, he did not see the distinction. From the outset, for example, he found his party bitterly divided on the protective tariff. Among Quebeckers, it was a sacred trust, the protector of jobs and fortunes. In the west, the Liberal Party's other stronghold, it was an abomination, a tax by the east on the struggling pioneers, compelling them to buy high-cost machinery from Brantford and clothing from Montreal and Valleyfield instead of paying half the price in nearby Minneapolis. King's skill at compromise is evident in this passage:

We take the position that to keep our country united, to keep Canada happy and contented, we must have regard for all shades and all parts of the country, and any policy that is extreme we must avoid. I say what I said in other provinces that nothing in the nature of free trade would be possible, for however it might appeal to some men in the west, it would breed discouragement and discontent in this part of the Dominion, and therefore would make for divisions instead of harmony. Similarly, I said, speaking in the west, that neither can a policy of higher and higher protection keep this country united. I do not admit for it that it would have the beneficial effect claimed for it, but even supposing it did, if the effect of it was to provoke an extreme movement in the western provinces, sooner or later, those effects would be felt in this part of the Dominion. That is why the Government has sought to find a course that will help to reconcile rather than to exaggerate the differences existing so far as tariff is concerned.

Source: House of Commons *Debates*, June 16, 1931.

So which side was he on?

As long as he was prime minister, King wrestled with such issues as conscription, the tariff, and provincial rights, and he did so with such success that, by the time he retired in 1948, he had held a prime ministership longer than any politician in the British Empire. Indeed, people insisted that running Canada was easy – and all the more so because it had been done by a fussy little bachelor with little charm and a resolute distaste for drama. For instance, King was so convinced that voters would condemn a smiling prime minister that he insisted that photographers record only his solemn moments. Inevitably, these became his dominant public pose. Over time, King's reputation has grown as Canadians appreciate what he accomplished. Canada, after all, is a very difficult country to govern, and King deserves a second look.

Though he would have loved to be admired as an orator, his wisdom was evident less in soaring rhetoric than in snatches of prudent advice. "The promises of yesterday," he warned Parliament, "are the taxes of today." In the international arena, King maintained that, whenever Canada ventured to the edge of war and peace, not raw emotions but "Parliament would decide":

It is for Parliament to decide whether or not we should participate in wars in different parts of the world, and it is neither right nor proper for any individual, for any group or individuals, to take any step which in any way might limit the rights of Parliament in a matter which is of such great concern to all the people of our country. We have felt and feel very strongly that, if the relations between the different parts of the British Empire are to be made of an enduring character, this will only be through a full recognition of the supremacy of Parliament, and this particularly with regard to matters which may involve participation in war.

Source: House of Commons *Debates*, July 7, 1942.

Mackenzie King left Canada much richer and more powerful and, on the whole, happier than he found it. Some have argued that he was the country's greatest prime minister. Certainly he was the most successful. Perhaps his success stemmed from the shrewdness evident in such statements as "not necessarily conscription but conscription if necessary" and "the great thing in politics . . . is to avoid mistakes." A successor, Lester Pearson, never forgot King's warning:

My boy ... I would just give you one piece of advice, to remember that in the course of human history far more has been accomplished for the welfare and progress of mankind in preventing bad actions than in doing good ones.

Source: Peter Newman, *The Distemper of Our Times: Canadian Politics in Transition, 1963-68* (Toronto: McClelland and Stewart, 1968), 52.

James Gray (1906—)

"Our World Stopped and We Got Off"

In *The Winter Years,* journalist James Gray wrote one of the best accounts of what it was like to be middle class and hopelessly out of work in Winnipeg during the Great Depression of the 1930s. Like other "reliefers," Gray was compelled to chop wood in the winter and pick dandelions in the summer while the clothes he needed to get any kind of office work became threadbare and ragged.

In this passage, Gray describes not the Thirties but the preceding Twenties, when the seeds of his own financial undoing were laid. While some people blamed the capitalist system for the Depression, more were like Gray. Typical of many Canadians, he had gambled on "making it" and he blamed only himself and bad luck for failure. And, to be fair, Gray's luck changed. After a few grim years, his writing ability won him a reporter's job at the *Winnipeg Free Press* and the chance to describe the Depression rather than live out its misery. He would become one of western Canada's most popular historians.

Money has an overweening importance to anybody who grows up in poverty, and our family knew nothing but poverty in Winnipeg during the First World War. From the time I was nine, and my brother Walter was six, we sold papers, ran messages, delivered groceries and laundry after school. If we never went hungry, there was never a time when what was wrong with our family could not have been repaired with $25 or $50.

The Winnipeg Grain Exchange in 1921 was on the threshold of its last great fling. The brokerage offices were crowded with speculators who bought and sold grain futures on margin. Outside, work was starting on a ten-storey addition that was to make it the biggest office building in the British Empire. The trading floor itself was a forest of temporary wooden beams and scaffolds, for it, too, was being enlarged. Here the shrieking voices of a hundred pit-traders created a din that, when the windows were open, could be heard clear over to Portage and Main. Behind the Monte Carlo façade was the actual business of ware-housing, transporting, and marketing the western grain crops. Incidental to the frenzy of speculation, the wheat crops did get marketed. It so happened that the company I went to work for was actually engaged in the market-ing business, and my employer never went into the wheat-pit. He was one of half a dozen vessel-brokers who obtained lake freighters for grain exporters and found exporters to charter the vessels.

My first job was running messages back and forth between our office and the telegraph offices on the trading floor. Soon I was helping with the books and learning eagerly how to run a typewriter, operate an adding machine, and make out insurance policies and invoices. The office opened at nine and closed whenever the day's work was done, usually along towards midnight. My job was as exhausting as it was exhilarating and at Christmas time I was amply rewarded with a $100 bonus. I ran all the way home clutching my envelope full of $5 bills.

When navigation ended on the Great Lakes in December, the vessel-brokerage business came to a dead stop. My employer went off to California; I enrolled in a correspondence course in accounting and picked up some extra money as a part-time bookkeeper in an option brokerage across the hall. Thereafter, promo-tions and pay raises came rapidly. By the time I was nineteen, there was nothing about the business I did not know or could not do, I was

making $150 a month, and my Christmas bonus reached $500. Only experienced brick-layers made more, and most bank accountants made less. In those days the banks refused to permit their employees to marry until they were earning $1,000 a year, a level that usually took ten years to reach.

The success I achieved only whetted my appetite for more. I bought a half interest in a couple of race-horses, fell for one swindle after another, sent good money after bad to pro-moters of oil wells in Louisiana, gold mines in Colorado, and silver mines in Ontario. In between times I took losing fliers in the grain market. That I did nothing but lose never con-cerned me, because ultimately I would make an investment that would repay all my losses. Besides, by 1926, I was otherwise preoccupied. I had acquired a nearly-new Ford sedan, smoked two-for-a-quarter cigars, and was squiring one of Eaton's prettiest cashiers. Her name was Kathleen Burns, and by that Christmas we were so much in love that we could discover no reason for not getting married. We did so, and I had a further incentive to get on with my fortune-making. Instead of buying furniture or a house, we bought a race-horse, with my employer as silent partner, and for the next year I coupled horse-training with my Grain Exchange employment. As a horse-trainer I was a monumental bust, but it was great fun.

Our daughter Patricia was born in 1928, and her arrival gave me still another incentive. But somehow I had slipped into a rut. My salary had stopped going up, my employer had brought his brother into the company, and my position steadily deteriorated. When a group of grain-brokers decided to finance a new stock-brokerage office on Portage Avenue, I hired on as margin clerk, statistician, and general factotum. Not a single partner or employee knew anything about the stock market or the brokerage business. We even had to bring in employees of other brokers to train us in the simplest procedures such as computing margins. On the basis of this all-pervading ignorance, we were prepared to advise everybody in town how to make and manage investments in the stock market. In the logic of 1928, we should have been eminently successful, but the project never got off the ground and the business closed a full year before the crash.

Instead of going back to the Grain Exchange, I decided the time had come to get into business for myself. The first chance that came along was a candy franchise, and for the first half of 1929 I was in the candy business. I worked eighteen hours a day servicing the candy stands and Kay worked almost as long filling bags with candy. We went broke in six months and I returned to the vessel-brokerage business with a different employer. A few months after the Wall Street crash I was offered a much better job as manager of the grain department of a new brokerage firm that was opening an office in Lethbridge.

I arrived in Lethbridge just before the Solloway Mills scandal broke. Brokers were being arrested all across the country for "bucketing" their customers' orders during the mining boom. They were more victims of circumstances than anything else. The banks

would not lend money on mining shares, and this prevented the brokers from financing their customers' margin purchases at a time when the customers were clamouring for mining stocks on margin. So the brokers sold stock on the exchange against their customers' purchases, a highly illegal action for which they went to jail.

By the time Kay had sold our furniture and brought Patty to Lethbridge, I had discovered some highly unsavoury things about an oil company my employers were floating. The more I probed into it, the more certain I became that the investors would lose their money. I quit in a panic, for fear I too would go to jail, and went back to Winnipeg to the job I had quit only a few months before. It was not until much later that I realized how lucky I was to get any kind of a job then. The brokerage failures turned hundreds out of jobs in Winnipeg. The break of the wheat market below a dollar and then below ninety cents brought hard times for the Grain Exchange, and, outside, the secondary effects of the stock-market crashes were becoming clear. But not to me.

That was the year of the miniature-golf craze. Like millions of others, Kay and I took up the game. The trouble was that the nearest course was miles away from home, and it was always crowded.

"You know," I said, "a guy could make a lot of money with a course like this near our place."

Kay pointed out that she could act as cashier during the day, if my mother would look after Patty, and I could run it at night. Our overhead would be small, and, if we got a quarter of the business the pioneer course was getting, we could clean up. We talked ourselves into it in no time. There was a small impediment. We had no money, or relatively little, compared to the capital required. The original operator egged us on.

"Why," he said, "there's nothing to it. Do it on credit! Your course will cost you $2,000. You might even do it for $1,500, and all you need is a couple of hundred in cash. Right now I'm taking in better than $200 a day. You won't do that good. But you could figure on a minimum of $100 a day. In fifteen days you'll pay for the course and you'll be set for next year."

It sounded wonderful. And it was as easy as that – almost. We rented a vacant lot, installed lights and a shack, and bought clubs and balls. No one demanded payment for the supplies. We were astounded at how good our credit was. Nevertheless, we spent all the money we had and borrowed more before the thing was finished. During the first week business was wonderful and we took in well over $500. Then came Labour Day, and nothing collapsed as quickly as miniature golf in September 1930. We closed the course in October with creditors clamouring for their money. So much of my pay was earmarked to repay loans that there was little left to live on.

Then the blow fell. On November 30 my employer went out of business. Nor was this all. By one of those queer twists of fate, two of my brothers were laid off on the same day. By a momentary stroke of good fortune, I managed to find a buyer for the golf course and he paid me enough to clean up most of my debts. But I still owed better than $300, which was more than I could have repaid even if I had had a job. And I had no job.

I have told this story in detail to make this point: I was a typical "child of the Twenties." What happened to me happened to everybody, more or less. What you became in life depended upon the job you settled into. You left school when you had to, though no earlier than fourteen, the legal limit. Then you got whatever extra education you needed at night schools or by correspondence courses. If your first job lacked opportunity for advancement, you quit and went elsewhere. It was not uncommon to make three or four false starts before settling into a permanent position, and no stigma attached to rolling stones.

Source: James Gray, *The Winter Years: The Depression on the Prairies* (Toronto: Macmillan, 1966), 9-13.

R. B. Bennett (1870–1947)

MAVERICK CAPITALIST

Richard Bedford Bennett was almost a caricature of the successful capitalist, from his striped trousers, cutaway coat, top hat, and spats to his early success as the Calgary lawyer for the Canadian Pacific Railway. With his personal wealth increased by a rich bequest from the heiress of the Eddy Match fortune, Bennett personally paid for the Conservative Party victory in 1930. Canadian voters, trapped in the first stages of the Great Depression, loved his booming self-confidence and his pledge to use high tariffs to force other countries to open their gates to Canadian exports.

Until it embraced an American-style dedication to the unfettered market, Canadian conservatism was a home for both nationalism and a willingness to use government to protect Canada's identity. Bennett reflected that Tory tradition. Though few gave him credit, Bennett was an activist prime minister. He almost doubled Canada's national debt and strained the constitution by spending federal revenues to help provinces relieve poverty. More millions vanished to save farmer-owned wheat pools. The "New Deal" he unveiled prior to the 1935 election – an ambitious program of legislation that included unemployment insurance and farm-marketing boards – was denounced by the Liberal opposition as unconstitutional and overturned after his defeat.

In the first of the selections below, a 1932 speech in Parliament supporting his government's legislation creating a Canadian Radio Broadcasting Commission, Bennett echoes the argument of Sir John Aird (1855–1938), president of the Canadian Bank of Commerce, that Canada's choice was "the State or the States." His case for a well-funded public broadcaster is still strong today. In the second selection, an extract from a speech in the 1935 election, Bennett sets out his view of the need for government intervention in the capitalist system.

In moving the second reading of the bill which stands in my name, I desire to intimate to the house that in a general way it follows the committee's report which was unanimously adopted a few days ago and it is based upon principles which the government believes should be adopted, because they fulfil two essential requirements without which

radio in Canada must fail in service to the Canadian people.

First of all, this country must be assured of complete Canadian control of broadcasting from Canadian sources, free from foreign interference or influence. Without such control radio broadcasting can never become a great agency for the communication of matters of national concern and for the diffusion of national thought and ideals, and without such control it can never be the agency by which national consciousness may be fostered and sustained and national unity still further strengthened. Other and alternative systems may meet the requirements of other countries, and in any case it is not my purpose to comment unfavourably upon those systems. But it seems to me clear that in Canada the system we can most profitably employ is one which, in operation and control, responds most directly to the popular will and the national need. In this stage of our national development we have problems peculiar to ourselves and we must reach a solution of them through the employment of all available means. The radio has a place in the solution of all those problems. It becomes, then, the duty of parliament to safeguard it in such a way that its fullest benefits may be assured to the people as a whole.

Furthermore, radio broadcasting, controlled and operated in this way, can serve as a dependable link in a chain of empire communication by which we may be more closely united one with the other in that enduring fellowship which is founded on the clear and sympathetic understanding which grows out of closer mutual knowledge.

No other system of radio broadcasting can meet these national requirements and empire obligations. Therefore, the parliament of Canada is asked to support the principle embodied in this measure.

Secondly, no other scheme than that of public ownership can ensure to the peoples of this country, without regard to class or place, equal enjoyment of the benefits and pleasures of radio broadcasting. Private ownership must necessarily discriminate between densely and sparsely populated areas. This is not a correctable fault in private ownership; it is an inescapable and inherent demerit of that system. It does not seem right that in Canada, the towns should be preferred to the countryside or the prosperous communities to those less fortunate. In fact, if no other course were possible, it might be fair to suggest that it should be the other way about. Happily, however, under this system, there is no need for discrimination; all may be served alike. Equality of service is assured by the plan which calls for a chain of high power stations throughout Canada. And furthermore, the particular requirements of any community may be met by the installation of low power stations by means of which local broadcasting service may be obtained.

Operation under the technical plan covered by the bill has been made possible by an arrangement between this country and the government of the United States, by which the necessary channels when required will be made available for effective domestic use.

I desire to acknowledge the friendly spirit which is manifest in this arrangement. I believe that the plan now suggested when in operation will permit Canada to enjoy a scheme of radio broadcasting unexcelled in any other country in the world.

Then there is a third reason to which I might refer, and one which I believe must commend itself to every hon. member in this chamber. The use of the air, or the air itself, whatever you may please to call it, that lies over the soil or land of Canada is a natural resource over which we have complete jurisdiction under the recent decision of the privy council. I believe that there is no government in Canada that does not regret to-day that it has parted with some of these natural resources for considerations wholly inadequate and on terms that do not reflect the principle under which the crown holds the natural resources in trust for all the people. In view of these circumstances and of the further fact that broadcasting is a science that is only yet in its infancy and about which we know little yet, I cannot think that any government would be warranted in leaving the air to private exploitation and not reserving it for development for the use of the people. It well may be that at some future time, when science has made greater achievements than we have yet a record of, it may be desirable to make other or different arrangements in whole or in part, but no one at this moment in the infancy of this great science would, I think, be warranted in suggesting that we should part with the control of this natural resource. I think, Mr. Speaker, that that is a third and adequate reason why we should proceed with the bill.

Source: House of Commons *Debates*, 1932, vol.3 May 1932, 3035-6.

I do not intend to trouble you just now with the history of the capitalist system. But, in my opinion, it is important that you should carefully examine the origin of capitalism, its place in the early days, and the theory upon which it operated. It would be helpful to a clearer understanding of some of our present difficulties if you were to trace the development [of capitalism] which carried the system from the simple practice of a simple theory to the complex practice of a theory strained and wrenched out of its original form. You would then see that for the old checks and balances which ensured the proper working of the original system, the system today has provided no counterpart within itself. You would agree that free competition and the open market system as they were known in the old days, have lost their place in the system, and that the only substitute for them, in these modern times, is government regulation and control. You would understand that past depressions were caused by maladjustments in the operation of this system, and were corrected only after intense suffering and hardship, that these depressions were so many crises, dangerous and difficult to surmount, but that, in comparison with them, this depression is a catastrophe, and therefore demands the intervention of the Government . . .

Selfish men, and this country is not without them – men whose mounting bank rolls loom larger than your happiness, corporations without souls and without virtue – these, fearful that this Government might impinge on what they have grown to regard as their immemorial right of exploitation, will whisper against us. They will call us radicals. They will say that this is the first step on the road to socialism. We fear them not. We think that their ready compliance with out programme would serve their interests better than any ill-timed opposition to it. We invite their co-operation. We want the co-operation of all . . .

The agencies of production, of manufacture, of distribution, of finance: all the parts of the capitalist system, have only one purpose and that is to work for the welfare of the people. And when any of those instruments in any way fails, it is the plain duty of a government which represents the people, to remove the cause of failure. This I do not say by way of threat. I have told you that we hope for the unanimous support of all classes, in this great and difficult task of reform, but I think it is only right to add that opposition from any class which imperils the future of this great undertaking we will not tolerate. The lives and the happiness and the welfare of too many people depend upon our success to allow the selfishness of a few individuals to endanger it.

Source: R.B. Bennett, *The Prime Minister Speaks to the People* (Ottawa, 1935), 18-19.

Irving Abella (1940–) and Harold Troper (1942–)

"NONE IS TOO MANY"

In the introduction to their book on Canada's refusal to accept Jewish refugees from Hitler's Europe, Irving Abella and Harold Troper refer to an anonymous senior official who, during "a rambling, off-the-record discussion with journalists in early 1945," was asked how many Jewish refugees would be admitted to Canada after the war. Troper and Abella write: "His response seems to reflect the prevailing view of a substantial number of his fellow citizens: 'None,' he said, 'is too many.'"

The official appears to have been F.C. Blair, who in 1936 became director of the immigration branch of the Department of Agriculture and was responsible for administering Canada's immigration policy before, during, and after the Second World War. Blair was adamantly opposed to the admission of Jewish refugees. In this he was not alone: he reflected the pervasive anti-Semitism of pre-war Canada. And, as Abella and Troper insist, Blair enforced policies approved by the Liberal government of William Lyon Mackenzie King.

The following passage from *None Is Too Many* captures the mixture of polite and pernicious anti-Semitism which animated Blair and those who shared his views and which condemned thousands of Hitler's victims to their deaths. Though Canada is not free from racism today, such blatant and cruel acts of mass discrimination have become rare.

For Blair the term "refugee" was a code word for Jew. Unless "safeguards" were adopted, he warned Thomas Crerar, Canada was in danger of being "flooded with Jewish people," and his task, as he saw it, was to make sure that the safeguards did not fail. Indeed, he was inordinately proud of his success in keeping out Jews. "Pressure on the part of Jewish people to get into Canada," he wrote, "has never been greater than it is now, and I am glad to be able to add, after 35 years experience here, that it was never so well controlled." Blair expressed a strong personal distaste for Jews, especially for "certain of their habits." He saw them as unassimilable, as people apart, as threatening people "who can organize their affairs better than other people" and so accomplish more. He complained bitterly that Jews were "utterly selfish in their attempts to force through a permit for the admission of relatives or friends." "They do not believe that 'No' means more than 'Perhaps.'" And Jews, he lamented, "make any kind of promise to get the door open but . . . never cease their agitation until they get in the whole lot." Blair saw a conspiracy behind all Jewish attempts to get their co-religionists into the country, "to bring immigration regulations into disrepute and create an atmosphere favourable to those who cannot comply with the law." Self-righteous and justifying, he commiserated with the traffic manager of the Canadian Pacific Railway: "If there is any surer way to close the door in their own face, I do not know of it."

But did Blair see himself as an anti-Semite? No, for he was, in his own view, just being realistic – realistic about Canada's immigration needs and about the unsuitability of the Jew to those needs. To keep Jews out of Canada, he would often argue, did Jews a favour, even if they could not see it. The arrival of Jews would create anti-Semitism in Canada, undermining the security of the existing Canadian Jewish community and little benefitting the new arrival. Those who saw anti-Jewish sentiment in Blair's position did so, Blair claimed, from self-serving motives. "I am sure," he declared, "the treatment received in Canada by Jewish people in no way warrants the charge of anti-Semitism. I suggest that those who hold such a view are putting it forward not on the ground of our past history but probably as an argument in favour of an open door policy, which under present economic conditions is impossible to adopt."

Blair was of course an anti-Semite. His contempt for the Jews was boundless. In a revealing letter to a strong opponent of Jewish immigration, Blair elaborated on the reasons for his prejudice:

I suggested recently to three Jewish gentlemen with whom I am well acquainted, that it might be a very good thing if they would call a conference and have a day of humiliation and prayer, which might profitably be extended for a week or more, where they would honestly try to answer the question of why they are so unpopular almost everywhere . . . I often think that instead of persecution it would be far better if we more often told them frankly why many of them

are unpopular. If they would divest themselves of certain of their habits I am sure
they could be just as popular in Canada as
our Scandinavians . . . Just because Jewish
people would not understand the frank kind

of statements I have made in this letter to
you, I have marked it confidential.

Source: Irving Abella and Harold Troper, *None Is Too
Many: Canada and the Jews of Europe, 1933-1948*
(Toronto: Lester and Orpen Dennys, 1983), 7-9.

Gwethalyn Graham (1913-65)

"REFUGEES: THE HUMAN ASPECT"

**Canada's response to the plight of German-Jewish refugees fleeing Nazism was one of the
darker moments of Canadian history. It is therefore all the more important to recognize those
few Canadians who bucked the tide of prejudice and indifference to urge a more generous
immigration policy. Among these was the author Gwethalyn Graham. One of her articles,
which appeared in *Saturday Night* in November 1938, began with the prescient assertion that
the aim of the Nazi government in Germany was to "wipe out" the Jews of Germany and
Austria. Poignantly chronicling the tragedy facing European Jews, she cried out to Canada to
take more active measures on their behalf.**

**Much of Graham's subsequent writing was also aimed at promoting tolerance and under-
standing among groups. Her book *Earth and High Heaven* focused on Jewish-Gentile relations.
Concerned with the deepening gulf between English and French Canadians, she collaborated
in 1963 with Solange Chaput-Rolland (1919-) to write *Dear Enemies/Chers ennemis*.**

There can be very few literate Canadians
today who do not realize that it is the
intention of the German government to wipe
out the Jews of Germany and Austria if the rest
of the world does not come to their rescue. Yet
because the average human being's capacity to
feel what he reads about but has not seen is very
limited, we appear to be largely unaware of the
urgent and desperate need of the refugees.

At this moment there are thousands upon
thousands of men, women and children who
are being herded like cattle from frontier to
frontier. *There is no place for them to go.* You
may be sure that if there were, they would not
be sitting on benches in Hyde Park and the
Tulleries, or sleeping in Victoria station and
the Gare du Nord, or waiting for hours each
day in the rooms of charitable organizations,
on platforms and docks, in foreign consulates,
or at the Home Office. You see them everywhere in London and Paris, the mother and
father sitting straight, looking at nothing, while

the children try to sleep with their heads in their parents' laps. Not very long ago the pattern of these people's lives was very like your own; they had roots like yours in their community, and thought of themselves as an integral part of that larger community, the German state. They believed they *were* Germans. As one of them said to me in London two months ago, "I don't suppose we remembered our Jewish blood much oftener than you think of your Scottish blood. We thought we were Germans, as you consider yourself Canadian."

Equipped with only newspaper and magazine-gained knowledge, I was totally unprepared for the chaos, the suffering, and the incredible muddle created by the daily arrival of hundreds of refugees in London. Forty thousand had already landed by the first of May; they seemed to be everywhere. You could spot them at social affairs, or in the street, by what we called the "refugee look." Rich or poor, they all had that blankness of expression which is a characteristic of people with no home, no money, no goal and nothing to work for . . . only a day-to-day existence made possible by English charity. All this has come about through no fault of theirs.

I have never seen such courage. There was one woman who had just come from Vienna to London, via Paris, with her two daughters, whom I met at the house of a mutual friend. She was tall, thin, vivacious and very witty. Her description of their flight from Vienna to Paris was actually funny. Eleven times between Vienna and the Swiss border what few possessions they had were searched, thrown on the floor and trampled upon. Three times they were forced to take off all their clothes for inspection by a Nazi policewoman. When at last they got to Paris, they spent three weeks sitting and waiting in various government offices hoping to obtain French passports. "Without a passport," she remarked, stirring her tea, "you are next door to non-existent. You can neither remain in a country nor leave it."

She began to ask questions about Canada. What were the people like, the climate, the countryside? Though one of her daughters was an industrial designer, the other an architect, she explained eagerly that of course they would do anything, anything at all. She herself was a very good cook, and they thought if worse came to worse, they could all do domestic work. When my hostess protested, she said calmly, "This is July, 1938. We have had time to adjust ourselves during the past five years. Ever since Hitler came into power in Germany, we knew it was going to happen."

They had only a little money. When she asked direct questions about Canadian regulations, I had not the courage to say, "There's no hope for you in my country," but made some confused statement about the High Commissioner's office. She realized then that they had been wrong in thinking there was one nation which would not fail them. With that same gallantry which I had encountered over and over again, she said, "Of course these are difficult times for everyone. There must be some place for us. We keep saying that to each other . . . there must be some place for us. We can't stay much longer in England because we have to get work. The Home Office is giving as many permits as possible, but there are so many refugees here."

She mentioned her husband once or twice but when I asked something about him, she said in a flat voice, "He's dead," and went on to talk of something else. My hostess explained next day that he had been beaten to death in a Nazi jail two days before that flight from Vienna to Paris.

The last I heard of her and her two daughters they had set out for Belgium on a four weeks' visa.

I remember an afternoon early in May when I was invited to the flat of some friends for cocktails. Besides the Scottish husband, Viennese Jewish wife, and her brother, there was one young Englishman named Peter, and myself. In the serene, civilized high-ceilinged room we talked desultorily of unimportant things until suddenly Lisa said to Peter, "I wish you'd see if you can get any information about Franz when you get back. He was arrested a month ago. We're afraid he's been murdered."

After a few brief questions and answers, our conversation continued, broken now and again by instructions from Lisa to go to such and such a Strasse and enquire at the café on the corner about a friend, or a relative. She wrote down the names of five people whom she wanted Peter to find out about. He was in a London bank, and was being sent over for a third time to try to transfer Jewish and non-Jewish capital from Vienna to Zurich by fair means or foul. To half the people whom Lisa or

her brother mentioned, he merely shook his head, and like the refugees, after a brief silence we would talk of something else. The whole scene was like a nightmare, at one time both unbearably real, and monstrously unreal. The conversation would switch without warning from painting, to torture and murder, or imprisonment without trial, then back to painting again.

At dinner parties and teas and cocktail parties the refugees I met used to question me about Canada until I came to dread any reference to my nationality and hoped that I would be taken for English. Up to the time of the Evian Conference, they believed that in Canada, a country liberal, democratic, tolerant, with immense unoccupied lands and a population not much larger than that of Greater New York or London, they might make another home. There, at least, no one would ever again write on their door during the night, "This Is The House Of A Jewish Pig," for their children to read when they came out to go to school in the morning.

With almost no exceptions, in the face of agony and privation beyond belief, the democratic nations represented at the Evian Conference played safe. For such overcrowded countries as England and France there was some excuse. For Canada there was no excuse whatever. These refugees are asking only some land of their own and a chance to live in decency and peace; they do not want charity, nor would they permit themselves to become a burden upon us.

With the refugee problem has come our first real opportunity for world leadership. We can continue to say, "Let George do it," but for once in our lives, George is not going to do it. There are no vast habitable but vacant spaces where the refugees can find a home, and the London Refugee Office set up by the Evian Conference is not going to be able to create such territories. If the present course of European events leads to the world disaster which now seems inevitable, it will be as much through our fault as anyone else's. Should the already over-crowded countries be forced to take in the refugees, we will have to pay dearly for the resultant chaos and hardship in the end.

Germany and Italy maintain that there is something inherently inefficient in the democratic system which makes unemployment and government relief inevitable. In their eyes our refusal to aid the Jews is regarded as proof in point. We, the democracies, have been forced into a position where we have to answer for the fate of the Jews of Germany and Austria. Either our system can be made to work through extraordinary necessity, and because it is a life and death matter to countless human beings, or we are clinging at terrible expense to an economic and political structure so weak and outworn that it will bear no additional strain.

By our behavior in this crisis our national character, our ideals and our sincerity will be judged. Those principles which we represent and which are fast disappearing in many countries may well be said to stand or fall by our conduct toward the refugees.

Source: Saturday Night, vol. 54, no. 2 (November 12, 1938), 8.

J.W. Dafoe (1866–1944)

"What's the Cheering for?"

Who Speaks for Canada? is generally a book about Canada. Sometimes, of course, Canada remembers that it is part of the world. John Wesley Dafoe never forgot it. Preoccupied though he was by the political and economic issues of the prairie provinces, the editor of the *Winnipeg Free Press* was a passionate internationalist. He had gone with Prime Minister Robert Laird Borden (1854–1937) to the Versailles Peace Conference in 1919 because he wanted Canada to have its own voice and its own view. He believed in the League of Nations and, with fading hope, in collective security as the only way to keep the world from war.

At the end of September 1938, Europe had passed through the most serious war scare since the Allied victory in 1918. Sudeten Germans, whipped up by Hitler's agents, had demanded autonomy within Czechoslovakia. Prague had conceded their demands. The Nazi dictator was not satisfied. **The whole territory had to be returned to Germany. France's Édouard Daladier and Britain's Neville Chamberlain hastened to Munich to appease Hitler. The Fuhrer emerged triumphant. Almost everywhere the news spread, there was rejoicing. Back in Britain, Chamberlain proclaimed "peace in our time" to roaring applause. In Ottawa, Prime Minister Mackenzie King dispatched a congratulatory telegram. Most Canadians agreed. Only in his cramped, disorderly editorial office did one man disagree.**

"What's the Cheering for?" spoke for Canada, but eleven months too early. By September 10, 1939, all of Czechoslovakia was under Nazi control, Poland had been invaded, and Canada was at war.

While the cheers are proceeding over the success which is attending the project of dismembering a state by processes of bloodless aggression, some facts might be set out for the information of people who would like to know what the cheering is about and who ought to be taking part in it.

I.

First we draw attention to this passage in a letter from the Berlin correspondent of the Economist, appearing in its issue of September 17:

"When Prague made concessions which would have more than satisfied the Sudeten Germans, had they desired to remain within the Republic, the pretence that they only wanted autonomy within the Czechoslovak State had to be abandoned. In fact, it was abandoned in Germany before Herr Hitler made his final Nuremberg speech – first when the Press was ordered to print dispatches, all dated from Nuremberg, declaring for partition (an English newspaper article provided incentive and text); and, secondly, when Herr Hitler

made a general statement in favor of the right of 'self-determination.' He was most emphatic, addressing the army on September 12, in his announcement that 'no negotiation, no conference, no agreement (Abmachung) gave us the natural right to unite Germans.' He was expressly referring to Austria; and he added that the right was vindicated, 'thanks to the soldiers.'

"Significantly, the only 'agreement' in question at the time of the Anschluss was the agreement concluded between the Fuehrer and Herr von Schuschnigg to respect Austria's independence. What, we may ask, would be the use of a similar agreement about Czechoslovakia – were there any chance of such an agreement – if, 'thanks to the soldiers,' the agreement would merely lead to further disagreements and the vindication, as in Austria's case, of the natural right to unite Germans?

"It is to be feared that, in these matters, the blunt-minded English people do not understand the Nazi psychosis, sometimes misnamed an ideology. The substance of this is that there are no limits to what may rightly be done in the name of unity, Aryanism, might, and other national values, real or ornamental. It is from this that the impressive single-mindedness of National-Socialism derives – the great thaumaturgy of doing-as-one-likes in pursuit of aims which, neither moral nor immoral, are always National-Socialist. From this single-mindedness also arise the apparent contradictions and anomalies of National-Socialist actions – the execution today of political enemies for shots fired in street riots six years ago, while shots fired on the other side are applauded; the impending trial of Austrian Separatists; and so on."

In this brief compass there is given the formula for Nazi aggression, which excludes as worthless agreements, engagements, pledges, guarantees, when they get in the way of desire for aggression and the power to effect it. Austria yesterday; Czechoslovakia today; What of tomorrow and the day after?

II.

To apply the formula to the events of only the last two years is to see how effectively it works in the absence of countervailing force. These need not be given in detail since this would be to repeat what has already appeared on this page; but they can be so grouped and summarized as to throw a penetrating light upon the manoeuvres of today and the consequences tomorrow.

Nazi Germany guaranteed the independence of Austria July 11, 1936, and destroyed it on March 11, 1938. The steps can be clearly identified: internal disturbances organized and directed from outside; the habitual misrepresentation in Germany of efforts by the Austrian authorities to maintain law and order as diabolical persecution of a minority; intervention by ultimatum to force the admission into the Austrian government of Nazi agents; further intervention by a second ultimatum demanding the transfer of power to Hitler's representatives; then the rape of Austria covered with a thin veil of legality by the pretence that the new government, established by these means, requested the assistance of German troops. The brazenness of these successive steps towards the destruction of a friendly and kindred power are undisguised!

III.

With Czechoslovakia more devious methods were necessary. First it was necessary to make protestations that Nazi Germany had no designs upon the territorial integrity of Czechoslovakia. Hence Herr Hitler's announcement in the Reichstag in March, 1936, that: "We have no territorial demands to make in Europe" (just as he now says that his demands upon Czechoslovakia are the last that he will make of Europe). Further, in this speech he went on to say that he favored, not force, but "a slow evolutionary development of peaceful co-operation" for the adjustment of "wrong relationships between the populations living in areas."

Though there has been friction between the Czechoslovakian government and the Sudeten Germans (or rather a section of them) since the peace treaty, the Nazi government did not come into the open as instigators of extreme courses by the minority until after Austria had been safety bagged.

On February 20 Herr Hitler, in his address to the Reichstag preparatory to the raid on Austria, declared that Germany charged herself with "the protection of those fellow-Germans who live beyond our frontiers and are unable to ensure for themselves the right to a general freedom, personal, political and ideological." The Czechoslovakian premier naturally interpreted this as implying a possible "attempt to intervene in our internal affairs, an attempt incompatible with the principle of the recognition of the sovereignty of other states," and declared the purpose of his country to defend "the attributes of its independence."

IV.

This was on March 4, 1938. Just one week later, on the day that the Nazi forces marched into Austria, Field Marshal Goering gave "a general assurance to the Czech Minister in Berlin – an assurance which he expressly renewed later on behalf of Herr Hitler – that is would be the earnest endeavor of the German government to improve German-Czech relations." This quotation is from a statement to the House of Lords on March 14 by Lord Halifax. Two days later Lord Halifax again noted these assurances in a statement to the House of Lords, and added:

"By these assurances, solemnly given and more than once repeated, we naturally expect the German government to abide. And if, indeed, they desire to see European peace maintained, as I earnestly hope they do, there is no quarter of Europe in which is more vital that undertakings should be scrupulously respected."

The recital, for the purposes of enlightenment, need hardly go further; the general course of events since March being within the knowledge of the public. Herr Hitler made no attempt whatever to "improve German-Czech relations"; on the contrary, once Austria was safely in his power, he tuned up the agitation of the Sudeten Germans to a degree which gave him the opening for the application of the formula of Nazi aggression on racial grounds, as described by the writer in the Economist. This writer, in the same article, states as something about which there is no doubt whatever, that the Nazi government from the first had no other intention than the wrestling, by force or duress in other forms, of portions of Czechoslovakia.

* * *

The doctrine that Germany can intervene for racial reasons for the "protection" of Germans on such grounds as she thinks proper in any country in the world which she is in a position to coerce, and without regard to any engagements she has made or guarantees she has given, has now not only been asserted but made good; and it has been approved, sanctioned, certified and validated by the governments of Great Britain and France, who have undertaken in this respect for the democracies of the world.

This is the situation; and those who think it is all right will cheer for it.

Source: Winnipeg *Free Press*, September 30, 1938.

Lorne Morgan (1897–1977)

A Theory of Permanent War

Lorne T. Morgan was a professor of political economy at the University of Toronto, one of those marvellous and memorable teachers who published very little but whose students could never forget his classes. One of those students was able to find a job only when war was declared in 1939 and the Royal Canadian Air Force accepted him for pilot training. A talented person had no role in peacetime but, with the war, Canada could afford to provide him with a complex and costly bomber and orders to devastate Germany. In 1943 word reached Morgan that his former student was dead. In his fury, he propounded the "Morgan Theory of Permanent War."

Homo the Sap – *homo sapiens* is the Latin name for our species – had apparently solved the problem of economic depressions by putting its people into uniform and sending them out to kill or be killed. In this famous satire, Morgan argued that capitalism could prosper only in a state of continuous warfare. Indeed, many Canadians feared victory in 1945 as much as they yearned for it because peace would cost them their jobs. In the end, governments took responsibility for post-war economic management and, some would argue, the Cold War against the Soviet bloc was the "Permanent War" Morgan had predicted.

Thus by irrefutable logic and utterly against my real nature, previous methods of thought, background, bias, religious training, and everything else, I am reluctantly driven to consider the idea of permanent war as the only possible solution to our economic ills. But I hasten to repeat that I do NOT mean war as it is being waged today, for our current struggle has got completely out of hand, is being waged unscientifically, and may yet lead to complete disaster. I advocate a scientific war, *every phase of which would be planned in advance, and which would be operated in strict conjunction with the business cycle*. It would be speeded up when the index showed a downward trend in business activity. Conversely, it would be slowed down when business approached a desired and pre-determined level of prosperity. It is theoretically possible that there might be brief armistices, something like a momentary rest between rounds, but that is highly unlikely in actual practice. Such a war must not be waged upon too large a scale, for excess profits taxes, shortages, priorities, the conscription of labour and excessive government interference, all combined would probably more than offset the advantages derived. On the other hand, it must be fought on a scale large enough to affect our economy directly and decidedly. If I may be allowed, momentarily only, to slip into the jargon of my Profession, this war would be meticulously regulated to ensure *the exact equation of Supply and Demand of both men and materials.* There is not an economic theorist from Adam Smith to John Maynard Keynes – except Karl Marx, and he was a ruddy Red and no Economist – who will deny that if such (here comes more jargon) a point of equilibrium could be achieved and maintained, we should enter into a period of Permanent Prosperity. After 5000 years of futile effort, civilized society would at long last have solved its economic problem. Economic Paradise would be on our door-step and, let me add, legitimately, for it otherwise would be unacceptable in Canada. Depressions, unemployment, poverty, suffering, bankruptcies, a heavy percentage of all crime and, above all, radicalism would vanish from the face of the earth, or at least from Canada, which is all that really matters. All this, and more, is to be had for the asking. But, throughout all history, new and great ideas have spread slowly. It was so with the intellectual gems of Galileo, Copernicus, Bacon, Descartes, Spinoza and countless others. Unfortunately, there is little reason to believe that it will be different with what I have chosen (perhaps somewhat immodestly) to call the Morgan Theory of the Permanent War. (For the sake of brevity, and in keeping with the best traditions of the Profession, I shall in future refer to the theory as the M.T.P.W.) Under the circumstances, therefore, I henceforth concentrate upon convincing only my own countrymen of the validity of my thesis. I shall confine myself to the strictest of logical analysis, adding just enough specific illustrations to make misunderstanding impossible to all except the most stupid of minds. With those, I am not concerned.

Let us assume that the Axis has been defeated and peace declared. I have already described the four possible alternatives, to wit: attempt to revert to 1939; adopt Fascism; develop a socialized economy; accept and put into practice the M.T.P.W. I have also pointed out just why the first three of these suggested programmes, or any combination of them, are either impossible or undesirable. Let us now consider in detail, therefore, the Morgan Theory of the Permanent War.

The first necessary step would be "to provoke an incident" leading to war with a nation in the western hemisphere. If the first provocation didn't work, we could keep right on provoking until we got what we wanted. History is full of accounts of the eventual fruitfulness of such a plan. The country chosen must of necessity be among those in the western hemisphere. European or Asiatic possibilities would involve too many complications. In the new world, we should have to placate only the United States, and this could be done without too much difficulty. That percentage of her population actuated by ethical considerations would doubtless be satisfied if the United States were made sole referee of the conflict, enforcing agreed-upon rules and regulations, as well as advising from time to time either or both belligerents. Thus she would hold a position of great prestige, and in time might earn the admiration and trust of even the Argentine. She is also powerful enough to prevent non-American nations from horning in on the show and complicating it with their imperialist machinations. This would further strengthen, without antagonizing her sister republics, the principles of the Monroe Doctrine. That section of her populace motivated by more material considerations could easily be mollified, as both contestants would undoubtedly purchase some of the necessary munitions of war from the United States. The stimulating effect of those purchases on the American economy would in all probability obviate the necessity of the United States hunting up an opponent for herself. This combination of profit and altruism has never before failed in its appeal, and there is no reason to believe it would in this case.

There is yet another reason, besides fear of foreign entanglements, which necessitates our proposed opponent being one of the Latin American republics, namely, Quebec's objection to "foreign" wars. Under already existing legislation, the Dominion Government could conscript and send men from Cape Horn to the North Pole (at least to this side of the Pole) without further provoking that province. Besides, exposed as she is to attack without the protection of the British navy, Quebec would really appreciate the necessity of whole hearted co-operation with her sister provinces in a joint military effort. For the first time since 1763, Quebec would be given an opportunity to prove the oft-asserted statement of her most partisan nationalists that she will fight to the last *habitant* to protect Canada's own shores in Canada's own wars. Thus by the one simple stroke of provoking war with a Latin American

republic we would simultaneously guarantee prosperity and settle what is one of the most baffling and threatening political problems in Canada. In itself, that is surely enough to recommend the M.T.P.W. to any intelligent Canadian. But there are other, and almost equally important, reasons for pursuing such a course, and these will be discussed in the ensuing paragraphs.

In the first place, a permanent war of the nature outlined above, would go far toward settling various Canadian constitutional and political problems in addition to the one just discussed. The British North America Act is definitely out of date today for the plain and simple reason that the Fathers of Confederation, as great as they undoubtedly were, could not anticipate Canada's needs in 1943. Up until the present time, our more pressing problems have invariably been met by the simple device of appointing a Royal Commission to go into the matter, and then shelving the Report. This worked well in the past. Today, however, the growing disjuncture between evolving economic forces and fixed political institutions has finally reached the danger point. We all know it, and appreciate it, but in time of peace we are completely unable to do anything about it. As a result, bickering between provinces on the one hand, and between the provinces and the Dominion government on the other, has come to be almost constant, and has only aggravated issues already serious. But since the outbreak of the present conflict, necessity has forced upon us steps we should have taken long ago. Today, for the first time, the Dominion government exercises power, albeit much of its extra-constitutional, compatible with the economic needs of the present century. This veritable revolution has been achieved within a remarkably short space of time, and has been accompanied by a minimum of squawks from Provincial Righters, for they don't dare to open their mouths in time of war. That necessary trend toward centralization of power should be even more marked in the future, provided we remain at war, for two of the doughtiest of Provincial Righters are now on the political side-lines. Nature permanently retired one, while the other is in at least temporary eclipse. The danger is PEACE accompanied by Canada's constitutional retreat from 1945 to 1867. The old constitutional setup didn't work before, and we were lucky in avoiding catastrophe. It won't work in the future, and, as sure as fate, we shall come a cropper. It is ironic, but peace within Canada demands war without.

In addition to the necessary *de facto* constitutional changes outlined above, we have witnessed an equally great political revolution going on beneath our very noses, almost unnoticed despite the fact that some maintain that these changes have been accompanied by emanations offensive to the olfactory organs. I refer to the change from a *political* to a *functional* system of government (political scientists likewise have their jargon). It is difficult to contrast concisely the two systems. Under the former, you usually become a member of Parliament, or Congress, because you are nominated by a Party which "sweeps to power."

This procedure may possibly account for some of the sweepings picked up. It is thoroughly Democratic in that it assumes one man to be as good as another in all things. Most remarkable results not infrequently ensue. It is quite possible for a prairie farmer who has never seen a body of water larger than an irrigation ditch, to become Minister of Fisheries; or for a doctor to become Minister of Transportation; or for a company union advocate to become Minister of Labour; or for an evangelist to become Premier. It is likewise possible for a foreign-born Member to introduce a Bill advocating the partition of his native country, despite the fact that the two nations happen to be allies in a moment of great danger from a common foe. All this is possible and more. (It should be emphasized at this point that the examples outlined above are purely fictitious possibilities, and that any fancied resemblance to living persons exists only in the reader's mind.) Nevertheless, Political Democracy somehow managed to work in the past.

Under the *functional* system, one is either elected or appointed to an administrative position because of proved competence in a particular field of activity. The usual criticism (why, I don't know) is that while the latter system is more efficient, it is for some reason or other, less representative. I do know, however, that the present trend in Canada is markedly from the political to the functional type of government, although still largely on a *de facto* rather than a constitutional basis. The exigencies of war forced this development. Whereas formerly the government operated through parliamentary procedure, today "dollar a year" men and other appointees wield enormous power without corresponding political responsibility. At the same time, Orders-in-Council have largely superseded Parliamentary legislation. Parliament today is in reality a sounding board for policies already worked out elsewhere, or a field of honour where personal vendettas are waged without mercy, scruples or even manners, much to the delight of the Readers of Hansard. A top-heavy government majority, with a consequent weakling of an opposition, speeds the trend. A permanent war would complete the transition within a very short period. Members of Parliament could then be returned to productive employment, and the country thus saved a considerable sum of money annually. Certainly, two Dominion governments are an unwarranted luxury, and that is exactly what we have today. The Rump was elected a long time ago by the people; the really operative element has since been appointed from Above. Peace will indubitably result in a demand for the return of democratic government, and it would be a crime to waste all the progress we have made in the opposite direction. Progress impossible in peace comes naturally from war. We don't even have to think about it, or do anything about it; it just comes.

Source: Lorne T. Morgan, "The Permanent War or Homo the Sap," in Hugh R. Innis, ed., *Selected Readings in Economics* (Toronto: Pitman, 1960), 20-4.

Joy Kogawa (1935—)

"WHAT DO I REMEMBER OF THE EVACUATION?"

Joy Kogawa is a Canadian novelist and poet. Born to a Japanese-Canadian family in Vancouver, she was among roughly twenty thousand Japanese Canadians who were forcibly evacuated from coastal areas of British Columbia in 1942. This action was taken because Canadian authorities feared that Japanese Canadians might prove loyal to Japan and engage in actions which could endanger national security during the war.

The relocation of Japanese Canadians, the forced sale of their property, and the eventual emigration of several thousand back to Japan after the Second World War is perhaps the gravest episode of minority oppression in twentieth-century Canada. Not one Japanese Canadian had been charged with, let alone convicted of, any act of sabotage; yet the evacuation went ahead.

Many observers feel that, far more than national security, virulent racist attitudes conditioned the atmosphere in which the evacuation took place. For years, both Japanese and Chinese Canadians on the west coast had endured racist fears of a "yellow peril" which threatened to overrun Canada. While no Japanese Canadians were executed, and the relocation camps ought not be confused with the barbaric Nazi-run concentration camps, relocation was a searing tragedy for Japanese Canadians.

Joy Kogawa's poem captures her memories, as a young teenager, of the evacuation and its trauma. Many years later, the federal government of Brian Mulroney (1939–) decided to issue a formal apology to Japanese Canadians for the internment and to pay restitution for lost property. An amount of $24 million was paid out, half to individual Japanese Canadians and the other half to help set up a Race Relations Foundation. The Foundation's mandate is to help in the fight against racism and racial discrimination, so that an episode like the Japanese internment will not happen again.

What do I remember of the evacuation?
I remember my father telling Tim and me
About the mountains and the train
An the excitement of going on a trip.
What do I remember of the evacuation?
I remember my mother wrapping
A blanket around me and my
Pretending to fall asleep so she would be
    happy
Though I was so excited I couldn't sleep
(I hear there were people herded
Into the Hastings Park like cattle.
Families were made to move in two hours
Abandoning everything, leaving pets
And possessions at gun point.
I hear families were broken up
Men were forced to work. I heard
It whispered late at night
That there was suffering) and
I missed my dolls.
What do I remember of the evacuation?
I remember Miss Foster and Miss Tucker
Who still live in Vancouver

And who did what they could
And loved the children and who gave me
A puzzle to play with on the train.
And I remember the mountains and I was
Six years old and I swear I saw a giant
Gulliver of Gulliver's Travels scanning the
    horizon
And when I told my mother she believed it
    too
And I remember how careful my parents were
Not to bruise us with bitterness
And I remember the puzzle of Lorraine Life
Who said "Don't insult me" when I
Proudly wrote my name in Japanese
And Tim flew the Union Jack
When the war was over but Lorraine
And her friends spat on us anyway
And I prayed to the God who loves
All the children in his sight
That I might be white.

Source: Eva C. Karpinski and Ian Lea, eds., *Pens of Many Colours* (Toronto: Harcourt Brace Jovanovich, 1993), 198-9.

Earle Birney (1904–95)

"TURVEY IS ENLISTED"

Perhaps it is appropriate that the best-known Canadian novel of the Second World War is about a soldier who never got to fight. Although, by the end of the war, the Canadian army needed conscription to fill its infantry battalions, it is still hard to explain why an army with 600,000 volunteers – among them the mythical Private Thomas Leadbeater Turvey – and only 76,000 casualties needed to force men to serve.

Born in Calgary and raised in the Rockies, Alfred Earle Birney was already a university lecturer when he joined the army. As a personnel-selection officer for the army, he understood the army's wartime manpower problems better than most. Although Turvey desperately wants to join his friend Mac and the Kootenay Highlanders, bad luck and his own innocence repeatedly get in his way. The opening passage is not only a satire on the army's futile attempts to put square pegs in round holes, it also reflects the number of jobs a man might hold in the frequently futile search for work in depression-ridden Canada.

A poet of eclectic skills and strong left-wing tendencies, Birney worked for the CBC after the war and in 1946 was appointed to the English department of the University of British Columbia where he spent the rest of his professional career. Though better known as a poet and literary critic than as a novelist, Birney created in *Turvey: A Military Picaresque* a character and a setting that almost anyone who ever served in the Canadian army could recognize.

Number Eight was a drawing of an envelope addressed to Mr John Brown, 114 West 78th, New York, N.Y. It had a New York postmark but no stamp. The squeaky sergeant had told them to draw in the missing part of each picture. Turvey licked his pencil point and tried to recall whether King George had a beard.

He had finished the stamp, except for one edge of perforation, when he remembered the American postmark. It ought to be George Washington. There was no eraser on the pencil he had been given. Turvey was in the midst of a leisurely probe of his trouser pockets when his head, coming up, was transfixed by the sergeant's amber stare. It was a stare of suspicion; it leapt in a straight beam from the sergeant's highstool, over the hunched and shirted backs of the other recruits, unmistakably and directly to him. Turvey blushed, made a show of scratching his behind, and returned to picture Eight.

Implanting a careful X over the implausible head of George, and an arrow to the margin, he began a profile which in spite of himself grew into the head of the sergeant. He shouldn't have put in the Adam's apple. Turvey was laying pencil to tongue again, wondering if the remaining eight pictures in Test One would be as tough, when, like the sudden shriek of chalk on a blackboard, the sergeant's voice scratched the heavy air:

"Lay down your pencils. Turn over the page and fold under. You are about to begin Test Number Two."

Turvey tried to go more quickly but the camel held him up. It was two-humped and had a guy riding it backwards. The sergeant had, with a precise maidenly firmness, made it very clear to them that in each set of four pictures, one and one only was wrong and to be crossed out. Since in the other three a man rode an animal frontwards, the camel picture must be wrong. Still, should you ride an elephant with your feet tucked under its ears? Or a horse with no knee-joints in its forelegs? The broad-beamed youth at the next barrackroom table broke wind suddenly and the roomful of silent sweating men stirred in sympathy, squirmed on the pitted benches, sighed as in dreams of anguish. But Turvey continued to regard the little parade of riders; the more he examined them the more he was convinced they were all wrong. All except the camel, maybe. If you rode a camel backwards you could see better. And you had the rear hump to hang on to; it was more pointed; you could get a grip on it. Turvey was neatly crucifying the mahout and his elephant when the gopher voice of the sergeant piped again, and they

were in Test Number Three. When it came to the arithmetic questions, Turvey remembered what Mac had said and was careful not to go too fast. Besides, he had caught a far glimpse, through the dusty window beside him, of a girl in the backyard of a store – no, it couldnt be – yes, and unbelievably, in a bathing suit, like a butterfly from the garbage can.

Once the O-testing was over, Turvey began to think his second day in the army much more enjoyable, though he hadnt found any Kootenay Highlanders yet. Yesterday he had stood in long dispirited line-ups before attestation clerks and then naked before staccato doctors. Now, though they had been filed out of the testing room into a big hall where he couldnt discover a window with a view of the girl, there was a lull. He got friendly with two Icelanders and had won a dollar-twenty from them shooting craps in a corner of the lavatory before he heard the bawling of his name and it was his turn to sit down before the Personnel Corporal in a dark corner of the bare hall.

He was a bulky balding chap whose questions came out tonelessly between sucks on a rooty pipe. Turvey was surprised at the number of large stiff papers the corporal had with TURVEY, THOMAS LEADBEATER already typed at the top. And now he was starting to fill out a new one in a big sloping hand, pronouncing each word as he traced it, much as if his arm were phonographic.

"Born thirteenth May nineteen-twenty-two Skookum Falls B.C. . . . white single nextofkin Mr Leopold Turvey Skookum Falls brother. No glasses righthanded. Ussssp?"

Turvey would not have ventured to halt the flow of the voice and bulbous pen if he had not decided that the last suck of the corporal's pipe was meant to be a question mark.

"Lefthanded, sir . . . except for hockey."

The corporal's pen wavered and his pipe hissed mildly.

"Wut about a rifle?"

Turvey smiled ingratiatingly. "Anyway you like, sir."

The corporal pouted his lips at the tip of his pipe and put a curvaceous R in the corner of the big sheet. "Dont call a corporal 'sir,' callum 'corporal.'" The voice was almost expressionless but Turvey detected a purr and decided he had said the right thing.

"Completed grade nine Kuskanee High at sixteen wotcha chief occupation civil life?"

Turvey thought carefully. "Well, I was chokerman in the Kootenays once. Just a two-bit camp." The corporal looked blank. "Then I was a bucker in Calgary."

"You mean you was a bronco-buster?" The edge in the corporal's voice betrayed a hint of unprofessional surprise.

"No, s –, no, corporal, on a bridge. You know – holdin a bat under the girder for the riveter. I was a sticker too." The corporal kept his eyes on the form, nodding as if he had known all along, but his bald head pinkened slightly and his pen halted. "That's fine. How long you, uh, stick?"

"At stickin? Not very long. I got to missin rivets with my bucket and a hot one set a big Swede on fire and he complained to the straw-boss. Then I rode the rods east and sorta bummed. Then I was scurfer in a coke plant. And I was a pouncer once, for a while."

The corporal twisted his ear as if he were having trouble hearing. His face had become a mask of distrust. Turvey felt sorry he had mentioned pouncing and he added apologetically:

"In a hat factory, Guelph. You know – sandpaperin up the fuzz on fedoras. Then I come to Toronto to join the Air Force, cause the war had started, but they wouldnt have me cause I hadnt matric and couldnt see enough green at night or somethin. So my pal Mac and I hit the freights to Vancouver to get in the Kootenay Highlanders but they was filled up. Then in Victoria we worked house-to-house gettin moths out of pianos. Then –"

But the corporal had taken the pipe out of his mouth and was holding it at a monitory angle, and his voice was a growl:

"Dont try no smart stuff here. I ast you wut cher *chief* occupation was. Wut did you do longest?"

Turvey thought rapidly. There was the time he was a popsicle-coater, and then assistant flavour-mixer, in that candy factory. But he quit after, what was it, four months? Got tired of the vanilla smell always on his clothes. Wanted to get east anyway and try the army again. The corporal was staring sullenly at his forms. What happened then? O yes, the army turned him down because he had a mess of hives and his front teeth were out and his feet kind of flat. So after a while he landed that tannery job. How long was he there? Gee, almost a whole winter!

"Wet-splittin."

The corporal's eyes rose, speckled and malevolent, but they saw only a round face beaming with the pleasures of recall and the tremulous smile of the young man anxious to please.

"I ran a machine scrapin fat off hides. Eastern Tannery, Montreal."

The corporal laid his pipe down (it had gone out), wrote "Machine Operator," and asked hurriedly:

"Any previous military experience?"

"Well, we started cadets in Kuskanee High but we never got rifles. But I was in the Boy Sc –"

"That's all. Wait on a bench atta back till the officer calls you, next man!" The corporal looked past him, mopped his veined head with a khaki handkerchief, and whanged his pipe spitefully against the table leg.

Source: Earle Birney, *Turvey: A Military Picaresque* (1949; repr. Toronto: McClelland and Stewart, 1963), 1-4.

Murray Peden (1923–)

"Gelsenkirchen"

Born and raised in Winnipeg, Murray Peden was not yet sixteen when the Second World War broke out. Like thousands of other young Canadians, he trained as a pilot under the British Commonwealth Air Training Plan and flew bombers over Germany. In 1944, at the age of twenty-one, he earned a Distinguished Flying Cross. His beautifully written *A Thousand Shall Fall* evokes the humour, terror, and frustration of young men at war. In this passage, he describes taking F Fox, an American-built B-29, to Gelsenkirchen and almost all the way back, one of tens of thousands of missions which were part of the Allied bomber offensive against Germany and from which thousands of other Canadians never returned.

After the war, Murray Peden became a lawyer and later the head of the Manitoba Securities Commission.

O n June 21st I learned in the morning that there was to be a war on that night, and that Peden's crew were on the battle order in F Fox. We went out and did our air test immediately. It was on this occasion, as I recall, that we were standing waiting for the crew bus when it pulled up at the dispersal next to ours and we saw Johnny Corke and his crew disembarking to climb aboard their aircraft. Johnny's engineer was a chap named Barber, and he was known to the ground crew to be meticulous in his requirements. One of the erks obviously thought him too damned meticulous. As he saw Barber alight from the rear step of the crew bus, I heard him call in a low voice to one of his mates: "Oi . . . 'ere comes Ali Barber and the 40 snags."

At 4:30 that afternoon we sat in the briefing room and watched in the usual strained silence as the curtains swished noisily open to reveal route tapes running to Gelsenkirchen, in the heart of the Ruhr. Someone in the crew muttered: "Christ, Happy Valley." I responded with supreme confidence, "Piece of cake." Our target was the Nordstern oil plant in Gelsenkirchen.

I really did not feel the confidence I had expressed as I looked at the big target map in front of us. Heavy flak areas on that map were marked with red circles. The Ruhr was one solid turnip-shaped blotch of red, many inches wide, and a foot long on our map; and it had a deep belt of searchlights all round it, denoted by a continuous broad blue border framing the whole blob. Ruhr trips had one good quality: they were short. That was their only redeeming feature. Happy Valley was probably the most heavily defended industrial area in Europe. Apart from the hundreds of flak batteries and the dense concentrations of searchlights, it was well protected by swarms of night fighters, and it was extremely difficult on such a short trip to mislead them by routing as to the intended target area. When I said "piece of cake" it was just so much whistling past the graveyard; but I was to be reminded of it later.

* * *

Takeoff was late these summer nights. It was just after 11:00 pm when the Aldis lamp's green flash sent F Fox roaring down the flarepath. We crossed the coast outbound near Cromer, and climbed steadily to 22,000 feet in the clear night air.

Once we hit the enemy coast, the ever-present strain mounted rapidly to the higher level that was the concomitant of being in the enemy's ball park, blindfolded by night. I always waited tensely for the first burst of flak to stab at us, hoping it would not be too close. Once that first burst came up, and I recovered from the violent start that the sudden flash in the darkness always caused, I breathed a little easier and began the game that every pilot had to play, changing altitude, course, and speed, to throw off the next burst, counting the seconds carefully and watching to see where that next burst came; then varying the course again, being careful not to "balance" the pattern with a nice symmetrical correction to the other side. The German predictors were quick to average symmetrical evasions and fire a burst at the appropriate moment along the mean track.

The human system is incredibly adaptive, and what constantly surprised me, when I thought about it in safety on the ground, was how matter of factly we could play this deadly game, and even derive a certain nervous satisfaction from it, watching shells burst two or three hundred yards away, at the very spot you would have been had you not changed course as the gunners were launching their speeding projectiles on their way.

* * *

At a point about 20 minutes from the target we began to approach an outlying belt of searchlights which stood before us on either side of our intended track in two great cones. I feared and hated those baleful blinding lights more than anything else the Germans used against us. While in themselves they seldom caused death – although there were reported cases of pilots, particularly at low level, apparently becoming completely disoriented by their glaring beams and diving into the earth – they were all too often the harbinger of death. A pilot trapped in a large cone had little chance of escape. For long seconds on end the dazzling glare would render him helpless, spotlighting him as the target and making it almost impossible for him to see his instruments and maintain any sense of equilibrium. Meanwhile the searchlights' accomplices, the heavy guns, would hurl up shells in streams, and all too frequently the aircraft would explode or begin a crazy, smoking dive to the ground.

As I watched these two cones warily, I noticed that they were remaining stationary for 30 seconds or so at a time, leaving a corridor between them, then abruptly moving together and establishing one giant cone right in the middle of what had been the safe passage. Twice I saw them do this, and twice when they came together in the centre they trapped a Lancaster attempting to slip by. Each time the Lancaster was destroyed. It was an unnerving spectacle to watch, particularly when your turn to run the gauntlet was fast approaching. It was Hobson's choice with a vengeance. You could not fly straight into either cone while they were standing separate; that was committing suicide; and detouring all the way around the outside would have involved a major departure from the prescribed track and thrown out the aircraft's time over target by several minutes. You had no practicable alternative but to take the black void between the two cones, knowing that the lights would swing inward and illuminate some part of the safe passage every few seconds. You headed for the open spot and prayed that you would get through. I chose a spot slightly right of centre and sweated. We were lucky.

Hardly had we cleared this hurdle than Stan came on the intercom again to report another contact, a close one. This time we were not left long in doubt. In less than a minute our rear gunner, Johnny Walker, spotted an aircraft directly astern at a range of about 300 yards. This was approximately where Stan had predicted the contact would be found, but it was another 30 seconds or more before Johnny Walker and Bert Lester confirmed that it was a Lancaster. Then, for a minute or two, we seemed to be holding the same relative positions. I was reluctant to weave away if I could avoid it, since Sam's navigation thus far had kept us dead on track, and I preferred not to mar his handiwork. However, after another minute, Johnny Walker reported that the Lanc had closed further and was now just about 200 yards astern.

"If he comes any closer, any closer at all," I said, "let me know, and I'll weave off to the side a bit."

It was at that precise moment that Fate dealt us a card off the bottom of the deck.

The Lancaster abruptly stood on its wingtip and dived away. Directly behind it, and now directly behind us and in perfect firing position, was a Messerschmitt 410 which had been stalking the Lancaster.

As Johnny Walker shouted a warning and began firing himself, the air around us was instantly filled with white flaming shells that flashed past our windows with horrifying speed, and F Fox shuddered heavily to the pounding of a hail of close range cannon fire. Through the back of my seat I felt a rapid series of staccato blows that jarred us like the strokes of a wild triphammer.

I had instinctively thrust the control column forward and twisted the ailerons to dive into a violent corkscrew; but in the second it took to initiate the manoeuvre, F Fox absorbed heavy punishment from the torrent of shells the Messerschmitt's cannons poured into us. Before I had 15 degrees of bank on, the starboard inner engine burst into great leaping flames and the intercom went dead.

As we rolled into the dive to starboard, the heavy vibration of a long burst fired from our mid-upper turret shook the instrument panel in front of me into a great blur; it was as though the instruments were mounted on the sounding strings of some giant lyre. With remarkable presence of mind, Bill ignored the tracers flying around his head, and moved to feather number three at the same time as he activated its fire extinguisher. I was dimly aware of his actions, and of the frightening flames that gushed out of the engine and were snatched back across the cowling as I rolled to begin my climb to port.

The firing ceased as suddenly as it had started – on both sides. With some difficulty I levelled up, after a fashion, and tried to take stock of the situation. F Fox was sickeningly sluggish and unresponsive; but for the next two minutes that problem paled into insignificance as I struggled to stop her swift descent, and watched Bill fight to get number three feathered so that we could get the fire under control. We had been told frequently that a fuel-fed fire, blown against the interior of the wing by the slipstream, could eat right through the main spar in as little as two minutes. If the main spar went, our chances of getting out of the aircraft as it cartwheeled earthward would be remote. Bill was unable to coax the recalcitrant propeller to feather properly, although the blades did rotate to the point where the propeller was turning over at a low speed.

Meantime J. B. had clambered back to find out what had happened in the rear of the aircraft. For all we knew, the four crew members behind the mid-upper might have abandoned the plane – or been killed.

F Fox continued to lose height, and without warning number three began to wind up. In moments it was up past its safe maximum and was overspeeding with a terrifying banshee wail. As it screamed itself into hysteria, the fire, which had been dying down, flared up in all its fury again.

Scared half out of my wits by the flames, and the knowledge that they were only inches away from enough gasoline to blow us into eternity, I tried vainly to remember what one did with an overspeeding propeller. In a moment Bill suggested throttling back the other three, and I strained to pull F Fox's nose up at the same time so that the overspeeding propeller would be carrying a substantial load.

It worked. Like a screaming circular saw suddenly deprived of power the propeller began to slow down, its terrifying note gradually subsiding like some manic thing being quieted. As it sank back below normal speed, we shifted the load onto the other three engines, staring appraisingly at number three and trying to gauge whether that fire would kill us with an explosion. Although it was not extinguished, it had subsided again with the propeller, so I turned my attention momentarily to the task of coaxing F Fox to hold height.

* * *

As we levelled up, the air around us was suddenly filled with a hail of tracers again, and once again I threw F Fox into a corkscrew. But this time we could only manage a travesty of the prescribed manoeuvre, and we would have died then and there but for the good shooting of Johnny Walker. A Ju 88, drawn by the irresistible sight of fire aboard a wounded prey, had stalked us and closed to finish us off. But the German pilot had reckoned without Johnny Walker. Hollering into the dead intercom in a fruitless attempt to warn me, Johnny drew a careful bead on the German and, in the face of the fighter's overpowering weight of fire, traded lead so accurately that the German was shortly forced to break off.

F Fox had absorbed more punishment in this second combat, although nothing like what she had taken the first time. She had lost even more of her characteristic responsiveness, and her struggle to fend off the clutch of gravity was palpably less successful. Another result of the second attack, however, was that it forced us to dive again, and this in turn had immediately started number three winding up. Once more the fire flared wickedly, ugly tongues of flame visible from a great distance at night, and again we went through our scary exercise, stalling the sluggish aeroplane to get the screaming propeller back under control. The second attack, therefore, inflicted additional structural damage upon us, re-kindled the fire in number three, and cost us altitude we could not afford to give away. It did one other thing: it convinced me that it would be foolhardy to try to make our way through the main flak and searchlight defences over the target in the condition we were in. Night fighters too were clearly in the stream in force. The Ju 88 had picked us up within minutes of the first attack, and I felt it would be simply asking for it to count on escaping from a third attack in our present condition. Although we were now no more than ten minutes away from the target, I coaxed F Fox into a gentle turn and reversed our course.

Bill went forward to get me a proper course from Sam, and again I surveyed the situation with what few crumbs of equanimity I could muster. Our most worrisome problem, apart from the smouldering fire which kept threatening to flare and spread, was the generally precarious performance of the aircraft. Flying on three engines with the fourth propeller properly feathered is one thing. It is quite another doing it with an engine which is windmilling and refuses to feather, and in an aeroplane which has been torn open and battered to the point where its aerodynamic efficiency has been seriously compromised. Pulling an aeroplane through the sky with an engine windmilling is much the same as pushing a stalled car while leaving it in gear. The drag is tremendous, and the net effect is to subtract and waste a substantial amount of your remaining power. When I turned F Fox about, we were down to 15,000 feet, having lost close to 7,000 feet in the two combats and the ensuing struggle with the burning engine. We were still losing height at about 500–700 feet per minute, were still without intercom, and were seriously limited as to manoeuvrability.

As Bill and I were setting the remaining three engines to the most power we felt we could call upon them to deliver for a protracted period, and trying to trim the aircraft into the best attitude for its sorry condition, I felt a tap an my shoulder and looked round to see Hembrow, the German-speaking special wireless operator, standing just behind my seat. He looked dishevelled and more than slightly shaken. (In fact he had been slightly wounded, with a cannon splinter in the back of the shoulder.) His terse message registered indelibly on my brain as he raised his voice and called above the noise: "The wireless operator's been hit . . . And I've been hit . . . And we all want to go home."

This trusting message, implying that I could somehow wash out the balance of the exercise, and ordain safe delivery to Blickling Hall despite fire, battle damage, and anything else that might follow, made me feel rather fatherly. I reached back and clapped him lightly on the shoulder and told him everything was okay, that we were heading for home.

Source: Murray Peden, *A Thousand Shall Fall* (Stittsville, Ont.: Canada's Wings, 1979), 308-406.

Jackie Robinson (1919–72)

"Il a gagné Ses Épaulettes" (by Dink Carroll)

Jackie Robinson was the first black American to play in baseball's major leagues, and one of the great ball players of his time. Ironically, Canada, and specifically Montreal, played a role in the dramatic blow against American racism.

Before calling him up to the Brooklyn Dodgers, general manager Branch Rickey decided Robinson would spend a year, 1946, with the Montreal Royals of the International League, a triple-A farm team for the Dodgers. Rickey wanted to be certain that Robinson had the right ability and character to handle the pressure of being the first black player in the major leagues.

That year was difficult, and Robinson encountered racism from fans in many cities, from opposing players, and even from some on his own team. But in Montreal, Robinson and his wife, Rachel, found a supportive environment. In Rachel's words, "Jack and I always attributed a great deal of our eventual success to the love and respect we received in Montreal. I was pregnant and Jack was on the road a lot of the time, and the neighbours did all they could to help me out. Even though I didn't speak French and they didn't speak English, we still got along . . . It was a big contrast to what we had experienced in the South where everything was segregated."

Robinson's outstanding play that year helped lead the Montreal Royals to the league championship. The front-page column by Dink Carroll of the *Gazette* captures some of the elation the Montreal fans felt for Robinson. As another columnist wrote, "It was probably the only day in history that a black man ran from a white mob with love instead of lynching on its mind."

The Royals are champions of everything they survey this morning in the world of baseball underneath the major leagues. For the first time in their long history they brought the top minor league honors to Montreal by beating the Louisville Colonels in the sixth game of the Little World Series at the Stadium last night, 2-0, to capture the best-of-seven classic by four games to two.

The season was closed out by unprecedented scenes in the Stadium, the deliriously happy mob of 19,171 paying customers refusing to leave the park for a full half-hour after the game was over.

They yelled for Clap Hopper, the Royals' manager. They yelled for Curt Davis, the veteran pitcher whose head and arm sponsored last night's shutout. They yelled for Jackie Robinson, the first Negro to break into organized baseball, who starred at second base for the club all summer. First Hopper and Davis appeared, coming out of the dugout still in uniform. The crowd chaired them and marched them triumphantly around the diamond. Jackie Robinson finally appeared in street clothes and they stormed around him, eager to touch him. They almost ripped the clothes from his back.

The crowd stood in line, forming a gauntlet, waiting until the players came out. They finally had to leave the park when the lights were turned out. The crowd sang, "Il a gagné ses epaulettes," as a tribute to Jackie Robinson.

Source: "Royals win Little World Series for first time in their history," *Montreal Gazette*, October 5, 1946.

W. O. Mitchell (1914–96)

A Boy's View of the Prairie

William Ormond Mitchell was born and grew up in Weyburn, Saskatchewan, a prairie town not unlike the setting for his 1947 classic novel, *Who Has Seen the Wind*. In that work, Mitchell tells about the growing up of a boy named Brian during the Great Depression of the 1930s and his exposure to birth, death, joy, tragedy, choices, and consequences. In the following selection, Mitchell sets a stage that any prairie dweller can recognize. Indeed, most would agree that no one has described the prairie better than W.O. Mitchell.

By the time of his death, Mitchell had become one of the best-known and most-beloved Canadian writers of his time.

Here was the least common denominator of nature, the skeleton requirements simply, of land and sky – Saskatchewan prairie. It lay wide around the town, stretching tan to the far line of the sky, shimmering under the June sun and waiting for the unfailing visitation of wind, gentle at first, barely stroking the long grasses and giving them life; later, a long hot gusting that would lift the black topsoil and pile it in barrow pits along the roads, or in deep banks against the fences.

Over the prairie, cattle stood listless beside the dried-up slough beds which held no water for them. Where the snow-white of alkali edged the course of the river, a thin trickle of water made its way toward the town low upon the horizon. Silver willow, heavy with dust, grew along the riverbanks, perfuming the air with its honey smell.

Just before the town the river took a wide loop and entered at the eastern edge. Inhabited now by some eighteen hundred souls, it had grown up on either side of the river from the seed of one homesteader's sod hut built in the spring of eighteen seventy-five. It was made up largely of frame buildings with high, peaked roofs, each with an expanse of lawn in front and a garden in the back; they lined avenues with prairie names: Bison, Riel, Qu'Appelle, Blackfoot, Fort. Cement sidewalks extended from First Street to Sixth Street at MacTaggart's Corner; from that point to the prairie a board-walk ran.

Lawn sprinklers sparkled in the sun; Russian poplars stood along either side of Sixth Street. Five houses up from MacTaggart's Corner stood the O'Connal home, a three-storied house lifting high above the white cottage to the left of it. Virginia creepers had almost smothered the veranda; honeysuckle and spirea grew on either side of the steps. A tricycle with its front wheel sharply turned stood in the middle of the walk.

* * *

Brian walked back towards his home. He did not turn down Bison Avenue where it crossed the street upon which the church was, but continued on, a dark wishbone of a child wrapped in reflection.

The wind was persistent now, a steady urgency upon his straight back, smoking up the dust from the road along the walk, lifting it and carrying it out to the prairie beyond. Several times Brian stopped: once to look up into the sun's unbearable radiance and then away with the lingering glow stubborn in his eyes; another time when he came upon a fox-red caterpillar making a procession of itself over a crack that snaked along the walk. He squashed it with his foot. Further on he paused at a spider that carried its bead of a body between hurrying thread-legs. Death came for the spider too.

He looked up to find that the street had stopped. Ahead lay the sudden emptiness of the prairie. For the first time in his four years of life he was alone on the prairie.

He had seen it often, from the veranda of his uncle's farmhouse, or at the end of a long street, but till now he had never heard it. The hum of telephone wires along the road, the ring of hidden crickets, the stitching sound of grasshoppers, the sudden relief of a meadow lark's song, were deliciously strange to him. Without hesitation he crossed the road and walked out through the hip-deep grass stirring in the steady wind; the grass clung at his legs; haloed fox-tails bowed before him; grasshoppers sprang from hidden places in the grass, clicketing ahead of him to disappear, then lift again.

A gopher squeaked questioningly as Brian sat down upon a rock warm to the backs of his thighs. He picked a pale blue flax-flower at his feet, stared long at the stripings in its shallow throat, then looked up to see a dragonfly hanging on shimmering wings directly in front of him. The gopher squeaked again, and he saw it a few yards away, sitting up, watching him from its pulpit hole. A suave-winged hawk chose that moment to slip its shadow over the face of the prairie.

And all about him was the wind now, a pervasive sighing through great emptiness, unhampered by the buildings of the town, warm and living against his face and in his hair.

Then for the second time that day he saw a strange boy – one who came from behind him soundlessly, who stood and stared at him with steady gray eyes in a face of remarkable broadness, with cheekbones circling high under a dark and freckled skin. He saw that the boy's hair, bleached as the dead prairie grass itself, lay across his forehead in an all-round cowlick curling under at the edge. His faded blue pants hung open in two tears just below the knees. He was barefooted.

Brian was not startled; he simply accepted the boy's presence out here as he had accepted that of the gopher and the hawk and the dragonfly.

"This is your prairie," Brian said.

The boy did not answer him. He turned and walked as silently as he had come, out over the prairie. His walk was smooth.

After the boy's figure had become just a speck in the distance, Brian looked up into the sky, now filled with a soft expanse of cloud, the higher edges luminous and against the blue. It stretched to the prairie's rim. As he stared, the gray underside carded out, and through the cloud's softness was revealed a blue well shot with sunlight. Almost as soon as it had cleared, a whisking of cloud stole over it.

For one moment no wind stirred. A butterfly went pelting past. God, Brian decided, must like the boy's prairie.

Source: W.O. Mitchell, *Who Has Seen the Wind* (Toronto: Macmillan/Seal Books, 1982), 3-12.

Gabrielle Roy (1909–83)

"RUE STE.-CATHERINE"

Long before the dramatist Michel Tremblay (1942–) proudly wrote in the ordinary language of Montrealers, Gabrielle Roy had set the pattern in her novels about life in Quebec and in francophone communities beyond its borders. Born in St-Boniface in Manitoba, Roy worked as a journalist before she established her reputation, both in English and in French, as one of Canada's best novelists. *Bonheur d'occasion* earned Roy the Prix Femina and, later, a Governor General's Award. More honours followed. Yet, at the same time, Roy's recording of the *joual* of ordinary speech shocked many well-educated Quebeckers who believed that the struggle to preserve French involved the protection of its classic purity.

"Have any of you guys ever walked on St. Catherine Street without a cent in your pocket and looked at all the stuff in the shopwindows? I guess so. Well, I have too. And I've seen some fine things, boys, as fine as you can see anywhere. I can hardly describe all the fine things I've seen while tramping up and down St. Catherine Street! Packards, Buicks, racing cars, sport cars. I've seen mannequins in beautiful evening dresses, and others without a stitch on. What can't you find on St. Catherine Street? Bedroom suites, with a doll in a silk nightie on the bed. Sporting-goods stores,

with golf sticks, tennis rackets, skis, fishing poles. If anyone has the leisure to play around with such things, it's us, eh? But the only fun we get out of it all is to look. And the grub! Have you ever passed one of those restaurants where they roast chickens in the window when your belly was flapping against your ribs? But that's not all, my friends. Society spreads everything out before us, all the finest things in the world. But don't get the idea that that's all. Ah no! They urge us to buy too. You'd think they were scared we weren't tempted enough. They're on our necks day and night to buy all this fancy stuff. Turn on the radio, and what do you hear? A bigwig from the loan company who wants to lend you five hundred bucks! Boy, you could buy a secondhand Buick with five hundred bucks! Or a fellow begs you to let him clean your old rags. You're stupid not to wear the latest styles. You're a fool not to have a frigidaire in your kitchen. Look at the paper. Buy all the products in the ads; the papers are full of them. Buy cigarettes, buy Holland gin, buy headache pills, buy fur coats! No one should be without these things! In this era of progress every man has the right to have a good time."

He rose and emerged into the light, a tall thin boy with narrow hips, red swollen eyelids, and large ears standing out from his head.

"That's what society gives us, temptations. From beginning to end that's all we get. The whole bloody circus is set up to tempt us. And that's how society, the dirty slut, gets a grip on us. Don't get any ideas into your heads, boys. Sooner or later we all fall for it. It requires no great temptation either to make us give up our wretched little lives. I know a guy who enlisted, do you know why?"

Putting his hand in his pocket he drew out a toothpick and stuck it in his teeth.

"To get a winter coat. He was tired of buying his clothes from the old-clothes men in Craig Street, wearing rags that stank of sweat and onions. One day he got the idea that he wanted a coat with brass buttons. And how he shines up those brass buttons nowadays, how he polishes 'em! They cost a pretty penny, eh?"

Source: Gabrielle Roy, *The Tin Flute*, trans. Hannah Josephson (Toronto: McClelland and Stewart, 1947), 57-8.

Moses Coady (1882–1959)

"THE LESSON OF THE TIDES"

Moses Michael Coady was born at North East Margaree in Nova Scotia and never forgot the desperate poverty of the fishing and farming communities of his youth. Educated by the Jesuits and ordained as a priest, Coady became a founder of the Antigonish movement, a program of adult education, marketing cooperatives, and self-help which was a beacon of hope during the years of the Great Depression and, in later years, a model development program carried to many parts of the Third World.

Critics and even admirers of the Antigonish movement believed that its key was Coady himself. A practical optimist, Coady shamed, cajoled, and inspired, never forgetting that bills had to be paid and insisting that political handouts exacted a bigger price than anything they could contribute. He was passionately committed to Canada, the Maritimes, his own St. Francis-Xavier University, and, of course, the beautiful valley of the Margaree.

We in the Maritimes are children of the sea. At no point in Nova Scotia are we farther than thirty miles from the ocean. Prince Edward Islanders are nearer still and the people in many parts of New Brunswick have grown up with the roar of the sea in their ears. We love the open sea. We have watched it in all its moods – bathed in it in our hours of play, battled against it in the pursuit of our livelihood.

Is it too much to hope that our people will acquire and have operating in their economic and social lives the venturesome spirit that prompts them to pit their energies against the angry ocean?

There is a great lesson to be learned from the coming and going of the tides that might be applied to our economic and social lives. Even our most beautiful bays and harbours lose much of their beauty in the ebb-tide. When the clear, healthy salt water goes out, it exposes to us the ugly clams, the slimy sea-weeds and jelly-like marine plants and fishes. Water-logged stumps and planks and hulks of ships are strewn chaotically before our view. The air is filled with unpleasant smells. Above all this ugliness the screaming scavengers, the gulls and the other sea-birds, wheel and circle in their search for prey.

Something similar happens in a rural community where the population is decreasing. The uglier features of the community show up. Those who go around hawking gossip and blue ruin are more in evidence and become dangerously influential in a society where the population is on the decline. Defeatism is everywhere in evidence because the community has fallen in manpower below the optimum of social performance. The country-side takes on the forlorn disorder of a deserted beach at ebb-tide.

But when a community's population is growing, it is like the full tide. All the ugly things disappear and there is life and beauty everywhere. The air is charged and invigorated with the right kind of emotions, making everyone enthusiastic, happy and ambitious. It doesn't take many people to bring a social flood-tide into rural communities. Sometimes half a dozen or more bright, energetic families will do it.

But the strange thing is that few people are ever interested in seeing the population grow in their communities, although there is every argument for wanting to see the population of rural communities increase. Unfortunately, there seems to be an instinctive opposition on the part of our people to strangers coming in to settle in their communities.

Nova Scotia has a population of 650,000; Holland, with an area half the size of Nova Scotia, has ten million, and the per capita economic position of Holland is as high as anywhere in the world.

Only with an increased and intelligent population will we in the Maritimes reach the flood-tide of economic and social development.

Source: Alexander F. Laidlaw, *The Man from Margaree: Writings and Speeches of M.M. Coady* (Toronto: McClelland and Stewart, 1971), 169-70.

Joey Smallwood (1900–91)

HOW TO VOTE FOR CONFEDERATION

Joseph Roberts Smallwood was the last Father of Confederation: in 1949 he led Newfoundland into Canada. A journalist at first, he was elected in 1946 to the Constitutional Convention charged with laying the groundwork for a referendum on Newfoundland's future. A dynamic speaker with a populist touch, Smallwood campaigned hard for Confederation. In one memorable speech, he told his fellow Newfoundlanders: "We are not a nation. We are a medium-sized municipality . . . left far behind in the march of time." The first referendum was indecisive; in the second, held in July 1948, Confederation narrowly won. After being elected leader of the provincial Liberal Party, Smallwood won the first provincial election in May 1949. He served as premier and dominated Newfoundland politics for over two decades.

Smallwood was both a passionate Newfoundlander and a passionate Canadian. He identified himself as a champion of his province, and of the underdog generally, though critics like John Crosbie (1931–) insist that his acquisitiveness was as scandalous as his arrogant use of power. Confederation gave Newfoundlanders a far higher standard of living but solved few underlying economic problems. In recent years the weakness of the fisheries has led to high seasonal unemployment and rising welfare dependency in the province. But it is not clear how staying out of Canada would have improved matters.

The following speech, delivered during the referendum campaign of 1949, is vintage Smallwood.

It is so simple. You won't find anybody's name on the ballot paper – not Joe Smallwood's, not Ches Crosbie's, not Peter Cashin's, nobody's. You will not be voting for me, and you'll not be voting to "give Ches a chance." Don't you bother about me or Ches or anyone else – you bother about yourself tomorrow, and you bother about your family, your children, or your grandchildren. You vote tomorrow to give them a chance! "Give Ches a chance," indeed! And how do you go about giving Ches a chance? By voting for responsible government

as it existed in 1933, with all the dole and dole bread. I don't think Ches was on the dole in 1933 – he didn't have to eat the dole bread. You had to, or your relatives or friends – but Ches didn't. And if responsible government as it existed in 1933 wins tomorrow, it's not Ches who'll have to go on the dole and eat the dole bread; not likely. You know who will be going on the dole. And that's what you will be voting for if you vote to give Ches a chance. Why should you do it? Have you thought it over? Have you found a good, sensible reason why you should give Ches a chance? Or anyone else except your own family?

Well, there you are, alone in that little polling booth, you and your conscience.

The choice is clear: responsible government as it existed in 1933, or Confederation with Canada. You make a last-minute decision between the two forms of government. You know what responsible government was like in 1933; the depression, the destitution, the dole, the disease. You know all about the tuberculosis and the beriberi. You know all about the brown dole bread. I don't have to remind you of the suffering under responsible government "as it existed in 1933." There may be a few youngsters around who don't remember anything about it – but you do. Even if you weren't on the dole and didn't have to eat the dole bread yourselves, your neighbours did, and you know all about it.

You ask yourself, "Will I mark this X for responsible government as it existed in 1933?" And you say to yourself, "Yes, I'll do it. I'm no namby-pamby – I'm tough, I am; I took it before, and I can take it again. I starved before, and I'm willing to starve again. I ate dole bread then, and I'm prepared to eat it now. I pulled in the belt in 1933, under responsible government, and I'm willing to pull it in again, and take whatever they hand out to me. I'll vote for responsible government as it existed in 1933!"

And with that, before you change your mind, you take the pencil and mark that X.

Then you fold up the ballot paper, as they told you to do, and you take it outside into the polling booth, and you push it down through the slot into the ballot box. You give it a couple of taps to make sure that it's gone into the box and can't be hooked out. You want to be sure that your ballot won't be hooked out by someone who is not prepared, as you are, to pull in the belt again. The deed is done! You've made your choice. You walk out of the polling station and make your way down the road to your home.

And as you go down the road, you meet a little boy, or a little girl, coming toward you.

If you have a conscience at all, you'll stop and you'll say, "Little boy (or little girl), I make my apology to you. I have just betrayed you. I have just voted for responsible government as it existed in 1933 – the dole, the dole bread, the tuberculosis and the beriberi. I was able to take it; I pulled in my belt – now it's your turn. I don't see why you should get off any more than I did and other children did in 1933 – but all the same, I suppose I should make my apology for condemning you in the polling booth today."

Source: Joseph Smallwood, *I Chose Canada: The Memoirs of the Honourable Joseph R. "Joey" Smallwood* (Toronto: Macmillan, 1973), 301-3.

Gratien Gélinas (1909–)

The Very Ordinary Dreams of Tit-Coq

One of Canada's best known dramatists and theatre producers, Gratien Gélinas was born in Saint-Tite in Champlain County. He became well known in Quebec in the 1930s as the creator of a series of popular reviews, *les Fridolinades*, which featured the legendary character Fridolin. Gélinas had a powerful influence on Quebec society, a social critic whose transcendant humanity made his questions gentle but absolutely insistent.

While *Bousille et les justes* (1959) and *Hier, les enfants dansaient* (1966) were powerful works, Gélinas will perhaps be best remembered for *Tit Coq* (1950), his play about a French-Canadian soldier in the Second World War. Tit-Coq embodies the fundamental decency and wit Gélinas always found among his fellow *Canadiens*. Just to be together with his child and his wife, heading out for an evening with his favourite uncle – that would be his dream of happiness.

PADRE: You didn't feel like marrying her, your Marie-Ange, before you left?

TIT-COQ: Feel like it? Every day of the week! But no. Me marry a girl . . . and she'd have a child of me while I'm to-hell-and-gone away, never in a hundred years! If my father was not with my mother when I was born in a charity ward or wherever it was, that was his business. But I, when my baby comes, I'm going to be right there at my woman's side. Yes sir! As close to the bed as I can get.

PADRE: I understand.

TIT-COQ: Damn right I'll be there. So that baby will know, as soon as he opens his eyes, who his father is. And I want to pinch his cheeks and bite his bottom as soon as he is washed. Not find him half grown two or three years old. I missed the first part of my life. O.K., let's forget it. But the second part, I don't want to miss a drop of it. And the little punk, he's going to have a cute little mug like his mother!

PADRE: And a heart in the right place like his father?

TIT-COQ: Except he's going to be a clean child, outside and inside. Not an alley-brat of a foundling, like me.

PADRE: So it's because you want to be near your baby when he's born that you're leaving . . . ?

TIT-COQ: A virgin and a martyr, yes.

PADRE: That's as good a reason as any.

TIT-COQ: Probably.

A Ukrainian family lines up at the gates of the immigration sheds in Quebec City in 1911. The railway will carry them westward to what Canadian agents billed as "The Last Best West." Homesteading anywhere was a gruelling ordeal and misguided advice from so-called experts did not help. However, the Ukrainians' homeland experience of dryland farming proved an enormous asset on the Canadian prairies. (National Archives of Canada, C 4745)

Children in a turnip field near Woodstock, New Brunswick, line up for a photograph. The eldest contrives to keep order, steady the dog, and comfort the youngest, responsibilities she has doubtless had for a good many of her few years. A large family was a blessing on the farm, where much work demanded many hands; in the cities, where most work was reserved for adults, children were a more costly blessing. In both environments, infant mortality would now strike us as appallingly high. (National Archives of Canada, PA 10724)

Would-be immigrants to Canada alongside the Komagata Maru, *a Japanese ship chartered to test a Canadian immigration rule requiring direct passage from India (this at a time when no shipping line provided such a route). Though Sikhs had been hardworking and successful in British Columbia, and many of the intended immigrants had served loyally in the British army, the white population cheered when the government, backed by militia and its new cruiser,* H.M.C.S. Rainbow, *barred the immigrants and sent the ship back to India.* (National Archives of Canada, PA 34015)

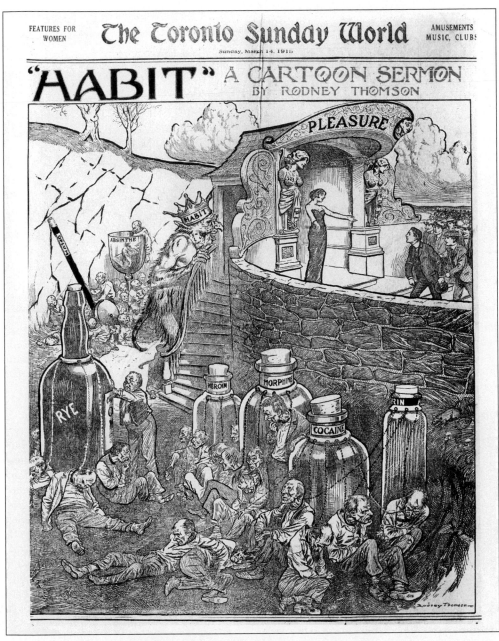

If Canadians were accused of taking their pleasures sadly or not at all, the image of pleasure was hardly alluring. When decent young men rushed through the doors, they would find themselves chained by Habit to perennial servitude. The Toronto Sunday World was a popular weekend magazine that evolved into the midcentury national favourite, the Star Weekly, before succumbing to television and changing reading habits.
(City of Toronto Archives, James Collection, 628)

Swimming class at the Lillian Massey Household Science Building at the University of Toronto, March 13, 1915. Ontario expected its provincial university to train its graduates to avoid drowning. Many of these women were two years away from winning the right to vote, and the arguments for women's suffrage – that the nation's mothers would bring family values and moral uplift to political affairs – would make some of their descendants cringe. (National Archives of Canada, PA 01386)

The grenade-filling station of Winnipeg's 8th Battalion in France, May 1916. Formed in 1914 from a peacetime militia regiment, the unit survived the gas attack at Ypres in 1915 and every other major battle of the Canadian Corps. On average, infantry soldiers lasted a year in battle before death or crippling wounds ended their lives. These men have two and a half more years of fighting ahead of them. (National Archives of Canada, PA 151)

Generations of Canadians grew used to seeing their northern landscape as the Group of Seven painted it. The inspiration for the Group of Seven was Tom Thomson (1877-1917), an Ontario-born and largely self-taught painter whose passion for art and for wilderness living combined during a summer in Algonquin Park in 1912 and ended when he drowned at Canoe Lake on June 8, 1917. The Jack Pine (1916-17) is a characteristic product of this period. (National Gallery of Canada)

Members of the Local 72 of the Ukrainian Social-Democratic Party assembled near Timmins, Ontario, on May Day, 1918, testing the tolerance of their English-speaking neighbours. While many Canadians welcomed the end of Tsarist tyranny, the Bolshevik decision to end the Tsar's war with Germany made his former subjects suspect in a Canada still utterly committed to Allied victory. Would freedom prevail, or patriotism? Or would both be outdistanced by the sun, fresh leaves, and wild flowers of a long-awaited spring? (Multicultural History Society of Ontario)

Lawren Harris (1885-1970) was one of the most gifted of the Group of Seven and, as a member of a wealthy family, the most free to pursue his genius. Unlike others, who preferred natural landscapes, Harris had an eye for urban scenes that few contemporaries regarded as worthy of an artist's vision. January Thaw: Edge of Town, *painted in 1921, records the sloppy weather that usually breaks the Canadian winter but leaves most people yearning for the next frost.* (National Gallery of Canada)

Emily Carr (1871-1945) was a West Coast artist who sought her own spirituality through interpreting the totems of the native peoples of British Columbia. Blunden Harbour, *with its unpeopled starkness, was one of her characteristic works.* (National Gallery of Canada)

To many Canadians, the Pre-Cambrian Shield country was captured forever by the Group of Seven. Their style suited the rocks, trees, and lakes of the region, particularly when the landscape was transformed by the strong colours of autumn. Arthur Lismer (1885-1969) was a member of the original group as well as a distinguished teacher. His October on the North Shore, Lake Superior was completed in 1927. (National Gallery of Canada)

The Alaska Highway, built in 1942-43 from northern British Columbia to Anchorage, was fortunately never needed to supply forces to resist a Japanese invasion. The road was virtually impassable by 1944, and only after the war was it completed by Canadian engineers. As a war artist, A.Y. Jackson (1882-1974) depicted the stubborn terrain and harsh climate of the Highway and its sparse traffic of army trucks. (National Gallery of Canada)

PADRE: God has been good to you, do you know that?

TIT-COQ: Oh yes . . . He didn't break his neck at the start, but, these last few months, he's been doing quite nicely! And I don't ask much more. Because, do you know what would make my life one hundred per cent successful?

PADRE: Tell me!

TIT-COQ: Maybe you'll laugh at me. Because if you don't understand, it just sounds mawkish.

PADRE: There'll be nothing to laugh at, I'm sure.

TIT-COQ: I don't see myself as a senator in parliament some day, nor a millionaire in a castle. No, when I dream, I see myself in a street-car, on a Sunday night about a quarter past seven; with my baby in my arms and, holding on to me, my wife, neat and tidy, diaper bag in her hand. And we're on our way to spend the evening at Uncle Alcide's . . . My uncle by marriage, but my uncle just the same. The little bastard all alone in life, gone and done with. In the streetcar there would be just a man like the rest, very plain with his grey hat, white scarf, wife and baby. Just like the rest. No more but no less! Some might call that a mighty dull future, but me, with that, I'd be right on the peak of the world.

Source: Gratien Gélinas, Tit-Coq, trans. Kenneth Johnstone (Toronto: Clarke, Irwin, 1967), pp. 37-8.

Anne Hébert (1916—)

PRECURSOR OF A NEW QUEBEC

Though no longer living in Quebec, Anne Hébert remains one of French Canada's most renowned authors. Born in Sainte-Catharine de Fossambault, a cousin of Hector de Saint-Denys Garneau (1912-43), she studied in Quebec and, like him, began publishing her poetry in the 1930s. She worked for Radio Canada and the National Film Board in the 1950s, partially sheltered from the crushing censorship of the Duplessis regime, but in 1954 she moved to Paris.

In Paris she began a career primarily devoted to the novel, of which *Kamouraska* (1970) is probably the best known. The title poem in *Le Tombeau des rois* (*The Tomb of the Kings*) is part of a collection of Hébert's poetry that appeared in 1953. It typifies the work of a poet who shuns the lush verbal imagery of her predecessors, seeking a spare modernist form in which each word must carry its own weight, in which the imagination has to work as hard as the poet.

THE TOMB OF THE KINGS

I have my heart on my fist
Like a blind falcon.

With the taciturn bird taking my fingers
A lamp swollen with wine and with blood,
I go down
Toward the tombs of the kings
Astonished
Scarcely born.

What thread of Ariadne leads me
Along the muted labyrinths?
The echo of footfall is swallowed there step
    by step.
(In what dream
Was this child bound by her ankle
Like a fascinated slave?)

The author of the dream
Presses on the thread,
So come the naked footsteps
One by one
Like the first drops of rain
At the bottom of the well.

Already the odor stirs in swollen storms
Seeps from the sills of the doors
Of the rooms, secret and round,
Where the enclosed beds are arrayed.

The still desire of the effigies draws me.
I gaze with astonishment
As set on the black bones
Shine the blue encrusted stones.

LE TOMBEAU DES ROIS

J'ai mon coeur au poing.
Comme un faucon aveugle.

Le taciturne oiseau pris à mes doigts
Lampe gonflée de vin et de sang,
Je descends
Vers les tombeaux des rois
Étonnée
À peine née.

Quel fil d'Ariane me mène
Au long des dédales sourds?
L'écho des pas s'y mange à mesure.

(En quel songe
Cette enfant fut-elle liée par la cheville
Pareille à une esclave fascinée?)
L'auteur du songe
Presse le fil,
Et viennent les pas nus

Un à un
Comme les premières gouttes de pluie
Au fond du puits.
Déjà l'odeur bouge en des orages gonflés
Suinte sous le pas des portes
Aux chambres secrètes et rondes,
Là où sont dressés les lits clos.

L'immobile désir des gisants me tire.
Je regarde avec étonnement
À même les noirs ossements
Luire les pierres bleues incrustées.

Several tragedies patiently wrought,
On the breast of the kings, laid out
In the guise of jewels
Are offered to me
Without tears or regrets.

Ranged in a single row:
The smoke of incense, the cake of dried rice
And my trembling flesh:
Ritual and submissive offering.

The golden mask on my absent face
Violet flowers by way of eyes,
The shadow of love makes me up with
    precise little strokes;
And this bird of mine breathes
And sobs strangely.

A long shiver
Like the wind that catches, from tree to tree,
Stirs seven great ebony pharaohs
In their solemn ornate casings.

It is only the depth of death that persists,
Feigning the last torment
Seeking its appeasement
And its eternity
In a light tinkling of bracelets
Vain rings games of elsewhere
Around the sacrificed flesh.

Craving the brotherly source of evil in me
They lay me down and drink me;
Seven times, I know the vise of bones
And the dry hand that seeks the heart to
    break it.

Quelques tragédies patiemment travaillées,
Sur la poitrine des rois, couchées,
En guise de bijoux
Me sont offertes
Sans larmes ni regrets.

Sur une seule ligne rangés:
La fumée d'encens, le gâteau de riz séché
Et ma chair qui tremble:
Offrande rituelle et soumise.

Le masque d'or sur ma face absente
Des fleurs violettes en guise de prunelles,
L'ombre de l'amour me maquille à petits
    traits précis;
Et cet oiseau que j'ai
Respire
Et se plaint étrangement.

Un frisson long
Semblable au vent qui prend, d'arbre en
    arbre,
Agite sept grands pharaons d'ébène
En leurs étuis solennels et parés.

Ce n'est que la profondeur de la mort qui
    persiste,
Simulant le dernier tourment
Cherchant son apaisement
Et son éternité
En un cliquetis léger de bracelets
Cercles vains jeux d'ailleurs
Autour de la chair sacrifiée.

Avides de la source fraternelle du mal en moi
Ils me couchent et me boivent;

Livid and gorged on horrible dream
My limbs unfettered
And the dead outside me, assassinated,
What glimmer of dawn strays here?
How is it then that this bird trembles
And turns towards the morning
Its blinded eyes?

Source: Anne Hébert, "The Tomb of the Kings," in *The Tomb of the Kings*, trans. Peter Miller (Toronto: Contact Press, 1967), 86-91.

Sept fois, je connais l'étau des os
Et la main sèche qui cherche le coeur pour le
    rompre

Livide et repue de songe horrible
Les membres dénoués
Et les morts hors de moi, assassinés,
Quel reflet d'aube s'égare ici?
D'où vient donc que cet oiseau frémit
Et tourne vers le matin
Ses prunelles crevées?

Source: Laurent Mailhot and Pierre Nepveu, eds., *Le poésie qûébécoise* (Montreal: Typo poésie, 1990).

Hilda Neatby (1904–75)

"So Little for the Mind"

Hilda Marion Neatby was a Canadian writer, historian, educator, and critic of the educational system. She is best known for her controversial book *So Little for the Mind*, first published in 1953. In it Neatby launched an attack on progressive and child-centred educational approaches. She claimed that these led to a watered-down curriculum which left the best students under-challenged. In a sense her book anticipated by three decades the conservative reaction against the various educational reforms of the 1960s and 1970s. Those reforms, typified by the Hall-Dennis report in Ontario, argued for a looser educational system with more student and community involvement, equal educational opportunity and outcomes, fewer requirements, and less emphasis on discipline and regulation.

The back-to-basics movement of the 1980s emerged as a reaction to the perceived excesses of the student-centred educational reform movement. We present here a portion of the introduction to Hilda Neatby's book, which outlines her basic positions. Whether one agrees with her or not, Neatby's arguments are echoed today by many Canadian politicians, educators, and parents.

The twentieth century school is faced with a tremendous threefold task.

First, it must accept, and afford some sort of training for, every child above a very low intellectual level. This has meant an enormous and rapid increase in numbers in all schools, and a vast increase in the numbers of intellectually incompetent in the high schools. Somehow all these future citizens must receive education or training appropriate to their capacities.

Secondly, the school must convey to these swollen numbers a mass of information useful and even essential to them, information of which their grandparents never dreamed. They must learn the rules of health, the principles of a balanced diet, safety regulations, traffic laws, the operations of public services and utilities, the use and hazards of modern domestic equipment, and literally hundreds of other matters. Much of this practical instruction may be unnecessary and even absurd. Most of it should be learned in the home. But some school instruction in these matters is probably inescapable, time-consuming though it may be.

Thirdly, the school should, in addition, convey to all, insofar as they are capable of receiving it, the intellectual, cultural and moral training which represents the best in a long and honourable tradition of Western civilization. On the proper performance of this task depends the future of our society. Informed individuals outside the progressive schools speak of the crisis in civilization with seriousness and intelligence. Progressive educators have apparently not even heard of it; they continue blandly to socialize for a society which threatens every moment to cease to exist.

Looking back over the past generation or two, it seems obvious that the true "pragmatist," that is the really practical and forward looking man or woman, would have used the great resources of the schools, public interest, increasing wealth, improved buildings, up-to-date equipment, adequate teacher training, more effective methods of teaching, to fulfil this threefold obligation. They would have realized that all the new resources and all the new enthusiasm would be barely enough to meet the heavy new responsibility of teaching the multitudes and of imparting an ever-increasing mass of useful, practical information, without neglecting the task, now more essential than ever, of offering mental discipline and intellectual and spiritual enrichment. They did not see either the challenge or the opportunity. They took the easy way out. Instead of using their enormous new resources in material equipment, knowledge and skill to cope with their tremendous task, they frittered them away in making school life easy and pleasant, concentrating on the obvious, the practical, and the immediate. Democratic equalitarianism encouraged the idea of a uniform low standard easily obtainable by almost all. Special attention was given to all physical, emotional and mental abnormalities, but the old-fashioned things called the mind, the imagination and the conscience of the average and of the better than average child, if not exactly forgotten, slipped into the background. As a result the much maligned traditionalist is now retorting with some pretty vigorous criticisms of progressive education as he sees it.

It is frankly anti-intellectual. There is no attempt to exercise, train and discipline the mind. This is old-fashioned language, now forbidden by the experts, but its meaning is still clear to the literate person. The traditionalist firmly and even brutally conveyed a body of facts which must be learned precisely, and which provided, as it were, the material of thought. Or he might demonstrate the process of thought through the admittedly painful process of causing the pupil to memorize a mathematical proposition and its proof. True, the matter often began and ended with memorizing, and never reached the stage of thinking. The progressivist noted this, but instead of taking over and doing the thing properly he threw up the sponge. Because, he argued, intellectual training is difficult and painful and many fall by the wayside, throw it out altogether. Failures spoil the record! The denial by the schools of the duty of intellectual training is neatly reflected by the current fashion of lightly dismissing in argument an unanswerable proposition as "a question of semantics."

Progressivism is anti-cultural. This is quite in keeping with the revolutionary, pseudo-scientific materialist fashions of the day. In this scientific age we find that everything, not just educational methods, but everything, is better than it used to be. It is the pride of the machine age that we can now understand, manipulate and control men as we do machines. Why should we look at the evidence of human joys, sorrows, failures, and achievements in the past? It would almost be an admission of defeat. We manage everything better now. No one actually says this; and even progressivists can enjoy good (if traditional) music or painting. But the result of progressivism has been effectively to cut off many if not most of our pupils from any real enjoyment or understanding of the inheritance of western civilization; and certainly from any sense that the achievements and values of the past are a trust to be preserved and enriched for the future. Culture in its traditional sense of intellectual and moral cultivation is as unfashionable as is scholarship.

Finally, progressive education is, or has been, amoral. There is something of a reaction today, but for a generation it has been unfashionable, to say the least, to speak openly of right and wrong actions. Teachers take cover instead under "desirable" and "undesirable" "attitudes" or "responses." But these are not enough. The pupil soon learns the meaning of desirable and thinks, quite rightly, that in a democratic society he has as much right to desire as anyone else. Even the elementary discipline of establishing rules which the child was required to keep was questioned. True, rules certainly existed in practice; but pragmatic theory frowned on all external control and therefore rules were enforced uneasily and with a bad conscience. The general tendency of the progressive approach has been to weaken respect for law and authority as such, and to dull discrimination between right and wrong, by the teaching, implied if not expressed, that "desirable" actions on the part of the child (actions pleasing to others) will bring "desirable" responses (actions pleasing to him). It is no doubt often true that honesty is the best policy, but no one ever learned honesty from that maxim. Pragmatism is certainly not entirely responsible for the flabby morality of today, but it has lent itself with enthusiasm to the general trend of the times. The current reaction which kindly allows "idealism" in the progressive school has added to the intellectual confusion without establishing any clear moral principles. In a democratic society which must ultimately rest on the morality of individuals with every opportunity for, and incentive to immorality, this seems strange indeed.

Judged by their fitness for the individuals and for the society which they serve, our progressive methods are neither pragmatic nor progressive in any true sense of these words. The industrial challenge of today is to tool up and increase production by all means. We are not doing this in the educational world. We are, it is true, offering innumerable "special" courses but the special course, by definition, is a tool for a narrowly prescribed purpose. The unknown demands of the future must be met by a general education calculated to produce an informed, intelligent, adaptable, and loyal but not servile worker; in the words of Cromwell which still apply in peace as in war, the man who "knows what he fights for, and loves what he knows." Are the schools giving pupils such a knowledge of their civilization, its history, its philosophy, its achievements and its failures, that they are ready to refuse the evil and to choose the good; that they may play an adequate part in its growth and in its enrichment? Are they building morale by telling the pupils frankly how real and earnest modern life is, telling them not in a cruel or a morbid way, but with the calm common sense that they bring to training in habits of health or regard for the traffic lights? The plain truth is that they are not doing these things. They are carefully avoiding the essential issues.

The sensible and fair thing is surely to let children know by experience in school that life may be difficult and disagreeable as well as delightful and simple; that theirs is a world for workers, and that work demands their best effort; and to help them to acquire in school such firm habits and such clear principles as will enable them, whether they gain or lose the world, to do their duty in it with diligence and with intelligence. Nothing could be less practical or progressive than the current fashion of keeping those who should be achieving the age of discretion in ignorant, if contented immaturity.

Source: Hilda Neatby, *So Little for the Mind* (Toronto: Clarke-Irwin, 1953), 13-19.

E. J. Pratt (1882–1964)

"Towards the Last Spike"

Newfoundland-born, raised in a series of Methodist manses in outport Newfoundland, Edwin John ("Ned") Pratt trained for the ministry and was ordained in Toronto, but his life was spent teaching at Victoria College at the University of Toronto, initially in psychology and then, much more appropriately, in English. He became English-speaking Canada's most renowned and successful narrative poet. The young Pratt concentrated on Newfoundland and Maritime themes. Later, he turned to stirring episodes in Canada's history, such as the martyrdom of Father Jean de Brébeuf (1593-1649) and, in this extract of a much longer poem, the construction of Canada's first transcontinental railway.

The building of the Canadian Pacific Railway was, Pratt argued, a triumph of the stubborn Scottish character, whether in the titanic battle by surveyors and engineers with muskeg and mountains, or in the no less desperate struggle by capitalists to find the finances and by politicians to quell rebellious followers. George Stephen (1829-1921), the Montreal financier, had appealed to his fellow directors with the war cry of the clan Grant, "Stand Fast, Craigellachie!" The site where the lines from the Pacific and the Atlantic met, in the middle of the Rockies, would be christened Craigellachie.

THE GATHERING

"Oats – a grain which in England is generally given to horses, but in Scotland supports the people" – DR SAMUEL JOHNSON. *"True, but where will you find such horses, where such men?"* – LORD ELIBANK'S REPLY AS RECORDED BY SIR WALTER SCOTT.

Oatmeal was in their blood and in their
  names.
Thrift was the title of their catechism.
It governed all things but their mess of
  porridge
Which, when it struck the hydrochloric acid
With treacle and skim-milk, became a mash.
Entering the duodenum, it broke up
Into amino acids; then the liver
Took on its natural job as carpenter:
Foreheads grew into cliffs, jaws into juts.
The meal, so changed, engaged the follicles:
Eyebrows came out as gorse, the beards as
  thistles,
And the chest-hair the fell of Grampian
  rams.
It stretched and vulcanized the human span:
Nonagenarians worked and thrived upon it.
Out of such chemistry run through by genes,
The food released its fearesome racial
  products: –

The power to strike a bargain like a foe,
To win an argument upon a burr.
Invest the language with a Bannockburn,
Culloden or the warnings of Lochiel,
Weave loyalties and rivalries in tartans,
Present for the amazement of the world
Kilts and the civilized barbaric Fling.
And pipes which, when they acted on the
  mash,
Fermented lullabies to *Scots wha hae*.
Their names were like a battle-muster –
  Angus
(He of the Shops) and Fleming (of the
  Transit),
Hector (of the *Kicking Horse*), Dawson,
'Cromarty' Ross, and Beatty (Ulster Scot),
Bruce, Allan, Galt and Douglas, and the
  'twa' –

Stephen (Craigellachie) and Smith
  (Strathcona) –
Who would one day climb from their Gaelic
  hide-outs,
Take off their plaids and wrap them round
  the mountains,
And then the everlasting tread of the Macs,
Vanguard, centre and rear, their roving eyes
On summits, rivers, contracts, beaver,
  ledgers;
Their ears cocked to the skirl of Sir John A.,
The general of the patronymic March.

Source: Margaret Atwood, ed., *The New Oxford Book of Canadian Verse in English* (Toronto: Oxford University Press, 1983), 80-2.

Ralph Gustafson (1909–1995)

"In the Yukon"

Old as it is, the dense wilderness is the world at its beginning, untouched and unspoiled and glorious in its grandeur. And all of it without the burden of history.

Few short poems say as much about the Canadian wild as Ralph Gustafson's "In the Yukon." Gustafson grew up near Sherbrooke, Quebec, studied at Bishop's University in Lennoxville, and taught in that university's English department for his entire academic career. Physically and poetically, he ranged across the second-biggest country of the world, including the westernmost of Canada's northern territories, while remaining based in Quebec's Eastern Townships. He published many volumes of poetry and won the Governor General's Award for Poetry in 1974.

In Europe, you can't move without going
down into history.
Here, all is a beginning. I saw a salmon jump,
Again and again, against the current.
The timbered hills a background, wooded
green
Unpushed through: the salmon jumped,
silver.
This was news, was commerce, at the end of
the summer
The leap for dying. Moose came down to
the water edge
To drink and the salmon turned silver arcs.
At night, the northern lights played, great
over country

Without tapestry and coronations, kings
crowned
With weights of gold. They were green.
Green hangings and great grandeur, over
the north
Going to what no man can hold hard in
mind.
The dredge of that gravity, being without
experience.

Source: A.J.M. Smith, ed., *Modern Canadian Verse in English and French* (Toronto: Oxford University Press, 1967), 123-4.

Wade Hemsworth (1916—)

"THE BLACKFLY SONG"

Newcomers to Canada may think of it as a land of ice and snow, short summers, and vast emptiness. Such impressions would be incomplete, however, without taking account of the dominant resident of Canada's northern woods, the blackfly. Resistant to most repellents and any weather short of a prolonged hot, dry spell, the tiny blackflies can drive large animals into blundering encounters with cars, trucks, and people. Their remorseless attacks can leave skin bleeding and painful from even a few minutes' exposure.

Wade Hemsworth was an Ontario Hydro worker. His popular song, written in 1949 while Hemsworth was exploring near James Bay, captures the experience of anyone who has served a summer in the north, whether in a survey crew, a railway gang, or in reforestation. When unions have the bargaining power, blackfly control is a requirement for forestry or construction operations.

'Twas early in the spring when I decide to go
For to work up in the woods in North Ontario,
And the unemployment office said they'd send me through
To the little Abitibi with the survey crew.

CHORUS:
And the blackflies the little blackflies
Always the blackfly no matter where you go.
I'll die with the blackfly a picking my bones
In North Ontario, In North Ontario.

Now the man Black Toby was the captain of the crew,
And he said, "I'm gonna tell you boys what we're gonna do.
They want to build a power dam and we must find a way
For to make the little Ab flow around the other way."

CHORUS

So we survey to the east and we survey to the west,
And we couldn't make our minds up how to do it best.
"Little Ab, little Ab, what shall I do?
For I'm all but goin' crazy on the survey crew."

CHORUS

It was blackfly, blackfly everywhere.
A-crawlin' in your whiskers, a-crawlin' in your hair;

A-swimming' in the soup, and a-swimming' in the tea;
Oh the devil take the blackfly and let me be.

CHORUS

Black Toby fell to swearin' cause the work went slow,
And the state of our morale was gettin' pretty low.
And the flies swarmed heavy – it was hard to catch a breath,
As you staggered up and down the trail talkin' to yourself.

CHORUS

Now the bull cook's name was Blind River Joe;
If it hadn't been for him we'd never pulled through,
For he bound up our bruises, and he kidded us for fun,
And he lathered us with bacon grease and balsam gum.

CHORUS

At last the job was over: Black Toby said: "We're through
With the little Abitibi and the survey crew."
'Twas a wonderful experience and this I know,
I'll never go again to North Ontario.

CHORUS

Source: Elizabeth Mouland, ed., *Tracing One Warm Line: Poetry of Canada* (St John's: Breakwater Books, 1994), 188-9. Copyright 1957, Southern Music Publishing Company (Canada) Ltd.

Félix-Antoine Savard (1896–1982)

"Wild Geese"

Félix-Antoine Savard, priest and writer, was one of Quebec's best-known popular writers. Born in the Saguenay, his imagination fired by the Charlevoix region, Savard combined practical leadership in the colonization of the Abitibi region with deep study of the classics. His novel *Menaud, maître-draveur*, published in 1937, reads like an epic poem, with its powerful central character driven to his tragic end through the cycle of the seasons. From the 1940s, Savard was dean of arts at Laval University, a fellow of the Royal Society of Canada, and a passionate defender of French Canada's traditions.

Savard's essay on wild geese speaks to both a reality and a symbol. To many Canadians, the V-shaped flights of Canada geese are harbingers of the change of the seasons. To Savard, they represent more – a dependable sense of direction, a sharing of leadership, and the fidelity of animals who share the misfortunes of each member, staying with any bird that is sick or injured during the flight.

A beautiful poem could be written about their transcontinental wings, their punctual and rectilinear flight, their finetuned travels, their loyalty to their native reeds.

And then there is the tenacity of their love; enlivening their hard-working feathers, it stabs at the wind and fog with its stubborn, obstinate, invincible beak. This hardened, imperturbable flesh flies or, put another way, prevails over its own weight, moving with the agility of desire through the eddies of the inextricable night along its lucid, infallible course.

They arrive in the spring, at night, on the south wind, through the sky's upper passageways.

Through the sky's upper passageways, through the great aerial space, condescending only to make the traditional stops in the odd marine meadow, intending no more than to nest in the tundra reeds. They haughtily and instinctively scorn the cities, the fields, the waters, the woods and everything natural, human or other that does not fit into their designs of love.

They advance in angular formation, an ensemble, joined to the lead goose by an invisible thread. Tirelessly, they maintain this mysterious geometry, each independently craning towards its own destiny, but always united, always oblique, ceaselessly brought back by social instinct to that single precise point that signifies direction, solidarity, unanimous penetration into the hard air and the dangerous journey.

Theirs is a democracy we would do well to study, their collective will straight and firm, their light-hearted obedience to the discipline of alignment, the virtue of the captain goose who, once his government is exhausted, cedes his place to another and simply takes up the rear. No concern beyond his own eurhythmy, no recompense beyond the song of his wings behind other wings and the victory of space traversed.

And, after days and days of transmigration, at the night wind's extremity, the shores finally gleam, and the ruddy sands at the base of Cap Tourmente finally appear – a love stop before the ultimate vast nesting lands. And then the winged triangle fragments and the geese fall, confused, rowdy, beating down like the blinding downpour of an April dawn.

This is where they make love, swinging, pirouetting in precise balance, feathers blooming, wings offering wings all the passion and joy of enraptured hearts before the long days of cloistered nesting among the northern reeds.

The nuptials begin when the shore welcomes spring and the great marine purge summons the green warmth rising from the denuded river. Movement, love, joy, winged life perpetually beating above the silt, incantatory and fertilizing flight over an inert mass waiting to be born: it is mid-May and spring is being hatched in all its fullness.

Ripe, oviferous, intoxicated by the liquid enveloping all that surrounds them, the geese now await their departure. They listen to the great penetrating hum; they sound out the wind, watch the immense blue waves rolling before them, carrying sap, perfumes,

exhalations. They spend long hours on the rocky sands of the isles, ready, palpitating, spreading their feathers, opening their wings to the stream of life that arouses their flesh. The hour comes at last, and their flight takes shape anew. In long strips, above the isles, the fields, the shores, above the garden of spring, they sway like the branch of a flowering apple tree. Then, one night, with the wind, the great wind of the sea, the great wind of the woods, the deep wind of space, they disappear.

The final stage of their journey, the longest, the hardest. Pointing north, the geese have realigned with the meridian of love; and endlessly beneath them, vegetation, waters abounding, countless lakes amid branched rivers.

Lofty, imperturbable, they battle against themselves, against the still raging squalls, their sharp beaks tenacious in the icy wind. They battle against the night, exalted by the constellations flying above, charmed by the hum in the syrinx of their wings. They blindly battle against everything, fortified by their charge: fragile shells, precious treasure of the future, sole destiny of a long-coursing race.

They are invincible because their love for the familial nest is heroic, set at the ends of the earth, among three distaffs, somewhere in the home of the tundra.

Admirable, admirable, intrepid and loyal. What marvels you teach me!

Source: André Morency, ed., *L'Abatis* (Montreal: Fides), 29-32.

Donald Creighton (1902–79)

"THE EMPIRE OF THE ST. LAWRENCE"

Donald Grant Creighton was probably English-speaking Canada's premier historian during much of his lifetime. An instructor and professor at the University of Toronto for forty-four years, he came to believe that Canada had been formed because it lay along the St. Lawrence and the Great Lakes transportation system and had been extended by the man-made Canadian Pacific Railway to the Pacific. Those who had fought for this transportation system, be they the Montreal merchants of the 1830s or his special hero, Sir John A. Macdonald, were the heroes of Canada; those who opposed it, be they Louis-Joseph Papineau's Patriotes or George Brown's mean-spirited Grits, were Canada's enemies. While many more people read his two-volume biography of Macdonald, the book that defined his approach to Canadian history was *The Empire of the St. Lawrence*, published in 1956.

Creighton's "Laurentian" thesis and his Tory nationalism influenced generations of Canadian historians but he had critics too. Few in twentieth-century Canada sympathized with the wealthy Montrealers or their railway. Further, Creighton had no respect for Quebec nationalism or regional discontent, and these elements of his thinking attracted much hostility. What no one denied, however, was the old-fashioned elegance of Creighton's writing and the irascible passion of his patriotism.

Chance flung the first English colonists on the edges of the Atlantic seaboard and opened the single great eastern waterway of the interior to the French. In the history of the different economies, of the cultural patterns which were to dominate North American life, these were acts of first importance. For each cultural group, the English and the French, fell heir to one of America's geographic provinces, and both these regions had their laws, their promises and their portentous meanings. Of the two, the Atlantic seaboard conformed more nearly to the geographic conditions of western Europe, which had been for centuries a forcing-house of nations. It was, for North America, a fairly small and compact area, sharply defined by obvious natural frontiers. From the coastline the land stretched westward to rise at last in the ridges of the Appalachians, which were unbroken from the St. Lawrence valley to the Floridas, save where the Hudson-Mohawk system gave access to the west. It was a boundary; but during colonial times it was not a barrier in the sense that it confined a restless and ambitious people determined upon its assault. Because they shaped the courses of the rivers, the mountains helped to focus the attention of the English-

Americans upon that other boundary of the Atlantic seaboard, the ocean. Their faces were turned east rather than west; and during the greater part of the colonial period, the commercial energies of the population were concentrated in the numerous short rivers, in the bays and sounds and harbours which fretted the coastline, and sought their objectives eastward on the sea. For New England especially, whose economy was based upon its fisheries, the pull of the coastline and the submerged continental shelf beyond it, was enormous. The prohibitions, the invitations and the varieties of this seaboard empire directed, in a kindly fashion, the energies of an adaptive people. While the land configuration concentrated their pursuits, the climate and soil gave them variety. The area meant stolidity, gradual settlement, the inescapable necessity to produce and the possibility of diversified production. Seaward, it meant a commercial empire which would cease to be imperial because it would inevitably become oceanic.

The river up which Cartier ventured gave entrance to the totally different dominion of the north. It was a landscape marked off from the other geographic provinces of the new continent by the almost monotonously massive character of its design. A huge triangle of rocky upland lay bounded by a river and a string of giant lakes. It was a solemn country, with that ungainly splendour evoked by great, crude, sweeping lines and immense and clumsy masses. The marks of age and of terrific experience lay heavy upon it. It was an elemental portion of the earth, harshly shaped by the brutal catastrophes of geological history. The enormous flat bulk of the Precambrian formation was not only the core of the whole Canadian system, but it was also the ancient nucleus of the entire continent. It lay, old and sombre and ravaged, nearly two million square miles in extent. The ice masses, during the glacial period, had passed over and beyond it, and they had scarred and wrenched and altered the entire landscape in their advance and their retreat. Scouring the surface of the Shield itself, pouring boulder clay into the valleys to the south, the ice sheets had hollowed the beds of new lakes and had diverted the courses of ancient rivers. There was left a drainage system, grand in its extent and in the volume of its waters, but youthful, wilful and turbulent. The wrinkled senility of the Precambrian formation was touched by a curious appearance of youth. The countless meaningless lakes and lakelets, the intricately meandering rivers and spillways, the abrupt falls and treacherous rapids, which covered the face of the Shield, seemed to express the renewal of its primitive strength. To the south, below the Shield, the ice masses had throttled the waters into new lakes and had dammed the St. Lawrence into a long southern loop, leaving Niagara, the Long Sault and Lachine as evidence of the novelty of its course.

The Canadian Shield and the river system which seamed and which encircled it, were overwhelmingly the most important physical features of the area. They were the bone and the blood-tide of the northern economy. Rock and water complemented each other, fought each other's battles and forced each other's victories. The Shield itself, a huge lop-sided triangle, whose northern points were Labrador and the Arctic east of the Mackenzie, occupied over one-half of the land area which was to become the Dominion of Canada. For the French and for their successors it was unescapable and domineering. It hugged the north shore of the St. Lawrence as the river issued from the continent. Westward, in the centre of the lowlands of the St. Lawrence, the good lands began to peter out a hundred miles north of Lake Ontario in the scarred, blank rock, thin soil sheet and towering evergreens peculiar to the Shield. Relentlessly it followed the north shore of Lakes Huron and Superior and at last struck north and west for the Arctic Ocean. Its long, flat, undeviating plateau effected the complete severance of the St. Lawrence lowlands from the western plains. In the east it helped, with the northern spurs of the Appalachians, to cut off Acadia from Quebec. Settlement starved and shrivelled on the Shield; it offered a sullen inhospitality to those occupations which were traditional in western Europe and which had been transferred by the first immigrants to the Atlantic seaboard of North America. But from the beginning it exercised an imperious domination over the northerners, for though it was a harsh and an exacting country, it offered lavish prizes to the restless, the ambitious and the daring. It was an area of staples, creating simple trades and undiversified extractive industries; and its furs, its forests and its minerals were to attract three great assaulting waves of northerners. Fur was the first great staple of the north. And with the fur trade, the Precambrian formation began its long career in the Canadian economy as a primary, instead of as a subsidiary, economic region. It was upon these ancient rocks that the central emphasis of the Canadian system was placed at first, and the initial importance of the Shield is of deep significance in the history of the economy of the north.

To the south lay the lowlands of the St. Lawrence. Here the intense winters of the Precambrian formation were softened and the hot, bright summers flamed more slowly out of long springtimes and faded gradually into reluctant autumns. North of the lakes, the lowlands stretched from Quebec city to Georgian Bay – a narrow but slowly, broadening band of fertility, crowded a little oppressively by the sombre masses of the Shield. South and west, beyond the river and the lakes, they lapsed easily into the central lowlands of the continent and the basin of the Mississippi. In the centre of this rich region lay that immense organization of waters which issued from the continent by the river of Canada; and this drainage system, driving seaward in a great, proud arc from Lake Superior to the city of Quebec, was the fact of all facts in the history of the northern half of the continent. It commanded an imperial domain. Westward, its acquisitive fingers groped into the territory of the plains. Aggressively it entrenched upon the dominion of the Mississippi. It grasped the Shield, reached southward into the valley of the Hudson and at last rolled massively seaward between sombre approaches which curved away southward into the Maritimes and rose north-eastward past Quebec and Labrador to Newfoundland.

It was the one great river which led from the eastern shore into the heart of the continent. It possessed a geographical monopoly; and it shouted its uniqueness to adventurers. The river meant mobility and distance; it invited journeyings; it promised immense expanses, unfolding, flowing away into remote and changing horizons. The whole west, with all its riches, was the dominion of the river. To the unfettered and ambitious, it offered a pathway to the central mysteries of the continent. The river meant movement, transport, a ceaseless passage west and east, the long procession of river-craft – canoes, *bateaux*, timber rafts and steamboats – which followed each other into history. It seemed the destined pathway of North American trade; and from the river there rose, like an exhalation, the dream of western commercial empire. The river was to be the basis of a great transportation system by which the manufactures of the old world could be exchanged for the staple products of the new. This was the faith of successive generations of northerners. The dream of the commercial empire of the St. Lawrence runs like an obsession through the whole of Canadian history; and men followed each other through life, planning and toiling to achieve it. The river was not only a great actuality: it was the central truth of a religion. Men lived by it, at once consoled and inspired by its promises, its whispered suggestions, and its shouted commands; and it was a force in history, not merely because of its accomplishments, but because of its shining, ever-receding possibilities.

For something stood between the design and its fulfilment. There was, in the very geography of the region itself, a root defect, a fundamental weakness, which foreshadowed enormous difficulties, even though it did not pre-determine defeat. In the centre, by Lake Ontario and the lower reaches of the river, the drive of the great waterway was unquestioned and peremptory. But this power was not indefinitely transmissible, and the pull of a system stretching over two thousand miles was at long last relaxed and weakened. The outer defences of the St. Lawrence contradicted its inward solidity; its boundaries were not bold and definite, but a smudged faint tracery. Between the valley of the St. Lawrence on the one hand and the valleys of Hudson Bay, the Mississippi and the Hudson river on the other, the separating heights of land were low and facile; and over these perfunctory defences invasions might pass as easily as sorties. The river's continuity was broken at Niagara: it stumbled and faltered at the Cascades, the Cedars and Lachine. As it drove east and north past Quebec and into its immense estuary, the river was caught, its influence narrowed and focused by the uplands of the Shield to the north and the rolling highlands of the Appalachians below. There were breaks and obstacles; and over both its seaward approaches and its continental extremities the hold of the river closed and again relaxed, uncertainly and unconvincingly. Yet for all its inward contradictions and its outward weakness, the river was a unit, and its central entrance was dominated by the rock of Quebec and the island of Montreal.

Source: Donald Creighton, *The Empire of the St. Lawrence: A Study in Commerce and Politics* (Toronto: Macmillan, 1956), 3-7.

Frank R. Scott (1899-1985)

"W.L.M.K."

Frank R. Scott was a poet, socialist, and professor of law who made an enormous contribution to Canadian cultural and political life.

In his poem "W.L.M.K." (1954), Scott expresses the familiar view of Canada's seemingly dullest and yet most enduring national leader, William Lyon Mackenzie King. From 1921 to 1948, King was prime minister for all but five years. During that period, Canada developed from a debt-burdened, deeply divided, self-governing colony into a major middle power with the world's second-highest standard of living.

Yet most Canadians would have echoed Scott's complaints about a leader who avoided dynamic leadership, whose principles seemed to be made of jelly, and whose chief ingenuity was in knowing how to avoid making decisions and in travelling a little behind public opinion. The discovery, after King's death in 1950, that he had been a fervent believer in spiritualism, communicating with his dead mother and with various prominent figures of the past, made King even more embarrassing to Scott and other Canadians of his era. Yet, in retrospect, the Canada King left to his heirs seems uniquely blessed and united. Perhaps Canadians have always had trouble appreciating the virtues of their leaders. And certainly Canada is a lot harder to manage than it seemed to King's contemporaries.

How shall we speak of Canada,
Mackenzie King dead?
The Mother's boy in the lonely room
With his dog, his medium and his ruins?

He blunted us.

We had no shape
Because he never took sides,

And no sides
Because he never allowed them to take
    shape.

He skillfully avoided what was wrong
Without saying what was right,
And never let his on the one hand
Know what his on the other hand was
    doing.

The height of his ambition
Was to pile a Parliamentary Committee on a
    Royal Commission,
To have 'conscription if necessary
But not necessarily conscription',
To let Parliament decide –
Later.

Postpone, postpone, abstain.

Only one thread was certain:
After World War I
Business as usual,
After World War
Orderly decontrol.
Always he led us back to where we were
    before.

He seemed to be in the centre
Because we had no centre,
No vision
To pierce the smoke-screen of his politics.

Truly he will be remembered
Wherever men honour ingenuity,
Ambiguity, inactivity, and political longevity.

Let us raise up a temple
To the cult of mediocrity,
Do nothing by halves
Which can be done by quarters.

Source: Margaret Atwood, ed., *The New Oxford Book of Canadian Verse in English* (Toronto: University of Toronto Press, 1982), 92.

Ringuet (1895–1960)

MONTREAL IN THE 1950S

Montreal was long the great cosmopolitan metropolis of Canada: the meeting point of French and English, the centre of Canada's wealth and much of its manufacturing, and the home of its richest as well as poorest people. Created as a military outpost for New France, developed as a fur-trading centre, it was totally French until the Conquest of 1760, predominantly English-speaking through much of the nineteenth century, and overwhelmingly francophone by the end of the twentieth.

Ringuet was best known for his 1938 novel, *Trente arpents*, the final stage of that celebration of rural life that had begun with Arthur Buies (1840–1901) and Louis Hémon (1880–1913). His real name was Philippe Panneton. Born in Trois-Rivières, he trained as a doctor but in 1946 began a diplomatic career, first as cultural attaché in Brazil and later as ambassador to Portugal, where he died. His description of Montreal, written about 1956, describes a city that remains recognizable today.

ontreal? To anyone arriving from France, Montreal is a very American city. But to those coming from the United States – and let me point out that I didn't say, as they so often do in France, "to anyone coming from America," which is nonsensical – so, to anyone arriving from the United States, Montreal is indubitably a French city. At least its eastern half, the half that is in fact closer by several kilometres to the French coast. Depending on whether you find yourself in the French-Canadian or the Anglophone half, you French will feel more or less at home. Signs are sometimes in French, sometimes in English. Some are even in both. Not that anything gets repeated. It's just that the signs are a bit like certain French Canadians of whom a journalist once jokingly said, "They are perfectly bilingual, speaking English and French at the same time!" And these are the Montrealers whom the French usually find it difficult to understand in their first weeks here. None of this, however, changes the statistically proven fact that, in sheer numbers, Montreal is the second largest French city in the world. The majority here speak French. And the fact that a certain number of Montrealers don't understand the language or understand it poorly can't take away the city's much beloved title. Does everyone in Marseille speak the *langue d'oïl*?

Mount Royal, a city park, is forever the heart of Montreal. And since Montreal is an island, there is the river, one which takes itself pretty seriously. It is laden with boats during the four months of the year in which the ice isn't forcing it to hibernate. With its canals, it conveys ocean-going vessels to the heart of the continent; towards the factories of Toronto, the mills of Chicago, the silos of Fort William. Montreal, meanwhile, is growing. Its outskirts are being peopled by the suburban dwellings of small home owners: civil servants and labourers.

And the city has revived several theatres, just when we thought for a second that movie houses had killed off live theatre forever. Some of these movies, by the way, are Canadian. Theatre troupes that only recently were amateur are now professional. Didn't we send a sampling of our actors to Paris five years ago and didn't the French approve? Our writers are publishing, having come out of their provincial rut. And, a fact not to be scoffed at, I don't think there's another North American city in which you can find a coq au vin so perfectly basted with such excellent Burgundy. You even have a dozen excellent caterers from which to choose.

French can be heard on the radio. The bus driver will announce Lagauchetière and Carrières Streets in a Normandy accent. And Montreal hasn't forgotten that she descends from a country called New France or that she belongs to a province whose motto is *"Je me souviens"* (I remember).

Source: Michel Le Bel and Jean-Marcel Paquette, *Le Québec par ses textes littéraires, 1534-1976* (Montreal: Fernand Nathan, 1979), 202-3.

Irving Layton (1912—)

"FROM COLONY TO NATION"

Canadians are not particularly prone to think positively about themselves. Deep down, they are as proud as anyone about what they have done, individually and collectively, but they tend to wait for the rest of the world to celebrate their achievements. Since their closest neighbours, the Americans, and the French and British are largely preoccupied with themselves, Canadians often have a long and frustrating wait for approval. Others might describe the Canadian frame of mind as a national inferiority complex.

Irving Layton, born in Romania and raised in Montreal, was one of a highly talented group of young poets who shaped Canada's post-war literary life. A proud Jew and no shrinking violet, he displayed a brutal vulgarity that shocked and secretly delighted Canadians who already suspected that they were closer to Layton's description than they cared to admit. Like most Canadians, Layton had to admire the grandeur of the land to which his parents had brought him, but what kind of a people would make a national symbol of their red-coated policeman, tax themselves heavily to preserve the rural idiocy of the family farm, and favour the wisdom of the censor over the insight of the poet? Yet Layton's scolding did not keep Canadian universities from giving him employment and the means for a moderately licentious life.

A dull people,
but the rivers of this country
are wide and beautiful

A dull people
enamoured of childish games,
but food is easily come by
and plentiful

Some with a priest's voice
in their cage of ribs: but
on high mountain-tops and in thunderstorms
the chirping is not heard

Deferring to beadle and censor;
not ashamed for this,
but given over to horseplay,
the making of money

A dull people, without charm or ideas,
settling into the clean empty look
of a Mountie or dairy farmer
as into a legacy

One can ignore them
(the silences, the vast distances help)
and suppose them at the bottom

of one of the meaner lakes,
their bones not even picked for souvenirs.

Source: F.R. Scott and A.J.M. Smith, *The Blasted Pine* (Toronto: Macmillan, 1956), 3-4.

John Diefenbaker (1895—1979)

CANADIAN NATIONAL POLITICS

When he became prime minister in 1957, John George Diefenbaker bore little resemblance to the succession of Conservatives who had held power since Confederation. A son of German and Scottish parents, he had grown up in pioneer-era Saskatchewan and forged his career as a successful defence counsel and leader of the tiny, fragmented provincial Conservative Party.

When Diefenbaker first sought the Tory leadership, critics mocked his Germanic name and scorned him as a prairie windbag. In 1956 he won despite them and in 1957 he became prime minister. Not since his hero, Sir John A. Macdonald, had there been such talk of a national vision; not since Laurier had there been bolder national rhetoric. Here is Diefenbaker in February 1958, on his way to the greatest electoral mandate Canadians had ever given a political leader:

This party has become the party of national destiny. I hope it will be the party of vision and courage. The party of one Canada, with equal opportunities to all. The only party that can give to youth an Elizabethan sense of grand design – that's my challenge. The faith to venture with enthusiasm to the frontiers of a nation; that faith, that assurance that will be provided with a government strong enough to implement plans for development.

To the young men and women of this nation, I say, Canada is within your hands. Adventure. Adventure to the nation's utmost bounds, to strive, to seek, to find and not to yield. The policies that will be placed before the people of Canada in this campaign will be ones that ensure that today and this century will belong to Canada. The destination is one Canada. To that end I dedicate this party . . .

Source: Speech in the Winnipeg Civic Auditorium, February 12, 1958, in Michael Bliss, ed., *Canadian History in Documents* (Toronto: Ryerson Press, 1966), 334-5.

As prime minister, Diefenbaker believed that he had triumphed over the barriers his background had created for him, even in his own party. In 1958 *Maclean's* magazine quoted the new prime minister's defence of "un-hyphenated" Canadianism:

I am the first prime minister of this country of neither altogether English nor French origin. So I determined that that was the thing I was going to do. I never deviated from that course, and I determined to bring about a Canadian citizenship that knew no hyphenated consideration.

At university they used to laugh about this dedication to a certain purpose. I said: "You will never build a Canada on this basis, when every ten years a person has to register on the basis of his paternal origin. You will never build a Canada on that." If you look the records up you will see that I spoke on that at the university. And when I made my first speech in parliament in June of 1940, that was it, and on the 11th of August, 1944, I came back to it again and I said: "This is wrong." I said that those who served in the Canadian Armed Forces with "Canada" on their shoulderstraps, when

they came back, were going to have to register again according to their racial origins. Mr. Mackenzie King said he would join with me.

I said that I never thought of Roosevelt as a Dutch-American or General Eisenhower as a German-American, or Pershing as a German-American. I said that they were all Americans and that we were building up in Canada this hyphenated citizenship, and I said, "That is what I am going to change."

Well, I never deviated from this purpose. It's the reason I went into public life. That is what I said I was going to do. I am very happy to be able to say that in the House of Commons today in my party we have members of Italian, Dutch, German, Scandinavian, Chinese and Ukrainian origin – and they are all Canadians.

Source: *Maclean's*, March 29, 1958, 57-8.

Diefenbaker's defence of nationalism was characteristically convoluted but his love for his vision of Canada was unequivocal. His lack of ability in French did not prevent him from defending bilingualism and biculturalism, two concepts that seemed in the 1960s to offer reconciliation to the two cultural and linguistic solitudes of Canada. In his *Memoirs* he recalled a letter he had written to a student in 1964:

As to bilingualism and biculturalism these are two necessary and inescapable facets of Canadian nationality. Canada was conceived of by men of two different equally rich cultures, or two distinctive communities. Bilingualism and biculturalism are facets of Canadian life that cannot – and should not – be hidden or avoided. They are important, even vital, to Canada as a nation. But they are assets, not liabilities, positive factors, not negative ones.

They should be approached in the spirit of co-operation and mutual appreciation and never used as tools of narrow nationalism. They are too valuable to Canadians to be degraded by being used to further the ends of political expediency or as weapons in factional feuding.

Source: John G. Diefenbaker, *One Canada: Memoirs of the Right Honourable John G. Diefenbaker – The Tumultuous Years 1962 to 1967* (Toronto: Macmillan, 1977), 250-1.

Later, however, Diefenbaker was one of the few MPs of any party to oppose the Official Languages Act of 1969.

Georges Vanier (1888–1967)

"WE ARE ALL GOD'S CHILDREN"

Georges-Philéas Vanier was the first francophone governor general of Canada. After winning three decorations and losing a leg in the First World War, Vanier commanded the Royal 22nd Regiment and joined the Canadian delegations at the League of Nations and in London. During the Second World War Vanier served as ambassador to all Allied governments in exile in London. From 1944 to 1953 he was ambassador to France, and in 1959 he was appointed governor general.

Vanier brought a great deal of dignity to his position. His term in office was marked by the beginnings of the Quebec independence movement, including its terrorist arm. In his installation speech, Vanier focused on the reconciliation between English and French 200 years after the battle of the Plains of Abraham. Deeply influenced by his first-hand observations of the evils of intolerance in Europe, he symbolized and eloquently advocated the search for common purpose and unity among Canadians.

Mr. Prime Minister, my first words are a prayer. May Almighty God in his infinite wisdom and mercy bless the sacred mission which has been entrusted to me by Her Majesty the Queen and help me to fulfil it in all humility. In exchange for his strength, I offer him my weakness. May he give peace to this beloved land of ours and, to those who live in it, the grace of mutual understanding, respect and love.

I shall have the honour to convey to Her Majesty the message of devotion and loyalty to which you have given expression on behalf of the people of Canada. The recent visit of our Sovereign to this country, with His Royal Highness the Duke of Edinburgh, has made of the word loyalty a synonym of affection. The Queen has established with Canadians a bond personal rather than formal. Aptly does Shakespeare evoke this feeling in Henry VI: "My crown is in my heart, not on my head." Is it surprising that such a crown should find its way into our hearts as well?

We are deeply grateful, my wife and I, for the generous terms and the charming way in which you have welcomed us.

I am happy to pay tribute to my predecessor, the first Canadian governor-general.[*] He had to blaze a new trail and well has he done it. During seven and a half years, never sparing himself, he has laboured with fortitude and devotion in the service of his Sovereign and his country. His place is very high in the list of those who have had the honour to represent the Crown in Canada. From the bottom of my heart I thank him for the assistance and advice he has given me. I have no illusions about being able to equal his achievement.

We are indeed fortunate in being attached to the Crown which holds for the world a promise of peace. It is well to recall that the Queen is the symbol of the free association of member nations of the Commonwealth and as such is accepted as its head. The total area of the Commonwealth is estimated to be about fourteen and a half million square miles and its population something in the neighbourhood of six hundred and fifty millions.

Canada forms part of this mighty far-flung Commonwealth, which is composed of many races and creeds. What a power is there for good in the world, what a power to right many wrongs, to solve many problems, in amity, without recourse to arms! Does not the very thought of the Commonwealth's potential action conjure up a vision inspiring in scope and grandeur?

You have drawn attention, Mr. Prime Minister, to the significance of this day. How right you are. Two hundred years ago, a certain country won a battle on the Plains of Abraham; another country lost a battle. In the annals of every nation, there is a record of victories and defeats. The present Sovereign of the victorious country, Sovereign also of Canada now, returns to the same battle-field, two centuries later, and presents colours to a French-speaking regiment, which mounts guard over the Citadel

---

[*] Vincent Massey (1887-1967)

of Quebec, a regiment of which Her Majesty is colonel-in-chief.

And how is the battle of 1759 commemorated? By a monument, erected in 1828, to the memory of both commanding generals, who died in action. It bears the inscription in Latin: "Valour gave them a common death, history a common fame, posterity a common monument." Is there a better way to heal the wounds of war, to seal the bonds of peace?

The sixty thousand French Canadians of 1759 have become several millions. For two thousand years, more or less, the annals of history proclaim the fame and glory of Great Britain and France. The future of Canada is linked with this double fabulous heritage. Canadians of Anglo-Saxon and French descent, whose two cultures will always be a source of mutual enrichment, are an inspiring example of coexistence. They go forward hand in hand to make Canada a great nation, hand in hand also with Canadians of every origin, with their heritages, irrespective of race or creed. We are all God's children.

Each one of us, in his own way and place, however humble, must play his part towards the fulfilment of our national destiny. To realize how mighty this destiny will be, let us lift our eyes beyond the horizon of our time. In our march forward in material happiness, let us not neglect the spiritual threads in the weaving of our lives. If Canada is to attain the greatness worthy of it, each of us must say, "I ask only to serve."

Source: George Cowley and Michel Vanier, eds., *Only to Serve: Selections from Addresses of Governor General Georges P. Vanier* (Toronto: University of Toronto Press, 1970), 4-5.

Jean-Paul Desbiens (Frère Untel) (1927–)

ON "JOUAL"

As a priest, writer, and philosopher, Jean-Paul Desbiens played an important role in setting the stage for Quebec's Quiet Revolution. His book *Les Insolences du Frère Untel* (The Insolences of Brother Anonymous), a scathing critique of Quebec's educational system, was first published in 1960. The Church sent him out of Quebec in 1961, but he returned in 1964 to work first as a reformer in the Ministry of Education and later as a school principal and columnist for *La Presse*. In this selection from *Les Insolences du Frère Untel*, Desbiens attacks the use of "joual" on the part of French-speakers.

"Joual" is a term from popular French slang deriving from a mispronunciation of the word for horse, "cheval." It is a language spoken by the man on the street, the average Quebecker. Over the past generation there has been an interesting debate within French Quebec on the merits of "joual." Some analysts have seen it as a patois articulating the authentic voice of the people of Quebec, and it has been popularized in the songs of Robert Charlebois (1945–) and the plays of Michel Tremblay (1942–). Desbiens is solidly hostile to joual, seeing it as an "absence of language" and as related to a general ignorance on the part of the younger generation of French Quebeckers. What is the purpose of preserving French in North America, he asks, if the language has been debased and robbed of its sophistication and precision?

We are proud of being vanquished, we play and work as vanquished men. We laugh, we weep, we love, we write, we sing as the vanquished. All our moral and intellectual life can be explained by this single fact, that we are cowardly and dishonoured vanquished men.

LEON BLOY

In October, 1959, André Laurendeau published a short column in *Le Devoir* in which he qualified the speech of French Canadian students as "joual talk." He, not I, invented the name. It was well chosen. The thing and the name are alike, both hateful. The word joual is a summary description of what it is like to talk joual, to say *joual* instead of *cheval*, horse. It is to talk as horses would talk if they had not long since plumped for the silence and the smile of Fernandel.

Our pupils talk joual, write joual, and don't want to talk or write any other way. Joual is their language. Things have gone so far that they can't even tell a mistake when it is shown them at pencil point. "The man what I talk to," "We are going to undress themselves," and the like do not bother them. In fact such expressions seem elegant to them. It is a little

different when it comes to mistakes in spelling, and if a lack of agreement between noun and adjective or the omission of an *s* is pointed out, they can identify the error. But the vice is deeply rooted at the grammatical level, and on the level of pronunciation. Out of twenty pupils whose names you ask at the opening of school, not more than two or three will be comprehensible the first time. The others will have to repeat theirs. They say their names as if they were confessing a sin.

Joual is a boneless language. The consonants are all slurred, a little like the speech of Hawaiian dancers, according to the records I have heard. Oula-oula-oula-alao-alao-alao. They say *chu pas apable* for *je ne suis pas capable.* (I am not able.) I can't write joual down phonetically. It can't be fixed in writing for it is a decomposition, and only Edgar Poe could fix a decomposition. You know the story where he tells of the hypnotist who succeeded in freezing the decomposition of a corpse – it's a wonderful horror story.

Joual, this absence of language, is a symptom of our non-existence as French Canadians. No one can ever study language enough, for it is the home of all meanings. Our inability to assert ourselves, our refusal to accept the future, our obsession with the past, are all reflected in joual, our real language. Witness the abundance of negative turns of speech in our talk. Instead of saying that a woman is beautiful, we say she's not bad-looking; instead of saying that a pupil is intelligent, we say he's not stupid; instead of saying that we feel well, we say we're not too bad.

The day it appeared I read Laurendeau's comment to my class. My pupils realized that they spoke joual. One of them said, almost proudly, "We've founded a new language." They saw no need to change. "Everybody talks like us," they told me. Some said, "People would laugh at us if we talked differently from the others." One said – and it is a diabolical objection – "Why should we talk otherwise when everybody understands us?" It's not easy for a teacher, taken unaware, to answer this last proposition, which was made to me one afternoon.

Of course joual-speakers understand each other. But do you want to live your life among joual-speakers? As long as you want merely to chat about sports and the weather, as long as you talk only such crap, joual does very well. For primitives, a primitive language is good enough; animals get along with a few grunts. But if you want to attain to human speech, joual is not sufficient. You can make do with a board and some whitewash if you want to paint a barn, but finer tools are necessary for the Mona Lisa.

Now we approach the heart of the problem, which is a problem of civilization. Our pupils speak joual because they think joual, and they think joual because they live joual, like everybody around here. Living joual means rock-'n'roll, hot dogs, parties, running around in cars. All our civilization is joual. Efforts on the level of language don't accomplish anything, these competitions, campaigns for better French, congresses, all that stuff. We must act on the level of civilization, which is easy to say, but what can we do? What can a teacher, buried in his school, do to halt the decay? His efforts are ridiculous. Whatever he accomplishes is lost an hour later. From four o'clock on, he is in the wrong. The whole culture contradicts him, contradicts what he defends, tramples on what he preaches, makes fun of him. I am not old, I am not very peevish. I like teaching, and yet I despair of teaching French.

* * *

The Quebec Government ought to require respect by law for the French language in the names of companies and in their advertising. I understand that manufacturers and big trading companies must at some time or other appear before the Government to be registered or be legally recognized. That's the time the Government should lie in wait for them. "Give yourselves French names, advertise in French, or we don't know you," it can say. Then we would have no more Thivierge Electric, or Chicoutimi Moving, or Turcotte Tire Service. If these two spheres, titles and advertising, were watched as closely as Laurentide Park, the language would be saved right there. But will the Government be realistic enough to do that?

We can be practical and still lack realism; shall we ever have a Government that will not be satisfied to be practical, and so in the end be made a fool of, but that will be realistic? Who can estimate all the harm practical people have done us by lack of realism?

* * *

I had already published three or four letters in *Le Devoir* in which I had expressed my views, and numerous readers had been writing in during some five months, when the matter of *O Canada* suddenly came up. There was a fine rumpus. I had conceived the idea of asking my students (11th year commercial) to write the first stanza of our national anthem, later on I asked the 10th and 11th year in science. The result of this inquiry was distressing beyond all expectation. We expected some mistakes in spelling, but we were really flabbergasted by what we got. Here are bits of the joual version: *Au Canada, taire de nos ailleux,* for *O Canada, terre de nos aïeux* (Land of our fathers). For *Ton front est ceint de fleurons glorieux* (Thy brow is wreathed with glorious flowers) we got *Ton front est sain, ton front essaim, ton front est sein de flocons,* and several other variations. *Et ta valeur de foi trempée* (thy valor tempered by faith) came out *Et cavaleurs de froid trempé, de voir trembler, de foie tremblay,* and so on. (They were like the girl who sang "And laid him on the green," in The Bonny Earl of Moray every time as "Lady Mondegreen.")

Laurendeau remarked, "No use getting angry. But might we ask a few questions? *Taire de nos ailleux* makes nonsense, but could it have some hidden meaning? And *cavaleurs de foi tremblée,* could that mean us, cavaliers of shaky faith maybe?"

* * *

Just considering our weakness in French is not enough. We must also consider the almost complete lack of any civic or patriotic education in our schools for the past twenty years, the incompetence and irresponsibility of many of our teachers, the incompetence and irresponsibility of our Department of Public Instruction. But only an anti-clerical would take our Department to task. So then we have the best system of education in the world. The *Jeunesse Ouvrière Catholique* report doesn't show that, but never mind. We are a hundred and fifty years ahead of all other countries as to the essential thing (which is Heaven), aren't we? The proof that all is well lies in the absence of any quarrels over the schools since 1867. Another proof is that the Council of Public Instruction meets only once in fifty-two years. The last meeting before this year's was in 1908, and then they met only to congratulate each other, promoting each other to sainthood. We have nightmare programs and incredible textbooks. Just take a look at Verhelst's *Essentials of Philosophy,* and see what a Belgian canon can accomplish when he undertakes to sweat out philosophy to the glory of God (evidently) and the salvation of souls (evidently).

My inquiry on *Au Canada* showed that there is no more patriotic education in the schools. I think it showed a few other things. I have proof now that almost everywhere in the Province they've begun to write and explain our national anthem. It's a beginning. And I also have the proof that I can reach the teachers through *Le Devoir*.

Good old *Devoir*, brotherly old *Devoir*, cheers! Cheers for good old Filion!* They've been saying that you grow old and prudent. No matter, you struck a stout blow for freedom.

And cheers for you, Laurendeau, so sensitive and human, and for all the staff of *Le Devoir*. How I would like to meet a bishop of whom I would want to say, Cheers, good old bishop! I don't say there aren't any, but I've never met one.

Source: Jean-Paul Desbiens, *The Impertinences of Brother Anonymous*, trans. Miriam Chapin (Montreal: Harvest House, 1962), 27-36.

---

* Gérard Filion, publisher of *Le Devoir*.

Part Four
1960 to the Present

Leonard Cohen (1934–)

"THE ONLY TOURIST IN HAVANA TURNS HIS THOUGHTS HOMEWARD"

Leonard Cohen grew up in Westmount, graduated from McGill, and was the youngest of a group of gifted Montreal poets. At the same time, as an equally gifted composer, entertainer, and novelist, Cohen became the best known of Canada's modern poets and one of the most accessible. Conservative in technique, often escapist in theme, self-deprecating but proud in person, Cohen has provoked considerable criticism from his fellow poets, partly because of his poetic style but also because of his commercial success.

What did a Canadian think about in Havana in April 1961, only months after Fidel Castro's Marxist revolution? In these times, how many wonderful Canadian nationalist fantasies were on the verge of becoming true? In 1961 it was already apparent that asbestos, the fireproof white fibre much used in construction, was a carcinogen. A New Party (renamed the New Democratic Party) was about to be born as a marriage between the Canadian Labour Congress and the old Co-operative Commonwealth Federation (CCF). Smelting pig-iron in backyard furnaces was the latest scheme of China's Maoists. Teaching sex in the schools was still a radical idea in 1961, and while the St. Lawrence Seaway had been opened in 1959 by President Dwight Eisenhower and Queen Elizabeth II, arguments about tolls and maintenance continued.

Come, my brothers,
let us govern Canada,
let us find our serious heads,
let us dump asbestos on the White House,
let us make the French talk English,
　not only here but everywhere,
let us torture the Senate individually
　until they confess,
let us purge the New Party,
let us encourage the dark races
　so they'll be lenient
　when they take over,
let us make the CBC talk English,
let us all lean in one direction
　and float down

to the coast of Florida,
let us have tourism,
let us flirt with the enemy,
let us smelt pig-iron in our back yards,
let us sell snow
　to under-developed nations,
(Is it true one of our national leaders
　was a Roman Catholic?)
let us terrorize Alaska,
let us unite
　Church and State,
let us not take it lying down,
let us have two Governor Generals
　at the same time,
let us have another official language,

let us determine what it will be,
let us give a Canada Council Fellowship
   to the most original suggestion
let us teach sex in the home
   to parents,
let us threaten to join the U.S.A.
   and pull out at the last moment,
my brothers, come,
our serious heads are waiting for us
   somewhere

like Gladstone bags abandoned
   after a *coup d'état,*
let us put them on very quickly,
let us maintain a stony silence
   on the St. Lawrence Seaway.

Source: Leonard Cohen, "The Only Tourist in Havana Turns His Thoughts Homeward," in Eli Mandel and David Taras, eds., *A Passion for Identity: Introduction to Canadian Studies* (Toronto: Methuen, 1987), 66-7.

Tommy Douglas (1904—86)

The Case for Universal Health Insurance

The Co-operative Commonwealth Federation, precursor of the New Democratic Party, came to power in Saskatchewan in 1944 under the leadership of Thomas Clement Douglas. At that time, no one could claim that his socialist government would bankrupt the province, for Saskatchewan was already as bankrupt as a province could be. In twenty years, Douglas's government paid down Saskatchewan's debt and gave its people pioneering social legislation, especially in the field of health care. Canadians gained national medicare in 1968 because the Saskatchewan CCF had fought the medical profession and the Liberal opposition to establish a plan.

For Douglas, a former bantamweight boxer and a Baptist minister, medicare was a personal crusade. Afflicted since boyhood with a painful bone disease, he had experienced charity medicine first hand; he knew that doctors' bills had been far beyond the means of his working-class family. In 1947 his government pioneered Canada's first universal hospital insurance plan. The idea of pre-paid medical insurance was tested in the Swift Current health district, and by the end of the 1950s Douglas was ready to proceed. A deluge of propaganda from private insurance companies and the medical profession flooded Saskatchewan. Opponents, even in his own party, condemned medicare as premature, unfair to doctors, too expensive for a poor province.

When Douglas rose in the legislature on October 13, 1961 to speak on his government's plans, he displayed his typical speaking style – a few jabs at the overly comfortable, some easily understood arguments, and a prophetic vision. Despite a physician's strike in 1962 and the defeat of the CCF in 1964, Douglas's final sentence proved absolutely correct.

I want to point out, Mr. Speaker, that the cost of a medical care plan is not a new cost to the people of Saskatchewan. The people of this province now are spending $18 million to $20 million a year for medical care. This is not a new cost. It is a different distribution of the cost – that is all. This money had to be paid before. Doctors of this province had to be paid. Everything has had to be paid for – their staff, X-ray technicians, lab technicians, these things all had to be paid for. But they have been paid for by those who were unfortunate enough to be ill. We are now saying they should be paid for by spreading the cost over all the people. We propose that the family tax, which we admit is a regressive tax, since there is a flat rate on every family, and therefore bears no relationship to ability to pay, should be kept as small as possible. We propose that the balance of the cost – probably two-thirds of the cost – ought to be raised by factors which have a measure of ability to pay.

Maybe this is why the Liberal press have been so vehement in their attacks on this plan. It may be that some of them begin to suspect that they are going to have to pay a part of the medical bill of some other people who are not able to pay their own.

Yesterday the Leader of the Opposition sneered at the idea of "I am my brother's keeper." He said, "There isn't much cream in Saskatchewan." I want to suggest that the *Leader-Post* and the *Star-Phoenix*, the Sifton interests and the Leader of the Opposition have fattened quite a bit during the term of the CCF government in office, and it will certainly not hurt them at all to make some contribution towards the medical care for those less fortunate than themselves.

It seems to me to be begging the question to be talking about whether or not the people of this province, or the people of Canada can afford a plan to spread the cost of sickness over the entire population. This is not a new principle. This has existed in nearly all the countries of western Europe – many of them for a quarter of a century. It has been in Great Britain since 1948; it has been in New Zealand since 1935; it has been in Australia. The little state of Israel that only came into existence in 1948 has today the most comprehensive health insurance plan in the world. It has more doctors, and nurses and dentists per thousand of its population than any other industrialized country or any country for which we can get statistics.

It is not a new principle. To me it seems to be sheer nonsense to suggest that medical care is something which ought to be measured just in dollars. When we're talking about medical care we're talking about our sense of values. Do we think human life is important? Do we think that the best medical care which is available is something to which people are entitled, by virtue of belonging to a civilized community? I looked up the figures and I found that, in 1959, the people of Canada spent $1,555 million, or eight percent of their personal expenditures on alcohol and tobacco. I would be the last person to argue that people do not have the right, if they want to, to spend part of their income for either alcohol or tobacco or entertainment, or anything else. But in the same period of time, the people of Canada spent $944 million for medical and dental care, or four and one-half percent of their income expenses. In other words, in the year 1959 we spent almost twice as much on luxuries such as tobacco and alcohol as we spent on providing ourselves and our families with the medical and dental care which they require.

If we can afford large sums of money for other such things as horse-racing, and many other things, and we do – I'm not arguing against them – then I say we ought to have sufficient sense of values to say that health is more important than these things, and if we can find money for relatively non-essential things, we can find the money to give our people good health.

I want to say that I think there is a value in having every family and every individual make some individual contribution. I think it has psychological value. I think it keeps the public aware of the cost and gives the people a sense of personal responsibility. I would say to the members of this House that even if we could finance the plan without a per capita tax, I personally would strongly advise against it. I would like to see the per capita tax so low that it is merely a nominal tax, but I think there is a psychological value in people paying something for their cards. It is something which they have bought; it entities them to certain services. We should have the constant realization that if those services are abused and costs get out of hand, then of course the cost of the medical care is bound to go up.

I believe, Mr. Speaker, that if this medical care insurance program is successful, and I think it will be, it will prove to be the forerunner of a national medical care insurance plan. It will become the nucleus around which Canada will ultimately build a comprehensive health insurance program which will cover all health services – not just hospital and medical care – but eventually dental care, optometric care, drugs and all the other health services which people require. I believe such a plan operated by the federal and provincial governments jointly will ultimately come in Canada. But I don't think it will come unless we lead the way. I want to say that when the history of our time is written, it may well be recorded that in October 1961, the Saskatchewan legislature and the Saskatchewan people pioneered in this field and took a first step towards ultimately establishing a system of medical care insurance for all the people of Canada . . .

The government believes that health is too important to be left to the chance that the average family will have the necessary money to buy health services. I believe that if we put this health plan into operation it will have the same history as the Hospital Insurance Plan. I am convinced that inside two or three years both the doctors who provide the service and the people who receive the service will be so completely satisfied with it that no government will dare to take it away.

Source: L.D. Lovick, *Till Power Is Brought to Pooling: Tommy Douglas Speaks* (Lantzville, B.C.: Oolichan Books, 1979), 133-43.

Fernand Ouellette (1930–)

"Language, History, and Memory"

At some point in the 1960s, some serious shifts in identity began. People who had called themselves "Canadien" or "Canadien-français" started using the name "Québécois." Perhaps it was a phenomenon of the generations, with people of a certain age making the change while their older relatives did not. If the Quiet Revolution meant secularization and a sudden new faith in the potential of the Quebec state, it also brought a new approach to language. The older conservative nationalism had accepted that the language of power in Quebec might well be English. No longer. Within a state where francophones were a majority, what was more democratic and essential for the survival of French than to declare it the only official and, ultimately, the only visible language? North American life would be lived in French as well as English.

Fernand Ouellette, born in Montreal and co-founder with Jacques Godbout (1933–) of *Liberté*, made his living and his reputation as a producer at Radio-Canada. He was honoured for his essays and his poetry though he refused the 1970 Governor General's Award for his *Les Actes retrouvés*. In 1964 he launched his manifesto in a language struggle which continues to rage in Quebec to this day.

We know that North America can be thought of in French, since we've been doing it from the start. We know there's no such thing as a continental vocation. Does Cambodia not have the right to coexist with China? Denmark with Germany and France? We're completely at home in North America and we belong to its future. Being a small people may imply less power, but not a lack of quality. Our uniqueness is already a great richness for those who believe in something other than the dollar. And so we have the urgent task of remaking our society, rethinking it as North American French, as Québécois. Only then will French become the language of daily life. It will involve a complete and foundational vision, a resurrection, and a lot of stereotypes will have to disappear. An enormous effort will have to be made when it comes to the economy, of course, to reassert ourselves and to gain real power. But if our politicians, our technocrats, our union leaders and our academics don't begin to see the gravity of the language problem, they're likely to find themselves with greater economic power, undoubtedly, but leading a people in the process of disappearing. Our great "humanists" want so much to be realistic and serious that they have become unconscious agents of the genocide of their own people. Our language is a social organism as urgently in need of attention as the economy. We need to politicize the language problem in Quebec immediately. In this day and age, the clergy no longer preserve the language, since language is no longer the guardian of the faith. Those who speak of "racism" or of "dictatorship" have no understanding of existence, nor of politics, nor of history. Can one think of a more realistic act than to refuse to die? For many, however, to refuse to die is not practical. Defeatism undoubtedly seems a more positive attitude. To be civilized is to be practical and pragmatic like the Anglo-Saxons. The word "practical" is their vessel, containing the purest refinement of spirit ever found in a can. Certainly, we wish to be practical, but in French. Our perception of the world is a manifestation of French and North American cultures. We feel America. We have it under our skin. And it isn't allergic to our language. We Quebec poets prove it. Quebec will become the image of what it makes of itself. For it is no longer by turning to the past that we will find the courage to live in the present. Our will to live has too long been supplanted by our memory of having been. This incessant return to dead events has only created in us a desire to survive. When it is no longer a question of surviving, but of living, the present and the future alone will become forces for life. We must dissociate history from memory. Our history must be made with our hands. Let the nation that has lived in memory return to memory. We are another people and we have other hopes.

Source: Michel Le Bel and Jean-Marcel Paquette, *Le Québec par ses textes littéraires, 1534-1976* (Montreal: Fernand Nathan, 1979), 246-8.

The Royal Commission on Bilingualism and Biculturalism

TWO NATIONS OR MANY?

Arguably the most important royal commission in Canadian history, the Royal Commission on Bilingualism and Biculturalism was created by Prime Minster Lester Pearson in 1964 as a response to the rise of separatism in Quebec and the terrorism of the Front de Libération du Québec (FLQ). The two chief commissioners were André Laurendeau (1912–68) and Davidson Dunton (1912–87). Laurendeau was a former editor of *Le Devoir* and a prominent Quebec journalist; Dunton was an Ontario university administrator and former president of the Canadian Broadcasting Corporation.

The B & B Commission's central idea was that French Quebeckers should be made to feel that they had a political home in the federal government equal to that in Quebec and the

National Assembly, and, to achieve this end, it would ultimately recommend that a policy of official bilingualism be implemented in the federal government and all federal institutions. Yet there was another side to the commission's work. Among the commission's ten members were Paul Wyczynski, a Polish-born professor at the Université de Montréal, and J.B. Rudnycki, a Ukrainian-speaking professor at the University of Manitoba. Their influence was noticeably increased when delegations from the so-called "Third Force" – Canadians of neither French nor English origin – politely but firmly reminded the commission that the "other ethnic groups" would not settle for less than cultural equality.

In the first selection below, an excerpt from their preliminary report issued in 1965, the commissioners offer a few cautious words on "other" Canadians, words that, in due course, would grow into an entire book in the final report and in the 1970s would flower into the policy of multiculturalism. In the second selection, also from the preliminary report, the commissioners express their sense of urgency about the future of Canada and stress the necessity of accommodating the aspirations of French Canadians and Quebec within Confederation. This might seem old news now; it appeared very new to most Canadians at the time.

A great majority of Canadians of other than French or British origin speak English, use it regularly in their daily lives, and are more or less integrated to the English-speaking society. A much smaller number speak French and tend to become associated with the French-speaking society. A comparatively few, who live in groups where their own language is commonly used, speak little or no French or English. Of the great number that habitually use one of these languages in their working lives, some are anxious also to maintain their own language and the cultural heritage that goes with it; others are content to see their children grow up just like Canadians of British or French origin, or have themselves been fully integrated. Still, as already noted, and particularly at the preliminary hearing in Ottawa, we were struck by the number of representatives of those groups who spoke fluently in both English and French.

A good number of these Canadians spoke to us, on many different occasions, of the very serious and sometimes thorny problems they are facing in Canada. We thus began to understand and measure the importance of the cultural riches which they brought with them and which they wish to preserve. We know their difficulties a little better, but also their pride and their feeling of belonging to Canada. For instance, when Canadians of Ukrainian origin vigorously stood up against the idea of "two founding races" it was because they were deeply conscious of having themselves cleared and opened great stretches of territory in Northern Ontario and the Prairies, and of having contributed in this way to the "founding" of a part of modern Canada.

Representatives of certain ethnic groups have already made known their demands which, on the whole, are quite moderate; some of them appear in Part Two of this report. It should be understood of course that we shall be continuing our study of these claims in our final report. The question we are asking ourselves here is somewhat narrower: what role do the other ethnic groups play in the crisis which is threatening to tear Canada apart today?

It is difficult to describe the character of a segment of the population that is so diverse: each ethnic group has its own original language and culture. And even within one group, because of factors of geography or individual characteristics, many divergences are to be found. These people's experiences of "Canada" differ in both time and space; it is a long step from an immigrant's grandson born in Montreal, to someone who has himself had to live through the traumatic experience of being transplanted onto the Prairies. If it is not always easy for Canadians of the two traditional cultures to come to grips with the meaning of their own heritage, what shall we say of the Canadian of a different origin for whom integration has been sometimes a dramatic experience?

Moreover, some of these groups did not present themselves to us at the regional meetings. We met very few Canadians of German or Dutch origin, relatively few Poles, Italians or Finns, but many Ukrainians. Finally, among those who participated in the discussions, reactions differed greatly from one minority to another. With a few exceptions these groups only became numerous many years after Confederation. Nevertheless, it seems that the immigrants – except those who settled in Quebec – have not always been aware that they were entering a bilingual and fundamentally bicultural country; a number even remarked that Canada has been presented to them as a unilingual country using the English language, or even as simply a British colony. For this reason the demands of French Canadians seemed to them to be a new and in many ways surprising fact.

Consequently the theory of "equal partnership" seems suspect to them; they see in it an attempt to manufacture an "aristocracy" from which they would be excluded. In reaction, some of them would like to define Canada as a collection of minorities among whom it would be unfair to choose only one, whether it be one or other of the two most important, and endow it with a privileged status; it would be better, in their opinion, to accept the fact of the multiplicity of cultures and recognize only one language of communication, English, except perhaps in Quebec, where the principal language would be French. And thus, by way of a detour and with a new set of arguments, we are back to the concept of Canada as an English country with the French enclave of Quebec.

However, the argument put forward above has another aspect: if it is true that certain recent immigrants are scarcely conscious of the fact that they belong to a bilingual and bicultural country, it seemed to us equally clear that other Canadians are not yet fully aware of the relatively new presence among them of these people. It seems to us that an evolution is needed in the thinking of Canadians of British and French origin; they are no longer the only ones in Canada, and they will have to take this very important human factor into account.

Here and there the idea of a "melting pot" after the American pattern entered into the discussions. Others – Ukrainians in particular – took delight in emphasizing "multiculturalism" as the distinctive characteristic of Canadian society. However, it seemed to us that the prototype of the United States cast a spell over the opinions of several ethnic groups: the picture of a vast country where the national goal is to create a vital unity without taking into account all the languages and cultures.

There were certainly other voices and other opinions. A varied range of views was offered to us, bearing witness to the efforts being made to work the other ethnic groups into a really Canadian context, distinct from the "melting pot" or "balkanization." On several occasions we saw evidence of a great longing for all to pull together for the unity of the country and to participate in Canadian life in accordance with contemporary needs. But we could not say that the other ethnic groups proposed a clear, consistent and definite formula. They, too, are trying to find themselves in the present troubled waters; they, too, must carry on an examination of collective conscience in the most genuine way.

To the degree that the demands of certain ethnic groups make awareness of the fundamental duality of the country more difficult, to that extent they aggravate the state of crisis in Canada. Above all, they provide new arguments for the partisans of a "One Canada." Nevertheless, the study of problems facing Canadians of other than British or French origin gives rise to a number of questions which make it possible to evaluate better the present situation in Canada and to judge more fairly the difficulties we are experiencing.

All that we have seen and heard has led us to the conviction that Canada is in the most critical period of its history since Confederation. We believe that there is a crisis, in the sense that Canada has come to a time when decisions must be taken and developments must occur leading either to its breakup, or to a new set of conditions for its future existence. We do not know whether the crisis will be short or long. We are convinced that it is here. The signs of danger are many and serious.

The ways in which important public and private institutions now operate strongly dissatisfy a very significant part of the Canadian population, while the other part remains largely indifferent to this situation, or does not even know of its existence.

A strong impression we drew from our contacts with thousands of French-speaking Canadians of all walks of life and of all regions of the country was the extent to which, for most of them, questions of language and culture do not occur in the abstract. They are rooted in the experiences of daily life, in jobs, in meetings, in correspondence with public and private corporations, in the armed forces. They are inseparably connected with the social, economic and political institutions which frame the existence of a people and which should satisfy their many needs and aspirations. The opinions we heard were often the result of ordinary individual and collective experiences; hence our conviction that they can hardly be changed by simple appeals to abstract ideas like "national unity." It seemed to us that the dissatisfaction and the sense of revolt came from aspects of reality rather than from doctrines that had been preached.

At the same time we were confronted constantly by English-speaking Canadians, including many expressing sentiments of goodwill, who seemed to have no realization of the daily experiences that cause the discontent among so many of their French-speaking fellow citizens. Nor do most understand the underlying trend toward the increasing autonomy of Quebec and the strengthening of the belief among her people that she is now building herself into a distinct form of nationhood with full control of all her social and economic institutions. What is grasped is frequently rejected. Thus there exists a deep gulf, with unawareness on one side, and strongly rooted feeling on the other.

We are convinced that it is still possible to rectify the situation. But a major operation will perhaps be unavoidable. The whole social body appears to be affected. The crisis has reached a point where there is a danger that the will of people to go on may begin to fail.

This is an initial diagnosis, not a prophecy. We describe what we saw and summarize what we heard, without the least feeling of defeatism, for the Canadian situation has, most fortunately, another aspect. Most of the people we met love Canada. We believe that once they are aware of the danger threatening it, they will apply themselves to removing the causes. Nevertheless, the crisis appears to us to be an undeniable fact.

Canada has lived through other and less profound crises before, which have brought to the surface very different concepts about the country held by French-speaking and English-speaking Canadians. We found the memories of these past events very much alive, especially in French Canada. Thus a sense of grievance can accumulate with each successive conflict no matter how it has been resolved.

Canada was of course born out of warfare between the "two founding peoples" as it was born also out of the white man's imposition of his culture upon the original Indians and Eskimos. From the Indian point of view, French and English both have the same title to the land – conquest. Quebec tends to feel that the French were settlers and the English invaders. We have indicated before that even these ancient battles have not ceased on both sides to motivate present behaviour. The youths who destroy monuments in Quebec want history re-written – at least for the future. An English Canadian looking at this early period usually either wants to restore the monuments, and thus symbolize a return to the status quo; or else he remembers principally the granting of representative government, the coming of responsible government, and the other constitutional achievements which have made present day Canada a "nation," giving wide opportunities to its citizens for self-development and occupying a significant place in world affairs. Lord Durham is to the French the great assimilator; to the English the great decolonizer.

Conflicts since Confederation are well known, although viewed from totally different aspects by the two main participants. Riel, the "murderer," was hanged; Riel, the defender of minority rights, was judicially murdered. Manitoba was endowed at its birth by an English-dominated federal Parliament, with the two official languages and separate schools; but the local Manitobans took away these rights, and when the Government in power at Ottawa proposed to force the schools back on the unwilling Manitobans, the people in Quebec voted solidly for a Laurier who rejected compulsion. Yet to Quebec the Manitoba experience proves that "les Anglais" everywhere are untrustworthy, and that when the chips are down the majority always wins. Regulation 17 in Ontario, adopted in 1913, severely limiting the use of French as a language of instruction in separate schools, was repealed by a later Ontario government; but this change of heart did little to restore [sic: alleviate] the animosity originally aroused by the Regulation. Conscription in 1917 and again in 1942 appeared to many in English Canada as a necessity for a nation committed to victory in crucial wars; but in Quebec it seemed to drag a peaceful people into conflicts of prime concern only to those of British descent.

These earlier conflicts, however, were settled by one means or another. But they are not unrelated to the present crisis. On the contrary, it seems to us that, recorded in the memory of the "nations" in the form of synthetic opinions ("The French Canadians are never satisfied," or "The English Canadians will never understand us"), these half-resolved old conflicts are coming together again – this time in a less spectacular but nevertheless deep-rooted crisis, which may be, over and above anything that is new, the product and consummation of all the past resentments. The previous conflicts did not seriously threaten the fundamentals of the state. The crisis today is of a different order. There has never been the feeling, except perhaps among a few individuals and groups, that the fundamental conditions for the existence of the Canadian people were in jeopardy.

This time, as we have noted on many occasions throughout these pages, the themes of the situation are complex and difficult to define because they are global. It is not only one aspect of Canadian life that is at issue; the vital centre is in danger: we mean the will to live together, at least under present conditions.

What is at stake is the very fact of Canada: what kind of country will it be? Will it continue to exist? These questions are not matters for theoreticians only, they are posed by groups of human beings. And other groups by refusing to ask themselves the same questions actually increase the seriousness of the situation.

The chief protagonists, whether they are entirely conscious of it or not, are French-speaking Quebec and English-speaking Canada. And it seems to us to be no longer the traditional conflict between a majority and a minority. It is rather a conflict between two majorities: that which is a majority in all Canada, and that which is a majority in the entity of Quebec.

That is to say, French-speaking Quebec acted for a long time as though at least it had accepted the idea of being merely a privileged "ethnic minority." Today, the kind of opinion we met so often in the province regards Quebec practically as an autonomous society, and expects her to be recognized as such.

This attitude goes back to a fundamental expectation for French Canada, that is, to be an equal partner with English-speaking Canada. If this idea is found to be impossible, because such equality is not believed in or is not acceptable, we believe the sense of deception will bring decisive consequences. An important element in French-speaking Quebec is already tempted to go it alone.

We are conscious of the fact that no one can foretell future events, and that even as we write this report the picture keeps changing. Since the appointment of the Commission in July 1963, many accommodations have been negotiated. Adjustments have been made in federal-provincial relations that have met certain of Quebec's particular demands. Joint federal-provincial programs, so much a part of our recent constitutional history, have given way to opting out devices; federal pension plans have been adapted to Quebec's needs, and tax sharing has greatly enlarged the freedom of Quebec. The public funds available for use by the people of Quebec through their government have in effect increased substantially. The visit of Her Majesty in October 1964 exposed forces and disclosed attitudes which caused serious reflection on all sides. The climate of opinion, particularly in the Province of Quebec, seems to change rapidly and we cannot foretell what new directions it will take. Nevertheless, in spite of the importance of these events and adjustments, we are convinced the opinions we heard spring from attitudes too deeply rooted for them to have been modified in any significant or permanent way. Thus, we must reiterate that we have found overwhelming evidence of serious danger to the continued existence of Canada.

On the other hand we are not blind, nor do we think any Canadian should be, to hopeful aspects in the situation. In spite of present differences in outlook Canadians of different origins have much in common. They share many facets of a great common European tradition; and they maintain many connections across the Atlantic. They have lived together for 200 years. Geography and conditions of life in the northern half of North America have a common influence on them. They join in a common love for their land as such. Abroad, English-speaking and French-speaking Canadians have often found that they have more in common with each other than with citizens of other countries. All Canadians are members of a modern, technologically advanced society, with all that this implies in problems and in opportunities. The advances taking place in Quebec, while they may increase the sense of competition between French and English-speaking Canadians, may also give them more to talk about together than ever in the past.

We think that there are grounds for hope in the signs we discovered of evolving attitudes among English-speaking Canadians. The number of those who understand the issues seems to be increasing; the number who wants to understand appears to be growing still more rapidly. In Quebec the very vigour of developments may reduce the frustrations felt by many people, and at the same time, lead them to put less blame on the English-speaking majority in Canada, and to accept more responsibility for themselves. During the year we have noted in New Brunswick in particular, but also in other parts of Canada, positive signs of better understanding of the aspirations and needs of the French-speaking minorities. In our opinion, there is substantially more comprehension in English Canada of the need for adjustments than there was a few years ago.

It is hardly possible to travel across Canada from coast to coast, and to talk to literally thousands of Canadians of different origins and background, as we have done, without being struck by the enormous potentialities of this country and its people. It seemed to us again and again that current problems between the peoples of Canada are impeding great advances. A solution to the dilemma posed by duality would, we are sure, release immense energy and creative power. Vitality could then come from the very differences and tensions among Canadians. The extra power released could be turned to making Canadian life as a whole better for all its citizens: to economic and social improvements; to increasing opportunities for the individual as a human being whatever his language; to enhancing Canada's contribution to all humanity. Then the potentialities of the two cultures, English and French-speaking, with the enriching contributions from those of other origins, each working in its own way for common purposes, could be enormous.

Wide-ranging negotiations, however, will be necessary between the major groups of Canadians. We believe that Canada will live and thrive if there can be a satisfactory matching between the minimum of what French-speaking Canadians consider as vital, and the maximum that English-speaking Canadians will accept. In our final report we hope to make recommendations about adjustments and accommodations that seem reasonable and fair. However, any necessary changes can be introduced and become effective only if, on each side, there is an insistent, driving desire to understand the other, and to consider the common good.

But it appears to us that there are some vital prerequisites to a positive outcome of the present state of crisis. There must be important changes in attitudes.

In particular we suggest that all Canadians examine closely the concept of democracy itself. Too often, it has been reduced to the simple game of majority versus minority. Some English-speaking citizens before the Commission invoked the "law of the majority" as though they were brandishing a threatening weapon; some French-speaking people, who had complained bitterly of the consequences of this "law," expressed the desire to make use of it to their own advantage in a more or less independent Quebec.

It is true that, on a number of occasions, this rule has played its part in Canadian history, leaving behind bitter memories among those who felt its weight. And the fact that a cultural majority can always have recourse to it may appear to a minority to represent a threat to its liberty. But that way of looking at things is so incomplete that it becomes a caricature.

It does not take into account the constitutional guarantees a cultural minority may obtain. It overlooks the fact that we live in a federation, one result of which is that the division of authority between Ottawa and the provinces reduces the "English majority" to the state of a minority in Quebec, in connection with provincial matters, while it gives the "French minority" the status of a majority; the consequences of this fact should be considered, for example, in the fields of education and natural resources. To reduce the function of a parliamentary democracy to a simplified game of numbers is to reason in the abstract. As a matter of fact, decisions made in Parliament (as for that matter, in the Legislative Assemblies) are the result of a rather complicated and subtle process: discussions or compromises within cabinets and parties in which both groups are represented; political considerations and economic influences of various kinds; federal-provincial bargaining in certain cases, and so on. Lastly, in a great number of matters, ethnic and cultural factors never arise or have little importance. It seems urgent that observations of this kind concerning the political system be thoroughly examined. In any case, this is a task we shall be taking up in the hope on our part of gaining a better idea of how cultural equality may be achieved, without unfairness to any one and without any open break.

From evidence so far accumulated, it appears to us that English-speaking Canadians as a whole must come to recognize the existence of a vigorous French-speaking society within Canada, and to find out more about the aspirations, frustrations and achievements of French-speaking Canadians, in Quebec and outside it. They must come to understand what it means to be a member of a minority, or of a smaller partner people, and to be ready to give that minority assurances which are unnecessary for a majority. More than a century ago, Sir John A. Macdonald wrote to an English-speaking friend: "Treat them as a nation and they will act as a free people generally do – generously. Call them a faction and they become factious." They have to face the fact that, if Canada is to continue to exist, there must a true partnership, and that the partnership must be worked out between equals. They must be prepared to discuss in a forthright, open-minded way the practical implications of such a partnership. To some extent, they must be prepared to pay by way of new conditions for the future of Canada as one country, and to realize that their partner of tomorrow will be quite different from their partner of yesterday.

On the same evidence, it seems to us that French-speaking Canadians for their part must be ready to respond positively if there are to be truly significant developments toward a better partnership. It would be necessary for French-speaking Quebecers to restrain their present tendency to concentrate so intensely on their own affairs, and to look so largely inward. Problems affecting all Canada are their problems too. They would need to beware of the kind of thinking that puts "la nation" above all other considerations and values. They too, like the English-speaking, should forget the conquest and any psychological effects they think it left. They would have to avoid blaming English-speaking Canadians for shortcomings which are their own; and at times, to remember that English-speaking Canadians have their feelings too. They, as well as the English-speaking, must remember that, if a partnership works, each party must give as well as get.

All ten of us are convinced that in the present situation there is a grave danger for the future of Canada and of all Canadians. There are those who feel that the problems will lessen and go away with time. This is possible, but, in our view, it is more probable that unless there are major changes the situation will worsen with time, and that it could worsen much more quickly than many think.

There are hopeful signs; there are great possibilities for Canada. But we are convinced at the present time that the perils must be faced.

Source: A Preliminary Report of the Royal Commission on Bilingualism and Biculturalism (Ottawa: Queen's Printer, 1965), 125-8 and 133-9.

Al Purdy (1918–)

"THE COUNTRY NORTH OF BELLEVILLE"

Born in the tough farming country north of Belleville, Ontario, that he describes in his best-known poem, Al Purdy began writing at the age of thirteen but he would not be recognized as a serious poet for another forty years. Meanwhile, he worked his way across the country as a labourer, served in the Royal Canadian Air Force during the Second World War, and settled

afterwards in the Ontario town of Ameliasburgh, still a labourer. He developed a distinctive poetic voice, gruff, colloquial, wry, inspired by the everyday and the past.

Purdy belongs to a generation of Canadian writers and artists whose work is imbued with nationalist sentiments. He possesses an extensive knowledge of Canadian geography and history, and his poetry both chronicles and explores the meaning of Canada, including such disparate topics as hockey, the shooting of D'Arcy McGee, implementation of the War Measures Act in 1970, and our ancestors and the land on which they lived. He is a raconteur who speaks to and about Canadians. In 1965 he received the Governor General's Award for Fiction for *The Cariboo Horses*.

"The Country North of Belleville" (1965) recalls the defeat of farm settlement on land where the Precambrian Shield pushed south to cross the St. Lawrence River around Kingston. Shallow, thin soil and a generous crop of boulders defied settlers and condemned most of them to a meagre livelihood. Today, casual visitors barely notice the signs of past despair, but this was the background that shaped Purdy and others like him.

Bush land scrub land –
       Cashel Township and Wollaston
Elzevir McClure and Dungannon
green lands of Weslemkoon Lake
where a man might have some
       opinion of what beauty
is and none deny him
          for miles –

Yet this is the country of defeat
where Sisyphus rolls a big stone
year after year up the ancient hills
picnicking glaciers have left strewn
with centuries' rubble
          backbreaking days
          in the sun and rain
when realization seeps slow in the mind
without grandeur or self deception in
          noble struggle
of being a fool –

A country of quiescence and still distance
a lean land
        not like the fat south
with inches of black soil on
        earth's round belly –
And where the farms are
        it's as if a man stuck
both thumbs in the stony earth and pulled

        it apart
        to make room
enough between the trees
for a wife
        and maybe some cows and
        room for some
of the more easily kept illusions –
And where the farms have gone back
to forest
        are only soft outlines
        shadowy differences –

Old fences drift vaguely among the trees
        a pile of moss-covered stones
gathered for some ghost purpose
has lost meaning under the meaningless sky
        – they are like cities under water
and the undulating green waves of time
        are laid on them –

This is the country of our defeat
        and yet
during the fall plowing a man
might stop and stand in a brown valley of the furrows
        and shade his eyes to watch for the same
        red patch mixed with gold
        that appears on the same

        spot in the hills
        year after year
        and grow old
plowing and plowing a ten-acre field until
the convolutions run parallel with his own brain –

And this is a country where the young
               leave quickly
unwilling to know what their fathers know
or think the words their mothers do not say –

Herschel Monteagle and Faraday
lakeland rockland and hill country
a little adjacent to where the world is
a little north of where the cities are and
sometime
we may go back there
                to the country of our defeat
Wollaston Elzevir and Dungannon
and Weslemkoon lake land
where the high townships of Cashel
      McClure and Marmora once were –
But it's been a long time since
and we must enquire the way
      of strangers –

Source: Russell Brown, ed., *The Collected Poems of Al Purdy* (Toronto: McClelland and Stewart, 1986), 56-7.

George Grant (1918–88)

"LAMENT FOR A NATION"

George Parkin Grant was a leading Canadian philosopher. A professor of religion and philosophy at McMaster University and then Dalhousie, he combined Canadian nationalism with a broader conservative concern for the Western world's future in the face of liberal capitalism and technological imperatives – threats that in Canada's case were inseparable from the reality of continentalism. Continentalism reflects a view that regards consumption as the dominant concern; a Canadian border that impedes consumption becomes increasingly irrelevant.

Grant's views were grounded in a deep religious traditionalism, which challenged American liberalism and modernism. His Red Tory Canadian nationalism is a key element of the Canadian cultural and political landscape, most persistent and comfortable in corners of the Progressive Conservative Party but also discoverable in other parties.

In *Lament for a Nation*, published in 1965, Grant pondered the implications of the Diefenbaker era for Canada. He lamented the seemingly unstoppable power of continental liberalism in defeating the essentially conservative thrust of Canadian nationalism. The passage presented here, from the conclusion of *Lament for a Nation*, demonstrates the bittersweet blend of irony and despair that infused Grant's defence of an independent, conservative Canada.

Perhaps we should rejoice in the disappearance of Canada. We leave the narrow provincialism and our backwoods culture; we enter the excitement of the United States where all the great things are being done. Who would compare the science, the art, the politics, the entertainment of our petty world to the overflowing achievements of New York, Washington, Chicago, and San Francisco? Think of William Faulkner and then think of Morley Callaghan. Think of the Kennedys and the Rockefellers and then think of Pearson and E. P. Taylor. This is the profoundest argument for the Liberals. They governed so as to break down our parochialism and lead us into the future.

* * *

Many levels of argument have been used to say that it is good that Canada should disappear. In its simplest form, continentalism is the view of those who do not see what all the fuss is about. The purpose of life is consumption, and therefore the border is an anachronism. The forty-ninth parallel results in a lower standard of living for the majority to the north of it. Such continentalism has been an important force throughout Canadian history. Until recently it was limited by two factors. Emigration to the United States was not too difficult for Canadians, so that millions were able to seek their fuller future to the south. Moreover, those who believed in the primacy of private prosperity have generally been too concerned with individual pursuits to bother with political advocacy. Nevertheless, this spirit is bound to grow. One has only to live in the Niagara peninsula to understand it. In the mass era, most human beings are defined in terms of their capacity to consume. All other differences between them, like political traditions, begin to appear unreal and unprogressive. As consumption becomes primary, the border appears an anachronism, and a frustrating one at that.

The disadvantages in being a branch-plant satellite rather than in having full membership in the Republic will become obvious. As the facts of our society substantiate continentalism, more people will explicitly espouse it. A way of life shaped by continental institutions will produce political continentalism. Young and ambitious politicians will arise to give tongue to it. The election of 1963 was the first time in our history that a strongly nationalist campaign did not succeed, and that a government was brought down for standing up to the Americans. The ambitious young will not be slow to learn the lesson that Pearson so ably taught them about what pays politically. Some of the extreme actions of French Canadians in their efforts to preserve their society will drive other Canadians to identify themselves more closely with their southern neighbours than with the strange and alien people of Quebec.

Of course continentalism was more than a consumption-ideology. In the nineteenth century, the United States appeared to be the haven of opportunity for those who had found no proper place in the older societies. Men could throw off the shackles of inequality and poverty in the new land of opportunity. To many Canadians, the Republic seemed a freer and more open world than the costive colonial society with its restraints of tradition and privilege. The United States appeared to be the best society the world had ever produced for the ordinary citizen. Whatever the mass society of prosperity has become, the idea that the United States is the society of freedom, equality, and opportunity will continue to stir many hearts. The affection and identification that a vast majority of Canadians have given to the publicly expressed ideals of such leaders as Roosevelt and Kennedy is evidence of this.

Continentalism as a philosophy is based on the liberal interpretation of history. Because much of our intellectual life has been oriented to Great Britain, it is not surprising that our chief continentalists have been particularly influenced by British liberalism. The writings of Goldwin Smith and F. H. Underhill carry more the note of Mill and Macaulay than of Jefferson and Jackson. This continentalism has made two main appeals. First, Canadians need the greater democracy of the Republic. To the continentalists, both the French and British traditions in Canada were less democratic than the social assumptions of the United States. In such arguments, democracy has not been interpreted solely in a political sense, but has been identified with social equality, contractual human relations, and the society open to all men, regardless of race or creed or class. American history is seen to be the development of the first mass democracy on earth. The second appeal of continentalism is that humanity requires that nationalisms be overcome. In moving to larger units of government, we are moving in the direction of world order. If Canadians refuse this, they are standing back from the vital job of building a peaceful world. After the horrors that nationalistic wars have inflicted on this century, how can one have any sympathy for nationalism? Thank God the world is moving beyond such divisive loyalties.

* * *

Ancient philosophy gives alternative answers to modern man concerning the questions of human nature and destiny. It touches all the central questions that man has asked about himself and the world. The classical philosophers asserted that a universal and homogeneous state would be a tyranny. To elucidate their argument would require an account of their total teaching concerning human beings. It would take one beyond political philosophy into the metaphysical assertion that changes in the world take place within an eternal order that is not affected by them. This implies a definition of human freedom quite different from the modern view that freedom is man's essence. It implies a science different from that which aims at the conquest of nature.

The discussion of issues such as these is impossible in a short writing about Canada. Also, the discussion would be inconclusive, because I do not know the truth about these ultimate matters. Therefore, the question as to whether it is good that Canada should disappear must be left unsettled. If the best social order is the universal and homogeneous state, then the disappearance of Canada can be understood as a step toward that order. If the universal and homogeneous state would be a tyranny, then the disappearance of even this indigenous culture can be seen as the removal of a minor barrier on the road to that tyranny. As the central issue is left undecided, the propriety of lamenting must also be left unsettled.

My lament is not based on philosophy but on tradition. If one cannot be sure about the answer to the most important questions, then tradition is the best basis for the practical life. Those who loved the older traditions of Canada may be allowed to lament what has been lost, even though they do not know whether or not that loss will lead to some greater political good. But lamentation falls easily into the vice of self-pity. To live with courage is a virtue, whatever one way think of the dominant assumptions of one's age. Multitudes of human beings through the course of history have had to live when their only political allegiance was irretrievably lost. What was lost was often something far nobler than what Canadians have lost. Beyond courage, it is also possible to live in the ancient faith, which asserts that changes in the world, even if they be recognized more as a loss than a gain, take place within an eternal order that is not affected by their taking place. Whatever the difficulty of philosophy, the religious man has been told that process is not all. *"Tendebantque manus ripae ulterioris amore."*[*]

Source: George Grant, *Lament for a Nation* (Toronto: McClelland and Stewart, 1970), 88-97.

---

[*] Virgil, *Aeneid* (Book VI): "They were holding their arms outstretched in love toward the further shore."

Farley Mowat (1921–)

SPEAKING OUT ON VIETNAM

For many Canadians, opposition to the American war in Vietnam was a defining moment. The Canadian anti-war movement, like its American counterpart, had many strands, ranging from those who saw the war as a mistake to those who denounced it as the behaviour of an arrogant, racist power bent on using Cold War hysteria for imperialistic ends. These arguments were employed in the United States, too, but in Canada there was another ingredient in the mix: nationalism.

Farley Mowat is a well-known novelist who served with distinction as a Canadian infantry officer in Italy during the Second World War. A fierce crusader for the native people, the Arctic, and the environment generally, he is also a forceful nationalist, and in the 1960s he used language associated with Nazi Germany to attack American actions in Vietnam. Writing in 1967, he insisted that "the balance of reasoned action" lay with Russia and China. He could not have foreseen that only a year later Soviet tanks would rumble into Prague, that in 1980 the Soviet Union would invade Afghanistan, and that the Communist regimes of Eastern Europe would crumble from within by 1989.

The American presence in Vietnam and the undeclared war being waged there by the United States constitutes one of the most blatant acts of aggression the world has seen since the destruction of Hitler's Third Reich.

The United States is guilty of the invasion and occupation of South Vietnam. It has no moral, and only highly suspect legal claims to support its presence there. It entered Vietnam at the invitation of, and to provide support for, the corrupt and undemocratic oligarchy controlled by the Diem family. It is of more than incidental interest that this represented the 27th time since 1934 that U.S. military forces had been openly employed to establish, strengthen or support dictatorships in foreign countries, and to prevent the evolution of democratic systems. Nevertheless, the great rallying cry and justification of the United States in its actions against other nations has always been, and remains, the contention that it is the great champion of democracy. In all honesty, we cannot help but ask ourselves: democracy for whom?

* * *

Concentration camps have been established for Viet Cong prisoners and suspects. There is as yet no concrete evidence to show that these camps have reached the appalling depths of degradation which characterized Belsen and Dachau, but there is ample evidence, almost entirely provided by the U.S., witnessing the fact that the torture of prisoners is standard procedure amongst South Vietnamese and U.S. forces. Almost daily (and with a terrifying lack of concern) the United States press publishes photographs of Viet Cong prisoners or "suspects," men and women and youths who are hardly more than children, being knifed in the belly; kicked in the head; drowned in streams or buckets of water; and being otherwise tortured by South Vietnamese troops, while United States troops look on; or by American soldiers themselves.

This may be the first war in history which has seen the aggressors publish, in their own press, such candid pictures of atrocities being committed on the enemy by their own troops. It is a development that bears thinking about. As a commentary on the ethics which seem to motivate the United States in its actions in Vietnam, it speaks all too clearly.

In terms of what the United States has done, and is doing, in South Vietnam, by its own public admission, the atrocities perpetrated by Mussolini in Ethiopia become mere childish peccadillos and the German treatment of Belgium in two World Wars becomes an act of civility!

The United States is guilty of beginning and of waging an undeclared war against North Vietnam. The largest, most powerful industrial and military nation on earth is waging an aspect of total war against one of the world's smallest, poorest, and least industrially developed nations. I say "aspect" of total war because the United States has not yet invaded North Vietnam on the ground. But from the air the United States had even by December 15, 1965, dropped an announced tonnage of bombs on North Vietnam which was almost double the tonnage dropped on Great Britain during World War II by the Germans.

* * *

The United States is engaged in an aggressive war which is heavy with racist overtones. It is not too much to suggest that a nation which has produced the widespread Alabama mentality would have little difficulty in persuading itself that the murder of great numbers of

Asiatics does not really constitute a crime against humanity. When we examine the war in Vietnam we cannot, no matter how we try, escape the feeling that if the Vietnamese were "white" they would not get the treatment being meted out to them by the United States. It seems certain that the American public would not stand for the atrocities being committed by their forces, and being portrayed so graphically in their press, if the victims were white men. The point is that they are not white. They are no more white than were the "gooks," the name, it will be remembered, which the Americans gave to the Koreans during that unsavoury adventure.

* * *

I say this to Canadians. If we are a nation; if we are people who place any value on ethics or morality, then we must take an unequivocal stand against the actions of the United States in Vietnam. Our Government will not act for us, since it is demonstrably subject to the will of the United States. We must therefore act individually and declare, publicly and privately, in any and all company, as frequently as possible, despite reprisals and the dangers of reprisals, that the United States is guilty of a great crime against mankind. That she is perpetrating a fearful wrong. And that we, individually and collectively, will have no part of her military adventure in Vietnam. And that we condemn her for that adventure, before the eyes of all the world.

I am a veteran of the war against Hitler. I am not a communist. At one time, during the Stalin era, I believed that we in the west were in serious danger from a militant world communism which would deprive us of our liberty. I no longer nurture this fear. I believe now that the balance of reasoned action has swung away from our side, and lies with Russia and, perhaps, with China. I believe that both these countries are determined not to engage the west in warfare, recognizing that a new world war would be suicide for the human species. Russia certainly, and China probably, know that the Third World War will be the last.

We do not.

The United States of America, and its flaccid, parasitic allies (which must include Canada) has now become the major threat to world peace and, by extension, to the survival of mankind. I am afraid that if there is a third world war – the United States will start it. I, personally, am not prepared to give any further credence to the protestations of the Government of the United States that it seeks peace in the world. I believe it seeks power – world power – and that it will use all means at its disposal, including the greatest and most destructive military machine the world has ever known, to achieve its unstated ends. Those who choose to adhere to Washington, on the principle that it is better to be on the side of the winner than the loser, are deluding themselves. In the future which threatens us . . . there will be only losers.

Source: "Farley Mowat Speaks Out on Vietnam," *Canadian Dimension*, vol. 4, no. 4 (May-June 1967), 30-2.

Harold Cardinal (1945–)

"The Mystery of the White Man"

Harold Cardinal is an Indian leader and author. Born in Alberta, he served as president of the Indian Association of Alberta from 1968 to 1977, the youngest person to occupy this post. In response to the "assimilationist" Indian policy announced by the federal Liberal government in a White Paper of 1968, Cardinal helped draft "Citizens Plus," a "Red Paper" which rejected the assimilationist option. He also published *The Unjust Society*, an angry response to the "just society" theme of the Liberal Party's 1968 campaign.

The following selection is typical of Cardinal's writing. With a blend of satire and angry commentary, he turns the table on white Canadians, who often act as commentators on First Nations issues and problems. Cardinal takes the perspective of an aboriginal Canadian analysing the problematic aspects of white society.

An Indian, who probably wasn't joking at all, once said, "The biggest of all Indian problems is the white man." Who can understand the white man? What makes him tick? How does he think and why does he think the way he does? Why does he talk so much? Why does he say one thing and do the opposite? Most important of all, how do you deal with him? As Indians, we have to learn to deal with the white man. Obviously, he is here to stay. Sometimes it seems a hopeless task. The white man spends half of his time and billions of dollars in pursuit of self-understanding. How can a mere Indian expect to come up with the answer?

The white man has some good qualities. Over the centuries he has managed to work out some quite acceptable concepts of morality, justice, democracy, freedom, equality, and so on, none of them new to the Indian, but all decent, solid thinking. But the white man is a paradox. On the one hand, he professes almost fanatic commitment to high ideals; on the other, he disdains those same ideals in practice. He believes in the concept of unity. He believes in a God and adheres to a monotheistic religion. Yet even in the area where he could offer most, in the one area where he could exemplify unity – in his religion – he is ridiculously fragmented. He preaches love and brotherly concern and manufactures napalm and hydrogen bombs – and who doubts he will use them?

The white man seems unable to understand, or perhaps he is unwilling to accept, the fact that another man may believe differently, that another man's religion may be valid.

I know this is not a new discovery about the white man. But it continues to puzzle the Indian. The white man feels compelled to pray for the salvation of another's soul, and if that soul won't go along, just as compulsively condemns it to eternal damnation. And while he preaches brotherly love and tolerance, he often simultaneously directs his place of worship to become an all-white sanctuary.

In his social doctrines he stresses his belief in equality and elaborates on the need for and the value of diversity. But confront him with a diversity in colour of skin, confront him with some different values, and see how long he stays a champion of diversity. He believes in equality, but apparently believes the white man is more equal than the Indian. He just doesn't make sense. Study of the white man will make a great field for future Indian psychologists and psychiatrists . . .

Despite the white man's righteous and indignant assertions that he has no feeling of prejudice against the Indian, we know that his true feelings surface when there is confrontation. We will believe the white man when his actions match his words.

Luckily Indians have resilience to match their stoicism. We will survive the stupidities of bigotry, the indignities of condescension, and the gushing of the do-gooders, but we admit to deep and penetrating wounds inflicted by the white man's attitude toward our women.

The word *squiew* in Cree means woman (or lady, if you prefer that delicate locution). No Indian word has been so abused and perverted. On the white man's tongue, *squaw* is a dirty word used to describe any Indian woman. The connotation is one more appropriately drawn from the term *whore*, another white word our people dislike. To match our

feelings when we hear our wives, mothers, sweethearts, and daughters called squaws, lump your white wives, daughters, mothers, and sweethearts under the general connotation of whore.

But you white men still are far ahead of us in actual abuse and perversion of our women, never mind the terminology. In too many areas Indian women are regarded by every passing stray white tomcat as easy prey. Nor is this attitude confined to white trash. Many God-fearing, good, solid, middle-class white citizens mouth self-righteous concern about the supposedly lax morals of Indians and at the same time conveniently overlook the actions of their fun-loving sons or brothers or husbands.

The despoliation of our women by unthinking, unfeeling, self-indulgent whites stands as the most degrading insult inflicted upon our people. The white social institutions of Canada seem blind to the situation. Turn the tables and see what would happen. Imagine a carousing invasion of one of your suburbs by roistering young Indian males in search of white girls for easy conquest. Like the white man's forked tongue, his morality comes in double standards.

We don't know where to start to correct this situation. The institution of the law might seem an appropriate place, but there is a saying among Indians: "If a white man rapes an Indian woman, he gets a suspended sentence or goes free, but if an Indian rapes a white woman he receives the lash and sentence of life imprisonment." Aside from the implication that the double standard has pervaded the hallowed courts of Canadian justice, we might suggest that the comparative availability of high-cost legal aid to whites and to Indians represents another perversion of the concept of equality.

White people have a long way to go on this one. They might start by banning the use of the word *squaw*. Indian women are as moral as white women or women of any other colour. This is a cultural trait, an individual trait, not a race or colour characteristic. Our people had rigid moral codes before the white man found his way across the ocean. We will match our girls' character against your best team of debutantes any day.

Much has been written on prejudice. American bookstores are full of bitter and clever books by talented black authors. This is a step in the right direction, but it will take another several generations of goodwill and soul-searching to wipe out the black or the red colour line.

From the beginning, the Indian accepted the white man in Canada. We allowed him differences. We helped him overcome his weaknesses in trying to make his way in our environment. We taught him to know our world, to avoid the pitfalls and deadfalls, how to trap and hunt and fish, how to live in a strange environment. Is it too much to ask the white man to reciprocate?

An Indian looks at nature and sees beauty – the woods, the marshes, the mountains, the grasses and berries, the moose and the field mouse, the soaring eagle and the flitting hummingbird, the gaudy flowers and the succulent bulbs. He sees an overall fitness, an overall collective beauty, but he looks deeper. He sees the beauty of the individual components of the big picture. He sees the diversity of the various elements of the entire scene. He admires the grace of a leaping deer, the straight-line simplicity of the pines the deer leaps through, the jagged, three-dimensional thrust into the sky of the rugged peaks, the quick silver flash of a trout on the surface of a wind-rippled take. He turns a sensitive ear to the faraway eerie wail of the loon and the nearer snuffling grunt of a bear pawing at a ground squirrel's den, and he blends them into the whispering of grasses and the bolder talk of the tall pines. He feels the touch of wind against his cheek and the coolness of the mist above the rapids. He surveys the diversities of nature and finds them good.

An Indian thinks this might be the way of people. He knows that whites and Indians are different. He knows that there are differences even within these larger groups, differences between Scot and Ukrainian, between Cree and Iroquois. He knows there are differences between man and his brother, red or white.

To the Indian this is the natural way of things, the way things should be, as it is in nature. As the stream needs the woods, as the flowers need the breeze, as the deer needs the grasses, so do peoples have need of each other, and so can peoples find good in each other. Indians are close to nature, so it is natural for them to see the bigger world in terms of the small world they do know. They know that men of different cultures and races have much to offer one another. We offer our culture; we offer our heritage. We know it is different from yours. We are interested in your culture and your heritage; we want you to discover ours.

Source: William and Christine Mowat, eds., *Themes in Canadian Literature: Native Peoples in Canadian Literature* (Toronto: Macmillan, 1975), 96-101.

Lester B. Pearson (1897–1972)

ON FEDERALISM

Of all Canada's prime ministers, none brought a greater international reputation and wider experience to the post than Lester Bowles Pearson. The son of a Methodist minister, he was a veteran of the First World War, an athlete, and a history lecturer when he joined Canada's young Department of External Affairs. His appointments in Ottawa and overseas marked him as a shrewd judge of character and circumstances. Behind the scenes, he was one of the brilliant post-war class of diplomats who helped design the United Nations in 1945 and the North Atlantic Treaty Organization in 1949.

Brought into politics by Prime Minister Louis St-Laurent (1882–1973), he served as secretary of state for external affairs from 1948 to 1957, earning the Nobel Peace Prize for his role in resolving the Suez Crisis of 1956. Chosen leader of the defeated Liberal Party in 1957, he showed little genius for electoral politics but impressive wisdom in grasping the divisive crisis which faced French- and English-speaking Canadians, and he struggled to reconcile the divisions during his time as Canada's eighteenth prime minister, from 1963 to 1968. As in diplomacy, his preference was for the accommodation and compromise Canadians had preached to the world. His successor, however – Pierre Elliott Trudeau – would prefer clarity and confrontation.

In the first of the selections that follow, Pearson explains his view of the nature of Confederation; in the second, he articulates his strategy of cooperative federalism as a response to the challenge of Quebec separatism.

Confederation was our declaration of faith in the destiny of a united Canada. It was also our declaration of independence from the United States. We would go it on our own on this continent from coast to coast, first as part of the British empire and later as an independent nation of the Commonwealth of nations. We knew at the time that such a declaration, based on such a faith, would involve an economic price. We were ready then in Canada to pay that price – and I hope and believe we are still ready to do so – namely, the price of being Canadian.

Confederation, however, also involved another price which too many of us either forget or do not wish to pay, because perhaps it is inconvenient for us to so pay it. Confederation meant the rejection not only of political and economic annexation by the United States, but also of the American melting pot concept of national unity. Confederation may not have been technically a treaty or a compact between states, but it was an understanding or a settlement between the two founding races of Canada made on the basis of an acceptable and equal partnership.

I began to talk about "co-operative federalism" in the early sixties before we took office. By that I meant that instead of trying to concentrate power in Ottawa we should try to make arrangements with the provinces for joint undertakings where the constitution allowed, while seeking always to maintain a more or less standard level of services for all Canadians.

This approach seemed to me to be particularly valuable in view of the developing national feeling in Quebec aroused by Lesage's Quiet Revolution. The intensity of that feeling made it clear that if we failed to contain and destroy separatism by coming to terms with the Quiet Revolution, that if we failed to treat Quebec as the heart of French culture and French language in Canada, as a province distinct in some respects from the others, we should have the gravest difficulty in holding our country together. But we could not give Quebec constitutional rights denied to the other provinces. While I judged that there could be no special status for any one province, there were other ways in which the position of French-speaking Canadians could be acknowledged . . . Although the federal government had to retain intact certain essential powers, there were many other functions of government exercised by Ottawa which could be left to the provinces. By forcing a centralism perhaps acceptable to some provinces but not to Quebec, and by insisting that Quebec must be like the others, we could destroy Canada.

Source: John A. Munro and Alex I. Inglis, eds., *Mike: The Memoirs of the Right Honourable Lester B. Pearson* (Toronto: University of Toronto Press, 1975), vol. 3: 67, 138-9.

René Lévesque (1922—87)

"An Option for Quebec"

René Lévesque was one of the most popular political leaders in Quebec. First rising to prominence as a journalist, he entered Quebec provincial politics as a Liberal in 1960 and subsequently held several portfolios. He was largely responsible for the decision of the Quebec government to nationalize private electric companies and merge them in the state-controlled Hydro Québec.

Lévesque soon became impatient with his party's constitutional stand and demanded increased powers from Ottawa. He left the Liberal Party in 1967 and in 1968 created the Parti Québécois to rally separatist forces. Though he led the party to electoral victories in 1976 and 1981, he failed to win majority support in the 1980 referendum when he lost to federalist forces by a 60-40 margin.

Lévesque's brand of independence for Quebec tried to soften the option for uneasy Quebec voters. He developed the idea of "sovereignty-association," which meant a form of political independence combined with an economic association with Canada. While he was unsuccessful in the referendum, the ensuing political and constitutional options emanating from Quebec have continued to include post-independence links with Canada.

In 1968 Lévesque published a best-selling book entitled *Option Québec* which outlined both the argument for Quebec sovereignty and a vision for the new country. In this passage from the book, Lévesque sets out the political, cultural, and psychological arguments which are often been made as justifications for Quebec independence.

W e are *Québécois.*

What that means first and foremost – and if need be, all that it means – is that we are attached to this one corner of the earth where we can be completely ourselves: this Quebec, the only place where we have the unmistakable feeling that "here we can be really at home."

Being ourselves is essentially a matter of keeping and developing a personality that has survived for three and a half centuries.

At the core of this personality is the fact that we speak French. Everything else depends on this one essential element and follows from it or leads us infallibly back to it.

In our history, America began with a French look, briefly but gloriously given it by Champlain, Joliet, La Salle, La-Vérendrye . . . We learn our first lessons in progress and perseverance from Maisonneuve, Jeanne Mance, Jean Talon; and in daring or heroism from Lambert Closse, Brébeuf, Frontenac, d'Iberville. . . .

Then came the conquest. We were a conquered people, our hearts set on surviving in some small way on a continent that had become Anglo-Saxon.

Somehow or other, through countless changes and a variety of regimes, despite difficulties without number (our lack of awareness and even our ignorance serving all too often as our best protection), we succeeded.

Here again, when we recall the major historical landmarks, we come upon a profusion of names: Étienne Parent and Lafontaine and the Patriots of '37; Louis Riel and Honoré Mercier, Bourassa, Philippe Hamel; Garneau and Édouard Montpetit and Asselin and Lionel Groulx . . . For each of them, the main driving force behind every action was the will to continue, and the tenacious hope that they could make it worth while.

Until recently in this difficult process of survival we enjoyed the protection of a certain degree of isolation. We lived a relatively sheltered life in a rural society in which a great measure of unanimity reigned, and in which poverty set its limits on change and aspiration alike.

We are children of that society, in which the *habitant*, our father or grandfather, was still the key citizen. We also are heirs to that fantastic adventure – that early America that was almost entirely French. We are, even more intimately, heirs to the group obstinacy which has kept alive that portion of French America we call *Québec*.

All these things lie at the core of this personality of ours. Anyone who does not feel it, at least occasionally, is not – is no longer – one of us.

But *we* know and feel that these are the things that make us what we are. They enable us to recognize each other wherever we may be. This is our own special wave-length on which, despite all interference, we can tune each other in loud and clear, with no one else listening.

On the other hand, one would have to be blind not to see that the conditions under which this personality must assert itself have changed in our lifetime, at an extremely rapid and still accelerating rate.

Our traditional society, which gave our parents the security of an environment so ingrown as to be reassuring and in which many of us grew up in a way that we thought could, with care, be preserved indefinitely; that "quaint old" society has gone.

This is how we differ from other men and especially from other North Americans, with whom in all other areas we have so much in common. This basic "difference" we cannot surrender. That became impossible a long time ago.

More is involved here than simple intellectual certainty. This is a physical fact. To be unable to live as ourselves, as we should live, in our own language and according to our own ways, would be like living without an arm or a leg – or perhaps a heart.

Unless, of course, we agreed to give in little by little, in a decline which, as in cases of pernicious anaemia, would cause life to slip slowly away from the patient.

Again, in order not to perceive this, one has to be among the *déracinés*, the uprooted and cut-off.

Today, most of us are city dwellers, wage-earners, tenants. The standards of parish, village, and farm have been splintered. The automobile and the airplane take us "outside" in a way we never could have imagined thirty years ago, or even less. Radio and films, and now television, have opened for us a window onto everything that goes on throughout the world: the events – and the ideas too – of all humanity invade our homes day after day.

The age of automatic unanimity thus has come to an end. The old protective barriers are less and less able to mark safe pathways for our lives. The patience and resignation that were preached to us in the old days with such efficiency now produce no other reactions than scepticism or indifference, or even rebellion.

At our own level, we are going through a universal experience. In this sudden acceleration of history, whose main features are the unprecedented development of science, technology, and economic activity, there are potential promises and dangers immeasurably greater than any the world ever has known.

The promises – if man so desires – are those of abundance, of liberty, of fraternity; in short, of a civilization that could attain heights undreamed of by the most unrestrained Utopians.

The dangers – unless man can hold them in check – are those of insecurity and servitude, of inhuman governments, of conflicts among nations that could lead to extermination.

In this little corner of ours, we already are having a small taste of the dangers as well as the promises of this age.

The dangers are striking enough.

In a world where, in so many fields, the only stable law seems to have become that of perpetual change, where our old certainties are crumbling one after the other, we find ourselves swept along helplessly by irresistible currents. We are not at all sure that we can stay afloat, for the swift, confusing pace of events forces us to realize as never before our own weaknesses, our backwardness, our terrible collective vulnerability.

Endlessly, with a persistence almost masochistic, we draw up list after list of our inadequacies. For too long we despised education. We lack scientists, administrators, qualified technical people. Economically, we are colonials whose three meals a day depend far too much on the initiative and goodwill of foreign bosses. And we must admit as well that we are far from being the most advanced along the path of social progress, the yardstick by which the quality of a human community can best be measured. For a very long time we have allowed our public administration to stagnate in negligence and corruption, and left our political life in the hands of fast talkers and our own equivalent of those African kings who grew rich by selling their own tribesmen.

We must admit that our society has grave, dangerous, and deep-rooted illnesses which it is absolutely essential to cure if we want to survive.

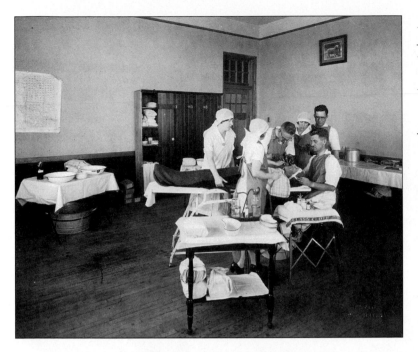

A travelling medical team performs an operation in rural Alberta in the 1920s. The equipment, conditions, and procedures all look primitive, but wartime experience had indicated that many patients fared better if medical care could be brought closer than if they had to travel to more sophisticated facilities. Prairie communities also struggled with the costs of medical care. The region led the way in developing cooperative solutions that culminated, by the 1960s, in the series of comprehensive health-insurance policies Canadians call Medicare. (National Archives of Canada, C 29449)

If the Victorians discovered childhood as a time of innocence and fun as well as of preparation for the burdens of adulthood, the new twentieth century discovered scientific motherhood. In a carefully posed photograph, staff at Toronto's Hospital for Sick Children lecture mothers on nutrition and lay out three balanced meals, while children wait their turn to be weighed and measured. (National Archives of Canada, C 91260)

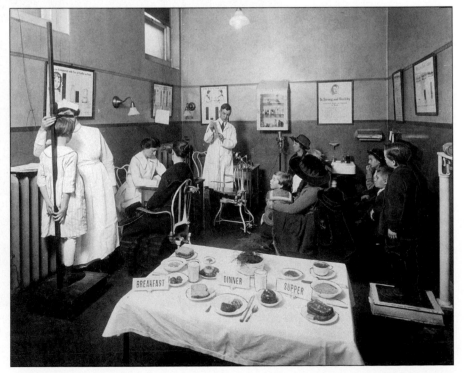

Canadians share a belief that there is something both idyllic and virtuous in growing up on a farm. Early rising and chores met the most demanding standards, but bare feet, plenty of space, and a casual attitude to schooling were blessings in the eyes of most city children. A farmer with a healthy brood expected to turn them into useful workers as soon as possible, though routinely, in English-speaking Canada, only the eldest inherited the land. (National Archives of Canada, WS 261)

Hochelaga was one of Montreal's eastern suburbs in 1929 when Marc-Aurèle Fortin (1888-1970) painted this landscape. It was a mainly French-speaking place of homes, factories, churches, and patches of countryside not yet devoured by brick and stone. The artist was one of his generation's most popular painters, in demand for church illustrations and domestic art. (National Gallery of Canada)

Any traveller in rural Ontario will soon recognize the characteristic gabled farmhouse, often on the crest of a hill, where generations of farm families grew up, tended the land, and spread their offspring across the continent. This was Carl Schaefer's background, too. Born in 1903, he painted his Ontario Farmhouse *in 1934.* (National Gallery of Canada)

Unemployed men parade during the Depression of the 1930s. Municipalities had to fund relief; those with the highest unemployment either went bankrupt or found desperate means to squeeze their hungry citizens. Single unemployed men were told to move on – and they then became transients, with no claim on any other municipality. The Depression experience persuaded a generation of Canadians that, whatever the constitution said, Ottawa had to play a major role in supporting the sick, the poor, and the out-of-work. (National Archives of Canada, C 29397)

Mayor Camillien Houde warns a Montreal crowd in March 1939 that war would bring conscription back to Quebec. Houde was right, though the war was almost over before 13,000 Canadian conscripts were sent over to fill the ranks of a battered Canadian army. Meanwhile, Houde had been interned for opposing National Registration in 1940 and the rest of Canada had voted in 1942 to relieve Ottawa of no-conscription pledges made to Quebec in the months before the outbreak of war on September 10, 1939. These events would long be remembered bitterly in Quebec. (The Gazette, National Archives of Canada, PA 110919)

Miller Brittain (1912-68) caught this image of longshoremen in his native Saint John in 1940. A social realist, he attended the Art Students League in New York in the 1930s and there was influenced to record the people other artists ignored – the day labourers and, sometimes, the drunks and derelicts of his city. (National Gallery of Canada)

Japanese Canadians from Vancouver unloading their possessions at Slocan, then little more than a ghost town in the interior. The evacuation of 21,000 people who had offended their neighbours only by their racial origins was a shameful event that provoked a few brave protests at the time and, fifty years later, a full national apology and compensation. (National Archives of Canada, C 47396)

Yellow quarantine signs are distant memories now for most Canadians, but they were medicine's response to communicable disease for generations. Until the Salk vaccine, poliomyelitis, or infantile paralysis, was a terrifying calamity which killed quickly or left survivors severely crippled or confined for years to an iron lung. This boy shares emergency post-war housing in Toronto in August 1947. (National Archives of Canada, PA 93671)

Quidi Vidi is an outport just north of Newfoundland's capital, St. John's. This is how it looked before Newfoundlanders narrowly voted to enter Confederation in 1949. The narrow inlet is rimmed by a church, fishermen's homes, sheds, landing stages, and "flakes," platforms where the catch was salted and dried. (Newfoundland Archives, VP 1487)

While television has robbed Canadians of some of their illusions about politics, an old-fashioned belief persists that a righteous person can somehow get elected to Parliament, come to Ottawa, denounce the misguided rascals who are misgoverning the country, and win the power to do it right. One major beneficiary of that belief was Saskatchewan's John Diefenbaker, Member of Parliament from 1940 to 1979 and prime minister from 1957 to 1963. (National Archives of Canada)

Now, a human society that feels itself to be sick and inferior, and is unable to do anything about it, sooner or later reaches the point of being unacceptable even to itself.

For a small people such as we are, our minority position on an Anglo-Saxon continent creates from the very beginning a permanent temptation to such a self-rejection, which has all the attraction of a gentle downward slope ending in a comfortable submersion in the Great Whole.

There are enough sad cases, enough among us who have given up, to show us that this danger does exist.

It is, incidentally, the only danger that really can have a fatal effect upon us, because it exists within ourselves.

And if ever we should be so unfortunate as to abandon this individuality that makes us what we are, it is not "the others" we would have to blame, but only our own impotence and resulting discouragement.

The only way to overcome the danger is to face up to this trying and thoughtless age and make it accept us as we are, succeeding somehow in making a proper and appropriate place in it for ourselves, in our own language, so that we can feel we are equals and not inferiors. This means that in our homeland we must be able to earn our living and pursue our careers in French. It also means that we must build a society which, while it preserves an image that is our own, will be as progressive, as efficient, and as "civilized" as any in the world. (In fact, there are other small peoples who are showing us the way, demonstrating that maximum size is in no way synonymous with maximum progress among human societies.)

To speak plainly, we must give ourselves sufficient reason to be not only sure of ourselves but also, perhaps, a little proud.

Source: René Lévesque, *An Option for Quebec* (Toronto: McClelland and Stewart, 1968), 14-17.

Claude Ryan (1925–)

"THE CANADIAN SOLUTION"

In the lifetime of its founder, Henri Bourassa, *Le Devoir* never advocated the cause of an independent Quebec. Nor would it under the long editorship of Claude Ryan. A solemn, devoutly Catholic, and liberal-minded man, Ryan managed *Le Devoir* from 1964 to 1978, turbulent years for Quebec and Canada. His calm, logical editorials and his balanced style made the newspaper an opinion leader in Canada as well as among Quebec's intellectuals. Passionately committed to Quebec and to its full rights and powers within Confederation, Ryan argued, as he does in this 1964 article, that Quebec not only needs its place in the Canadian economy but also has a role in the country as a whole. But note that, for Ryan, this is no more than a hypothesis.

It is an argument, not for Canada for the sake of Canada, but for Canada for the benefit of Quebec. It anticipates the claim of Quebec Premier Robert Bourassa (1933–96) that, for Quebec, Confederation is profitable. If the hypothesis is wrong . . .

Persuaded to enter politics as a Liberal, Ryan inherited the party leadership after René Lévesque had formed Quebec's first Parti Québécois government. He was the leader of the successful "No" side in the 1980 referendum, although federal Liberals like Pierre Elliott Trudeau and Jean Chrétien claimed the credit. Ryan, in turn, took the blame for losing the 1981 election. Later, he served as Bourassa's minister of education and campaigned, in his quiet, dignified way, for the development of a Quebec which could tolerate minority rights.

There are for French Canadians two ways of approaching the Canadian problem.

One consists of identifying French Canada with Quebec and examining all our problems in relation to the interests of Quebec. At the heart of this hypothesis Quebec is first and foremost. It is necessary to pursue it and defend it, putting all other considerations in second place: that is the thesis of "by itself and for itself" dear to M. Lévesque.

In this perspective the Canadian dimension appears a last resort. It is a rupture of the homogeneous order which would exist if Quebec was alone and completely master of its destiny; it is thus a weight from which it is necessary to strain in order to liberate oneself. Some are still prepared to accept the Canadian reality, provided that this reality does not hinder in any way the progress of Quebec, and that it serves Quebec's interests. Others have already concluded that the Canadian reality is injurious to Quebec, that it is necessary to put an end as soon as possible to an experiment which, in every way, has never been faithfully put to the test.

Between these two opinions there exists a difference of degree, not of nature. The two opinions accept, without discussion, the ideal of the primacy of Quebec. They separate at the chapter on means and strategy. In the long run the two opinions are destined to unite.

The second approach consists in envisaging the French-Canadian problem at the level of the whole country, that is, to begin with the Canadian hypothesis.

At the heart of this hypothesis there is a place for a loyal admission of the difficulties that have sorely tried the French Canadians in Confederation. There is equally room for an explicit recognition of the special position that Quebec – as the principal political expression of the French fact in Canada – ought to occupy in the Canadian body politic.

But the perspective remains Canadian. Canada is accepted not as a last resort from which one would like to be liberated, but as a valuable political reality which one wants to improve. This viewpoint is not that of a supporter of a unitary system, but rather of a federalist. For him the federal régime is the one that best fits our geographic, historic, economic, and political conditions. Without wishing this régime to survive at any price, he rejects the global and defeatist interpretations that some propose about the history of the last century.

This viewpoint also takes account of the evolution which has taken place in English-Canadian opinion in the last quarter-century. Those who adhere to this thesis believe that it is possible and desirable to reform our federation in a manner that will become effective and acceptable to Canadians of both languages. They see that this reform ought to be made up of conversations and faithful agreements between the two groups. They wish to obtain this objective by the road of dialogue rather than by the method of ultimatums. But they recognize at the outset that it is within the Canadian body politic that they look for a solution.

It is impossible, unless one wants to outsmart someone, to pretend to be inspired by both hypotheses. A newspaper should choose one of the two and defend it with courage and clarity. It should do this with the maximum loyalty and frankness. It should give all viewpoints a reasonable opportunity for expression in the news columns. But it would betray its mission if it avoided choice.

We choose the Canadian hypothesis for three principal reasons. The first reason relates to the very tradition of *Le Devoir*. The newspaper, under its first three directors, was a great Canadian newspaper. Henri Bourassa never wanted to limit his horizons to the province of Quebec. He considered that the whole of Canada was his country, that he ought to be at home everywhere in this country. Georges Pelletier also attached a great importance to Canadian realities. He liked to approach the most complex problems, for example those of transport, with an objectivity and a rigour that would have prevented him from closing them within a narrow compass. The third director, Gérard Filion, was of rural origin, but he had learned early at the school of the Catholic Union of Farmers the need for co-operation with the rest of the country. He was often severe toward Ottawa centralizers, but never negative or closed with regard to Canada itself.

The second reason lies in the economic order. It is sufficient to glance at a map of the country in order to establish that Quebec and Canada are tied together in many ways. Quebec's economy presents two important characteristics. It needs external markets for the dispersal of its products. It needs capital from outside for the development of its resources. Why should we say no to Canada today if that must only mean saying yes to others tomorrow? One does not deny his history for the simple pleasure of hypothetically changing partners.

Our most important motives lie in the political order. On the condition that Quebec enjoys all the autonomy which it needs to develop its own life and institutions, we believe that the preservation of the Canadian tie offers precious advantages. The first of these advantages is surely the possibility of maintaining and developing the French way of life in the rest of the country. *Le Devoir* has always maintained an attitude of solidarity with the French minorities in the other parts of the country. Whatever could have been said on this subject for some time, the present direction of *Le Devoir* holds that we must continue to support our compatriots in the other provinces. We refuse to join the prophets of doom who affirm, without ever having worked assiduously with these groups, that the French minorities of the other provinces are doomed to extinction.

The second advantage is less immediate, but no less obvious. Canada offers us the chance of constructing a new type of political society, that is, a society whose political boundaries will be advantageous for the development of different cultures without being rigidly or exclusively conditioned by one culture alone. We are convinced that this type of society can be revealed as more advantageous to the cultivation of fundamental liberties, in the long run, than societies calculated too closely on the single reality of a particular culture. In affirming this conviction we are conscious of enunciating an ideal which is far from having been attained in the Canadian reality. But the difficulties and the checks of the past are not yet decisive enough to justify pure and simple abandonment of the ideal which presided at the birth of Confederation.

A durable political society is built neither on impulses nor on vague desires, but on rational ideas, on a certain conception of man and of life in society, on an objective assessment of reality. Nothing proves that men nourished in different cultures are incapable of

co-operating on a certain conception of political life. The entente is surely more difficult when several cultures are called upon to cohabit, but it is not for all that purely and simply impossible.

That being said we insist on adding three qualifications.

We have said advisedly "the Canadian hypothesis." We have not spoken of dogma. It is possible that we are mistaken. If that is the case, the facts will indicate it to us in the proper time and place. Placed before the evidence we will not have the pretension of preventing history from fulfilling itself. But while waiting, the logic of events obliges us to fight firmly and frankly for the success of our hypothesis.

In choosing the Canadian hypothesis we are not opting for the status quo. If this hypothesis is to be realized, substantial modifications in the constitution of our country and in the functioning of our political institutions will have to be carried out. It will be necessary to rethink our federalism, to adjust it profoundly. It will be necessary to avoid the errors of the past, to correct the injustices of yesterday, to foresee new methods of work which will realize completely the equality of cultures.

Finally our choice will not prevent us in the least from approaching in Quebec the problems of Quebec. In the order of jurisdiction where it is and must remain (and even in certain areas become) sovereign, Quebec has the right to our first allegiance. It will have it without restriction. In the discussion of the problems of education, social security, and the development of our resources and of our economy we will not act in the fashion of "Canadians at large" who would like to solve our problems using norms borrowed from elsewhere rather than by the realistic examination of our situation and our resources. We will think and speak as Québécois without misplaced pride, but without false humility.

These positions seem to us to conform best to the true reality of French Canada.

Source: "The Canadian Solution," in William Kilbourn, *Canada: A Guide to the Peaceable Kingdom* (Toronto: Macmillan, 1970), 238-41. Originally published in French as editorials in *Le Devoir*, September 18 and 19, 1964.

Frank R. Scott (1899-1985)

ON THE WAR MEASURES ACT

Frank R. Scott, introduced in the previous section of this book, was a life-long civil libertarian. For example, when Quebec's popular and conservative premier, Maurice Duplessis (1890–1959), used his power to put a man out of business because he disapproved of the man's religious beliefs, Scott sued him and won his case in the Supreme Court, which ordered Duplessis to pay his victim for his losses.

In the 1960s Scott had good reason to be happier. Both Quebec and Canada adopted many of the reforms he had campaigned for all his life, from medicare to bilingualism. But some people wanted an even more radical change – an independent Quebec – and they thought that the right way to achieve their goal was to spread terror. Members of a small, loosely organized Front de libération du Québec stole weapons, blew up mailboxes, and, in October 1970, kidnapped the British trade commissioner, James Cross, and kidnapped and later murdered Quebec's minister of labour, Pierre Laporte. Montreal was in turmoil as young nationalists celebrated. Some veteran nationalists wanted a newly elected Robert Bourassa to hand power over to them so they could strike a deal with the FLQ. Instead, Bourassa asked Ottawa for help. Prime Minister Pierre Elliott Trudeau proclaimed the War Measures Act. Using some of this legislation's sweeping powers, the government banned the FLQ and ordered the army to help Quebec police during the crisis. The vast majority of Canadians, including 84 per cent of Quebeckers, agreed. So did Frank Scott.

Many supporters of civil liberties were appalled by the War Measures Act. They thought that Trudeau had acted too harshly, or that the FLQ threat was too small to warrant such a heavy-handed response. But, as usual, Frank Scott spoke his mind though many old friends would never forgive him. Yet his argument, set out in the selection below, is in a great Canadian tradition. Without civil government, there are no civil liberties. Quebeckers had elected a government only months before; to let it be threatened by violence was, for Scott, intolerable.

Global Attack on Our Institutions

Quebec is in grave trouble. Therefore Canada also is in trouble. Therefore all Canadians who are concerned about the future of our common country must try to understand what is happening and be willing to help.

In many parts of the world there are revolutionary movements attempting to overthrow existing societies. Some of them deserve to be overthrown. Others, of which Quebec is one, do not need a violent upheaval because not only are they in full evolution but other more humane means of changing their institutions are available. For example, the legitimate activities of the Parti Québécois, which aims to prove by democratic means that the majority in Quebec is in favor of independence, are not in question now. This party has existed for some years, it is distinct from the FLQ, and its activities are not rendered illegal by the proclamation of the War Measures Act.

It is not separatism in Quebec that is outlawed, it is a determined and well-organized revolutionary movement applying new techniques of terror aimed at the polarization of our society and the fracturing of those elements which enable Canadian federalism to exist at the moment and give assurance that it can exist in the future. It is a global attack upon all institutions in our present system.

CHE GUEVARA FAILED

If an organization like the FLQ were to enter Ontario or British Columbia, aiming to overthrow the social system by force, we all know it would have no chance whatever of success. Che Guevara tried this in Bolivia, a country where the native population was infinitely more oppressed than it is in Quebec, and no one would support him. But in Quebec the same kind of revolutionary movement has more success. We must ask ourselves why this is?

Obviously one reason is that an FLQ type of movement, whose philosophy and tactics are not specifically French Canadian but are merely showing now in French Canada, has more support in Quebec because it feeds on nationalism and the general notion of Quebec independence. This term also needs understanding, because sincere people in Quebec who say they are indépendantistes or séparatistes are not necessarily aiming at a new independent state totally unrelated to its surrounding communities.

The intelligent separatist knows that Quebec would not be a viable country without a great many of the economic and political contacts it now has with English Canada and with North America. René Lévesque himself has said he favors independence in order that Quebec might by herself think out her proper role in North America, and then, as it were, re-enter into a Canadian federalism adjusted to meet this new situation.

OPTIONS OFFERED

There is at the moment in Quebec a government newly elected which clearly offered the Quebec people an option on staying within Confederation and working out the necessary adjustments without a break in the fundamental relationship. This government represents the great majority of the Quebec electorate, and must be considered as the only authoritative voice of Quebec. It was this government, with the full support of the city government of Montreal, which requested Mr. Trudeau to give him emergency aid.

In the light of this double request, how could a federal prime minister have possibly refused to respond? It may well be debated and should be debated, whether the War Measures Act is the right kind of emergency legislation for this kind of emergency or whether the particular measures were not too severe. Mr. Trudeau himself knows this, and has suggested the necessity of a new substitute statutory power to deal with something less than the War Measures Act was intended to deal with. But at that moment when this request came Ottawa could scarcely have refused to acquiesce without laying itself open to a charge of gross irresponsibility towards the most important centre of French Canadian culture in Canada.

All this surely is clear. It is equally clear that the present emergency provides no ultimate solution for the problems out of which the emergency arose. The FLQ could not have developed from mere extremist propaganda to emotional appeal, with considerable support at least among the youth in the universities and schools, if it did not play upon basic aspirations in the people. This youth, as represented by the organization of its teachers, 70,000 strong, is by no means in support of the methods of the FLQ, but is in support of its fundamental aim of an independent Quebec though not necessarily of its brand of socialism.

FUNDAMENTAL CHOICE

Quebec is therefore facing and will continue to face its fundamental choice: does it believe that the future of its language and culture in North America is better secured by steady growth within Canadian federalism?

Or does it really believe that its future is better secured by creating a small independent fortress state which is not likely to begin its life without social and economic upheavals possibly forcing its government towards totalitarianism and cut off from the expanding centres of French culture outside Quebec?

It is a tragedy, in Pierre Trudeau's otherwise remarkable handling of the problems of a prime minister in Canada in these difficult days, that he has been led into economic policies which have imposed particular hardships upon Quebec and the youth of Quebec. If there was any province in which unemployment should have been carefully avoided, so as not to make it worse than in other parts of Canada, it is Quebec. Yet it is precisely in Quebec that unemployment is worst and is likely to grow more serious. This is no time to ask whether Quebec is receiving more favorable treatment than other provinces in monetary terms. It must receive better treatment if its problems are worse than those of other provinces.

The purpose of economic planning is to equalize economic benefits as far as possible across the country. They are extremely unequal now in Quebec. There must be economic measures taken to open opportunities for employment and for youthful careers in Quebec, and in the French language, if we are to have any hope of reducing the frustration and alienation which feed the FLQ. Some imaginative action on the part of Ottawa fully supported by all provinces of Canada is more necessary because it is obvious that the FLQ by its subversive activities, deliberately designed for this purpose, has probably frightened investors who might otherwise have put private money into Quebec resources.

REALISM NEEDED

What is needed in this situation above all is a sense of realism, and much good will. The realist who knows his facts will understand that nothing, not even the FLQ terrorism, will prevent the more creative and imaginative minds in Quebec from continuing their struggle to improve their cultural position and to enlarge their individual opportunities as members of the French-speaking community.

This is the essential issue. Either Quebec is going to produce some kind of French culture in North America, of which every person in Quebec can be proud, and all persons outside also appreciative and respectful, or it is not worth trying. Surely all English Canada must believe they ought to succeed in this effort. They must not be deflected from this purpose by the activities of terrorists whose primary aim is not so much the expansion of a culture as the achievement of political power for Maoist or Communist ends.

More and more people are coming to believe that the capitalist system, with its structures and values, is an obstacle in the way of developing a truly humane French culture, as it is to the development of a humane English culture in Canada. This problem both communities in Canada are tackling, though in my opinion with not sufficient vigor. We are accustomed to accept great injustices, partly because we did not really see them, and partly because we did not think there was any way of overcoming them easily. This time has passed. The productivity of modern technology could rehouse the population that needs better housing, could feed the people who have insufficient food, and could give employment to all who honestly sought it, in useful and inspiring activities, if we put the resources at our command to this great social purpose. But the present profit-seeking organization of the economy renders this extremely difficult. An increasing appreciation of this fact is the source of the revolutionary activities of so many people.

We have witnessed, in several parts of Canada resulting from the crisis in Quebec, young people expressing support for the FLQ. This does not necessarily mean that they like violence, nor that they support the tactics of kidnapping and murder. What it does mean, in my opinion, is that they support the global attack of the FLQ upon the false values, the corporate structure, the brainwashing of advertising, that everyone can see is a characteristic of our present economic system. In whatever means we take to deal with the present crisis in Quebec, and whatever new measure we adopt to prevent its recurrence, we must never forget this profound new widespread outlook, formerly held only by avowed socialists.

I still believe that we can hold off the violent revolutionaries while we apply ourselves to the solution of the problems which they rightly emphasize. I think to imagine that there are quick solutions to these problems is juvenile, and to label our society as nothing but oppressive and aggressive and violent is oversimplifying and greatly exaggerating. By comparison

with almost any previous condition of the human race in any part of the world, our present society contains as many humanitarian and democratic activities as have ever been seen before. It is therefore a question of the speed of change and the degree to which one trusts the processes, cumbersome though they may, in our present democratic institutions.

Source: Originally published in the *Montreal Gazette*, October 24, 1970; repr. in Michiel Horn, ed., *Frank R. Scott: A New Endeavour: Selected Political Essays, Letters, and Addresses* (Toronto: University of Toronto Press, 1986), 126-30.

Pierre Elliott Trudeau (1919—)

On Quebec Nationalism and Separatism

Pierre Elliott Trudeau was one of Canada's longest-serving and most intriguing prime ministers. He was certainly the prime minister with the greatest claim to being an intellectual, having studied at the Université de Montréal, Harvard, and the London School of Economics, written influential essays on law and politics, and taught law at the Université de Montréal in the 1960s.

In his early career he was a reformer and a man of the left, a critic of the conservative nationalism of Quebec Premier Duplessis, and a founder of the progressive Quebec review *Cité libre*. Along with labour leader Jean Marchand (1918–1988) and journalist Gérard Pelletier (1919–1997), he entered national politics to demonstrate that federalism was a viable option for Quebeckers. He was first elected as a Liberal MP in 1965, rose rapidly to become minister of justice, and then succeeded Lester Pearson as leader in 1968. His first election campaign was marked by "Trudeaumania," in which his unconventional personal and political style captivated Canadian voters. With the exception of a few months in 1979, he served as prime minister from 1968 to 1984.

A foe of nationalism since his days at the London School of Economics, he was determined to create an alternative to Quebec nationalism and the emerging separatist movement in Quebec by reforming Canadian federalism, entrenching official bilingualism, and repatriating the British North America Act, Canada's constitution, from Britain. His staunch opposition to Quebec independence, and the intellectuals who kept such dreams alive, earned him the

enmity of many Quebeckers, especially opinion leaders and artists, though he enjoyed continued electoral success in his native province. Excerpts from an article in which he set out his
views on Quebec nationalism, "The New Treason of the Intellectuals," appear below.

The New Treason of the Intellectuals

We must accept the facts of history as they are. However outworn and absurd it may be, the nation-state image spurred the political thinking of the British, and subsequently of Canadians of British descent in the "Dominion of Canada." Broadly speaking, this meant identifying the Canadian state with themselves to the greatest degree possible.

Since the French Canadians had the bad grace to decline assimilation, such an identification was beyond being completely realizable. So the Anglo-Canadians built themselves an illusion of it by fencing off the French Canadians in their Quebec ghetto and then nibbling at its constitutional powers and carrying them off bit by bit to Ottawa. Outside Quebec they fought, with staggering ferocity, against anything that might intrude upon that illusion: the use of French on stamps, money, cheques, in the civil service, the railroads, and the whole works.

In the face of such aggressive nationalism, what choice lay before the French Canadians over, say, the last century? On the one hand they could respond to the vision of an overbearing Anglo-Canadian nation-state with a rival vision of a French-Canadian nation-state; on the other hand they could scrap the very idea of nation-state once and for all and lead the way toward making Canada a multi-national state.

The first choice was, and is, that of the Separatists or advocates of independence; an emotional and prejudiced choice essentially – which goes for their antagonists too, for that matter – and I could never see any sense in it. Because either it is destined to succeed by achieving independence, which would prove that the nationalism of Anglo-Canadians is neither intransigent, nor armed to the teeth, nor so very dangerous for us; and in that case I wonder why we are so afraid to face these people in the bosom of a pluralistic state and why we are prepared to renounce our right to consider Canada our home *a mari usque ad mare*. Or else the attempt at independence is doomed to failure and the plight of the French Canadians will be worse than ever; not because a victorious and vindictive enemy will deport part of the population and leave the rest with dwindled rights and a ruined heritage – this eventuality seems most unlikely; but because once again French Canadians will have poured all their vital energies into a (hypothetically) fruitless struggle, energies that should have been used to match in excellence, efficacy, and persistence a (hypothetically) fearsome enemy.

The second choice, for the multi-national state, was, and is, that of the Constitutionalists. It would reject the bellicose and self-destructive idea of nation-state in favour of the more civilized goal of polyethnic pluralism. I grant that in certain countries and at periods of history this may have been impossible, notably where aggressive nationalism has enjoyed a crushing predominance and refused all compromise with national minorities. Was this the case in the time of Papineau and the *patriotes*? I doubt it; but the fact remains that the upshot of this "separatist" uprising was an Act of Union which marked a step backward for minority rights from the Constitutional Act of 1791.

As a matter of fact, this second choice was, and is, possible for French Canadians. In a sense the multi-national state was dreamed about by Lafontaine, realized under Cartier, perfected by Laurier, and humanized with Bourassa. Anglo-Canadian nationalism has never enjoyed a crushing predominance and has never been in a position to refuse all compromise with the country's principal national minority; consequently, it has been unable to follow the policy perhaps most gratifying to its arrogance, and has had to resign itself to the situation as imposed by the course of events.

* * *

As I have already said earlier in this article, we must separate once and for all the concepts of state and of nation, and make Canada a truly pluralistic and polyethnic society. Now in order for this to come about, the different regions within the country must be assured of a wide range of local autonomy, such that each national group, with an increasing background of experience in self-government, may be able to develop the body of laws and institutions essential to the fullest expression and development of their national characteristics. At the same time, the English Canadians, with their own nationalism, will have to retire gracefully to their proper place, consenting to modify their own precious image of what Canada ought to be. If they care to protect and realize their own special ethnic qualities, they should do it within this framework of regional and local autonomy rather than a pan-Canadian one.

For the incorporation of these diverse aspirations the Canadian constitution is an admirable vehicle. Under the British North America Act, the jurisdiction of the federal State of Canada concerns itself with all the things that have no specific ethnic implications, but that have to do with the welfare of the entire Canadian society: foreign affairs, the broader aspects of economic stability, foreign trade, navigation, postal services, money and banking, and so on. The provinces, on the other hand, have jurisdiction over matters of a purely local and private nature and those that affect ethnic peculiarities: education, municipal and parochial affairs, the administration of justice, the celebration of marriage, property and civil rights, and so forth. Nevertheless, in keeping with the fact that none of the provincial borders coincide perfectly with ethnic or linguistic delineations, no provincial government is encouraged to legislate exclusively for the benefit of a particular ethnic group in such a way as to foster a nation-state mentality at the provincial level. On this point the record of

Quebec's treatment of its minorities can well stand as an example to other provinces with large French, German, Ukrainian, and other minorities.

I have no intention of closing my eyes to how much Canadians of British origin have to do – or rather, undo – before a pluralist state can become a reality in Canada. But I am inclined to add that that is *their* problem. The die is cast in Canada: there are two main ethnic and linguistic groups; each is too strong and too deeply rooted in the past, too firmly bound to a mother-culture, to be able to engulf the other. But if the two will collaborate at the hub of a truly pluralistic state, Canada could become the envied seat of a form of federalism that belongs to tomorrow's world. Better than the American melting pot, Canada could offer an example to all those new Asian and African states already discussed at the beginning of this article, who must discover how to govern their polyethnic populations with proper regard for justice and liberty. What better reason for cold-shouldering the lure of annexation to the United States? Canadian federalism is an experiment of major proportions; it could become a brilliant prototype for the moulding of tomorrow's civilization.

Source: Pierre Trudeau, *Federalism and the French Canadians* (Toronto: Macmillan, 1968), 164-5, 177-9.

Trudeau's opposition to Quebec independence seemed to have suffered a setback when in 1976 Quebec elected the sovereignist Parti Québécois under René Lévesque. For many Canadians, the unthinkable had happened. A frail, divided independence movement, which had claimed, at most, 13 per cent of Quebeckers in the early 1960s, had been transformed into a majority government. Canada's future was at risk.

Trudeau should have been among the victims; after all, he had been elected in 1968 partly because Canadians believed that he had the answer to Quebec's disaffection. Yet Trudeau was defiant. With the same icy logic and utter calm with which he faced other crises in his political career, the prime minister stated the issues and rallied an anxious and divided country. Trudeau's November 17th speech, reprinted below, demonstrated his extraordinary ability to seize public opinion.

Negotiation Yes Appeasement No

To some Canadians last week's election in Quebec has given rise to many hopes. To many other Canadians it has been a cause of great concern, but to all it has posed many questions, and I believe it is incumbent upon me, as Prime Minister of this nation, to try, by way of response to some of these questions, to try to take stock of the current situation.

The first fact that we must acknowledge is that democracy is in good health in Quebec, and that is good news.

When a young party less than 10 years old, fighting only its third general election, can take power, while respecting the democratic liberties, I think this phenomenon has few equals in the world today. It is a victory for thousands of party workers who, with no support other than their faith in an idea, and in their belief in political morality, have taken the Parti Québécois into power. That is a victory for them, but it is also a source of satisfaction for the great majority of Quebeckers who believe in the democratic process, many of whom certainly will hope to use that process to defeat the very ideas of the Parti Québécois in their day.

The second fact is that Quebec does not believe in separatism. Now, this proposition, perhaps apparently paradoxical, is very easy to demonstrate. The Parti Québécois was defeated in 1970 and again in 1973, those two elections when it advocated the separation of Quebec. But it won in 1976 when it repeated over and over again that the issue was not separation of the provinces but sound administration of that province.

Thus the separatists themselves do not believe that separatism has the support of Quebeckers, and that, for me, is the second piece of good news.

The third fact: Quebeckers have chosen a new government; not a new country. Mr. Lévesque has no mandate to bring in separation, nor, of course, do I, nor do I have the desire to ask for such a mandate. Consequently, the federal government and the provincial government will have to co-operate together within the framework of the Constitution, continuing to serve to the utmost the interest of the people of Quebec, just as the federal Government, in co-operation with the other provincial governments, seeks to fulfil and serve the interests of the peoples of the other provinces.

But now within provincial jurisdiction, the Quebec Government has a very important priority, and will have to face many serious internal problems. The school questions, the stability of investments, management-labor relations, to mention only three of the more serious of those as an example. But for other problems, those which come under the jurisdiction of both levels of government, for those problems, the solution can only come through close co-operation with the federal Government . . .

I do want, however, to issue a caution, particularly for those who think that more decentralization, or a new separation of powers would solve our present worries. I say it is a grave illusion to believe that those who seek the breakup of Canada would suddenly cease to pursue their objective simply because the provincial governments have increased their powers in some areas, say, communications or immigration or fiscal powers, or cultural matters.

The question facing us is much more profound. The stakes for Canadians are much more important and the question is this: can Francophones of Quebec consider Canada as their country, or must they feel at home only in Quebec? And you know as well as I know that a new sharing of power between Ottawa and the provinces will never give the answer to that particular question, will never make a Francophone feel more at home in Toronto or in Vancouver than he does in Quebec.

Quebeckers, like citizens of the other provinces, are proud. They seek personal fulfillment in a free and independent way. The central question, therefore, is whether this growth of freedom and independence is best assured by Canada, or by Quebec alone. Canadians must think about this brutal question now. Not only think of solving it in words, but by deeds and through their attitudes. In the area of language problem, of course, but also in the very important areas of regional disparity and social justice.

With the victory of the Parti Québécois, we can no longer afford to postpone these questions by one generation, to put the problem aside for the next generation of Canadians, and in this sense, the crisis is real; the crisis is now, and the challenge is immediate. I believe that Canada cannot, indeed, that Canada must not survive by force. The country will only remain united – it should only remain united – if its citizens want to live together in one civil society.

History created this country from the meeting of two realities; the French and the English realities. Then these were enriched by the contributions of people from all parts of the world, but this coming together, this meeting, this encounter of realities, though at times difficult to accept, and hard to practice, this encounter has, itself, become the fabric of our life as a nation, the source of our individuality, the very cornerstone of our identity as a people.

Our forefathers willed this country into being. Times, circumstance and pure will cemented us together in a unique national enterprise, and that enterprise, by flying in the face of all expectations, of all experiences, of all conventional wisdom, that enterprise provides the world with a lesson in fraternity.

This extraordinary undertaking is so advanced on the road to liberty, so advanced in the way of social justice and of prosperity, that to abandon it now would be to sin against the spirit; to sin against humanity.

I have known René Lévesque for many years, some 20 years. I personally know many of his colleagues. I respect their intelligence and their dedication. We all believe in equality; we all want liberty and equality and democracy for the citizens of this country, but we disagree profoundly on the means to be employed.

My disagreement with Mr. Lévesque, dating back some 10 years, arises out of my conviction that there is room in Canada for all Canadians. He, on the other hand, probably not without regret – perhaps even with sadness – he, on the other hand, believes the opposite. He has, therefore, surrounded himself with a strong core of blood brothers, and he speaks to the rest of Canada as one speaks to good neighbors.

For myself, I believe that it is possible to be, at the same time, a good Canadian and a good

Quebecker. Just as it is possible to be a good Canadian and a good Nova Scotian, or a good British Columbian. And I will fight to the end against anyone who wants to prevent me from being both.

Today I am addressing all Canadians, as I have since I have taken office. I am speaking to you as to my fellow citizens. I am speaking to you of a deeper brotherhood than that of blood, of a fraternity of hope and of charity in the scriptural sense, for if the Canadian nation must survive, it will only survive in mutual respect and in love for one another.

Each of you, each of us, must work toward that goal with our every fibre in the reality of our daily lives. You can be assured that, as your Prime Minister, and as a consequence, as your servant and fellow Canadian, I will continue to work toward these objectives with all my strength.

Source: *Globe and Mail*, November 17, 1976.

Marie-Claire Blais (1939–)

"AU PENSIONNAT"

Marie-Claire Blais won early recognition as one of Quebec's greatest novelists. In 1965 she won the Prix France-Canada for *Une saison dans la vie d'Emmanuel*. *Manuscrits de Pauline Archange*, from which this extract is taken, won the Governor General's Award for Fiction in 1968.

While the Catholic Church has faded with astonishing suddenness from the ordinary lives of Quebeckers, generations who grew up before the mid-1960s were shaped by their schooling with the Christian Brothers or the many orders of nuns. Blais may not be the most sympathetic of witnesses to Quebec history before the Quiet Revolution, but she makes it easier to understand why the great superstructure of the Church would disappear with so few regrets.

The scents of breakfast come wafting from the refectory; but the breakfast is not for us, not yet. It is for the novices, who have been at prayer all night. Lips glued against my white veil, I eat off tiny scraps of lace as I walk along the corridors, passing beggars slouched against the steps, waiting for the remains of our yesterday's stew. They watch us humbly as we dis- appear toward the chapel. At the first stroke of the clapper, all knees drop onto the cold flagstones; at the second, I rush to my seat and open a missal brimming with funereal or saintly pictures, little photographs of dead people smiling amid the flowers of a frozen spring: here is Uncle Sébastien disguised as a handsome, immortal young man, and nearer to me still, Séraphine in her first-communion dress, her face half hidden by a bunch of roses held in one hand.

We emerge from the chapel two by two, taking care not to let our elbows touch, because that is a sin. Mother Sainte-Gabrielle announces that "we must clean out the classrooms before filling our stomachs." We scrub the blackboards, we scrape the inkstains off the floorboards with a razor blade, and Mother Sainte-Gabrielle stands over us, wearing an ironic, weary expression. Oh, what a dismal task a tyrant's is! How dreary never to receive any homage but the animal supplication of those thin faces, without hatred, without love! To look down at all those bowed heads inside which so much hypocrisy is furtively concealed! But there is the second bell for breakfast, at last! The big bowl of gruel is carried in past our noses, its reek made bearable by familiarity. Bless us, O Lord, and that which we are about to eat; there is no knowing if one is quivering with nausea or hunger, but one must eat. The tall Mother in charge of the refectory, a bearded Argus, dips her spoon parsimoniously into the boiled garbage before her: at the sound of her tongue smacking behind her black lips – "Hmmm, what delicious gruel" – we gulp down the contents of our bowls with a feeling of deliverance, for an initial void recedes, leaving its place to another, and this well-digested inward absence already feels a little less like the hunger of the evening before. We have eaten, prayed, done the novices' dishes, ah, Mother Sainte-Gabrielle, can we have permission now to leave the room?

"You can go at twelve, after classes."

"I want to go now, Mother."

"No."

All morning Mother Sainte-Gabrielle will continue to eye her victims with tenderness. She pretends to forget the torture she is inflicting on those lower bowels that God has so unfortunately created, she even forces herself to suffer with us, refusing to leave the room herself until midday. (Hence the almost winged urgency with which we see her vanishing up toward the second floor, her face red, her lips tightly pinched over her inner mystery.) She comforts us by telling us "that the body is nothing, a mere appearance of vanity, nothing more." It would be nice to believe her, oh how nice!

But one acquires the habit of living with a body thus slighted and humiliated. As we walk through the big girls' dormitory, in the morning, we are sometimes witnesses to strange scenes. "Quicker, walk quicker," Mother Sainte-Gabrielle cries, but the eye of memory flicks avidly open, capturing forever the image of a young girl sobbing on her knees beside her bloodstained bed, while the nun standing near her seems to be hiding in her round, magnanimous eyes the murderer, the incurable monster whose thoughts one can read.

"Give me something, Mother, it's running all down my legs . . ."

"It's a punishment from God, do as best you can with toilet paper."

"You must flatten your chest with a wide band of elastic so as not to tempt the devil."

"You must wear a corset and pull your stomach

in against your spine." That's the life the big girls lead, and we feel pity for their bodies subjected to those hard regulations. In the meantime, Mother Sainte-Gabrielle d'Egypte keeps her jealous eye on us too. One by one, she takes away from me the books that Mlle Léonard brings.

"That's not the sort of book for you. You'd far better read the *Imitation of Jesus Christ.*"

Later, she was to wait until night to seize our secret diaries, our exercise books full of poems. Why should we have the right to make our inner landscapes fruitful, the right to think and even to live, when she, from the moment of her entry into the convent, had renounced all hope, all vanity? And it was not the fear of God alone that haunted her compulsive brain – in which the waves had nevertheless now ceased to flow, leaving only a tempest of obsessions, a paralyzed impulsion toward the shore of life; there was also the terror of man. She was to say one day, during class, with a snort of disgust, that "all men are pigs," and then, astonished by this outburst, become suddenly silent, one hand up to her mouth. The smallest girls listen to her. They consent perhaps to her disgust. But I escape, I fly toward Jacquou and our gully, toward the explosive dazzle of that day in the trees. That summer will never come again, or that summer and miraculous autumn when Séraphine was beside me in our games. And now I see no one to love. I find that one of my classmates has slipped me a note during school: "Pauline Archange, wate for me in the recriation yard, we can skip roap together, signed, Augustine Gendron who loves you," but cruelly I draw away from Augustine and the poverty she exhales. During recreation I stand in the hole made by the courtyard and gaze up at the sky. I am bored.

Source: Marie-Claire Blais, *The Manuscripts of Pauline Archange*, trans. Derek Coltman (New York: Farrar, Straus and Giroux, 1969), 96-8.

Judy LaMarsh (1924–1980)

WOMEN IN POLITICS

Judy LaMarsh was a lawyer and politician who served in several federal Liberal cabinets from 1963 to 1968. She was known as a controversial minister and a strong advocate of the welfare state. During her tenure as minister of health and welfare, the Canada Pension plan was implemented and the outline of Canada's medicare system was designed.

Judy LaMarsh was a successful politician before feminism had begun to open doors for women in politics. As secretary of state in 1968, she helped establish the Royal Commission on the Status of Women. And, if the job of being a woman in politics is not easy today, it was far more difficult in the 1960s. LaMarsh resisted being labelled as someone responsible only for women's issues. But she faced harsh scrutiny and a host of ingrained prejudices and systemic barriers throughout her career. The following account from her memoirs gives us a feel for the travails she went through.

In the years I was present in Ottawa as a parliamentarian, I remember only one case in which a woman served as chairman of a committee. She was a Senator and a co-chairman at that. It was Senator Muriel Fergusson and her committee was a special committee on the Canada Pension Plan. There are no women serving among the officers of the House of Commons, nor of the Senate, nor have there ever been any. To my knowledge, Senator Nancy Hodges of British Columbia was the first woman Speaker in the Commonwealth, and there has been one since in Manitoba, but never in Ottawa. Although there have been two women ministers, there have only been two women parliamentary secretaries, both of them to the Department of National Health and Welfare. The parliamentary Librarian is a man, Legal Counsel to both Houses are men, and although there are and have been first-rate women on the interpreters' staff and on the Hansard reporters' staff, they never have a woman chief. To my recollection, the nurse is the highest appointment to the House staff occupied by a woman.

Nor do women fare better in institutions connected with Parliament, notably the fourth estate. There are very few women reporters assigned to Ottawa. I do not remember a political columnist who was a woman, save the late Judith Robinson and Margaret Aitken (herself three times elected to the House). The press gallery does not permit women to attend its gala yearly function, the Press Gallery Dinner. Members of the Gallery broke this cardinal rule by inviting all women members (four of us) to the 1967 dinner, to which, for the first time, women members of the Gallery itself were also allowed to come. That oversight was rectified in 1968, when only the women gallery members were permitted to attend. I cannot understand why women are excluded; it is a very staid affair, neither as drunken as repute has it nor as hilarious. On the 1967 occasion, my own escort, a columnist from a Toronto paper, was glum while sober and not in evidence while not. Since I was one of the main targets of the lampooning of the evening, I suppose it was only simple justice that I should be given the opportunity to listen to the skits in person. We women members had been indifferent to the invitation when it was received, but felt we must all go in order to acknowledge this progressive step taken by the Gallery members. Perhaps the ratio of four women to the five hundred male guests was what made the members decide in 1968 that they could not proffer another invitation.

Public life in Ottawa revolves about time-hallowed institutions, both that of Parliament and the life that surrounds it. Across Wellington Street from the Parliament Buildings, broods the haven of the Establishment, the Rideau Club. Its members are all men. It serves indifferent food and is no particularly attractive sight, but the advantages of its membership are that it has proximity to Parliament and that it is "in" to belong to it. It has had this aura since its founding. Women are permitted on the premises, but only as guests and only at the dinner hour or later. Within the past few years, profound change has taken place, for the Rideau Club has established a ladies' dining room, so that wives or women guests may come onto the premises during the daylight hours. The premises are not equal; they are separate. From time to time the Government of Canada engages a dining room in the Rideau Club for an official or semi-official function. At one of these, hosted by Paul Martin for a foreign dignitary, two women, Pauline Jewett and Margaret Konantz, both then members of Parliament, were invited as guests. But this was a luncheon, and as the two members entered the lobby and prepared to climb the winding staircase and take their seats officially, they were apprehended and barred from the Club, it being only noontime. It did not matter that they were members of Parliament; they were only women!

Another of Ottawa's venerable institutions is the Royal Ottawa Golf Club. Set in a beautiful sweep of the Gatineau Hills, it is actually located in Hull, not in Ottawa. It does permit women members to join and they swarm about its fairways. But when, in the spring of 1968, one of its oldest and most respected lady members died, the club management refused to lower its flag as tradition called for, explaining that this mark of respect was tendered only to men!

Within the Government itself, there are, of course, plenty of women in stenographic positions, some even in special positions as executive secretaries. Most ministers have one. There was, however, only one executive assistant (the summit of the appointive staff positions) who was a woman. She was Mary Macdonald of Pearson's staff. Mary had been with the Prime Minister from his days in External Affairs. She was devoted to him, she was interested in women's rights, and she did whatever she could to impress upon the P.M. the recognition of women. While she did not, in fact, perform the function of executive assistant, she did have the title and the salary that went with it. There are more than thirty Deputy Ministers in Ottawa, and countless others who occupy an equivalent position in the Government pecking-order and pay scale. Only one of these was a woman.

* * *

I grew tired of being the woman's watchdog. I grew tired of having the role thrust upon me simply because I was a woman. I was paid exactly what my male colleagues were paid, although many of them did not perform one-fifth of the work I did for the Government or for the Liberal party. I was particularly bitter about a Supreme Court of Ontario judgment released in early 1968. The case involved a policewoman in Northern Ontario who was paid less than her colleagues because, as a woman, she did not perform the same duties as they, and also because she did not have the same dependants to provide for! In the words of Mr. Justice Fergusson, of that Court, this inequality conforms to "all the rules of civilization, economics, family life and common sense." This is Ontario, in 1968!

* * *

I was always expected to be present when we had women's delegations attending upon the Cabinet. I was, further, expected to be particularly diligent in attending conventions of the party's women, and to make regular rounds in speaking to any and every women's organization which proffered me an invitation. I was the usual invitee whenever any organization, anywhere in Canada, held its annual "ladies night." I was asked to fashion shows, award dinners, and meetings of the professions in which women were a dominant group. My clothes, my stockings, my wigs were a matter of public discussion. (Until Pierre Elliott Trudeau, I do not remember any other member's style of dressing ever in the public print.) My weight, my age, my home, my cooking, my hobbies, my friends, my tastes, my likes and dislikes, all became public property to a degree suffered by none of my colleagues, including the Prime Minister. I was two or three times named "Woman of the Year" (not because of anything I did which was important, but because more lines of type appeared about me than about any other woman). Reporters followed me into the hairdressers, photographers tagging along.

Executive women followed me into washrooms, wives clustered about me in airports to receive me as I stumbled, bedraggled and exhausted, from an aircraft for yet another meeting. Children and teachers wrote me for recipes and for tips on how to get along as a woman. Columnists asked me about anything and everything – except about my job. Women's magazines and women's pages featured articles about me – sometimes without bothering to interview me. Cartoonists delighted in sketching me and my clothes and swelling girth. And always the whispers and speculation about my sex life – how much, and with whom? Every member with a pack of eager school-children visiting sought out the lady minister to talk; every member with a group of women politicians in tow asked me to meet with them; every woman politician from another country who visited Ottawa was at once shown in to me. I could not stop without being recognized and spoken to, my purchases eyed, the prices I was paying assessed. I could not walk down the street in Ottawa, or elsewhere, without being constantly on parade. Although most of these encounters were pleasant, the curiosity of the public took the greatest toll of me of anything in politics. For a while I talked freely on television and to the press, hoping that once my views were thoroughly known, I would be an object of curiosity no longer, but the publicity seemed to increase it. When first elected to Parliament, I was approached by Gerald Waring, a columnist and reporter to my hometown newspaper. One of the first things he asked me, as we sat in the noisy madhouse of the parliamentary cafeteria, was, "Are you a politician, or a woman?" Just as though the two were mutually exclusive! And that inquisitiveness only reflected what others thought.

Pearson never considered my sex when he invited me to undertake countless by-election appearances, nor to undertake the Truth Squad, not when I assumed the backbreaking duties that would have broken the health of most of my colleagues. Although he offered me National Health and Welfare, a big, busy department with much to be done, he was breaking no new ground, for he knew that women have been appointed to similar posts all over the free world. And when he appointed me as Secretary of State, he was only following the appointment of Ellen Fairclough earlier to that same post. Pearson could not, for instance, have conceived of me as the Minister of Energy (although I am sure I know as much about the subject as say Jean-Luc Pepin or Joe Greene when first appointed), nor as Labour Minister (although the most successful of American Cabinet Secretaries, of the miserable two so far appointed, were appointments made by F.D.R. – Frances Perkins to Health and Welfare, and Oveta Culp Hobby to Education), nor as Justice Minister (although I had practised in far more courts than Lucien Cardin and P. E. Trudeau combined). Whether in law, the military, or in politics, I always resisted an appointment to a position to "hang the lace curtains." But wherever there is a challenging job to be done which I can do without regard to my sex, I am eager to try. Whenever I am pushed by

direction of my superiors in office or by public opinion to appear a woman's representative, I simply do not know what to do. My feelings of resentment and frustration multiply; I find I can operate as a person, but I do not know how to operate as a woman.

For a long time, I was not really aware that I was an object of such intense scrutiny, so far as my private life was concerned; or if aware, it simply didn't hit home. I have seen articles about me which deal at length with the jealousy of my colleagues' wives (although never with those with whom I became fast friends), with the fact that I travelled with several young men on my staff (although I was always careful not to travel with any one young man), and with other barely hidden and not very pleasant suggestions. I am no more saint than anyone else, but I cannot say I have heard the same rampant speculation about my male colleagues and their friends. Scandal is the first weapon, the most continuous one, and the last weapon used against a woman anywhere, and particularly one of political prominence. I have had repeated to me by friends, families, and foes the most horrendous stories of my personal life. I have been accused of the full spectrum of sensual impropriety – funny had it not been so malicious. Perhaps the curiosity is natural, but it was so intensified in my case that it became a cardinal factor in my decision to retire.

I am a private person and I desperately sought privacy. When one can no longer bear the heat in the kitchen, one leaves it. Even as a private person I have found that my views are sought from time to time by newspapermen. (Why? Because there is "always a story in me," according to them.) I have been charged by some of them with being a publicity-seeker, when in fact I shun it when I can. I admit to being publicity-prone, but that is no more my fault than if I were accident-prone. I long to live quietly, but I have lost the secret of how to do it. It appears that to make a living I must stay on display as a public property. The first woman federal Member of Parliament, Agnes MacPhail, wrote, "The misery of being under observation and being unduly criticized is what I remember most. Visitors in the Gallery couldn't help seeing one woman among so many men, but they made no effort to disguise the fact that I was a curiosity and stared whenever I could be seen." After forty-five years, that soul-destroying public avidity is unchanged. The public still devours its own, and I have found that it is only in Niagara Falls people accept me as I am and leave me alone. Where there are twenty-five men, the public's interest is split; when there is one woman, she becomes a focus for criticism and for curiosity.

Source: Judy LaMarsh, *Memoirs of a Bird in a Gilded Cage* (Toronto: McClelland and Stewart, 1970), 301-2, 316-19.

Alden Nowlan (1933–83)

"Ypres: 1915"

At the frontline Belgian city of Ypres in April 1915, Canada's First Contingent faced its baptism of fire. As clouds of chlorine gas rolled towards them, French and Algerian troops broke and fled. Canadians, on the right, found their flanks open and struggled desperately to restore the line. On April 24th, it was their turn to attract German fury. Artillery shells and massed infantry, with gas as an added horror, drove the Canadians from their positions. Yet somehow, at the cost of 6036 men, half their unit's fighting strength, the raw Canadians staged a fighting retreat and finally held. Ignoring the confusion and mistakes of any formation in its first battle, the British official communiqué announced: "The Canadians had many casualties but their gallantry and determination undoubtedly saved the situation."

Those words gave comfort to a country that had survived the bloodiest battle of its history so far. For Alden Nowlan, a New Brunswick poet and writer, the memory of Ypres was special. He was right. The image of Canadians marching steadfastly past fleeing Algerians was as phoney as another legend of the Great War, that of the "Crucified Canadian." And there were other soldiers – British, Indian, and French – who fought as valiantly as Canadians (more than half of whom were British-born in any case). But Nowlan's picture of Private Billy MacNally from the south end of Saint John rings true, too.

The age of trumpets is passed, the banners hang
like dead crows, tattered and black,
rotting into nothingness on cathedral walls.
In the crypt of St. Paul's I had all the wrong thoughts,
wondered if there was anything left of Nelson
or Wellington, and even wished
I could pry open their tombs and look,
then was ashamed
of such morbid childishness and almost afraid.

I know the picture is as much a forgery
as the Protocols of Zion, yet it outdistances
more plausible fictions: newsreels, regimental histories,
biographies of Earl Haig.
        It is always morning
and the sky somehow manages to be red though the picture
        is in black and white.
There is a long road over flat country,
shell holes, the debris of houses,
a gun carriage overturned in a field,
the bodies of men and horses,
but only a few of them and those
always neat and distant.
        The Moors are running
down the right side of the road.
The Moors are running
in their baggy pants and Santa Claus caps.
The Moors are running.
        And their officers,
Frenchmen who remember
Alsace and Lorraine,
are running backwards in front of them,
waving their swords, trying to drive them back,
weeping
        at the dishonour of it all.
The Moors are running.

And on the left side of the same road,
the Canadians are marching
in the opposite direction.

The Canadians are marching
in English uniforms behind
a piper playing "Scotland the Brave."

The Canadians are marching
in impeccable formation,
every man in step.
The Canadians are marching.

And I know this belongs
with Lord Kitchener's moustache
and old movies in which the Kaiser and his general staff
seem to run like the Keystone Kops.

That old man on television last night,
a farmer or fisherman by the sound of him,
revisiting Vimy Ridge, and they asked him
what it was like, and he said,
There was water up to our middles, yes,
and there was rats, and yes,
there was water up to our middles
and rats, all right enough,
and to tell you the truth
after the first three or four days
I started to get a little disgusted.

Oh, I know they were mercenaries
in a war that hardly concerned us.
I know all that
Sometimes I'm not even sure that I have a country.

But I know they stood there at Ypres
the first time the Germans used gas,
that they were almost the only troops
in that section of the front
who did not break and run,
who held the line.

Perhaps they were too scared to run.
Perhaps they didn't know any better
   that is possible, they were so innocent,
those farmboys and mechanics, you have only to look
at old pictures and see how they smiled.
Perhaps they were too shy
to walk out on anybody, even Death.
Perhaps their only motivation
was a stubborn disinclination.

Private MacNally thinking:
You squareheaded sons of bitches,
you want this God damn trench
you're going to have to take it away
from Billy MacNally
of the South End of Saint John, New Brunswick.
And that's ridiculous, too, and nothing
on which to found a country.
      Still
it makes me feel good, knowing
that in some obscure, conclusive way
they were connected with me
and me with them.

Source: John Robert Colombo, *How Do I Love Thee: Sixty Poets of Canada (and Quebec) Select and Introduce Their Favourite Poems from Their Own Work* (Edmonton: Hurtig, 1970), 94-6.

Roderick Haig-Brown (1908–1976)

BRITISH COLUMBIA

Born in England, Roderick Haig-Brown came to the American west in 1926 and was quickly captivated by the hunting and fishing and the unspoiled beauty of the Rockies. In 1931 he emigrated to British Columbia and, in the harsh economic climate of the 1930s, managed to make a living by logging, trapping, guiding and, as he found his voice, writing. Haig-Brown became part of the Canadian tradition of nature writing, particularly for children. *Starbuck Valley Winter* and *Saltwater Summer*, its sequel, were widely acclaimed and the latter won a Governor General's Award in 1948. Among adults, Haig-Brown found his audience in his writing about sports fishing. *A Primer of Fly Fishing* remains the standard work on the subject.

Haig-Brown annoyed fellow British Columbians by his emphasis on conservation and his opposition to the rip n'run style of exploitation common in the west and supported by workers and their families for the sake of short-term "jobs." In this article, his love of British Columbia is apparent. So is his concern for its future.

Flying into it, as most modern visitors are likely to, from any direction except the west, the province is a spectacular array of mountain ridges, seamed and furrowed with snow, more or less heavily timbered on the lower slopes, the deep and narrow valleys floored by the reflected blue or steel-grey of the long lakes. Settlements are scattered and tiny, the few roads to be seen climb out of nothing into emptiness. Then there is the long let-down over the widening green of the Fraser delta, black city smog clinging along the mountain slopes, and the luxurious spread of settlement at the edge of the Gulf of Georgia. At night the transition is even more dramatic from occasional dim and tiny lights scattered through black immensity to the jewelled glare of neon and mercury vapor and ribboned headlights laid out in a pattern of unlikely beauty for miles on every side.

As a quick impression, it conveys as much truth as any other. But people are living and working out among those mountains, along those narrow valleys, out over the spread of the interior plateau, up the long coastal inlets. The rich glow of lights, the formidable concentration of settlement down in the southwest corner of the province is the yield of a hundred years of men burrowing into the mountains, stripping trees from the timbered slopes, raking the coastal seas, fighting the inland rivers, threading narrow ways through the canyons, chancing cattle among the gentler hills and kindlier valleys. Nearly a million people live on those eight hundred square miles of delta lands and the same lands produce ninety-seven per cent of the dairy products and fifty per cent of the farm value that comes from the whole province. Considerably less than a million people are scattered over the other 365 thousand square miles, where the mountains rear up and the lakes form and the rivers run down.

British Columbia was a hard place to discover and a hard place to explore. The first explorers were more concerned with finding a passage to China and the Indies through the upset scenery than with finding anything useful in the country itself. In fact they were singularly unimpressed with the looks of the place and at times quite bitter about it. Captain George Vancouver, who put an end to the myth of the Northwest Passage in the early 1790s and explored the entire coast of British Columbia in the course of doing so, was addicted to such phrases as: "the shores put on a very dreary aspect, chiefly composed of rugged rocks, thinly wooded with small dwarf pine trees," thus anticipating the scathing "rocks and Christmas trees" of later coast settlers. In June of 1792, among the islands at the northern end of the Gulf of Georgia, he found "as gloomy and dismal an aspect as nature could well be supposed to exhibit," though he was again thankful for the trees which "screened from our sight the dreary rocks and precipices that compose these desolate shores." As a writer he lacked the angle that makes the tourist folder.

Alexander Mackenzie, who came to the province by land, was somewhat more phlegmatic about it all; but even he, his canoes broken and his men numbed with cold and half-drowned, had few doubts about the quality of the first stream he found across the continental divide: "The evil nature of our small river, which we called the Bad River, was such that we were four full days longer in reaching the big water." Simon Fraser, discovering his great river, had rough words for it: "I scarcely ever saw anything so dreary; and seldom so dangerous in any country . . . whatever way I turn, mountains upon mountains, whose summits are covered with eternal snows, close the glooming scene." Even David Thompson, the kindliest and most receptive of all the explorers, had his moments of doubt on the western slope of the Rockies: "The scene of desolation before us was dreadful, and I knew it. A heavy gale of wind, much more a mountain storm, would have buried us." And then, as he and his men came down into the floor of the Columbia Valley: "We are pygmies among the giant pines and cedars of this country, some of them forty feet in girth and reaching two hundred feet without a branch."

This inhospitable land that so overawed the early explorers was supporting at this time a native population of at least seventy thousand people, many of them in some degree of comfort and security, with a high level of cultural advancement. It took another eighty years, annihilation of the sea otters, decimation of the fur seal herds, the discovery of gold, reduction of the native population (through disease) by some sixty per cent, union with Canada and a transcontinental railroad to build a white population comparable in size to that of their aboriginal predecessors.

As settlement developed it gradually became apparent that this was, after all, a rich and generous land; there were soft and gentle places among its awesome mountains; the mountains themselves had a beauty that inspired affection as well as fear. Richer than gold and more lasting were the zinc and lead of the Kootenays and the copper of the Coast Range. More valuable than beaver skins were the great Douglas firs and red cedars of the coastal forests and the salmon that ran to every river and stream. Farmers boldly dyked and drained the flood plain of the Fraser delta and found themselves with land that would grow almost anything; others in the Okanagan Valley were soon growing tree fruits of superb quality. A pioneer's life was never, anywhere, made up of roses and rapture or lilies and languor, nor even of beer and skittles, but in British Columbia it had worthwhile compensations. The climate was kindly enough, at least in the southern parts and along the coast. Work in the woods or the mines or the fisheries was a source of ready cash, while the dream of independence in the small farm or logging operation, the fishboat or trapline was never too far from probability. For recreation, there were fish to be caught in the streams and lakes, game to be hunted in the hills. Signs of growth and development were evident everywhere and in spite of periodic setbacks no British Columbian doubted them. Logging companies grew massive with the power of steam and sawmills worked into the night; the "white Empresses" of the C.P.R. sailed for the Orient from Vancouver and the proud fleet of coastal steamships grew ever larger, faster, and more luxurious; mines became richer and more sophisticated, the Fraser valley grew the finest dairy products, the Okanagan the finest fruit in the world.

It is rather easy to think of the development of British Columbia as a series of engineering triumphs; the Cariboo Road of Colonel Moody's Royal Engineers, the driving of the C.P.R. through the Fraser canyons and the passes of the Rockies and the Selkirks, the Fraser valley dykes, the logging railroads – often little miracles of ingenuity – the Hell's Gate fishways, the Aluminum Company's Kemano project, the miles upon empty miles of hard-topped highways built in the years since World War Two, the great hydro projects under construction on the Columbia and at Portage mountain – all these represent a good measure of the faith needed to move mountains and confirm the impression of the early explorers that this was indeed a difficult country. But engineering miracles are commonplace on the North American continent and reflect little of the individuality and meaning of a state or province.

In British Columbia there has always been a gallantry about the job and a shoddiness about the end result. The logger, the province's true aristocrat, stands large and bold against the background of his ravaged acres. The hardrock miner, courageous, skilful, and hard handed, moves on, leaving his ghost towns and tailings and abandoned millsites as scars upon the hillsides. The fisherman, proud and independent, struggles in the chaos of a disorganized industry. Farmland, brought to full fertility through three or four lifetimes, makes easy money for the real estate speculator. The construction worker manoeuvres his mighty machines in frantic haste through mud and dust and rock to leave behind him drowned and derelict forests, arrogant mills, and ill-planned cracker-box towns. Enormous log rafts among the coastal inlets, the seine boat fleets, white-face cattle driven down the Chilcotin or spread over the rolling hills of the Nicola Valley, tourists flanked by huge dead fish, loneliness of deep forest and mile-high glacier, gold of poplar and tamarack, desolate black of spruce, reflections in quiet lakes, rock and snow reared against the sky, surge of Pacific surf and watery glint of muskeg miles, all these things, too, are the pictured, familiar face of British Columbia.

Yet far more than all this, the province is an idea of pleasure and rich living, elegant houses hung on the rocks in West Vancouver, money made from nothing, as it always has been, in the big buildings downtown, retirement in Victoria, pleasure boats, year around golf, equitable climate generally, and in contrast with the rest of Canada, easy living.

The other side of this picture is the province's long tradition of militant unions, from the time of the early coal miners to the International Woodworkers, United Fishermen, United Mine Workers, and many others of today. Owing much to British trade unionism and the British Labour Party it has been, for the most part, a strong and successful movement, balancing the easy successes of capital let loose in the broad and fruitful field of natural resources. From the time of Amor de Cosmos and his war upon the "Family-Company-Compact," this view has had expression in the legislature, though usually in opposition. Without its counterbalance and the determined humanity of such men as Ernest Winch, who sat in the B.C. Legislature from 1933 until his death in 1957, the province would have been little better than a playground for economic imperialists, with the spoils going unfailingly to the strong.

Even as it is, British Columbia remains something of an anachronism. Until the last few years the mountains had effectively restricted development to a few favourable areas. Modern machinery and modern technology have suddenly opened up new areas and these are among the last on the continent available for old-fashioned industrial empire-building. Stakes, in the form of capital investment, are high; but the returns, in the form of long-term claims on natural resources, are almost beyond calculation.

Living out the final stages of nineteenth-century concepts in the latter half of the twentieth century, it has so far spared little attention for much beyond physical development. The pragmatic values of education are recognized in some degree and the university at Point Grey has become a great, though overburdened, school; it is now supported by two younger institutions, the universities of Victoria and Simon Fraser, and a growing list of regional colleges. The province's greatest collective artistic endeavour, the Vancouver International

Festival, has faded into steady decline through lack of municipal and provincial support. Yet the province has better artists in almost every field than it deserves or is aware of, and in this may be the real promise of change and growth. British Columbia has the wealth, energy, and newness to become the most enlightened and humanitarian of all the provinces. If the vision has become blurred in the rush of prosperity, it can still be renewed in the calmer times of consolidation.

Source: Roderick Haig-Brown, "British Columbia: Loggers and Lotus-Eaters," in William Kilbourn, *Canada: A Guide to the Peaceable Kingdom* (Toronto: Macmillan, 1970), 124-8.

Northrop Frye (1912–91)

ON CANADIAN IDENTITY

Northrop Frye was perhaps Canada's greatest literary critic. During a long career at the University of Toronto, he carved out a niche as an internationally respected analyst of literary subjects ranging from the Bible to William Blake and other English poets to Canadian literature.

In the latter field, Frye's talent has been to identify the essential elements which have created the Canadian cultural imagination. In this selection, Frye wrestles with the link between national unity and uniformity. Reflecting on his own background in the bilingual towns of Sherbrooke and Moncton, he argues that political unity need not require cultural uniformity.

The question of Canadian identity, so far as it affects the creative imagination, is not a "Canadian" question at all, but a regional question. An environment turned outward to the sea, like so much of Newfoundland, and one turned towards inland seas, like so much of the Maritimes, are an imaginative contrast: anyone who has been conditioned by one in his earliest years can hardly become conditioned by the other in the same way. Anyone brought up on the urban plain of southern Ontario or the gentle *pays* farmland along the south shore of the St. Lawrence may become fascinated by the great sprawling wilderness of Northern Ontario or Ungava, may move there and live with its people and become accepted as one of them, but if he paints or writes about it he will paint or write as an imaginative foreigner. And what can there be in common between an imagination nurtured on the prairies, where it is a centre of consciousness diffusing itself over a vast flat expanse stretching to the remote horizon, and one nurtured in British Columbia, where it is in the midst of gigantic trees and mountains leaping into the sky all around it, and obliterating the horizon everywhere?

Thus when the CBC is instructed by Parliament to do what it can to promote Canadian unity and identity, it is not always realized that unity and identity are quite different things to be promoting, and that in Canada they are perhaps more different than they are anywhere else. Identity is local and regional, rooted in the imagination and in works of culture; unity is national in reference, international in perspective, and rooted in a political feeling. There are, of course, containing imaginative forms which are common to the whole country, even if not peculiar to Canada. I remember seeing an exhibition of undergraduate painting, mostly of landscapes, at a Maritime university. The students had come from all over Canada, and one was from Ghana. The Ghana student had imaginative qualities that the Canadians did not have, but they had something that he did not have, and it puzzled me to place it. I finally realized what it was: he had lived, in his impressionable years, in a world where colour was a constant datum: he had never seen colour as a cycle that got born in spring, matured in a burst of autumn flame, and then died out into a largely abstract, black and white world. But that is a factor of latitude rather than region, and most of the imaginative factors common to the country as a whole are negative influences.

Negative, because in our world the sense of a specific environment as something that provides a circumference for an imagination has to contend with a global civilization of jet planes, international hotels, and disappearing landmarks – that is, an obliterated environment. The obliterated environment produces an imaginative dystrophy that one sees all over the world, most dramatically perhaps in architecture and town planning (as it is ironically called), but in the other arts as well. Canada, with its empty spaces, its largely unknown lakes and rivers and islands, its division of language, its dependence on immense railways to hold it physically together, has had this peculiar problem of an obliterated environment throughout most of its history. The effects of this are clear in the curiously abortive cultural developments of Canada, as is said later in this book. They are shown even more clearly in its present lack of will to resist its own disintegration, in the fact that it is practically the only country left in the world which is a pure colony, colonial in psychology as well as in mercantile economics.

The essential element in the national sense of unity is the east-west feeling, developed historically along the St. Lawrence-Great Lakes axis, and expressed in the national motto, *a mari usque ad mare*. The tension between this political sense of unity and the imaginative sense of locality is the essence of whatever the word "Canadian" means. Once the tension is given up, and the two elements of unity and identity are confused or assimilated to each other, we get the two endemic diseases of Canadian life. Assimilating identity to unity produces the empty gestures of cultural nationalism; assimilating unity to identity produces the kind of provincial isolation which is now called separatism . . .

I grew up in two towns, Sherbrooke and Moncton, where the population was half

English and half French, divided by language, education and religion, and living in a state of more or less amiable Apartheid. In the Eastern Townships the English-speaking group formed a northern spur of New England, and had at a much earlier time almost annexed themselves to New England, feeling much more akin to it than to Quebec. The English-speaking Maritimers, also, had most of their cultural and economic ties with New England, but their political connexion was with New France, so that culturally, from their point of view, Canada stopped at Fredericton and started again at Westmount. There were also a good many Maritime French families whose native language was English, and so had the same cultural dislocation in reverse.

As a student going to the University of Toronto, I would take the train to Montreal, sitting up overnight in the coach, and looking forward to the moment in the early morning when the train came into Levis, on the south side of the St. Lawrence, and the great fortress of Quebec loomed out of the bleak dawn mists. I knew that much of the panorama was created by a modern railway hotel, but distance and fog lent enchantment even to that. Here was one of the imaginative and emotional centres of my own country and my own people, yet a people with whom I found it difficult to identify, what was different being not so much language as cultural memory. But the effort of making the identification was crucial: it helped me to see that a sense of unity is the opposite of a sense of uniformity. Uniformity, where everyone "belongs," uses the same clichés, thinks alike and behaves alike, produces a society which seems comfortable at first but is totally lacking in human dignity. Real unity tolerates dissent and rejoices in variety of outlook and tradition, recognizes that it is man's destiny to unite and not divide, and understands that creating proletariats and scapegoats and second-class citizens is a mean and contemptible activity. Unity, so understood, is the extra dimension that raises the sense of belonging into genuine human life. Nobody of any intelligence has any business being loyal to an ideal of uniformity: what one owes one's loyalty to is an ideal of unity, and a distrust of such a loyalty is rooted in a distrust of life itself.

Source: Northrop Frye, *The Bush Garden: Essays on the Canadian Imagination* (Toronto: Anansi, 1971), i-ii.

Margaret Atwood (1939–)

"Survival"

Margaret Atwood, poet, novelist, and critic, is one of Canada's most respected writers. *The Circle Game*, a book of her poetry, won the Governor General's Award in 1966; a generation later, her novel, *The Handmaid's Tale* (1985), won another Governor General's Award and was a runner-up for the Booker Prize. With others of her generation, she established Canada as an important contributor to English literature worldwide. Her novels have frequently focused on the dilemmas facing women in modern society, often set in her native Toronto and with backgrounds furnished from a childhood growing up as the daughter of a professor of forestry.

In *Survival*, written at the height of a period of English-Canadian nationalism and at the outset of an era of strong feminist awareness, Atwood advanced a striking, pessimistic, and controversial claim about the essential nature of much Canadian writing. More people have read *Survival* than agree with it, but it has inspired many good arguments and a lot more reading. What better service can a distinguished author do for her colleagues?

I'd like to begin with a sweeping generalization and argue that every country or culture has a single unifying and informing symbol at its core. (Please don't take any of my oversimplifications as articles of dogma which allow of no exceptions; they are proposed simply to create vantage points from which the literature may be viewed.) The symbol, then – be it word, phrase, idea, image, or all of these – functions like a system of beliefs (it is a system of beliefs, though not always a formal one) which holds the country together and helps the people in it to co-operate for common ends. Possibly the symbol for America is The Frontier, a flexible idea that contains many elements dear to the American heart: it suggests a place that is new, where the old order can be discarded (as it was when America was instituted by a crop of disaffected Protestants, and later at the time of the Revolution); a line that is always expanding, taking in or "conquering" ever-fresh virgin territory (be it The West, the rest of the world, outer space, Poverty or The Regions of the Mind); it holds out a hope, never fulfilled but always promised, of Utopia, the perfect human society. Most twentieth century American literature is about the gap between the promise and the actuality, between the imagined ideal Golden West or City Upon a Hill, the model for all the world postulated by the Puritans, and the actual squalid materialism, dotty small town, nasty city, or redneck-filled outback. Some Americans have even confused the actuality with the promise: in that case Heaven is a Hilton hotel with a coke machine in it.

The corresponding symbol for England is perhaps The Island, convenient for obvious reasons. In the seventeenth century a poet Called Phineas Fletcher wrote a long poem called *The Purple island*, which is based on an extended body-as-island metaphor, and, dreadful though the poem is, that's the kind of island I mean: island-as-body, self-contained, a Body Politic, evolving organically, with a hierarchical structure in which the King is the Head, the statesmen the hands, the peasants or farmers or workers the feet, and so on. The Englishman's home as his castle is the popular form of this symbol, the feudal castle being not only an insular structure but a self-contained microcosm of the entire Body Politic.

The central symbol for Canada – and this is based on numerous instances of its occurrence in both English and French Canadian literature – is undoubtedly Survival, *la Survivance*. Like the Frontier and The Island, it is a multifaceted and adaptable idea. For early explorers and settlers, it meant bare survival in the face of "hostile" elements and/or natives: carving out a place and a way of keeping alive. But the word can also suggest survival of a crisis or disaster, like a hurricane or a wreck, and many Canadian poems have this kind of survival as a theme; what you might call "grim" survival as opposed to "bare" survival. For French Canada after the English took over it became cultural survival, hanging on as a people, retaining a religion and a language under an alien government. And in English Canada now while the Americans are taking over it is acquiring a similar meaning. There is another use of the word as well: a survival can be a vestige of a vanished order which has managed to persist after its time is past, like a primitive reptile. This version crops up in Canadian thinking too, usually among those who believe that Canada is obsolete.

But the main idea is the first one: hanging on, staying alive. Canadians are forever taking the national pulse like doctors at a sickbed: the aim is not to see whether the patient will live well but simply whether he will live at all. Our central idea is one which generates, not the excitement and sense of adventure or danger which The Frontier holds out, not the smugness and/or sense of security, of everything in its place, which The Island can offer, but an almost intolerable anxiety. Our stories are likely to be tales not of those who made it but of those who made it back, from the awful experience – the North, the snowstorm, the sinking ship – that killed everyone else. The survivor has no triumph or victory but the fact of his survival; he has little after his ordeal that he did not have before, except gratitude for having escaped with his life.

A preoccupation with one's survival is necessarily also a preoccupation with the obstacles to that survival. In earlier writers these obstacles are external – the land, the climate, and so forth. In later writers the obstacles tend to become both harder to identify and more internal; they are no longer obstacles to physical survival but obstacles to what we may call spiritual survival, to life as anything more than a minimally human being. Sometimes fear of these obstacles becomes itself the obstacle, and a character is paralyzed by terror (either of what he thinks is threatening him from the outside, or of elements in his own nature that threaten him from within). It may even be life itself that he fears; and when life becomes a threat to life, you have a moderately vicious circle. If a man feels he can survive only by amputating himself, turning himself into a cripple or a eunuch, what price survival?

* * *

Certainly Canadian authors spend a disproportionate amount of time making sure that their heroes die or fail. Much Canadian writing suggests that failure is required because it is felt – consciously or unconsciously – to be the only "right" ending, the only thing that will support the characters' (or their authors') view of the universe. When such endings are well-handled and consistent with the whole book, one can't quarrel with them on aesthetic grounds. But when Canadian writers are writing clumsy or manipulated endings, they are much less likely to manipulate in a positive than they are in a negative direction: that is, the author is less likely to produce a sudden inheritance from a rich old uncle or the surprising news that his hero is really the son of a Count than he is to conjure up an unexpected natural disaster or an out-of-control car, tree or minor character so that the protagonist may achieve a satisfactory *failure*. Why should this be so? Could it be that Canadians have a will to lose which is as strong and pervasive as the Americans' will to win?

It might be argued that, since most Canlit has been written in the twentieth century and since the twentieth century has produced a generally pessimistic or "ironic" literature, Canada has simply been reflecting a trend. Also, though it's possible to write a short lyric poem about joy and glee, no novel of any length can exclude all but these elements. A novel about unalloyed happiness would have to be either very short or very boring: "Once upon a time John and Mary lived happily ever after, The End." Both of these arguments have some validity, but surely the Canadian gloom is more unrelieved than most and the death and failure toll out of proportion. Given a choice of the negative or positive aspects of any symbol – sea as life-giving Mother, sea as what your ship goes down in; tree as symbol of growth, tree as what fills on your head – Canadians show a marked preference for the negative.

You might decide at this point that most Canadian authors with any pretensions to seriousness are neurotic or morbid, and settle down instead for a good read with *Anne of Green Gables* (though it's about an orphan . . .) But if the coincidence intrigues you – so many writers in such a small country, and *all with the same neurosis* – then I will offer you a theory. Like any theory it won't explain everything, but it may give you some points of departure.

Source: Margaret Atwood, *Survival: A Thematic Guide to Canadian Literature* (Toronto: Anansi, 1972), 31-3.

Antonine Maillet (1929–)

"LA SAGOUINE"

**Born at Buctouche, New Brunswick, Antonine Maillet is the dominant figure in Acadian liter-
ature. She achieved her status by imagining a new language that combines "ancient and
sonorous words" and literary expressions. *Pélagie-la-charette* (1979) won the Prix Goncourt
and became a bestseller in France, but *La Sagouine* (1971) is even closer to the Acadian spirit. La
Sagouine, a poor woman who cleans floors for a living, seems weak and helpless but, like the
Acadians, she is tough enough to win in the end. What better self-image for a people victimized
as much by their fellow French-speaking neighbours as by English-speaking Maritimers and
by British soldiers who drove them into exile two and a half centuries ago? Her strength of
spirit is clearly displayed in the 1972 story reproduced below, "Two Saints."**

**Antonine Maillet gave a voice to the Acadians characterized by wisdom, humour, restraint
and anger, lucidity, and patience. She writes from the collective memory of her people. Maillet
has lived outside the Acadian community, teaching literature and folklore at l'Université Laval.
She has been honoured by becoming a Companion of the Order of Canada.**

I often used to go around to Sarah's to get my
fortune read; not so much to learn about
my own life as about hers. For this Sarah was
one of your fortune-tellers who likes to chat
and between club and diamond spin you a yarn
and drop an opinion or two and rummage
around in family history. She knew your Great-
Uncle Jaddus, she did, the one who had the one
girl and then eleven boys ... eleven boys, Great
God yes, one on top of another. Ah! they really
knew how to do things in those days! And she
knew the old sorcerer from Rivière à Hache,
the one who could just as well burn you a
church right down to the ground as go bury
himself stark naked in the middle of a field of
wild mustard not a hundred feet from the
graveyard. Ah yes, they were something else

again, that race of devils was, and you can only
hope that on the Other Side there'll be some
kind of a Good Lord to look after them ... And
then she knew the Sagouine young, too.

I was afraid Sarah would start talking about
something else as she sat there shuffling the
cards, so I pounced on the ace of spades when
it dropped all hot from her fondling fingers.

"So you knew the Sagouine young, did you?"

"Knew her young and knew her old, aye,
and then too the wee bit in between when a
person's, as you might say, astraddle life like a
cow's back."

And Sarah let spurt from her throat and
eyes that big laugh she got from her father who
held it himself from a line of ancestors who

reached this land jumping across the ice-floes in the bay. Was it the thought of a Sagouine astride a cow's back that set off her laughter, or was she already thinking of something else?

"I knew the Sagouine at the time of her squabble with La Sainte," she says to me. "And that was something, that was. Too bad you missed that."

The old witch was making my mouth water. To think I'd lived so close by and missed it all.

But little by little I got the whole story or what was left of it as Sarah unravelled her ragged memories.

Once a week back in those prosperous times the Sagouine used to open up her stall of old rags and hand-me-down clothes which she sold at bargain prices, though her customers bargained for them just the same, for the pleasure of it. Because it would have been an insult to everyone, and to the Sagouine in particular, to step up and pay cash without bartering, like the bigwigs. No, where the Sagouine comes from you call each other names and haggle and it's all part of the business.

You haggled over the prices but also over the quality of the goods, though nobody was the least in the dark as to where they came from. They could have told you with their eyes shut that was the banker's shirt or the doctor's coat on the back of Henri Big-Belly or Francis Motté.

But don't you go thinking that the Sagouine was a thief. No, she was a beggar. Yes, she begged, as is the right of any poor slave of the Good Lord who never got more out of belong-ing to the Church than three drops of water at baptism and a slap at confirmation. It was all to the honour of her bump of business acumen then if, from the fruits of her begging on behalf of the shivering poor of the parish, she managed to mount a small trade that allowed her to live with respect and dignity.

That's about how the Sagouine saw things anyway, and the way La Sainte began to see them too one fine day without letting on to anyone.

The entry of La Sainte on the rag market was the hardest blow the Sagouine ever received in her life. Up till then the Catounes and Pitounes of the place had gladly disputed with the Sagouine another commercial activity which on occasion, by necessity, she also practised. But the Sagouine was of an age to understand that in that particular trade there was room for a little competition. Whereas in business, the success of the one is the bankruptcy of the other. That much the Sagouine knew. And it wasn't long before the facts began to bear this out.

Day by day she saw La Sainte adding more and more orange crates to her stand and filling them up with bundles of old clothes. And she was forced to watch, powerless, as business boomed for this brazen upstart who didn't even deign to begin at the bottom of the ladder like everyone else with socks and underwear.

No, right off the bat the hussy was dealing in coats and dresses as if to the manner born. And next breath making so bold as to move right into hats! Yes Ma'am, hats, if you please! And no one there but could recognize the feathers of Dominique's wife's bonnet and the vicar's fur hat. And O Sweet Holy Mother of God! A fox! A fox piece, I tell you! If that isn't a shame to stoop to selling foxes to the poor likes of us who haven't ever even slept in a feather bed yet. A fox! The Sagouine choked on it. It was just too much this time, really too much. And she closed up shop and went down to the shore to mull things over.

Had to find a way to put that big cow back in her place. But the Sagouine saw straight away that it wouldn't be easy. How to get under the skin of a woman who had sworn off all the sins of the flesh for so long? She didn't drink, the old bat, didn't smoke, or dance, or go gallivanting around either, naturally, saint that she was. La Sainte? Phooey! The Sagouine didn't have much book learning but she wasn't born yesterday either, and she judged there was plenty of grimacing under that guise of saintliness. Prissy stuck-up plaster saint paddling in holy water, the Sagouine exclaimed with a roar of laughter.

Then she sobered up. A saint who goes around stealing other folks' business deserves the same treatment . . . But how do you set about stealing somebody's saintliness? Sitting there, feet buried in the sand and head bowed with heavy thoughts, the Sagouine lifted her eyes and saw a heron pass by with his long beak stuck onto his long neck. Along he strode, disdainful and superb, waggling his precious behind with the dignified air of someone on their way to sing vespers. The Sagouine

contemplated this shore-bird an instant, then leaping up and yanking her feet out of the sand, let out a tremendous "Hah!" and lit out for the church.

You might have assumed that the Sagouine's first steps in the paths of sanctity would be difficult and gauche. That would be to misjudge a woman who from force of circumstance had been obliged to change her profession at least seven or eight times in her life. And besides, churches were something she knew a little about after all. For years now she had scrubbed out the sisters' chapel and the floor of the parish hall.

So she took to her new *métier* with the same flair as to the others, throwing herself into it heart and soul, belly and guts. As she used to say, either you're a saint or you're not, and the Sagouine was never one to do things by halves. She fitted herself out with a Sunday missal, two hymn books, and the usual array of medals, rosaries and scapulars guaranteed to ward off sickness, bad weather and unrepentant death. She gave up smoking, ceased to chew, quit swearing – yes by the Dear Lord Jesus Christ she did – and even abstained from sounding off from door to door about the conduct of her worst enemy, La Sainte. It was the most sudden and total metamorphosis ever seen on this stretch of coast since the time of the great rains.

It was La Sainte who was the most amazed. The most outraged. For here was someone filching the only thing that was truly hers, stealing her paradise, from her who had renounced the things of this world. It was an insult to God and his saints and a rank injustice to someone who had never missed a First Friday or Sunday Vespers or Public Prayers, Prayers with three rosaries one after the other, interspersed with intentions that La Sainte improvised as the spirit moved her for the dying, the sinners and the renegades of the parish. This time she'd cook up a prayer there'd be no mistaking for the intention of those pushy barbarians who figure they can take over other people's paradises just like that. She'd put that rag-seller back in her place, she would!

... But poor La Sainte didn't have a chance to put anyone in their place since her own, there in the front pew as prayer leader, had already been taken. Though she couldn't believe her eyes she was forced to admit that it was really the Sagouine up there at the lectern announcing the intention for the first decade of the rosary: "Let us pray," she declaimed, "that the men of this parish heretofore see fit to do their duty. Our Father who art in Heaven . . ."

So that's how the Sagouine got her business back, for La Sainte understood that she would have to choose between earth and heaven. She chose heaven and left the earth to the Sagouine who, the next day, sold her medals and her scapular along with her socks and coats and underwear.

And that's the story Sarah told me in bits and pieces as she ran her long fingers between heart and spade, laughing her big white-toothed laugh and shuffling her memories with the deck.

Source: Originally published as "Les Sargaillounes," in *Par derrière chez mon père* (Éditions Leméac, 1972); repr. in Richard Teleky, ed., *The Oxford Book of French Canadian Short Stories* (Toronto: Oxford University Press, 1983), 219-24, trans. Philip Stratford.

David Lewis (1909—81)

On "Corporate Welfare Bums"

It was a calculated risk, but when David Lewis began the 1972 election campaign with a furious attack on "welfare bums," he got nationwide attention. Of course, the "bums" were not unemployed people, living hand to mouth on social assistance, but some of the richest corporations in Canada, collecting enormous government subsidies and deferring taxes on their huge profits while lecturing politicians on squandering public money on health and social services. Credit for the actual strategy should belong to a Polish-born economic researcher, Boris Celovsky, but it was Lewis who became the passionate purveyor of the argument.

Born in a Polish ghetto, David Lewis came to Canada at the age of twelve. In a few years he swept through school and McGill University to a coveted Rhodes scholarship in 1931. He inherited his democratic socialism from his father but his brilliance made him the chief theorist and national organizer of the Co-operative Commonwealth Federation (CCF), Canada's left-wing party. Enemies of the party used his Jewish origins in a vicious campaign that blunted the CCF's prospects. In 1950 Lewis turned to the practice of law but he was instrumental in fashioning the alliance between labour unions and the CCF which created the New Democratic Party (NDP) in 1962.

Elected in 1962, he became one of Parliament's best debaters. In 1971 he was chosen leader of a deeply divided and floundering party, and his 1972 campaign allowed the NDP to hold the balance of power in Ottawa until the 1974 election. All in all, Lewis and his party deserve credit for helping to forge the policies and institutions that have made Canada "a kinder and gentler society."

Within the last twenty years or so we have built in Canada what I have described as the corporate welfare state . . .

The corporate welfare state seems to have begun in the late forties as governments attempted to face the trauma of turning the economy from war production to peacetime production without the major economic crises that followed the First World War.

From its humble beginnings it grew into a system of grants and tax concessions of massive proportions. The growth of the corporate welfare state derived from an approach to economic development which worships at the Shrine of the Gross National Product. One ad hoc policy was piled on top of another. Each new government, and almost every new cabinet minister, added to the list of give-away programs, oblivious to what had been done before and probably unaware of what others were doing.

The system has become so complex and expensive that we must stop and ask what we are accomplishing.

The government itself docs not evaluate the effectiveness of its programs. And anyone who asks questions is charged with being against whatever the programs are intended to achieve.

The critics of present regional-development policies are accused of being against regional development. Jean Marchand tells the premiers of the Atlantic provinces that if the criticism of the incentives grants to private industry continues, the money will be cut off. The prime minister is more credible. On September 16, 1972, he told his Halifax audience: "If people don't like them [regional-expansion grants] we'll give them all to Quebec." Opposition politicians are accused of being against the Maritimers or of being anti-Quebec.

Those who question the effectiveness of the government's grants and tax concessions to the extractive industry are labelled by the minister of Finance as builders of ghost towns in northern Ontario. Those who ask about the shipbuilding subsidy are accused of intending to dismantle the shipbuilding industry.

This negative attitude is the best proof of the government's uneasiness that the system is not working. The government is conveniently forgetting that they are the trustees of *our* tax money. It is not enough to show in the public accounts that our money was disbursed according to the accepted accounting principles: the columns of revenues and expenditures may well add up, although the auditor-general gives us an annual glimpse of some strange additions. What concerns you and me is simply who is putting the money in, who is getting it out, and what good it does.

Whatever the government says about its achievements, we know that prices are going up, as are the numbers of unemployed; that as many are living below the poverty line now as twenty years ago; that regional disparities are just as pronounced as ever; that taxes for middle-income Canadians are increasing; that corporations are getting away with a smaller and smaller share of the tax burden and that their profits are getting bigger.

This is the result of the government's economic and fiscal policies and the grant strategy. No amount of promises to the needy at election time will make the wrong policies right; nor will it lessen the enormous price we have to pay for them.

If the programs, whatever they are, do not deliver, or at least do not come close to the target, they must be scrapped. The game of using successes in individual cases as proof of general achievement is a crude device of deception. Promises of better things to come, repeated for years and years, are a cruel hoax on those who are hoping and waiting . . .

Moreover, there is not a known case of prosecution against a recipient corporation for misrepresentation or misuse of government grants. You and I know of many cases where unemployed workers have been dragged into court for drawing ten or one hundred dollars more than the rules allowed.

Does this mean that all cases involving billions of dollars of grants to corporations were handled properly, to the letter? Hardly. But we will never know, nor will we ever get our money back.

However, we do know that the billions of dollars doled out to the corporations leave us with the same problems we had before the corporate welfare state was really launched . . .

The needs of our country and our people are undisputed. Even the Liberal government recognizes them in that it speaks about justice and the eradication of regional disparities. But Mr. Trudeau believes that private enterprise is the *main* vehicle to achieve these ends. Mr. Stanfield believes corporations are *essential* to the process of building our country.

I say it is the government's responsibility to do the job. Governments are elected by people; corporations are not. Governments must answer to the people; corporations must answer only to their boards.

For this reason I reject the solutions of the past. I oppose unbridled giveaways to corporations, programs without strategy, evaluation or fair returns to the people of Canada.

I believe that every Canadian has the right to share fairly in the wealth of our country, regardless of where he lives. But I emphatically do not believe that private enterprise alone can be relied upon to make these rights a reality. If it could, poverty and regional disparity would not have arisen in the first place.

Free enterprise has a role in our society. But its role must be in accord with the objectives of our people. Only where this role contributes to our well-being should we give encouragement through the use of public funds.

In the last eight years, the federal government gave away $3.5 billion to industry in the form of grants and other subsidies, and approximately twice as much in income-tax concessions – a total of $10 billion to the corporations, most of them large and wealthy. Despite all this corporate welfare, hundreds of thousands of Canadians are jobless, and millions are living in poverty. Messrs. Trudeau and

Stanfield talk about the importance of "business confidence." With profits rising every year, I don't believe we have to cater any longer to this bromide. It is the confidence of ordinary Canadians, especially those people who have no jobs and no future, that concerns me. No matter what statistical trickery the government may choose to use, half a million people, and often more, are being sacrificed to the powerful gods of the free-enterprise myth. And millions more are squeezed by high taxes, high interest rates and the rising cost of food and shelter.

The government must stop its haphazard give-away programs. It must start with concrete and detailed objectives to develop a strategy.

A fair distribution of income should be the first and paramount goal. In this wealthy nation there is no reasonable excuse for poverty to ravage whole regions and whole segments of the population.

Source: David Lewis, *Louder Voices: The Corporate Welfare Bums* (Toronto: James Lewis and Samuel, 1972), 104-7.

Tom Connors (1936–)

"Sudbury Saturday Night"

Though Sudbury would probably prefer to be known for its university, hospitals, elegant Science North education centre, and even new government offices that now employ far more people than the nickel mines, the old image is hard to shake. Tom Connors's song recalls the hard reality of mining town life, where getting drunk with the gang on a Saturday night made

it possible to face the mine or the mill on Monday morning. The International Nickel Company, or INCO, has been one of the town's major industries for most of this century.

"Stompin' Tom" Connors was born in Saint John, grew up as an orphan in Prince Edward Island, and then lived the life of an itinerant worker that would inspire most of his songs. A Canadian patriot, Connors consciously describes the everyday lives of average Canadians. Why criticize fellow workers for spending their leisure time as they please?

Refrain:
The girls are out to Bingo and the boys
    are gettin' stinko.
We think no more of I.N.C.O. on a
    Sudbury Saturday Night.
The glasses they will tinkle when our eyes
    begin to twinkle
And we think no more of I.N.C.O. on a
    Sudbury Saturday Night.

With Irish Jim O'Connell there and Scotty
    Jack MacDonald
There's honky Fred'rick Hurgel gettin' tight,
    but that's all right.
There's happy German Fritzy there with
    Frenchy gettin' tipsy
And even Joe the Gypsy knows it's Saturday
    tonight.

Now when Mary, Ann and Mabel come to
    join us at the table
And tell us how the Bingo went tonight,
    we'll look a fright,
But if they won the money we'll be lappin'
    up the honey, boys,
'Cause everything is funny for it's Saturday
    tonight.

Refrain

We'll drink the loot we borrowed and
    recuperate tomorrow
'Cause everything is wonderful tonight, we
    had a good fight,
We ate the Dilly Pickle and we forgot about
    the Nickel
And everybody's tickled for it's Saturday
    tonight.

The songs that we'll be singin', they might be
    wrong but they'll be ringin'
When all the lights of town are shinin'
    bright and we're all tight,
We'll get to work on Monday but tomor-
    row's only Sunday
And we're out to have a fun-day for it's
    Saturday tonight.

Refrain

Source: Homer and Dorothy Hogan, eds., *Listen! Songs and Poems of Canada* (Toronto: Methuen, 1972), 62. Copyright Crown-Vetch Music Ltd (CAPAC).

Joni Mitchell (1943–)

"Big Yellow Taxi"

Born in Fort Macleod, Alberta, and raised in Saskatoon, Joni Mitchell began singing in Toronto coffeehouses in 1964. Her song "Big Yellow Taxi," with its memory of paradise lost, was an unusual anthem for youth, but it spoke to a generation in the 1970s which had already begun to question the value of "progress."

Canada's post-war prosperity fulfilled the dreams of people who had grown up scrimping, saving, and dreaming of owning a car and driving it on something better than mud roads, or even of enjoying the simple luxury of eating fresh fruit in the winter. No sooner were these marvels realized than their hidden costs were challenged. The song helped boost Mitchell to international stardom, but, more important, it contributed to an increasingly powerful environmental consciousness.

They paved paradise
Put up a parkin' lot
With a pink hotel, a boutique
And a swingin' hot spot
Don't it always seem to go
That you don't know what you've got
Till it's gone
They paved paradise
Put up a parkin' lot.

They took all the trees
Put them in a tree museum
And they charged the people
A dollar and a half just to see 'em
Don't it always seem to go
That you don't know what you've got
Till it's gone
They paved paradise
Put up a parkin' lot.

Hey farmer farmer
Put away that D.D.T. now
Give me spots on my apples
But leave me the birds and the bees
Please!
Don't it always seem to go
That you don't know what you've got
Till it's gone
They paved paradise
Put up a parkin' lot.

Late last night
I heard the screen door slam
And a big yellow taxi
Took away my old man
Don't it always seem to go
That you don't know what you've got
Till it's gone
They paved paradise
Put up a parkin' lot

I said, don't it always seem to go
That you don't know what you've got
Till it's gone
They paved paradise
Put up a parkin' lot . . .

Source: Homer and Dorothy Hogan, eds., *Listen! Songs and Poems of Canada* (Toronto: Methuen, 1972), 109. Copyright © 1970 Siquomb Publishing Corp.

Paul-Émile Cardinal Léger (1904–91)

"THE GAP BETWEEN THEM AND US"

Cardinal Léger was one of the most famous Canadian religious figures of the twentieth century, noted for his tireless devotion to the cause of the poor and disadvantaged in Quebec and throughout the country.

Cardinal Léger shocked Canadians when he announced in 1967 that he was relinquishing his episcopal seat in Montreal to undertake missionary work among lepers and the disabled in Africa. The contrast between the material comfort he was leaving behind and the humble, difficult life he was embracing in serving the cause of the world's truly unfortunate reminded many Canadians about the deeper message of Christ and the true meaning of religion. Upon his return from Africa, Cardinal Léger was a tireless promoter of Canadian foreign aid and sought to alert Canadians to the serious plight of many developing nations. This portion of an address to a well-heeled audience at the Empire Club was typical of those efforts.

And so my first words must be words of thanks: words of gratitude – gratitude for having asked me to speak to you today, gratitude for the kind memories so many of you have for me, gratitude for all those who have worked to support my work in Africa – for all those hours spent so unselfishly, for the gifts both large and small which have come from so many generous hearts, and for all the moral and spiritual support that so many of you have extended to me – for all this, and for so much more I thank you. And I thank you not only in my own name, but in the name of all those I have tried to serve, in the name of the poor and the lame, the blind and the paralysed, of the lepers and of the sick children. On behalf of all these people, I would like to thank those thousands and thousands of my fellow-Canadians who have helped to relieve the appalling scourges of hunger, disease, waste and premature death which afflict so many of our fellow human beings.

Sometimes, you know, we all get discouraged about our work, or our country – or just life in general. But sometimes when I am in one of these moods I think about our Canadian experience – with all its hesitations and even mistakes, yet, *also*, with its genuine idealism and spirit of respect for different points of view; I think about this experience, and I am proud to belong to a country which is still trying to create something new, a country which is looking forward to the future, a country, moreover, which being aware of its own tensions and difficulties is prepared to sympathize with the problems of less happy lands. We should take pride in this Canada of ours, and draw strength from what we have already accomplished in the past so that we may face the future confident and unafraid.

And part, of course, of the future which we are all going to have to face is the fact that most human beings in the rest of the world are not nearly so well off as we are. And, it is about these human beings, and my work with them that I have come to talk to you. But, first of all, you must realize that I can only talk to you on the basis of my own experience and background. I am not a diplomat, and I cannot really tell you anything about the political role of Canada and the African states. Nor again, am I an economist or a sociologist – I know nothing, in a first hand way, about the balance of trade or the interaction of social classes. After all, if you wanted to hear about any of these very important realities, there are lots of politicians, economists, and social scientists who could give you a much more authoritative talk than I could. But my life has been devoted to the preaching of the Gospel, of trying to bear witness, however imperfectly, to a spiritual and moral view of the world which led me finally to leave Montreal and to work in Africa. And what I want to do today is draw my work in Africa to your attention, and to try to show you why I think it is important to go on. Like St. Paul, a long time ago, I do not come to you "in lofty words of wisdom," but simply to give you an account of what I have tried to do, and how I see this work in relation to our responsibilities in the Western world, and our own vocation as Canadians.

* * *

It is difficult, I say, to make the reality of poverty and the degradation of disease on the enormous scale on which they exist, very real to ourselves. It was my own personal meditation on this kind of question which led me to resign as Archbishop of Montreal. I certainly had no idea that this decision of mine would have anything more than a symbolic value – I am enough of a realist to know that individuals can do very little. But this does not mean they are incapable of doing *anything*. I felt it was my calling to try to show that there are elements in our Western tradition which are concerned for more than the fast buck, elements which are really and practically concerned with the fate of the unfortunate, the halt and the lame. We all feel sometimes that we are cogs in a big machine, but the best elements in our tradition remind us that man is more than a play-thing of economic forces, and that our conduct and our decisions are not necessarily determined by greed, by lust and by hate. We are creatures who can work for good as well as for evil, and it is because I believe that most Canadians believe this that I still think it worth reminding you of the problems of the Third World.

It would have been wrong for me to have left Montreal if the Third World has no value; indeed I should have stayed in my Diocese if the problems to which I have tried to draw your attention are not real problems; truly, I made a mistake in leaving if I had thought that single-handed I would make a great difference to the African Continent. But what I have to say to you all today is, first of all, the Third World is important because it is made up of human beings like ourselves: secondly, that these human beings are up against real problems which through no fault of their own, they cannot solve by themselves; and thirdly, I have looked on my own contribution as having only a symbolic value, which I have always hoped might inspire at least some men of good will both in Canada and in Africa to work together in a rational way to help overcome unnecessary suffering and disease.

The Third World is important then, because it is made up of human beings, human beings who possess the same nature we do, people who are capable of suffering and of desiring, even as we suffer and desire, people who are condemned to a shabby, deprived and disease-ridden existence, and these are people for whom we have a moral and a religious obligation to care about. Because of the God we all believe in, because of the humanity common to us all, these people are our brothers, and part of my mission now is to try to keep that fact alive in your hearts. It is easy to forget them, so easy to say they do not matter, and if you find it uncomfortable to be reminded of them then I have done part of what I set out to do.

And these problems of the Third World are real problems. They are problems not because I say they are but because everybody who is willing to look beyond his own back yard knows they are. All the different organizations and committees of the United Nations trying to examine the situation as it really is tell us the same thing, that the gulf between the Third World and the small group of privileged nations to which Canada belongs is steadily widening. The problems are real, and I was, and I still am trying to keep this fact alive in your minds.

The people of the Third World, then, are valuable as human beings, and the problems they are up against are real problems, and it is within those given elements of the situation that you must try to see my own contribution. When I first went to Africa, I spent some time working with lepers and establishing centres for their treatment and care. With your help and support I was also able to set up a number of clinics for the treatment of other diseases. But I finally came to the conclusion that I would have to try to establish a work which could both serve an immediate need, and yet be capable of further development by the Africans themselves as they saw fit. And I have set up a Centre in Yaoundé for the treatment of children with polio.

The need this Centre is meeting is real, and is being partially met. But it is doing something more than meeting an immediate need. It is also the cell, or the foundation, of an all African Faculty of Medicine. Even as things are now, this Centre is the only serious facility of its type in five surrounding countries. But its importance is surely that it is taking root as an African project, and after the devoted labours of the Canadian doctors and nurses – who have been so generous in their services – has been finished, there will be a new generation of Africans to continue and advance their work. In this way Canada is represented to a part of the Third World not as a colonizing power, not as an industrial power greedy for natural resources, not as a political power anxious to secure client states as it pursues its power politics – no, but what I believe to be the true face of Canada has been revealed as a country which, in spite of its own difficulties and preoccupations, has had the generosity and the concern to support one of its fellow-citizens who has tried to serve his fellow human beings in a way which respected their dignity, which took account of their real needs, and helped them to build for a better future.

And so I would ask for your continued support and generosity, knowing that in some important sense I have tried to represent those values we all cherish as Canadians. That I have tried, furthermore, to represent the great spiritual heritage of the Jewish-Christian tradition which has always tried to reconcile the needs and legitimate demands of the community with the tenacious conviction that the individual human being is supremely important – that I have tried to represent this tradition in an environment which often seems suspicious of our efforts. But I ask for your support not because of anything I have managed to do, but because it is an opportunity to reaffirm your conviction that man can build as well as destroy. Let us ignore those prophets of doom, and let us help others to help themselves, let us make our contribution to easing the often intolerable burden of so many people in lands which seem so far away and strange, but which, in reality, are on our own doorsteps in this increasingly inter-dependent world.

Source: Paul-Émile Cardinal Léger, "The Gap Between Them and Us," *The Empire Club of Canada Addresses*, 1973-74 (Toronto, 1974), 224-32.

Pauline Julien (1933–)

"Les Femmes" ("The Women")

After a long struggle, Canadian women won the right to vote in federal elections in 1918 but it took until 1940 before women could vote in Quebec provincial elections. In a conservative Catholic society, all the old familiar arguments lasted a little longer. Women were too delicate and sensitive for the political arena, and perhaps not quite as mature and brave as the men. Besides, in their maternal role they already exercised enormous real power. In Quebec, an added argument was that votes for women was something that Protestants and English Canadians wanted: French-Canadian society was different. Nationalist newspapers like *Le Devoir* campaigned tirelessly against female suffrage.

A second revolution for women's rights began in the 1960s. In the atmosphere of Quebec's Quiet Revolution, the feminist struggle probably made more progress in changing values and institutions than it did in the rest of Canada. Among the leaders was Pauline Julien. Born in Cap-de-la-Madeleine near Trois-Rivières, she went in 1951 to Paris, where she studied acting and also began her singing career. Returning to Quebec in 1957, she popularized the songs of Kurt Weill and Bertolt Brecht. In 1964 she earned second place at the International Festival at Sopot singing Gilles Vigneault's "Jack Monnoloy." Pauline Julien soon became one of Quebec's most popular singers and songwriters, and a committed sovereignist. She was arrested briefly during the 1970 October crisis.

"Les Femmes," written in 1970, is a song that speaks to all women – and to men too: "in love, my love, together."

Women are always a little more fragile	Les femmes sont toujours un p'tit peu plus fragiles
They fall in love and have their hearts broken	Elles tombent en amour et se brisent le coeur
Women are always a little more anxious	Les femmes sont toujours un p'tit peu plus inquiètes
Tell me, gentlemen, do you really love them?	Dites-moi, messieurs, les aimez-vous vraiment
You create mothers so lovable	Vous les fabriquez mères toutes aimables
Mirrors of justice, thrones of wisdom	Miroirs de justice, trônes de la sagesse
Prudent virgins, arks of the covenant	Vierges très prudentes, arches d'alliance
Gentlemen you're dreaming	Vous *rêvez messieurs beaucoup*

Women are always trying to look a bit younger	Les femmes se font toujours un p'tit peu plus jeunes
While you so often look at sixteen-year-old girls	Vous r'gardez si souvent les filles de seize ans
Women are always a little more shy	les femmes sont toujours un p'tit peu plus timides
Could it be, gentlemen, that you talk too much?	Serait-ce messieurs que vous parlez trop
You christen them salvation of the infirm	Vous les baptisez salut des infirmes
Queens of the patriarchs, mystic roses	Reines des patriarches, roses mystiques
Mothers of wise counsel, merciful virgins	Mères du bon conseil, vierges clémentes
Gentlemen you're dreaming	Vous *rêvez messieurs beaucoup*
Women are always a little less significant	Les femmes sont toujours un p'tit peu plus légères
Men are always so extraordinary	Les hommes sont toujours tellement extra-ordinaires
Women, it is said, are perfectly frec	Les femmes, on le dit, sont parfaitement libres
As long as they abide by your laws	Mais, à la condition de bien suivre vos lois
You need them to be morning stars	Vous les exigez étoiles du matin
spiritual vases, spotless mothers	Vases spirituels, mères sans tache
venerable virgins, ivory towers	Vierges vénérables, tours d'ivoire
Gentlemen you're dreaming	Vous *rêvez messieurs beaucoup*
My God, how demanding women have become	Mon Dieu que les femmes sont devenues exigeantes
They no longer cry, don't even wait around	Elles ne pleurent plus, ne veulent même plus attendre
In love and elsewhere, they take what they want	En amour et partout, elles prennent ce qu'elles demandent
But tomorrow, my love, we will be happier together	Mais demain, mon amour, nous serons plus heureux ensemble
In love, my love	En amour, mon amour
Together	Ensemble

Source: Michel Le Bel and Jean-Marcel Paquette, *Le Québec par ses textes littéraires 1534-1976* (Montreal: Fernand Nathan, 1979), 349-50.

Margaret Laurence (1926–87)

"WHERE THE WORLD BEGAN"

Margaret Laurence is one of Canada's greatest twentieth-century writers. Perhaps her finest novel is *The Stone Angel*, published in 1964. It was the first of several works set in the town of Manawaka and involves characters ranging from Scottish pioneers to Metis outcasts.

Laurence was a recipient of the Order of Canada and honorary degrees from fourteen Canadian universities. She had wide literary interests, which included African literature and the writing of children's books. But, above all, Laurence was a fierce Canadian nationalist: her writing resonates with a concern for fashioning a Canadian voice that deals with Canadian themes and settings. This passion for the Canadian experience shines through clearly in the following selection.

A strange place it was, that place where the world began. A place of incredible happenings, splendours and revelations, despairs like multitudinous pits of isolated hells. A place of shadow-spookiness, inhabited by the unknowable dead. A place of jubilation and of mourning, horrible and beautiful.

It was, in fact, a small prairie town.

Because that settlement and that land were my first and for many years my only real knowledge of this planet, in some profound way they remain my world, my way of viewing. My eyes were formed there. Towns like ours, set in a sea of land, have been described thousands of times as dull, bleak, flat, uninteresting. I have had it said to me that the railway trip across Canada is spectacular, except for the prairies, when it would be desirable to go to sleep for several days, until the ordeal is over. I am always unable to argue this point effectively. All I can say is – well, you really have to

live there to know that country. The town of my childhood could be called bizarre, agonizingly repressive or cruel at times, and the land in which it grew could be called harsh in the violence of its seasonal changes. But never merely flat or uninteresting. Never dull.

* * *

When I was 18, I couldn't wait to get out of that town, away from the prairies. I did not know then that I would carry the land and the town all my life within my skull, that they would form the mainspring and source of the writing I was to do, wherever and however far away I might live.

This was my territory in the time of my youth, and in a sense my life since then has been an attempt to look at it, to come to terms with it. Stultifying to the mind it could certainly be, and sometimes was, but not to the imagination. It was many things, but it was never dull.

The same, I now see, could be said for Canada in general. Why on earth did generations of Canadians pretend to believe this country dull? We knew perfectly well it wasn't. Yet for so long we did not proclaim what we knew. If our upsurge of so-called nationalism seems odd or irrelevant now to outsiders, and even to some of our own people (*what's all the fuss about?*), they might try to understand that for many years we valued ourselves insufficiently, living as we did under the huge shadows of those two dominating figures, Uncle Sam and Britannia. We have only just begun to value ourselves, our land, our abilities. We have only just begun to recognize our legends and to give shape to our myths.

There are, God knows, enough aspects to deplore about this country. When I see the killing of our lakes and rivers with industrial wastes, I feel rage and despair. When I see our industries and natural resources increasingly taken over by America, I feel an overwhelming discouragement, especially as I cannot simply say, "damn Yankees." It should never be forgotten that it is we ourselves who have sold such a large amount of our birthright for a mess of plastic Progress. When I saw the War Measures Act being invoked, I lost forever the vestigial remains of the naive wish-belief that repression could not happen here, or would not. And yet of course I had known all along in the deepest and often hidden cave of the heart that anything can happen anywhere, for the seeds both of man's freedom and of his captivity are found everywhere, even in the microcosm of a prairie town. But in raging against our injustices, our stupidities, I do so *as family*, as I did, and still do in writing, about those aspects of my town which I hated and which are always in some ways aspects of myself.

The land still draws me more than other lands. I have lived in Africa and in England, but splendid as both can be they do not have the power to move me in the same way as, for example, that part of southern Ontario where I spent four months last summer in a cedar cabin beside a river. "Scratch a Canadian and you find a phony pioneer," I used to say to myself, in warning. But all the same it is true, I think, that we are not yet totally alienated from physical earth, and let us only pray we do not become so. I once thought that my lifelong fear and mistrust of cities made me a kind of old-fashioned freak; now I see it differently.

The cabin has a long window across its front western wall, and sitting at the oak table there, in the mornings, I used to look out at the river and at the tall trees beyond, green-gold in the early light. The river was bronze; the sun caught it strangely, reflecting upon its surface the near-shore sand ripples underneath, making it seem momentarily as though a whole flotilla of gold flickerings sailed there. Suddenly, the silver crescenting of a fish, gone before the eye could clearly give image to it. The old man next door said these leaping fish were carp. Himself, he preferred muskie, for he was a real fisherman and the muskie gave him a fight. The wind most often blew from the south, and the river flowed toward the south, so when the water was wind-riffled and the current was strong, the river seemed to be flowing both ways. I liked this, and interpreted it as an omen, a natural symbol.

A few years ago, when I was back in Winnipeg, I gave a talk at my old college. It was open to the public, and afterward a very old man came up to me and asked me if my maiden name had been Wemyss. I said yes, thinking that he might have known my father or my grandfather. But no. "When I was a young lad," he said, "I once worked for your great-grandfather, Robert Wemyss, when he had the sheep ranch." I think that was the moment when I realized something of great importance to me. My long-ago families came from Scotland and Ireland, but in a sense that no longer mattered so much. My true roots were here and would remain so, whatever happened.

I am not very patriotic, in the usual meaning of that word. I cannot say, "My country right or wrong" in any political, social, or literary context. But one thing is unalterable, for better or worse.

This is not only where my world began. It is also the land of my ancestors.

Source: James Foley, ed., *Themes in Canadian Literature: The Search for Identity* (Toronto: Macmillan, 1975), 98-103.

Robertson Davies (1913–95)

"WHAT MAY CANADA EXPECT FROM ITS WRITERS?"

Robertson Davies is considered by many Canadians to be the country's outstanding novelist. Following studies at Queen's University and at Oxford, Davies served for almost twenty-five years as editor and then publisher of the *Peterborough Examiner*. From 1960 to 1981 he taught at the University of Toronto.

While Davies published many outstanding essays, his main success was as a novelist. Perhaps his best-known novel is *Fifth Business*, part of a three-volume set known as the Deptford Trilogy (1970-75). This work, as well as most of his other novels, used the setting of small-town Ontario to deal with matters of the spirit and the mysterious forces of the human psyche.

Davies has long been concerned with understanding the link between Canadian literature and the Canadian experience. In this selection, he tartly analyses the role of the writer in the shaping and exposition of a distinctive Canadian identity, as well as in setting moral and intellectual standards.

I said that I would talk on the theme: What Does Canada Expect from Her Writers? The question is easily answered: Canada expects nothing from her writers. Let us rephrase the question to read: What May Canada Expect from Her Writers?

Canada may reasonably expect what other countries expect and get from a national literature. First, a sense of national character. Not, I hasten to say, of aggressive nationalism, of scorn-Britainism, of anti-Americanism, for these are negative qualities upon which nothing can worthily be built. Nor do I mean a projection of the picture of a typical Canadian of any kind, for literature of the first order does not deal with types, but with individuals. But as a people we are neither Englishmen who have been exported to the new world, nor are we Americans who, having been assembled on Canadian soil, pass as a native product while still looking like something conceived in Detroit. We have our own concerns, our own secrets, and our own dreams. Sometimes, to the Canadians who remember and ponder them, these dreams are restless, disquieting, and fearsome; sometimes they are foreshadowings of what is yet to be; sometimes they are assurances of personal conquests and new heights seized and held. It is upon these deeply personal things that our national character rests.

Second, we may expect from our writers that vigilance on behalf of intellectual freedom and moral vigour which Aleksandr Solzhenitsyn has shown heroically and in isolation in a country where those qualities are endangered. Endangered, as I have pointed out, because the government of his country fears them. Endangered and abraded in our land because it appears so often that Canada hardly realizes that these qualities exist, and does not know where to look for help in making them matters of acute and untiring national concern.

Last, we may expect from our writers a true depiction of what our life in Canada is. And of course I speak of the essence of that life, not its externals. That life cannot be described in terms of the problems of other countries, for even when we share those problems, they appear in our country as Canadian matters. Nor can our national life be described without saying some things that will distress tender-minded people who shrink from what is disagreeable. A great poet has said:

If way to the better there be
It exacts a full look at the worst.

But not, of course, at the worst alone. There is much in our life that lies in realms that can brace us, elate us, and make us laugh.

Canada has a literature now, and some parts of it may well be objects of national pride, and as I am myself a novelist, and must not therefore speak of the work of novelists, let me refer you to the work of some of our poets, which is poetry of a special fragrance, for it is our own. And in the future, we may, if Canada asks for it, expect from our writers works of the kind Solzhenitsyn speaks of in the great declaration to the world of which I have already spoken. They are, he says, works of pungency and luminosity, with completely irrefutable power to convince, works which cause the reader to be visited, dimly, briefly, by revelations such as cannot be produced by rational thinking.

Works like the looking-glass in the fairy tale, he says; you look into it and you see not yourself but, for one second, the Inaccessible, whither no man can ride, no man can fly. Ah, yes, but to have glimpsed the Inaccessible is, however imperfectly, to have gained access to it. Once we have *found* the mirror, we can return to it again and again.

And that, ladies and gentlemen, is what your writers can give you, if you want it, and let them know that you want it. But that decision rests not with the writers, but with you. And before you can ask us for what we have, it is first necessary to understand what we are.

Source: Robertson Davies, *One Half of Robertson Davies* (Markham, Ont.: Penguin, 1977), 140-2.

Joe Davidson (1915–85)

Old-fashioned Unionism

Union leaders in a liberal-democratic society are usually allowed one role by opinion leaders – to persuade their members to tighten their belts for the sake of the battle for higher productivity, lower inflation, and national prosperity. In this view, union demands, however reasonable in the past, are now unreasonable, excessive, and contrary to economic realities. Indeed, for some liberals, the most important freedom a worker needs is the right not to belong to a union at all.

Joe Davidson was not that kind of labour leader. Raised in Scotland, he never lost his accent or his commitment to trade union and socialist values. He emerged as leader of Toronto's postal sorters and rose to the presidency of the Canadian Union of Postal Workers (CUPW). If there was belt-tightening to be done, he insisted, it should be done by the rich, not by his members whose wages, despite a series of strikes and struggles, remained low. Arguably, in the effort to obtain security, dignity, and autonomy on the job for CUPW's members, Davidson and his successors won some battles but lost the war. Indeed, their militancy fostered mechanization and dehumanization of what once had been a respected job. At the same time, Davidson never wavered in loyalty to his members and his principles. His salary as a union president was no higher than that he would have earned on the job. If government negotiators grumbled at his stubbornness, they never doubted his integrity.

Near the end of his memoirs, written with Vancouver lawyer and novelist Bill Deverell, Davidson writes about wage controls, bosses, and his view of the role of unions and their leaders.

The practice of the so-called old-fashioned trade unionism can make a man unpopular with other union leaders as well as with management. I remember quite vividly a meeting of the ranking officers of the Canadian Labour Congress in the spring of 1975 in response to Finance Minister John Turner's proposals for voluntary wage restraint. Joe Morris and the rest of the CLC executive presented a list of ten demands which had been thrown together by the CLC executive the night before and proposed that we adopt them as the labour movement's "price" for accepting voluntary controls. The demands were quite extensive, including full employment policies, a greatly expanded housing program and several others which the Trudeau government was unlikely to accept. The CLC thinking seemed to be that it could have the best of both worlds, appearing flexible and reasonable in response to the government's campaign against inflation without actually having to take part. I was the only leader present to speak against the plan. I argued that wage controls in any form should be opposed outright as a matter of principle. The others greeted this intervention with silent scorn. Less than six months later the Trudeau government legislated wage controls and caught the trade union movement completely unprepared . . .

When wage controls and other legal restrictions on Canadian workers are the government's only answer to the country's deepening economic problems, the labour movement's response has to be fundamentally political. The CLC's ultimate power lies with its two million members; and until their voting and economic strength is organized and used to better effect, business and government will keep on calling the tune. The national day of protest on October 14, 1976, when more than one million Canadians struck in protest against wage controls, was an expression of the potential power of the labour movement, but in the minds of CLC leaders it was a one-shot affair and not a springboard to a larger organizing campaign.

My opposition to wage controls was and is based on both CUPW policy and my own brand of socialist philosophy. At an emotional level the hypocrisy of calls for belt-tightening from well-paid business and political leaders makes me angry. At the time the AIB program was announced, a postal clerk's annual wage was $9,500. I knew our members weren't living high off the hog on that, although certainly many Canadians were skimping by on even less. On the other hand, the more secure upper classes, who might reasonably be expected to show the way in belt-tightening, were not required to do so. The controls were expressed in percentages rather than an across-the-board dollar ceiling on allowable increases. Once again, as we have come to expect and resent, the generals were leading from the rear.

Socialists of all stripes have always believed that there must be a better way of organizing human affairs without relying so heavily on private property and the profit motive and all the evils that go with them. With this I agree, although experience and reading have taught me that there is no simple alternative. Undeserved privileges and management incompetence, inefficiency and abuse of power do not respect the boundaries between the public and the private sector or between capitalist and socialist countries. They can be found in every organization, whatever its ownership. Competition, if there is any, can provide a bit of a check on these tendencies, but another vital safeguard is good strong democratic unions. It seems a fact of life that managements will always be small self-serving elites, and there is precious little the average worker can do to eradicate that. Through strong, well-organized unions, however, we can try to keep those managers and owners on their toes and make them perform to a high standard in return for the privileges they always claim as rights.

This type of thinking does not endear me to those zealous supporters of communism or capitalism. Those on the far left claim that in some undefined way the workers can take complete power and tame or assimilate the other classes, but I have never been able to understand how. The capitalists and their growing army of technocrats and managers claim that their extravagant privileges and their power to tyrannize the lives of the workers are based on performance, personal ability and merit, but this too is a big lie which doesn't stand up to scrutiny. Untidy reality falls between those philosophical extremes and suggests to me that under any system workers will always need both strong unions and separate political parties devoted to their interests.

As the politicians of the right are pleased to remind us these days, there is no free lunch, but there is room for a much more honest and far-reaching debate about which groups are not pulling their weight. The solution to economic problems is not for the trade union movement to go into a shell, weakening and discrediting itself through tripartism and collaboration. Canadian workers must continue to fight hard to preserve the gains of the past and to force the decision-makers and administrators in the upper and middle classes to plan more sensibly and do more to earn their keep. We have to organize, challenge and keep the pressure for reform on them by every available democratic means.

In the Post Office, the CUPW will continue to demand public inquiries to expose the follies and miscalculations of the government and Post Office management. We will continue to demand a crown corporation in the full conviction that, despite the financial hazards involved, it will permit a saner administration, a better working life for postal workers and a better mail service for the Canadian public. We will ignore wage controls and by doing so push forward our demand for better performance from Canadian governments and Canadian business. If this is radicalism, then I am proud to be a radical. There is no other worthwhile or honourable course of trade union action.

The unfairness of the controls aside, there was nothing in the policies of the Trudeau government to suggest that sacrifices by Canadian workers through wage restraint would be put to good use. In particular, when the argument was made that union workers should hold back so that low-wage non-union workers could catch up, it was never explained to my satisfaction how the money would be transferred from one group to the other without sticking to the fingers of the employers in between. Equally fundamental was the fact that the government did not, and still does not, have any policy *requiring* that the profits extracted from Canadian resources and the labour of Canadian workers be reinvested to create productive employment and rising standards for all Canadians. In the absence of much stronger policies for equality among Canadians and great improvements in the organization of production, any submission by the organized labour movement to wage controls can only serve to shore up the irrationalities of the status quo.

Following the CUPW's long strike in December 1975, I was invited to address the New York City branch of the American Postal Workers Union to explain the ins and outs of wage controls and our situation in the Canadian Post Office. Until then I had never travelled in the United States and I was quite unprepared for the cultural gap. At the entrance to the large auditorium in the Statler-Hilton, I discovered an honour guard waiting to march me up the centre aisle to the platform, a ceremony I found altogether too military and pretentious for an ordinary mortal and union leader. I wandered around to a side door and slipped onto the stage unannounced, just as I would at any union meeting in Canada. When my turn came I began by assuring the diverse crowd of 4000 black, white and brown faces that most Canadians didn't talk like me. "I hope you'll be able to decipher this accent to hear a fellow postal worker's message," I said.

Instantly a voice from the floor piped up in a strong burr like mine; "That's no accent, Joe. That's a heritage." Suddenly feeling right at home, I went on for twenty-five or thirty minutes about the saga of the CUPW and Canada Post.

Toward the end of the speech, which was until then very well received, I launched into a talk about the limits of trade unionism and how workers need to be more involved in political action and the fight for socialism because the governments and the employers are lined up together against us. This was a straightforward statement of fact as far as I was concerned, but a frigid pall fell across the room as soon as the words left my mouth. "Before I go any further," I hastened to add, "let me explain what I mean by socialism. It's not a man with a big black beard, a bomb in one hand and a dagger in the other, calling for revolution. A socialist fights the injustices that are done, year in and year out, to the working people. Socialism is helping your fellow workers whenever you can and treating them the way you want to be treated." The tension began to lift. "But," I continued, "when it comes to turning the other cheek, I draw the line at bosses." Laughter and applause rippled through the audience, and we were all back on the same wavelength. When I sat down, the officer who had invited me, Moe Biller, came over and whispered, "Thank God you explained socialism so well, Joe. I didn't want a lynching on my conscience."

Source: Joe Davidson and John Deverell, *Joe Davidson* (Toronto: James Lorimer, 1978), 186-90.

Roch Carrier (1937–)

"THE HOCKEY SWEATER"

Roch Carrier is one of French Canada's most celebrated literary figures. He is a poet, novelist, and playwright but is perhaps best known for his short stories. He has had a varied career, making the transition from creative artist to senior public administrator. After serving as principal of the Collège Militaire Royal de Saint-Jean, he was appointed to head the Canada Council in 1994 and he remained in this post until 1997.

French-English relations is a recurring theme in his fiction. His story "The Hockey Sweater" is one of Canada's most famous short stories and has been issued as a children's book as well as an award-winning animated film. The simple yet powerful story links the Canadian passion with hockey to the ongoing tensions between the English and French, here represented by the Toronto Maple Leafs (and the Eaton Company) and the Montreal Canadiens. "The Hockey Sweater" tells what it was like to grow up French in small-town Quebec – or English in small-town Ontario.

The winters of my childhood were long, long seasons. We lived in three places – the school, the church and the skating-rink – but our real life was on the skating-rink. Real battles were won on the skating-rink. Real strength appeared on the skating-rink. The real leaders showed themselves on the skating-rink. School was a sort of punishment. Parents always want to punish children and school is their most natural way of punishing us. However, school was also a quiet place where we could prepare for the next hockey game, lay out our next strategies. As for church, we found there the tranquillity of God: there we forgot school and dreamed about the next hockey game. Through our daydreams it might happen that we would recite a prayer: we would ask God to help us play as well as Maurice Richard.

We all wore the same uniform as he, the red white and blue uniform of the Montreal Canadiens, the best hockey team in the world; we all combed our hair in the same style as Maurice Richard, and to keep it in place we used a sort of glue – a great deal of glue. We laced our skates like Maurice Richard, we taped our sticks like Maurice Richard. We cut all his pictures out of the papers. Truly, we knew everything about him.

On the ice, when the referee blew his whistle the two teams would rush at the puck; we were five Maurice Richards taking it away from five other Maurice Richards; we were ten players, all of us wearing with the same blazing enthusiasm the uniform of the Montreal Canadiens. On our backs, we all wore the famous number 9.

One day, my Montreal Canadiens sweater had become too small; then it got torn and had holes in it. My mother said: "If you wear that old sweater people are going to think we're poor!" Then she did what she did whenever we needed new clothes. She started to leaf through the catalogue the Eaton company sent us in the mail every year. My mother was proud. She didn't want to buy our clothes at the general store; the only things that were good enough for us were the latest styles from Eaton's catalogue. My mother didn't like the order forms included with the catalogue; they were written in English and she didn't understand a word of it. To order my hockey sweater, she did as she usually did; she took out her writing paper and wrote in her gentle schoolteacher's hand: "Cher Monsieur Eaton, Would you be kind enough to send me a Canadiens' sweater for my son who is ten years old and a little too tall for his age and Docteur Robitaille thinks he's a little too thin? I'm sending you three dollars and please send me what's left if there's anything left. I hope your wrapping will be better than last time."

Monsieur Eaton was quick to answer my mother's letter. Two weeks later we received the sweater. That day I had one of the greatest disappointments of my life! I would even say that on that day I experienced a very great sorrow. Instead of the red, white and blue Montreal Canadiens sweater, Monsieur Eaton had sent us a blue and white sweater with a maple leaf on the front – the sweater of the Toronto Maple Leafs. I'd always worn the red, white and blue Montreal Canadiens sweater; all my friends wore the red, white and blue sweater; never had anyone in my village ever worn the Toronto sweater, never had we even seen a Toronto Maple Leafs sweater. Besides, the Toronto team was regularly trounced by the triumphant Canadiens. With tears in my eyes, I found the strength to say:

"I'll never wear that uniform."

"My boy, first you're going to try it on! If you make up your mind about things before you try, my boy, you won't go very far in this life."

My mother had pulled the blue and white Toronto Maple Leafs sweater over my shoulders and already my arms were inside the sleeves. She pulled the sweater down and carefully smoothed all the creases in the abominable maple leaf on which, right in the middle of my chest, were written the words "Toronto Maple Leafs." I wept.

"I'll never wear it."

"Why not? This sweater fits you . . . like a glove."

"Maurice Richard would never put it on his back."

"You aren't Maurice Richard. Anyway, it isn't what's on your back that counts, it's what you've got inside your head."

"You'll never put it in my head to wear a Toronto Maple Leafs sweater."

My mother sighed in despair and explained to me:

"If you don't keep this sweater which fits you perfectly I'll have to write to Monsieur Eaton and explain that you don't want to wear the Toronto sweater. Monsieur Eaton's an *Anglais*; he'll be insulted because he likes the

Maple Leafs. And if he's insulted do you think he'll be in a hurry to answer us? Spring will be here and you won't have played a single game, just because you didn't want to wear that perfectly nice blue sweater."

So I was obliged to wear the Maple Leafs sweater. When I arrived on the rink, all the Maurice Richards in red, white and blue came up, one by one, to take a look. When the referee blew his whistle I went to take my usual position. The captain came and warned me I'd be better to stay on the forward line. A few minutes later the second line was called; I jumped onto the ice. The Maple Leafs sweater weighed on my shoulders like a mountain. The captain came and told me to wait; he'd need me later, on defense. By the third period I still hadn't played; one of the defensemen was hit in the nose with a stick and it was bleeding. I jumped on the ice: my moment had come! The referee blew his whistle; he gave me a penalty. He claimed I'd jumped on the ice when there were already five players. That was too much! It was unfair! It was persecution! It was because of my blue sweater! I struck my stick against the ice so hard it broke. Relieved, I bent down to pick up the debris. As I straightened up I saw the young vicar, on skates, before me.

"My child," he said, "just because you're wearing a new Toronto Maple Leafs sweater unlike the others, it doesn't mean you're going to make the laws around here. A proper young man doesn't lose his temper. Now take off your skates and go to the church and ask God to forgive you."

Wearing my Maple Leafs sweater I went to the church, where I prayed to God; I asked him to send, as quickly as possible, moths that would eat up my Toronto Maple Leafs sweater.

Source: Roch Carrier, *The Hockey Sweater and Other Stories*, trans. Sheila Fischman (Toronto: Anansi, 1979), 77-81.

Yvon Deschamps (1935—)

"The History of Canada"

What do Canadians know about their history? In each province, officials ensure that an appropriate version of the past is served, preferably in such a dreary form that little remains after the final exam – which in Quebec is compulsory and province-wide – except vague but powerful ideas of oppression, sacrifice, and triumph.

Yvon Deschamps is a Montreal-born actor, writer, and composer. Above all, however, he is a gifted comedian whose funny, sentimental descriptions of his fellow Montrealers draw laughter and tears from audiences who recognize the words and the accents of their own *quartiers*. Taking the role of the "little guy," Deschamps explains why history teaches him and his fellow French Quebeckers to hate the English. Readers will recognize Frontenac, Montcalm, and the Plains of Abraham. "Phits" is William Phipps, Frontenac's unsuccessful antagonist in 1690, and "Woulf" is General James Wolfe, who defeated Montcalm in 1759. The English might recognize themselves as "rough." After all, forcing the Acadians to live in New Brunswick is cruel and unusual punishment; so is sending the exiles of 1838 to Bermuda – in the middle of winter, no less!

I f some a'you have histories of Canada at home, make sure to tear out page 73 before any kids get their hands on it! Because, I tell ya, what happens on page 73 is sickenin'! *Les Anglais* arrive. And tha French hate those *Anglais* so much. It's really not that complicated, you know. I think they hated 'em as much then as we do now. That's for damn sure! Frontenac hated 'em so much that when he saw 'em comin' down the river, he got all nervy, he went crazy! He threw a fit! He ran all over the place, shootin' off cannons, bang, boom, boom, boom – so much that the English got scared and went away. Well, they came back. Oh yes, they came back on page 76, 'cause, ya know, those guys had one, they had the little book. They looked inside, and when they saw that, on page 75, Frontenac goes away and Montcalm takes over, they said, "We should go back on page 76, 'cause Montcalm, he won't get nervy, eh!" So, the reason they were such traitors – well, tha fact they arrive on page 76 doesn't bother me so much. That's their business. But what's most sickenin' 'bout it's that they arrange t'arrive just at tha bottom of the page. Now that's serious!

Yeah, 'cause that way they arrive on a Saturday night in July – I dunno if ya ever been

to Quebec City on a Saturday night in July, but in those days, it was the same as today. Go check it out next summer, you'll see. On a Saturday night in the month of July, there's no one 'round, see. They're all on the Plains a'Abraham. You can't see 'em. But they're there. The bushes shakin' over there? That's not the wind. No, no, no, no, no. There's a Québécois behind each bush, shakin' it. So, on that particular Saturday night, all the Québécois were on the Plains a'Abraham, each one shakin' his own bush. Montcalm, he was there too, but Montcalm was mounting the guard.

Naturally, in the book, they don't give the guard's name, for the sake of the parents an' all. You shouldn't get too carried away neither. So Montcalm was there and mounting the guard and he'd brought a guard dog with him, well the guard's dog, so while he's mounting the guard, his dog arrives: "Woulf, woulf, woulf!" So, he doesn't understand, and by the time he puts his clothes back on, an' all that, it's too late. He falls down dead as a stiff. It even happened so fast ya might say he was still stiff when he died. Well, we won't go into that.

That's when things started ta get scary. 'Cause those English, they was so rough, they arrive at tha bottom of page 76 and before they even get ta tha middle of page 77, they'd already deported the Acadians. To New Brunswick. Well, I dunno if ya ever been there, but it's not a place ta send people. Damn right, it isn't! And that's nothin'. On page 111, Lord Durham, he was a fine pig, he was. On page 111, right after the 1837 revolution, he took political prisoners, 'cause ya know in those days they was pretty rough. Nothin' holdin' them back. Not like today. He took political prisoners, eight a'them, he deported 'em to Bermuda! Right in tha middle a'winter! Couldn't take no underwear. Nothin'. Those guys, they're probably dead today.

Well, if that's not enough, they did worse'n that. On page 88 – we're at 88 now. Well, on page 88 that's when the Americans wanted to come up here. And the English didn't want 'em

to. They said, "No, no, no. Fight the Americans. We don't wanna see them here." Those *maudits Anglais* who stopped us from becoming Americans. I'll never forgive 'em for that! 'Cause, let's be honest, wouldn't it be great to be Americans! Things'd be fine. 'Cause those annoyin' young punks, ya know – we'd be jus' fine if we were Americans, 'cause if we were Americans, annoyin' young punks like you wouldn't be hangin' 'round. Old folks neither. Old folks'd be in Florida, young punks in Vietnam. An' things'd be jus' fine here, *Tabarnouche!* There'd be room for everyone.

Source: Michel Le Bel and Jean-Marcel Paquette, *Le Québec par ses textes littéraires 1534-1976* (Montreal: Fernand Nathan, 1979), 326-7.

Joe Clark (1939–)

"COMMUNITY OF COMMUNITIES"

Joe Clark, the youngest prime minister ever elected in Canada, took office in 1979 at the head of a minority Conservative government. His period in office was short-lived, and he was ousted as leader of the Conservatives by Brian Mulroney in 1983. Nevertheless, he continued as a prominent member of the Mulroney cabinet, identified with the progressive or "Red Tory" wing of the party.

Clark articulated a specific vision of Canadian identity. As a westerner, he impressed Canadians, particularly Quebeckers, by becoming fully bilingual. He may be best known for his description of Canada as a "community of communities," articulated early in 1979. With this phrase Clark asserted that Canada was truly a sum of all its diverse parts and that the absence of any overarching identity or ideology was in fact a virtue. His own origin in the small Alberta town of High River nurtured this sense of the value of small communities and the regional distinctiveness of Canada, including Quebec.

It's typical, I think, that our official emblem – the maple leaf – is not indigenous to two of our provinces and two of our territories. For there are thousands of happy and productive Canadian citizens who are most at ease when they speak neither of our two official languages. We are a nation that is too big for simple symbols. Our preoccupation with the symbol of a single national identity has, in my judgement, obscured the great wealth we have in several local identities which are rich in themselves and which are skilled in getting along with others.

If that truth has been lost on Ottawa's planners, it is not lost on the people of Canada, whether those people arc artists like Alden Nowlan or Monique Leyrac or W.O. Mitchell or Gordon Lightfoot or Emily Carr or any of the Group of Seven, whose work evokes their locale, or whether they are citizens who are starting heritage societies, starting history clubs, organizing walks through their own back yards. In an immense country, you live on a local scale. Governments make the nation work by recognizing that we are fundamentally a community of communities.

Of course the national government has to be strong, particularly on economic questions. But it must also be sensitive to the damage that neat theories can wreak upon a diverse country. There is nothing new to that view. Indeed, the successful Prime Ministers of Canada have incorporated that idea into the makeup of their governments, ensuring that every region had senior ministers who were strong enough to keep the government in touch with local realities. That is a fact of life in Canada to which we must return.

A second thing that is important is my view, and that of my party, that our economy in Canada is potentially one of the strongest in the world. We have in abundance resources which are elsewhere in short supply, whether of food or energy or minerals. Capital will come to us, and come to us in ways that we can control. So will as much population as we want. Our challenge in this country is not to cope with scarcity. Our challenge is to build on abundance. Other nations might well be forced, legitimately, to contemplate limits on growth. But our very different challenge here in Canada is to plan and to manage growth.

Finally, our people are ambitious. Whatever cultures we come from, whatever heritage we bring to these shores, we are all of us North American in aspiration. We want to build. We want to grow. Generally, the goals of Canadians are personal goals. A few people in our history have helped build our nation by consciously pursuing national goals, but many more have built this nation by pursuing the personal goals which the nature of this nation allows. The personal goal of most Canadians has been freedom and some security for their family. That caused the settlement of new regions, caused the immigration of new citizens, caused the transplanting of old roots to new ground. A policy designed to make the nation grow must build upon and must not frustrate the instinct of most Canadians to build a stake for themselves.

In the Korean War, Canadian soldiers found themselves a long way from home, with obsolete weapons and an abstract cause. Old-fashioned motives like comradeship and pride in their regiment kept them fighting. Here, three members of the Royal Canadian Regiment reflect on the night of October 23-24, 1952, after most of their company was wiped out during a Chinese attack on their position, Hill 355. These are men who have come very close to death. (National Archives of Canada, PA 128839)

Edge of the Woods, Gabriola Island, *painted in 1953, will remind most Canadians of their dream – realized or not – of a cottage by the water. Edward John Hughes (1913-) was a unique interpreter of British Columbia's landscape. Strong colours, balanced composition, and discreet evidence of human presence make his work easily identifiable.*
(Vancouver Art Gallery)

An Ottawa photographer superimposed a choir greeting Canada's centennial year on December 31, 1966, on a background of the floodlit Peace Tower of the Parliament Buildings. While most Canadians had approached their national centennial with suspicions of extravagance and folly, they soon discovered that they enjoyed the festivities more than they had expected. Events ranged from Expo 67 in Montreal to burning the last outhouses in one prairie community whose "centennial project" was a sewer system. (National Archives of Canada, PA 167992)

The Visitors was executed in 1967 by Jean-Paul Lemieux (1904-90), one of Quebec's most successful modern painters. The fur-clad trio, in vaguely old-fashioned dress, draw out memories of mid-winter family hospitality. (National Gallery of Canada)

I Triumphed and I Saddened With All Weather, *by the painter and mystic William Kurelek (1927-77), combines the hope and despair the elements bring to rural life. Rain floods a farmer's fields and delights his children with the chance to splash in the water. Kurelek was best known for beautifully illustrated books for children, but his work reflected his Ukrainian and Catholic heritage, his prairie boyhood, and a deeply moral view of the world.* (Confederation Centre Art Gallery, Charlottetown)

With her quilt entitled Reason over Passion, *completed in 1968, Joyce Wieland (1931- 1998) made a classic statement on the nature of the politician Canadians had embraced that year. Pierre Elliott Trudeau insisted that his approach to politics and government was guided by reason over passion, but his acceptance by many Canadians was described as "Trudeaumania," an emotional commitment to a man few voters bothered to study and whose policies many of them would soon reject. Wieland's own view may be imagined.* (National Gallery of Canada)

Montreal's Saint-Jean Baptiste Day normally opened a summer season of warmth, holidays, and fun. In the 1960s, it also became a day to publicize the growing force of Quebec nationalism. On June 25, 1968, emotions boiled over in rock-throwing violence when newly chosen Prime Minister Pierre Elliott Trudeau reviewed the traditional parade. As police try to calm the crowd, two children cling to each other and an adult. Canada was entering a frightening time. (National Archives of Canada, PA 152448)

When Prime Minister Pierre Elliott Trudeau proclaimed the War Measures Act in October 1970 to give his government extraordinary powers to deal with terrorism in Quebec, the move was hugely popular in all parts of Canada. Toronto cartoonist Duncan Macpherson suggested that many of the supporters would have favoured similar powers to suppress everything they hated about the permissive and liberal 1960s. Note that a censor has tried to alter the slogan "Hitler was Right." In such a climate, even a liberal newspaper felt nervous. (Duncan Macpherson, Toronto Star Syndicate)

Montreal's residential streets, with their steep staircases up to second-floor apartments, are the setting for a vigorous outdoor life once the warmth of summer finally arrives. Miyuki Tanobe, born in Japan in 1937, was already a trained artist when she came to Montreal in 1971. Her charming primitivist paintings catch the spirit of a city where so many languages and cultures enrich each other. (Galérie de l'art français, Montreal)

Canada is a country of three oceans and many huge lakes, and the stately tumbling of the waves on a sandy shore is a sight millions of Canadians can share. James B. Spencer, who painted Wave no. 4 in 1972-73, is a Nova Scotia artist born at Wolfville in 1940 and known for his magically real paintings of seas and mountains. (National Gallery of Canada)

A Canadian peacekeeper from Princess Patricia's Canadian Light Infantry keeps watch over the Green Line separating Greek- and Turkish-speaking Cypriots in Nicosia. While Canadians were enthusiastic about supporting peace when belligerents wanted to stop – or merely to rest – post-Cold War crises often required armed intervention across sovereign boundaries to stop large-scale violence. (Department of National Defence)

Part of southern Kwakiutl culture in British Columbia, this brilliantly painted sculpin mask was worn on the upper back of a dancer, whose sinuous motions imitated the movements of a fish. Traditional potlatch ceremonials became a criminal offence in 1884, a prohibition that had devastating consequences for native culture and that was not repealed until 1951.

So what we propose in this election campaign is not just a change in government, but a fundamental change in the very direction of this country, a change that would reflect the value of that cultural and regional diversity, that would build on the natural strengths of our economy, and would recognize that the best instrument of national achievement is the individual initiative of the private citizen and the private sector in this country.

Through the last decade, government has been properly concerned with services to citizens, and we now have a good basic system of services in place. But the challenge of this next decade is to make this nation grow in wealth and to make our people grow in understanding of the great good fortune that we have here in Canada.

We can do that.

I come, as your Chairman said, from the foothills of Alberta, and I have learned late the second language of our country, mais je peux le parler à High River sans danger, sans risque, mais avec le véritable avantage que maintenant je peux comprendre le Québec assez bien à communiquer les aspirations des Québécois aux Albertans, aux Ontarians et les autres Canadiens, et je peux, je crois, communiquer aux Québécois les aspirations, l'intérêt, la détermination des Canadiens des autres provinces de bâtir une pays avec le Québec. L'avenir du Canada est plus qu'une question de loi. C'est une question de volonté et de comprehension. Il y a deux jours j'étais applaudé quand j'ai défendu la bilinguisme devant un auditoire de la Colombie Britannique. Le peuple canadien a eu assez de toutes les querelles plus ou moins artificielles entre gouvernements. Ils cherchent un terrain d'entente. Ils cherchent des objectifs communes qui respectent la diversité des traditions de chacun.

The great need now, whether it is in constitutional policy or economic policy, is for momentum in this country. In constitutional terms, the fact is that a new national government *can* get agreement on several changes – more likely changes in practice than in law – but several changes and soon, and that will break the impasse of distrust. Once trust is restored to federal-provincial relations, we can begin toward the more profound reforms, reforms whose end purpose must be to confirm national leadership in economic development, and to confirm provincial leadership in the development of the cultures that are strong in the regions and the provinces of this country.

Source: Joe Clark, "Community of Communities," in *Building a Nation: The Empire Club of Canada Addresses, 1978-1979* (Toronto: The Empire Club of Canada, 1979), 320-2.

Peter Lougheed (1928—)

ALBERTA AND NATURAL RESOURCES

When they joined Confederation, western provinces had to wrestle control of their natural resources from Ottawa. After a long political and legal struggle, that goal was achieved by 1930 but interprovincial and international trade remained a federal jurisdiction. In the post-war years, Alberta's oil and natural gas resources gave the province a new source of wealth, particularly after the Diefenbaker government required Ontario to purchase higher-priced western oil and gas, leaving Quebec and the Atlantic region to buy on the international market.

The turning point came in the 1970s, when an international cartel, the Organization of Petroleum Exporting countries (OPEC), twice managed to force large increases in oil prices, causing major economic dislocation in consumer countries. Canada was not an OPEC member, but Alberta and Saskatchewan expected to reap a windfall as prices doubled and quadrupled. Instead, Ottawa proposed to tax western energy exports to subsidize imports in the east. One collateral benefit, Ottawa believed, would be to show Quebeckers the benefits of belonging to Confederation.

It was a classic Canadian regional struggle, with self-interest, selective memories, and power politics on both sides. After the first oil-price shock in 1973, a compromise was reached. In the second crisis in 1979, Joe Clark's short-lived government was defeated in the House of Commons as a result of its attempt to tax all energy consumers. The producing provinces were furious. Critics blamed Albertans, the lowest-taxed of any Canadians, for being greedy and selfish. Alberta's Conservative premier, Peter Lougheed, was the articulate spokesman of his province and region, setting out emotional and logical arguments that the west understood and echoed. In the national election, the federal Liberals, under Pierre Elliott Trudeau, regained power by sweeping the central provinces, and a new crisis developed. On July 25, 1980, Alberta offered its terms to the federal government, and on October 20th Premier Lougheed gave his version of the dispute to the Alberta Legislature. Shortly afterwards, the conflict reached its peak with the federal government's introduction of the National Energy Program, an initiative that, for many westerners, remains to this day a symbol of eastern Canada's exploitation of their region.

I believe it's important for members of the Assembly to have a report and accounting in some detail by the leader of the Alberta government at this time on developments over the past five months. I think there's no need for me to emphasize in this Assembly the significance of oil and gas revenues to our province. We're all aware that 55 per cent of our budget comes from natural resource revenues. We're aware that we utilize 70 per cent of natural resource revenues for current purposes and put aside only 30 per cent for the Heritage Savings Trust Fund. I believe all members of this Assembly do not need any reminder about the economic significance of oil and gas, and an active petroleum industry in terms of job security and stability and prospects for advancement. As we've mentioned, and as I mentioned at length a year ago, we have worked hard on our thrust of economic diversification, and we've made considerable progress. But as we said back in 1971, it would be a difficult task for a province with only 2 million people, distant from markets and tidewater, to fully realize its objective of economic diversification for some time. That, of course, has been compounded by the emphasis that has been placed during the decade of the '70s upon the area of energy, and oil and gas in particular. During the period 1974 to 1979, the whole matter of domestic pricing of conventional crude oil and domestic natural gas sales was established by way of agreement, after difficult negotiations, between the federal government and the government of the major producing province, which is Alberta.

I'm sure all hon. members are aware of the realities involved. The reality is simply this: under the Canadian constitution, Section 109, the provinces own the resources, and with the ownership go rights and jurisdictional positions. Of course that involves the determination of what resources should be developed, in what way, and the pace of that development.

Those are clearly the rights of the provinces, who own resources under our constitution. However, as we have said before, but important to repeat: when a province produces a resource and it moves from the wellhead into interprovincial trade, at that time the federal jurisdiction comes into play under the constitution. So you have the obvious balance in our nation today, where you have federal jurisdiction over interprovincial trade and provincial ownership rights. Quite clearly they have to be reconciled, and that has been the way between 1974 and 1979: a reconciliation by way of agreement. Neither party can dominate the other, therefore there has to be agreement. We've recognized that over the course of the years 1974-79 by agreeing to phasing in the price of oil to commodity value. We've agreed to selling our natural gas at less than the price at which we're selling our conventional oil, to encourage substitution among other reasons. That has been the history of the Canadian energy scene in that period of time.

I'd like to remind hon. members of the negotiations this government conducted last fall with the then federal administration under Prime Minister Joe Clark. That negotiation was conducted essentially with the same civil servants in senior capacity who are in place today in the federal Department of Energy, Mines and Resources. Inaccurate suggestions have been made that the delay in concluding those arrangements was the factor in terms of the approach of the government of Alberta, but that's not so. If you check *Hansard* on November 13, 1979, you'll recall our bringing forth a ministerial statement of our deep concern over a new approach being suggested by federal officials, the same federal officials that are in place today, of a wellhead tax on production, which is essentially a federal royalty on a provincial resource. That, among other factors, delayed the negotiations which were finally concluded, and an agreement was struck with the Clark administration on or about December 11, 1979.

It was an arrangement that we felt was good for Canada and good for Alberta, because it recognized the great benefits to our country of being self-sufficient in energy. It recognized too, as an approach, that it would assure the manufacturing complex in Ontario a significant competitive advantage. It would assure the manufacturing complex in Ontario something even more important than that: an assurance of energy supply, when the basic competitors across the border in the United States would not be able to have that assurance into the mid- and late '80s.

The benefits to our country – and almost every economic and academic analysis that has been made on this subject confirms that energy self-sufficiency for Canada in its multiplier effect and in its competitive position with the United States, is a very, very major economic plus for our country.

It's also clear, by almost every economic analysis that has been made, that it is not energy prices that in any way put the manufacturing complex in Ontario, or for that matter anywhere in Canada, into a competitive disadvantage. Almost all the manufacturing complex

involves a situation where energy is only 5 per cent or less of total energy costs. The facts are, and the analysis is clear, that in terms of a competitive situation only two or three industries are affected in any significant way. The fact is that the Alberta/Ottawa agreement of December 1979 did give a permanent position of competitive advantage as well as a determined effort to secure oil self-sufficiency for Canada with very significant benefits to this country, and I want to return to that.

We're aware of the decision of the voters of Canada on February 18, which saw a shift in support for the Clark administration in Ontario and certain other parts of the country but certainly not in western Canada. The support in western Canada on February 18 for the whole concept of approach to the provinces as reflected by the Clark administration is illustrated by the results of that day. The present federal government, as we all know, has no representation at all in the provinces of Saskatchewan, Alberta, and British Columbia, and nominally in Manitoba, with two seats. That is a situation that any Canadian looking at this matter should not ignore. It's a message to be very much aware of.

In that election, the federal Liberal government opposed the 18 cent a gallon tax at the pump. To set the record straight – because I had to do that on a number of occasions this summer; we're aware here, but it should be in the record of *Hansard* – the 18 cents a gallon at the pump was a federal Conservative government measure that had no relationship to the agreement we entered into with them over pricing at the wellhead of our conventional oil and natural gas.

The pricing agreement that was in existence between the federal government and the Alberta government was due to expire, as we adjourned this Legislature in late May, on June 30 this year. Now I have written down in my note here the word "negotiation," and I have some difficulty with the use of that term. There had been discussions and meetings between our Minister of Energy and Natural Resources and the federal Minister of Energy, Mines and Resources on the matter of oil and gas pricing. I believe our Minister of Energy and Natural Resources has been accurate in stating that it is really not appropriate to refer to these discussions as negotiations. They've really been a series of ultimatums by the federal minister.

In mid-June, after the Quebec referendum – because the federal minister was not prepared to get into discussions until that time – there was a meeting of some two days in duration in Ottawa between the Minister of Energy and Natural Resources of this province and the minister from Ottawa with no progress whatsoever and no effort to negotiate or compromise by the federal government. That's a very strong statement, but an accurate one. The decision was then made to extend the pricing agreement until the end of July this summer, to give the Premier of Alberta and the Prime Minister of Canada an opportunity to become involved in the whole matter of energy issues. I met with the Prime Minister for two days, on July 24 and 25.

The Minister of Energy and Natural Resources has tabled in the Legislature today, Mr. Speaker, a very important document. I ask our hon. members to consider it very carefully. I believe it's important that it be reviewed here at this time. It starts with an oil-pricing proposal over a four-year period and sets as its target not 85 per cent of the world price, which was the arrangement made with the Clark administration, but 75 per cent of the North American price. That is a very major compromise and concession, if you like, by the government of Alberta in an effort to make an arrangement with the federal government.

Some suggest that the use of the phrase "North American price," which excludes Mexico, gets into a situation with regard to the American decontrol that's insignificant. I suggest that's not valid. Any appropriate reading of that situation in the U.S. Congress indicates that we are therefore accepting a view of the U.S. Congress over the course of that four years of altering a position of full and complete decontrol, which is a distinct possibility. But in addition to that, we have dropped our target from 85 to 75 per cent of the North American price with all of the attendant benefits that would provide to Canadians.

It would continue a situation where Canada then would have a price for its conventional oil lower than any developed country. In terms of comparison, if you go to petroleum exporting countries such as the United Kingdom, you see that they are in fact selling their oil to their own citizens at the commodity value. So that is the position we have taken. In addition to that, we took the view that we would have natural gas pricing at 85 per cent of the cost of oil to encourage natural gas.

Then we made a number of important undertakings to increase oil and natural gas supply: first of all, substitution of natural gas for oil. The gas would be priced at the Toronto city gate at 65 per cent of the cost of Alberta oil. This means, of course, that it would be a very significant incentive to substitution in Quebec and the Atlantic provinces, and through Ontario and Manitoba, to shift to the use of natural gas for home heating and commercial heating wherever it was practical to do so. It would be economically valid to follow through on that for Canadians, having regard to our very seriously declining reserves of conventional crude oil and our supplies of natural gas that we have discovered.

In addition to that, the eastern pricing zone would be extended to include Quebec City, which would result in Alberta paying the cost of transporting natural gas to that new market. As part of this proposal, Alberta also offered to have an all-out effort to develop the oil sands of this province, an asset owned by the people of the province of Alberta. The view of most is that development off the shore of Newfoundland, which includes its jurisdictional difficulties, will take some time, and that the best possibilities for Canada in terms of new domestic supply come from accelerated development of oil sands plants. Alberta was therefore prepared to commit, by way of risk investment and equity financing, up to $7 billion in the proposed Alsands, Cold Lake,

and a third new oil sands plant. This would have resulted in Canadian ownership in these next three oil sands plants exceeding 50 per cent.

We also committed ourselves, even though the oil is not required for our own needs here in Alberta, to put in place the costly infrastructure for the plants, and an additional commitment of the facilities necessary to have a permanent work force in the Fort McMurray area to ensure continuous oil sands development. As part of this offer we were prepared to accept a royalty for the people of the province of Alberta, who own the resource, lower than the Syncrude royalty, and that is for both the Alsands and the Cold Lake projects. This would have resulted in the federal government receiving billions and billions of additional dollars in corporate taxation over the lifetime of the new plants.

In addition to that the government of Alberta agreed as part of this package, or was prepared to agree as part of this package, not to increase its royalty levels on conventional oil and natural gas, regardless of future price increases – and that was a significant long-term commitment – and that Alberta would continue its exploration, development, and enhanced recovery programs. such as the exploratory drilling and geophysical incentive program that you are aware of, our system of low royalties for new discoveries, and the very important area of enhanced recovery schemes and lower royalties for low-productivity wells.

In addition to this, Alberta was prepared to make other investments in Canadian energy self-sufficiency. We were prepared to provide the entire financing necessary, equity and debt financing, to ensure the construction of both the Quebec and maritime portions of the Q&M pipeline, designed to carry Alberta natural gas to eastern Quebec and the maritime provinces to replace imported high-cost foreign oil. We were prepared to expend hundreds of millions of dollars of additional funding to the Alberta Oil Sands Technology and Research Authority to stimulate the development of enhanced recovery schemes, a very important area, thereby increasing the recovery of oil from existing fields. We now get only some 38 per cent of production under existing methods from our existing conventional fields. So that's a very major area.

In addition to that, we were prepared to finance, upon the invitation of the federal government and the involved provinces, other energy projects such as eastern refinery conversions, western electric grids, and similar projects to assist Canada in its goal of energy self-sufficiency. We made a calculation, and said the advantages to the nation of these substitution programs and additional supply initiatives, including the Alsands and Cold Lake projects, would be to reduce Canada's dependence on foreign oil by approximately 600.000 barrels per day by 1988. In 1988 it's estimated it's going to cost Canada $15 billion in one year to import those 600,000 barrels of production per day. Today it's a $2 billion bill: by 1988, without that 600,000 barrels, it would be a $15 billion bill.

In addition to that, although it's not the responsibility of the government of Alberta, to use our funds to strengthen not just Alberta but all the west, we were prepared to commit by way of outright grant over $2 billion of unconditional funding to improve transportation for western Canada, not, as has been suggested, Mr. Speaker, as something we would determine in a jurisdiction of the federal government without the federal government involvement, but that the four western premiers would meet and establish priorities and the federal government or its appropriate agencies would then approve the projects. Now we said all of this subject to provisions with regard to taxation: first of all, that there not be a tax on natural gas exports, for reasons of which we're all acquainted here and I'll deal with that in a moment; or a wellhead tax, which we discussed, as I mentioned, last fall, on either oil or natural gas; or punitive taxation of an industry centred in this province that affected jobs in Alberta in a significant way.

Well that, in some considerable detail, was our proposal of July 25. The proposal was rejected in its entirety by the Prime Minister and the federal government. Many throughout all parts of Canada have assessed that proposal as being reasonable, generous, and in the best interests of Canadians. It was rejected in its entirety as a package proposal for energy self-sufficiency for Canada, in the interests of Canadian harmony, Canadian unity, and Canadian economic strength.

Mr. Speaker, on August 1 the province of Alberta moved to increase the price by $2 a barrel, which still left the value of our conventional oil being sold as it is today at approximately 50 per cent of its value. On October 2 the federal minister of energy came to Alberta to attempt to get Alberta to separate its position on the oil sands from that of the other aspects of energy in terms of conventional oil and natural gas and presented a proposal with regard to non-conventional pricing for the oil sands developments, and of course received the response he anticipated from our minister, that it was all that we presented on July 25, part of a total package.

We've accepted whatever opportunities have been available to try to get the message of self-sufficiency across, and the reasonableness and effectiveness of the Alberta proposal of July 25. We even went so far as commissioning a public opinion poll on these sorts of subjects, which is something we've never done before. We did that because a certain newspaper in a central city in a central province issued a statement to the effect that the positions being taken by the premier of Alberta were not supported even by his own citizens. That caused me some concern. The question was a good trick question. I'm used to it. From memory, it was: do you believe the exclusive jurisdiction over resources should be with the provinces or the federal government?

It was purely a trick question. This government has never, in any way, suggested exclusive jurisdiction. For example, we've accepted federal jurisdiction in the area of determining whether a particular resource is surplus to Canadian requirements, and in a number of other ways. In any event, it was important for us to get an assessment. I won't go into detail except to say that people throughout Canada, even a significant number of people in the province of Ontario, agree with and accept the position with regard to the ownership of the provinces relative to resources.

Mr. Speaker, I want to assure the Legislature that we have done and will continue to do everything we can to work out this situation on the basis of negotiations. However, indications are that the federal government is determined to move unilaterally in eight days, and try, no matter how it might be interpreted or presented, to take over control of Alberta resources to all intents and purposes. I sadly say that if they proceed on that basis, we will throw away, for as long as one could judge, our prospect of the economic potential for Canada, and what that means for us in terms of jobs and reducing employment by being oil self-sufficient, when many other countries in the world in the late '80s will not be able to. Throwing away an opportunity to create activity in this country will have a multiplier effect across all of Canada, and a very significant impact on the Canadian economy in all parts, with a strong west and a multiplier effect in the manufacturing centre. We're on the verge of throwing that opportunity away by the actions of the federal government. I hope I'm wrong, but today I can give this Legislative Assembly no indication other than that analysis.

Source: Alberta Hansard, October 20, 1980, 1142-6.

Peter Gzowski (1934—)

"HOCKEY WAS US"

Peter Gzowski is a journalist and arguably Canada's best-known broadcaster. The fact that his medium is radio and not television attests to the strength of CBC radio in Canadian culture. From 1982 to 1997 he was the host of the popular daily three-hour radio show, *Morningside*, and he has also been an active crusader on behalf of literacy.

One of his major passions is hockey. Indeed, for many Canadians and for many people in the world, hockey was for a long time synonymous with Canada. The first ice hockey game was played in Montreal in 1875, and the first organized hockey team was that of McGill University, in 1879. The National Hockey League was founded in 1909 (under a different name). Though most of the teams in the early NHL were American, all the players were Canadian. As international hockey developed in the 1920s and 1930s, Canadian teams routinely trounced those from the United States and Europe.

Hockey soon gained a powerful hold on the Canadian mind, even though the "official" national game was – and is – lacrosse. Hockey was well suited for the harsh winter climate. The Saturday night radio and television broadcasts of the NHL games became defining Canadian rituals, particularly in Montreal and Toronto. Broadcasters such as Danny Gallivan, René Lecavalier, and Foster and Bill Hewitt were as celebrated as any politician or entertainer. Stars like Maurice Richard or Gordie Howe defined excellence for generations.

In this selection from his book *The Game of Our Lives*, Peter Gzowski captures the passion of hockey both for youngsters playing in local rinks and ponds and for fans who admire the professional game.

In the winters of my boyhood, my life centred on a hockey rink in Dickson Park, across the road and down the hill from my parents' duplex apartment. The rink lay on a low stretch of the park, between the baseball diamond and a low, grey building used to exhibit farmers' wares during the fall fair. Even before freeze-up, workmen would set up boards around the rink's space, and the boards would stand there through the last days of autumn, pale against the darkening grass, waiting for the season to begin. Metal light standards sprouted along their edges. With the first frost, the workmen would begin to flood, so that well before Christmas we could skate, and each day after school and all day on weekends, until spring softened the ice, we would give our lives to our game.

Weekends were the best. I would wake early Saturday morning, and pad down the hall to the sunny kitchen at the back of the apartment, careful not to wake my parents. I would slither down the back stairs for the milk, reaching one goose-pimply arm out to clutch the cold bottles, from which, as often as not, the frozen golden Guernsey cream had pushed the tops. Then upstairs again for cereal with brown sugar and, if I felt leisurely, a piece of toast. Into my clothes: warm corduroy trousers, a plaid shirt and heavy sweater, thick woollen socks. Down the stairs again, where my skates and outer clothing had steamed overnight on the radiator. I would lace on the skates, stretching out my leg with each eyehole to get the laces tight enough to stop the circulation. A good pair of laces could be pulled tight enough to be looped around the ankles twice and tied in a double bow in front. Stand on the linoleum to get the feel. Up on the toes. Good. Then into coat and toque, earmuffs if the day was cream-popping cold, then on with the mittens – wool, unfortunately, with a hope of hockey gloves for Christmas – and out across the squeaky snow.

If I was lucky, I would get to the rink before anyone else. Then, I could move around by myself, revelling in the clean air and the early light, and the untrammelled freedom I would feel as my body swayed with the rhythm of my strides. My hockey stick was an extension of my body, swinging back and forth in front of me as I moved. Counter-clockwise I went at first, moving on the right wing along the boards and down along the end, making ever longer strides as I built up speed, digging in with the pushing foot, hearing the *rask, rask* as I glided into each step. Around the corners, crossing the right leg over the left, leaning into the turn, building up momentum for the straightaway, then harder even down the boards, bent at the waist, getting my shoulders into it. Head down, with the stick held horizontal in front. Dig, dig, then turn again, my body warming as I moved. Now some turns the other way. Kitty-corner across the diagonal of the rink, swerving around rough patches, skates biting into the good ice, bumping ratchet-quick across the choppy islands. Tighter turns now, smaller circles, raising the outer leg to swing with centrifugal force. Back onto the long stretch of open ice, glass smooth, its surface cleared by the overnight winds, exulting with jumps and hops, scissoring in the air, heading breakneck toward the boards to stop in a spray of snow and stand laughing and panting in the morning sun.

* * *

In 1949, I left both Galt and my boyhood, or at least the part of it that I had spent on skates. But my fascination with the game continued. At high school and university, and later, as I travelled about the country working on newspapers and magazines and eventually on radio and television, I followed it with interest and enthusiasm. Occasionally, I managed to turn my passion into part of my work. I wrote about hockey for most of the journals I worked for, though never, alas, as a full-time sports writer, and in broadcasting I seized every chance to talk to its latest stars or dig into its newest trends. Hockey was the common Canadian coin. Though the men who played it for a living came from what the sociologists called the lower or lower-middle classes ("66.2 per cent ranked 39 or less on the Blishen Socioeconomic Index for Canada," one study reported in the 1970s) the men – and sometimes the women – who followed it came from every class and every region. Wayne and Shuster made jokes about it on their own television shows and popped up as guests on *Hockey Night in Canada*. John Allen Cameron burst into his televised presentations of Cape Breton music to show himself proudly – and surprisingly gracefully – skating with the NHL Old Timers; on other shows and with other teams, other hosts repeated the same act, Allan Thicke in Vancouver with the Los Angeles Kings, Tommy Banks in Edmonton with the Oilers; in Montreal, Lise Payette, just before she left late-night television to become a Parti Québécois cabinet minister, strapped her ample body into goalie's pads and, with more bravado than good sense, let the Canadiens fire pucks at her.

Television was only one mirror of hockey's appeal. Hugh Hood, the Montreal novelist whose stated ambition was to write a fictional series of Proustian dimensions, took time out to write a worshipful book about Jean Beliveau. Mordecai Richler followed the Canadiens with as much passion as he delved into St. Urbain Street. Peter Pearson made a film with a vignette of the real Max Bentley. Rick Salutin wrote a play about *Les Canadiens*, "with an assist from Ken Dryden." Nancy White sang about hockey on CBC radio's *Sunday Morning*. Robert Charlebois wore a hockey sweater on the cover of his most popular album. When John Robert Colombo set about compiling the best-known Canadian images, he chose, among the grain elevators and Niagara Falls, Ken Danby's magical print "At the Crease." At *Maclean's*, the editors used to say, if there was no excuse to use the Queen on the cover, they could always get Gordie Howe.

Hockey was us.

Source: Peter Gzowski, *The Game of Our Lives* (Toronto: McClelland and Stewart, 1981), 79-84.

Michael Ondaatje (1943–)

"BURNING HILLS"

Michael Ondaatje, born in Colombo, Ceylon (now Sri Lanka), came to Canada from England in 1962 and soon emerged as one of the country's most admired poets, filmmakers, and editors. His poetic style combines the imaginary and the realistic in a freeze-frame cinematic style, and his novel *The English Patient* (1992) won him international recognition.

"Burning Hills," written in 1972, brims with images familiar to most Canadians who have ever known a summer cottage and its special invitation to nostalgia. Commonly, a cottage is a family hand-me-down, makeshift shack, bearing the marks of each generation's ambitions, mostly unfulfilled – a septic tank that backs up when it rains, a new roof that leaks a little more than the old, the rotting screen door that cries out to be replaced, someday. Cottages carry memories of childhood adventures and mishaps, of growing up and growing old. For a writer, a cottage promises escape – from telephone calls, friends, colleagues, enemies. But nature has its own interruptions, flies mostly, attracted to the man-made chemical weapons hooked to the ceiling. Summer in a cottage is a time for imaginings and memories.

So he came to write again
in the burnt hill region
north of Kingston. A cabin
with mildew spreading down walls.
Bullfrogs on either side of him.

Hanging his lantern of Shell Vapona Strip
on a hook in the centre of the room
he waited a long time. Opened
the Hilroy writing pad, yellow Bic pen.
Every summer he believed would be his
    last.
This schizophrenic season change, June to
    September,
when he deviously thought out plots
across the character of his friends.
Sometimes barren as fear going nowhere
or in habit meaningless as tapwater.
One year maybe he would come and sit
for 4 months and not write a word down
would sit and investigate colours, the
insects in the room with him.
What he brought: a typewriter
tins of ginger ale, cigarettes. A copy of
    StrangeLove,

of *The Intervals*, a postcard of Rousseau's
    The Dream.
His friends' words were strict as lightning
unclothing the bark of a tree, a shaved hook.
The postcard was a test pattern by the
    window
through which he saw growing scenery.
Also a map of a city in 1900.

Eventually the room was a time machine
    for him.
He closed the rotting door, sat down
thought pieces of history. The first girl
who in a park near his school
put a warm hand into his trousers
unbuttoning and finally catching the spill
across her wrist, he in the maze of her skirt.
She later played the piano
when he had tea with the parents.
He remembered that surprised –
he had forgotten for so long.
Under raincoats in the park on hot days.

The summers were layers of civilisation in
    his memory

they were old photographs he didn't look at
    anymore
for girls in them were chubby not as perfect
    as in his mind
and his ungovernable hair was shaved to the
    edge of skin.
His friends leaned on bicycles
were 16 and tried to look 21
the cigarettes too big for their faces.
He could read those characters easily
undisguised as wedding pictures.
He could hardly remember their names
though they had talked all day, exchanged
    styles
and like dogs on a lawn hung around the
    houses of girls
waiting for night and devious sex-games
    with their simple plots.
Sex a game of targets, of throwing firecrackers
at a couple in a field locked in hand-made
    orgasms,
singing dramatically in someone's ear along
    with the record
'*How do you think I feel / you know our love's
    not real*
*The one you're mad about / Is just a gad-
    about*
How do you think I feel'
He saw all that complex tension the way his
    children would.

There is one picture that fuses the 5 summers.
Eight of them are leaning against a wall
arms around each other
looking into the camera and the sun
trying to smile at the unseen adult photog-
    rapher
trying against the glare to look 21 and
    confident.
The summer and friendship will last forever.
Except one who was eating an apple. That
    was him
oblivious to the significance of the moment.
Now he hungers to have that arm around
    the next shoulder.
The wretched apple is fresh and white.

Since he began burning hills
the Shell strip has taken effect.
A wasp is crawling on the floor
tumbling over, its motor fanatic.
He has smoked 5 cigarettes.
He has written slowly and carefully
with great love and great coldness.
When he finishes he will go back
hunting for the lies that are obvious.

Source: Margaret Atwood, ed., *The New Oxford Book of Canadian Verse in English* (Toronto: Oxford University Press, 1982), 404-6.

Stan Rogers (1949—83)

"Northwest Passage"

Until his tragically premature death in a fire on an Air Canada plane, Hamilton-born Stan Rogers was perhaps the most successful popular poet and composer of modern Canada. He wrote beautiful melodies for songs that dramatized Canada's history and reflected the courage and dignity of ordinary people, from prairie farmers to Atlantic fishermen.

Among the songs that touched Canadian hearts and has already become a classic is "Northwest Passage." Sir John Franklin died in 1847 with the crew of two British ships in a tragic endeavour to demonstrate that there was a passage for shipping around the north end of the continent. The proof would come much later when the RCMP's Henry Larsen (1899–1964) took his little ship, the *St.-Roch*, west to east through the passage in 1940-42 and in both directions in 1944.

"Kelso" is Henry Kelsey (*c*.1667-1724), the first European to see the prairies, and Alexander Mackenzie (1764–1820), David Thompson (1770–1857), and Simon Fraser (1776–1862) were guided by natives through the vast sea of western mountains to reach the Pacific.

Ah, for just one time, I would take the
    Nortwest Passage
To find the hand of Franklin reaching for
    the Beaufort Sea
Tracing one warm line through a land so
    wide and savage
And make a Northwest Passage to the sea

Westward from the Davis Strait, 'tis there
    'twas said to lie
The sea-route to the Orient for which so
    many died
Seeking gold and glory, leaving weathered
    broken bones
And a long-forgotten lonely cairn of stones

Three centuries thereafter, I take passage
    overland
In the footsteps of brave Kelso, where his
    "sea of flowers" began
Watching cities rise before me, then behind
    me sink again
This tardiest explorer, driving hard across
    the plain

And through the night, behind the wheel,
    the mileage clicking West
I think upon Mackenzie, David Thompson
    and the rest
Who cracked the mountain ramparts, and
    did show a path for me
To race the roaring Fraser to the sea

How then am I so different from the first
   men through this way?
Like them I left a settled life, I threw it all away
To seek a Northwest Passage at the call of
   many men

To find there but the road back home again

Source: Elizabeth Mouland, ed., *Tracing One Warm Line: Poetry of Canada* (St. John's: Breakwater, 1994).

Pierre Berton (1920–)

"Dear Sam"

Pierre Berton is Canada's best-known writer of popular history as well as a journalist and television personality. His major mission has been to create a sense of excitement and passion in Canadian history through his series of books on topics ranging from the War of 1812 to the building of the Canadian Pacific Railway. Not surprisingly, Berton is a strong Canadian nationalist. But his nationalism has been typified less by shrill anti-Americanism than by attempts to identify and describe unique features of the Canadian experience.

A good example of Berton's approach can be found in the following excerpt of a letter to "Sam" (as in "Uncle Sam"). Berton outlines a variety of Canadian traits to try to explain Canada, with a mix of information and humour, to Americans. It is interesting that, when contrasting the American concern for liberty with the Canadian attachment to order, he recognizes the strong and weak points of both perspectives.

Dear Sam:

   Today is Constitution Day in Canada! That doesn't mean much to you, I know – I doubt if it will make your front pages – but it's a big thing for us. After centuries we've cut our last ties with Europe and we're officially independent; our Queen says so. In fact she's up there on Parliament Hill, saying it now with a very English accent. But then we're used to English accents in this country – to a babel of accents: English, French, Scottish, Irish, Ukrainian, Italian, and many, many others –

symbolizing those fierce ethnic and regional loyalties that hold us together as a distinctive people even as they tear us apart. A typically Canadian contradiction.

   Up on Parliament Hill they're singing "O Canada" in two languages and more than one version. They're also singing "God Save the Queen," because, you see, we still have a Queen and she's all ours, even if she drops in on us only occasionally from her home at Buckingham Palace. By another typically Canadian contradiction we have been made to believe that she is not the Queen of England, except when she's in England, but the Queen of Canada, even when she's not here. That allows us to be totally independent on this day of days: an odd business, when you think of it, since we have been insisting to you Americans for decades that we've really been independent all along.

But then, we were only acting like Canadians, confusing everybody, especially your countrymen, who can't see much difference between our two peoples.

I know you're confused yourself, because every time you visit this country you ask questions which indicate to us that we *are* a different people:

You want to know why you can't buy a six-pack in a Toronto deli. And why does the West hate the East? And why do people wear kilts at parties? And why are our streets safer than yours? And why did we let the Mounties get away with all those crimes? Why is Trudeau a pinko? What are family allowances? Why have we got movie censors? Why haven't we scrapped the National Energy Policy? How come there are no English signs in Montreal? Where are all the black people? Why don't our newspapers carry scandal columns? How come we mispronounce "about"? Where are the bottomless dancers? What does Precambrian mean? Why are our bankers so secure and also so cautious? What's a crown corporation? How come nobody owns a gun? Why didn't we have a revolution, like everybody else? Why don't we join up with the United States?

That last question is one you've asked more than once and it deserves an answer. The short answer is that we wouldn't mind, but only if you'd let us call the country Canada and retain the parliamentary system of government, along with our flag, anthem and official bilingual policy. I doubt if you'd go for that; and even if you did it wouldn't work. We really are quite different from you Americans, even though we talk and dress and look alike.

We *have* a distinct identity and your question requires a longer answer than the flippant one I just gave. I've been exploring that identity for most of my career. And now, on this damp April day, as Mr. Trudeau pops up on the tube sounding not the slightest bit pinkish, I'm going to borrow from my own researches into the epic moments of our past, and also from my travels from Nanaimo to St. Anthony, to try to explain, in a series of letters, why we act like Canadians.

I'm going back, first, to my own beginnings because that's where I originally began to see that our social attitudes were not the same as yours.

As you know, I was born and raised in the Yukon. My father left New Brunswick at the height of the Klondike gold rush, took advantage of a railway rate war, climbed the Chilkoot Pass, built a raft on the shores of Lake Bennett, and in the spring of 1898 floated down the Yukon River to Dawson City. He didn't talk much about those days, though I still remember his description of that long line of men on the Chilkoot – a human garland hanging across the chill face of the Pass – so tightly packed that, when an exhausted climber stepped out of line it took him hours to squeeze back in, cursing and hollering over the delay. He told me something else that I've never forgotten. He said that on the Canadian side of the border a man could lay down his pack, or even a sack of gold, in the middle of the trail and return for it in a week, knowing no one would touch it; such was the state of the law in the Canadian Yukon.

I know that many of your countrymen think the Klondike is part of Alaska and that it was once a wild and lawless place. What my father was trying to tell me was that, because of the Canadian passion for order and security, it was just the opposite.

I don't think I entirely believed him then. The silent films about the great stampede that Fred Elliott showed in his movie house in Dawson suggested the opposite. And I remember wondering, as a child, why *anybody* would want to leave a sack of gold lying around. But many years later, while digging into the history of the gold rush, I came upon an actual incident that suggested my father was not exaggerating. Let me set the scene for you:

The richest man in the Klondike was Big Alex McDonald, a huge, awkward prospector from Antigonish, Nova Scotia. He was so wealthy that he kept a bowl of nuggets on a shelf in his cabin to give away to visitors. His string of mules, each loaded with a hundred-pound sack of gold, was a familiar sight, moving in single file from his claim on Eldorado creek to the bank in Dawson City. One day, one of these mules broke away from the string, strayed into the hills and didn't turn up in Dawson for a fortnight.

This errant animal, stumbling about through the birches and aspens, brushing past trappers' cabins and prospectors' tents, stands for me as a symbol of Canadian probity. For it must have been seen and recognized by scores of men who had come to the north hoping to find a fortune. On its back, for the taking, was a treasure worth twenty thousand dollars. Yet nobody touched it: Big Alex got his mule back with the gold intact.

Let me remind you that in those days Dawson was really an American town on Canadian soil. Its population was at least three-quarters foreign. But nobody dared tangle with the Canadian concept of order and security.

This very Canadian mule illustrates our national preoccupation with peace, order and good government – by which, I must tell you, we Canadians generally mean "strong government." I'm afraid that those sturdy Canadian words, inscribed on parchment by the men we call the Fathers of Confederation, lack both the panache and the hedonism of the companion phrase in your own eloquent Declaration of Independence. But I must tell you, Sam, that life, liberty and the pursuit of happiness are lesser Canadian ideals. "Liberty" sounds awkward on the Canadian tongue; we use "freedom," a more passive-sounding word. When I was a soldier applying for a three-day pass, I asked for "leave," a word that suggests permission. Your G.I.s were granted "liberty," a word that implies escape.

But then, we were never a community of rebels, escaping from the clutches of a foreign monarch. For many decades, while you were entrenching, often through violence, the liberty of the individual to do his own thing, we remained a society of colonials. Basking in the security and paternalism that our constitutional phraseology suggests, we sought gradually and through a minimum of bloodshed to achieve our own form of independence.

To realize what we consider to be the best of all possible worlds, we Canadians have been prepared to pay a price. The other side of the coin of order and security is authority. We've always accepted more governmental control over our lives than you have – and fewer civil liberties.

But you, too, have paid a price. For the other side of the coin of liberty is licence and sometimes anarchy. It seems to many of us that you Americans have been willing to suffer more violence in your lives than we have for the sake of individual freedom.

Source: Why We Act Like Canadians: A Personal Exploration of Our National Character (Toronto: McClelland and Stewart, 1982), 12-15.

Thomas Berger (1933–)

"Fragile Freedoms"

Thomas Rodney Berger is a well-known British Columbia jurist and civil libertarian. From 1971 to 1983 he was a justice of the Supreme Court of British Columbia, and from 1974 to 1977 he served as the commissioner of the Mackenzie Valley Pipeline Inquiry. In the latter role, he emerged as an outspoken defender of the rights of Canada's First Nations. His report, *Northern Frontier, Northern Homeland*, argued against a pipeline through northern Yukon and for a ten-year moratorium on construction through the Mackenzie valley, pending a settlement of native land claims there.

Berger's stature as a civil libertarian and reformer was enhanced by publication of his *Fragile Freedoms: Human Rights and Dissent in Canada*. In this book, Berger analyses the landmark legal cases involving the violation of minority rights and civil liberties, and he stresses the role of the new Charter of Rights and Freedoms in ensuring that the transgressions of the past are not repeated.

Freedom is a fragile commodity in the world today. Everywhere human rights are beset by ideology and orthodoxy, diversity is rejected, and dissent is stifled.

Alexander Solzhenitsyn, Steve Biko, Lech Walesa, Jacobo Timerman – their names have made human rights one of the great issues of our time. They have given form and substance to the contest between freedom and repression. They and other brave men and women have been imprisoned and tortured, and some have been executed, for wanting to be free, and for believing that their countrymen should be free. They have claimed the right to question – and to challenge – the political ideas undergirding the regimes in their own countries. They speak for all mankind.

Mass deportations, terror and torture, racial prejudice, political and religious persecution, and the destruction of institutions from which people derive their sense of identity are assaults upon human dignity and the human condition that are odious to men and women everywhere. In the Western democracies, we especially cherish representative institutions and the rule of law, democracy and due process. These traditions affirm the right to dissent: in politics, in religion, in science and in the arts. We conceive of these rights as individual rights, but they are much more than that. They are the means whereby diversity is maintained, and whereby minorities can thrive.

Questions of human rights and dissent in Canada are linked to questions of human rights and dissent around the world. Our own successes and failures, our own attempts to accommodate minorities, are important not only to ourselves. If people of differing races, religions, cultures, and languages can live together harmoniously within a great federal state, perhaps they may learn to live together harmoniously in the wider world.

And what of the Canadian experience? What does our history say to us and to the world?

Canada has adopted a new Constitution and a Charter of Rights and Freedoms. In doing so, we have severed the last formal link to colonial dependency. Far more important, however, is the fact that this exercise in constitution-making has forced us to articulate our idea of Canada. For a Constitution does not merely provide the means of settling present disputes, it is a legal garment that reveals the values that we hold. It is a document expressing that decent respect which the present owes to the past; it is, at the same time, a document addressed to future generations.

A Constitution is not intended simply to divide up revenue and resources between the federal government and the provinces. Canada's new Constitution, like the British North America Act before it, divides legislative powers between Parliament and the provinces. This division is precisely that, a division of powers, powers exercised by a majority through the federal government or by a majority within each of the provincial governments. But every thoughtful person realizes that limits must be set to these powers: there must be guarantees for the rights of minorities and dissenters; there must be protection for those who would otherwise be powerless.

Although our notions of democracy and due process evolved in the ethnically defined nation-states of Europe, Canada is not such a nation-state. We have two founding peoples, English and French, within a single state; we have aboriginal peoples with an historic claim to special status; and we have a variety of ethnic groups and races who have immigrated to Canada. Thus, we have many linguistic, racial, cultural, and ethnic minorities. Each of them has a claim to collective as well as to individual guarantees under the new Constitution and the Charter of Rights and Freedoms, and each of them has a claim on the goodwill of the majority. For all of these minorities the right to dissent is the mainstay of their freedom.

In Canada, we have two great societies, one English-speaking, one French-speaking, joined by history and circumstance. When we look to our past, we can see that the central issue of our history has been the working out of relations between these two societies. No discussion of Canadian institutions can proceed except as a discussion of the evolution of relations between the English and the French on this continent. The dominant theme of the constitutional discussions that led to Confederation in 1867 was the accommodation of these two communities in Canada. This theme, though sometimes it recedes, still overshadows the continuing constitutional debate of our own time.

These two societies, today, have much in common. Both are urban, industrial and bureaucratic. Although their linguistic and cultural differences are still significant, and they are responsible for the creative tension that is the distinctive characteristic of the Canadian political scene, these differences no longer threaten either side. As Pierre Trudeau has remarked, "The die is cast in Canada. Neither of our two language groups can force assimilation on the other."

It was not always so. The conquest of New France by the British in 1759 led to a series of attempts to assimilate the people of Quebec. These attempts were stoutly resisted by Quebecers, and their population of 60,000 has grown to some six million, and their culture flourishes as never before. The history of the French Canadians of Quebec epitomizes the struggle of minorities everywhere.

Today, in every Canadian province, there is a minority that speaks either English or French, and this fundamental duality places the condition of minorities at the very centre of our institutional arrangements. At the same time, the diversity of our huge nation has given rise to many forms of dissent.

* * *

The Canadian Constitution has always recognized that we are a plural, not a monolithic, nation. This is one of the finest Canadian traditions. Refugees from every continent, immigrants of every race, peoples of all faiths, and persons seeking political asylum have all found their place in Canadian life. It is our good fortune not to be of one common descent, not to speak one language only. We are not cursed with a triumphant ideology; we are not given to mindless patriotism. For these reasons Canada is a difficult nation to govern; there is never an easy consensus. Yet, our diversity shouldn't terrify us: it should be our strength, not our weakness.

Along every seam in the Canadian mosaic unravelled by conflict, a binding thread of tolerance can be seen. I speak of tolerance not as mere indifference, but in its most positive aspect, as the expression of a profound belief in the virtues of diversity and in the right to dissent.

Many Canadians have championed the ideal of tolerance throughout our history. Who can forget the tortured figure of Louis Riel, who died insisting upon the rights of his people? Or the great Laurier, pleading the cause of the Franco-Ontarians during the First World War? Or Angus MacInnis, who insisted upon the rights of the Japanese Canadians during the Second World War when the whole of British Columbia – in fact, the whole nation – stood against them? Or John Diefenbaker, calling for an end to the persecution of the Jehovah's Witnesses during the Second World War; Pierre Trudeau, defender of civil liberties in Quebec during the 1950s under the Duplessis regime; Ivan Rand, a great judge and legal philosopher, who affirmed the rights of political and religious dissenters during the 1950s; and Emmett Hall, whose humane judgement in the Nishga Indians' case in 1973 opened up the whole question of Native claims in Canada?

I am not urging that we set up a national waxworks. But the Canadian imagination is still peopled almost exclusively by the heroes and heroines of other nations, and our knowledge of who we are has suffered as a result. The crises of times past have thrown into prominence many men and women who have articulated and defended an idea of Canada that has illuminated the Canadian journey.

These Canadians – men and women of courage and compassion – were committed to an idea of Canada that we can all share today, an idea that goes deeper than the division of powers, an idea more eloquent than any set of constitutional proposals, an idea that took root long before the present crisis and which will endure beyond it – a faith in fundamental freedoms and in tolerance for all peoples. This idea of Canada represents the highest aspiration of any nation, and it evokes the best in our Canadian traditions.

Source: Thomas Berger, *Fragile Freedoms: Human Rights and Dissent in Canada* (Toronto: Clarke, Irwin, 1982), ix-xvi.

Canadian Conference of Catholic Bishops

"SOME ETHICAL REFLECTIONS ON THE ECONOMIC CRISIS"

Religion in post-war Canada has fought a losing battle with materialism and secularism. Furthermore, its voice has often been identified with reaction against changes most Canadians have accepted and even welcomed – equality for women, greater ethnic diversity, freedom of sexual preference – and emptying pews have made some church leaders seek allies among the wealthy. Yet in 1983, as Canada's third major post-war recession left a million and a half people

without work, the Social Affairs Commission of the Canadian Conference of Catholic Bishops (cccb) struck a new note. Reflecting on the state of Canadian society against the background of the social teachings of the Catholic Church, the commission issued the document "Ethical Reflections on the Economic Crisis," which suggested that unemployment was a more serious problem than inflation.

The bishops urged the faithful to reflect on "the preferential option for the poor, the afflicted and the oppressed," an option simply described as favouring the needs of the poor over the wishes of the rich. The gospels also supported "the special value and dignity of work in God's plan." In contrast, the bishops noted, governments and corporations valued profitability and competitiveness over job creation, while the threat of joblessness forced workers to accept salary cutbacks.

The bishops and their "preferential option" provoked predictable outrage from governments and corporate leaders, most of whom questioned whether religious leaders understood economics, global markets, or the stress of meeting a payroll. Indeed, the outrage from national leaders, including Prime Minister Pierre Trudeau, probably did more to publicize the bishops' statement than anything they themselves could have done.

A s the New Year begins, we wish to share some ethical reflections on the critical issues facing the Canadian economy.

In recent years, the Catholic church has become increasingly concerned about the scourge of unemployment that plagues our society today and the corresponding struggles of workers in this country. A number of pastoral statements and social projects have been launched by church groups in national, regional, and local communities as a response to various aspects of the emerging economic crisis. On this occasion, we wish to make some brief comments on the immediate economic and social problems followed by some brief observations on the deeper social and ethical issues at stake in developing future economic strategies.

As pastors, our concerns about the economy are not based on any *specific political options*. Instead, they are inspired by the gospel message of Jesus Christ. In particular, we cite two fundamental gospel principles that underlie our concerns.

The first principle has to do with the preferential option for the poor, the afflicted, and the oppressed. In the tradition of the prophets, Jesus dedicated his ministry to bringing "good news to the poor" and "liberty to the oppressed." As Christians, we are called to follow Jesus by identifying with the victims of injustice, by analyzing the dominant attitudes and structures that cause human suffering, and by actively supporting the poor and oppressed in their struggles to transform society. For, as Jesus declared, "when you did it unto these, the least of my brethren, you did it unto me."

The second principle concerns the special value and dignity of human work in God's plan for Creation. It is through the activity of work that people are able to exercise their creative spirit, realize their human dignity, and share in Creation. By interacting with fellow workers in a common task, men and women have an opportunity to further develop their personalities and sense of self-worth. In so doing, people participate in the development of their society and give meaning to their existence as human beings. Indeed, the importance of human labor is illustrated in the life of Jesus who was himself a worker, "a craftsman like Joseph of Nazareth."

It is from the perspective of these basic gospel principles that we wish to share our reflections on the current economic crisis. Along with most people in Canada today, we realize that our economy is in serious trouble. In our own regions, we have seen the economic realities of plant shutdowns, massive layoffs of workers, wage restraint programs, and suspension of collective bargaining rights for public sector workers. At the same time, we have seen the social realities of abandoned one-industry towns, depleting unemployment insurance benefits, cut-backs in health and social services, and line-ups at local soup kitchens. And, we have also witnessed, first hand, the results of a troubled economy: personal tragedies, emotional strain, loss of human dignity, family breakdown, and even suicide.

Indeed, we recognize that serious economic challenges lie ahead for this country. If our society is going to face up to these challenges, people must meet and work together as a "true community" with vision and courage. In developing strategies for economic recovery, we firmly believe that first priority must be given to the real victims of the current recession, namely – the unemployed, the welfare poor, the working poor – pensioners, native peoples, women, young people – and small farmers, fishermen, some factory workers, and some small business men and women. This option calls for economic policies which realize that the needs of the poor have priority over the wants of the rich; that the rights of workers are more important than the maximization of profits; that the participation of marginalized groups takes precedence over the preservation of a system which excludes them.

In response to current economic problems, we suggest that priority be given to the following short-term strategies by both government and business.

First, unemployment rather than inflation, should be recognized as the number one problem to be tackled in overcoming the present crisis. The fact that some 1.5 million people are jobless constitutes a serious moral as well as economic crisis in this country. While efforts should continually be made to curb wasteful spending, it is imperative that primary emphasis be placed on combatting unemployment.

Second, an industrial strategy should be developed to create permanent and meaningful jobs for people in local communities. To be effective, such a strategy should be designed at both national and regional levels. It should include emphasis on increased production, creation of new labor intensive industries for basic needs, and measures to ensure job security for workers.

Third, a more balanced and equitable program should be developed for reducing and stemming the rate of inflation. This requires shifting the burden for wage controls to upper income earners and introducing controls on prices and new forms of taxes on investment income (e.g., dividends, interest).

Fourth, greater emphasis should be given to the goal of social responsibility in the current recession. This means that every effort must be made to curtail cut-backs in social services, maintain adequate health care and social security benefits, and above all, guarantee special assistance for the unemployed, welfare recipients, the working poor and one-industry towns suffering from plant shut-downs.

Fifth, labor unions should be asked to play a more decisive and responsible role in developing strategies for economic recovery and unemployment. This requires the restoration of collective bargaining rights where they have been suspended, collaboration between unions and the unemployed and unorganized workers, and assurances that labor unions will have an effective role in developing economic policies.

Furthermore, all peoples of goodwill in local and regional communities throughout the country must be encouraged to coordinate their efforts to develop and implement such strategies. As a step in this direction, we again call on local Christian communities to become actively involved in the six-point plan of action outlined in the message of the Canadian bishops on *Unemployment: The Human Costs*.

We recognize that these proposals run counter to some current policies or strategies advanced by both governments and corporations. We are also aware of the limited perspectives and excessive demands of some labor unions. To be certain, the issues are complex; there are no simple or magical solutions. Yet, from the stand-point of the church's social teachings, we firmly believe that present economic realities reveal a "moral disorder" in our society. As pastors, we have a responsibility to raise some of the fundamental social and ethical issues pertaining to the economic order. In so doing, we expect that there will be considerable discussion and debate within the Christian community itself on these issues. Indeed, we hope that the following reflections will help to explain our concerns and contribute to the current public debate about the economy.

Source: Social Affairs Commission of the Canadian Conference of Catholic Bishops, *Some Ethical Reflections on the Economic Crisis* (Toronto, 1983), 68-71.

Bryan Adams and Jim Vallance

"TEARS ARE NOT ENOUGH"

Moved by the plight of African victims of mass starvation and influenced by the efforts of artists in other countries, Canada's top musicians set out to help. On February 10, 1985 they met one afternoon in Toronto to record this song. The funds raised through its sales were directed to the Northern Lights for Africa Society, a charitable public foundation.

The fifty-two recording artists and entertainers who gave of their time and talent ranged (alphabetically) from Bryan Adams and Robert Charlebois to Anne Murray and Neil Young.

As every day goes by
How can we close our eyes
Until we open up our hearts?

We can learn to share
And show how much we care
Right from the moment that we start.

Seems like overnight we see
The world in a different light.
Somehow our innocence is lost

How can we look away,
Cause every single day,
We've got to help at any cost.

We can bridge the distance
Only we can make the difference
Don't you know that tears are not enough.

If we can pull together,
We can change the world forever.
Heaven knows that tears are not enough.

It's up to me and you
To make the dream come true
It's time to take our message everywhere
    you know.

C'est l'amour qui nous rassemble
d'ici a l'autre bout du monde.

Let's show them Canada still cares.
Oh, you know that we'll be there.
And if we should try together you and I,
Maybe we could understand the reasons why.

Source: Words by Bryan Adams and Jim Vallance; title by Bob Rock and Paul Hyde; music by David Foster.

Gil Courtemanche

"Les Yeux de la Faim" ("The Eyes of Hunger")

"Tears Are Not Enough" was not the only Canadian musical contribution to the fight against African famine in the 1980s. In Quebec, a French song entitled "Les Yeux de la Faim" was recorded by seventy-five artists and released in May 1985, with an accompanying video. The words were written by Gil Courtemanche, and the music by Jean Robitaille. The performers ranged from Normand Braithwaite and Yvon Deschamps to Gilles Vigneault (1928–) and Nanette Workman, and the proceeds from the song were directed to la Fondation Québec/Afrique.

While written independently, the two songs share the use of a recurring metaphor of eyes, visions, and tears. The lyrics do differ in one sense. The English song focuses on Canadians generally, using the word "we" and emphasizing a call to action. The French lyrics concentrate on describing the plight of the starving Africans, particularly the children, through use of the pronoun "ils." Both songs were clearly motivated by the same spirit of compassion and caring.

They don't cry any more	Ils ne pleurent plus
Have no more tears	N'ont plus de larmes
No more smiles, only eyes	Plus de sourire, juste des yeux
They only have eyes	Ils n'ont plus que leurs yeux
Only their eyes speak to us	Que leurs yeux pour nous parler
They don't move any more	Ils ne bougent plus
Have no more games	N'ont plus de jeux
No more laughs, only eyes	Plus de rire, juste des yeux
They only have eyes	Ils n'ont plus que leurs yeux
Only their eyes speak to us	Que leurs yeux pour nous parler
The children, the children who watch us	Les enfants, les enfants qui nous regardent
The children of destiny, the children of hunger	Les enfants du destin, les enfants de la faim
The children, the children who watch us	Les enfants, les enfants qui nous regardent
The children of tomorrow have the right to live	Les enfants de demain ils ont le droit de vivre

They only have eyes
That watch the killing winds
They only have eyes
And tears of sand

They don't sing any more
Have no more words
No more dreams, only eyes
They only have eyes
Only their eyes speak to us

They don't live any more
Have no more time, only eyes
They only have eyes
Let's not shut our eyes

The children, the children who watch us
The children of destiny, the children of hunger
The children, the children who watch us
The children of tomorrow have the right to live

The only have eyes
That watch the killing winds
They only have eyes
And tears of sand

Ils n'ont plus que leurs yeux
Qui regardent le vent qui tue
Ils n'ont plus que leurs yeux
Et des larmes de sable

Ils ne chantent plus
N'ont plus de mots
Plus de rêves, juste des yeux
Ils n'ont plus que leurs yeux
Que leurs veux pour nous parler

Ils ne vivent plus
N'ont plus de temps, juste des yeux
Ils n'ont plus que leurs yeux
Ne fermons pas les yeux

Les enfants, les enfants qui nous regardent
Les enfants du destin, les enfants de la faim
Les enfants, les enfants qui nous regardent
Les enfants de demain ils ont le droit de vivre

Ils n'ont plus que leurs yeux
Qui regardent le vent qui tue
Ils n'ont plus que leurs yeux
Et des larmes de sable

Source: Words by Gil Courtemanche, music by Jean Robitaille. Published and distributed by Chant de mon pays (Mont St-Hilaire, Quebec), 1985.

Gerald Caplan (1938–) and Florian Sauvageau (1941–)

THE PRINCIPLES OF PUBLIC BROADCASTING

When most Canadians are asked to identify those things that are uniquely Canadian, sooner or later the CBC, or public broadcasting, is mentioned. This is part of the general Canadian tradition of governmental funding for the arts, reflected in other institutions such as the National Film Board. From its creation in 1936, the CBC has been both revered and criticized by Canadians. It has also been the subject of countless government commissions and studies.

Certainly, the CBC has represented the Canadian commitment to public broadcasting as a basic element of government activity and policy. Beginning in the 1980s, in part because of the growth of the federal deficit and the recognition of the strength of market forces in leading to greater efficiency, the CBC has come under attack. One defence of the value of public broadcasting was contained in the 1986 Report of the Task Force on Broadcasting Policy, chaired by Gerald Caplan and Florian Sauvageau. Their report contained strongly nationalist recommendations. Caplan is an historian and activist in the New Democratic Party. Sauvageau is a journalist and professor of communications at l'Université Laval. We reprint here their conception of the principles of public broadcasting.

The concept of public broadcasting can be characterized in half a dozen principles. The first three all stem from one overriding idea – that public broadcasting provides radio and television programs for everyone, regardless of social status, place of residence or aesthetic preference. Commercial broadcasting, like any other commercial enterprise, will not cater to everyone, since some of the potential audience will always be too marginal to be worth reaching.

Thus, the first duty of the public broadcaster is to provide service to the entire sovereign territory of the nation where there are inhabitants to be served. Making transmission arrangements to serve sparsely populated areas is naturally not cost-effective, and the rationale for the CBC's Northern Broadcasting Service, to take a Canadian example, must be based on grounds other than audience ratings. Public broadcasting is a valuable service providing worthwhile experiences from which no citizens should be disenfranchised just because they do not live in a large built-up urban centre. In fact it is precisely those most remote from media of cultural expression, as in the far North, who most deserve an electronic window on the world beyond the confines of their own community. In this way public broadcasting is really no different from other basic social services such as education and health care, paid for at least in part out of general revenues.

The second duty of the public broadcaster is to provide programs that will appeal to all tastes. This is a highly controversial proposition, by no means universally supported by devotees of public broadcasting. In our view, it is properly interpreted to mean that a body of programs should appeal to the largest possible number of viewers or listeners, but not necessarily at the same moment. We disagree with those who argue programs should distinguish themselves from mainstream popular fare by appealing exclusively to minority audiences. At its best, public broadcasting should achieve both these objectives, yet must not be the captive of either extreme. Nor, one trusts, should it be axiomatic that a popular program cannot be a quality program, nor a quality one popular.

By the same token, audiences are not compartmentalized according to taste. In other words, watching a classical play one day does not prevent one from watching a serial situation comedy the next, or vice versa. So the public broadcaster should not treat the audience as though it were one homogeneous group wanting one kind of fare to the exclusion of all others. On the contrary, few viewers and listeners are the exclusive consumers of minority or majority interest programming all the time. And the public broadcaster must behave not only as though different members of the audience have different tastes, but as though each individual member has a range of tastes to be satisfied.

The third duty of the public broadcaster is to make programs that reflect the experience of all significant groups in society – women, visible minorities, natives and others who may be disenfranchised for social or economic reasons. Television, for example, must not be a medium that is mostly about well-to-do, white middle-class professionals, just as radio must not be a medium that is exclusively a vehicle for top-ten hits. This same principle extends to the provision of service, technically speaking, to those who might be disenfranchised because of some handicap, such as hearing impairment. Television is not therefore an eminently democratic medium just because it brings handsome doctors, rich lawyers and macho detectives into every living room in the land. Public television must strive to do more, by bringing a broad cross-section of society into the cultural mainstream.

A related but somewhat different principle, the fourth in this enumeration, concerns the contribution of public broadcasting to national consciousness or nation-building. This takes several forms. The most obvious expectation is that the public broadcaster will act as a rallying point for national sentiments, not by espousing any specific cause, such as national unity, but by providing shared experiences simultaneously to large numbers of people and by defining, exhibiting and explaining national events and trends, from sports finals to election coverage. It is an essential part of such activities that they utilize program production from different regions of a nation, so that individuals in disparate communities can learn about each other and communicate more effectively with one another. The public broadcaster is also expected to be the showcase *par excellence* for the nation's culture. In many cases this means acting as an agent of cultural development by providing work and exposure for talented performers, writers, producers, craftspeople, journalists and others.

Finally, in addition to these duties or responsibilities, the public broadcaster has an important privilege without which the notion of service to the public would be altered beyond recognition: that is, freedom from control by vested interests, whether political or financial. This privilege clearly includes the freedom to express certain opinions, especially journalistic ones, without fear of reprisal from politicians who would rather not hear themselves or their party taken to task for bad policies or acts of mischief.

But even a mature democracy can give no iron-clad guarantees that such reprisals will never be attempted, both because politicians are never happy to be criticized and because freedom of expression is never absolute. The restrictions on freedom of expression, and the related principle of operating at arm's length from the government of the day, are made even more complicated for the public broadcaster by the need to be accountable for the wise use of public funds. A public television or radio network cannot thus act capriciously or irresponsibly, not only because of the usual constraints on libel, obscenity and so forth, but also because such a network is a public institution, funded by the taxpayers who can, through their elected representatives, insist on an accounting from those who make the programming decisions. But the principle must be clear: it is a public broadcasting system we are discussing, not a state or government system.

The tension between the privileges of autonomy and the duties of accountability can never of course be resolved in the abstract. Such tension is an ever-present fact of life, and its management requires much vigilance and democratic goodwill. But the public broadcaster's freedom to program in a professionally responsible way brings with it more than just the right not to be a propaganda tool of government. In a more positive vein it is also intended to make room for a diversity of voices and opinions on the airwaves, by providing liberating working conditions for artists and program-makers.

Source: *Report of the Task Force on Broadcasting Policy* (Ottawa: Supply and Services, 1986), 261-3.

David Suzuki (1936—)

THE NATURE OF CULTURES

David Suzuki is a scientist, science educator, and broadcaster. Born in Vancouver, he experienced as a child the forcible evacuation of Japanese Canadians during the Second World War. His first career was as a geneticist at the University of British Columbia, where he conducted important work on the genetics of the fruit fly.

Suzuki gradually shifted his interests away from actual scientific research to science policy and science education. He emerged in the 1970s and 1980s as a leading defender of the environment while also alerting Canadians to the importance of linking ethical considerations to the practice of science. At the same time, he has been a passionate advocate of the value of science education for Canadians. His television series "The Nature of Things" has been an important source of science education in Canada and in many other countries.

In this introspective selection, Suzuki reflects on the differences between the culture of Japan today and that of the different generations of Japanese Canadians.

My genes can be traced in a direct line to Japan. I am a pure-blooded member of the Japanese race. And whenever I go there, I am always astonished to see the power of that biological connection. In subways in Tokyo, I catch familiar glimpses of the eyes, hairline or smile of my Japanese relatives. Yet when those same people open their mouths to communicate, the vast cultural gulf that separates them from me becomes obvious: English is my language, Shakespeare is my literature, British history is what I learned and Beethoven is my music.

For those who believe that in people, just as in animals, genes are the primary determinant of behaviour, a look at second- and third-generation immigrants to Canada gives powerful evidence to the contrary. The overriding influence is environmental. We make a great mistake by associating the inheritance of physical characteristics with far more complex traits of human personality and behaviour.

Each time I visit Japan, I am reminded of how Canadian I am and how little the racial connection matters. I first visited Japan in 1968 to attend the International Congress of Genetics in Tokyo. For the first time in my life, I was surrounded by people who all looked like me. While sitting in a train and looking at the reflections in the window, I found that it was hard to pick out my own image in the crowd. I had grown up in a Caucasian society in which I was a minority member. My whole sense of self had developed with that perspective of looking different. All my life I had wanted large eyes and brown hair so I could be like everyone else.

Yet on that train, where I did fit in, I didn't like it.

On this first visit to Japan I had asked my grandparents to contact relatives and let them know I was coming. I was the first in the Suzuki clan in Canada to visit them. The closest relative on my father's side was my grandmother's younger brother, and we arranged to meet in a seaside resort near his home. He came to my hotel room with two of his daughters. None of them spoke any English, while my Japanese was so primitive as to be useless. In typical Japanese fashion, they showered me with gifts, the most important being a package of what looked like wood carved in the shape of bananas! I had no idea what it was. (Later I learned the package contained dried tuna fish from which slivers are shaved off to flavour soup. This is considered a highly prized gift.) We sat in stiff silence and embarrassment, each of us struggling to dredge up a common word or two to break the quiet. It was excruciating! My great uncle later wrote my grandmother to tell her how painful it had been to sit with her grandson and yet be unable to communicate a word.

To people in Japan, all non-Japanese – black, white or yellow – are *gaijin* or foreigners. While *gaijin* is not derogatory, I find that its use is harsh because I sense doors clanging shut on me when I'm called one. The Japanese do have a hell of a time with me because I look like them and can say in perfect Japanese, "I'm a foreigner and I can't speak Japanese." Their reactions are usually complete incomprehension followed by a sputtering, "What do you mean? You're speaking Japanese." And finally a pejorative, "Oh, a *gaijin*!"

Once when my wife, Tara, who is English, and I went to Japan we asked a man at the travel bureau at the airport to book a *ryokan* – a traditional Japanese inn – for us in Tokyo. He found one and booked it for "*Suzuki-san*" and off we went. When we arrived at the inn and I entered the foyer, the owner was confused by my terrible Japanese. When Tara entered, the shock was obvious in his face. Because of my name, they had expected a "real" Japanese. Instead, I was a *gaijin* and the owner told us he wouldn't take us. I was furious and we stomped off to a phone booth where I called the agent at the airport. He was astonished and came all the way into town to plead our case with the innkeeper. But the innkeeper stood firm and denied us a room. Apparently he had accepted *gaijin* in the past with terrible consequences.

As an example of the problem, Japanese always take their shoes off when entering a *ryokan* because the straw mats (*tatami*) are quickly frayed. To a Japanese, clomping into a room with shoes on would be comparable to someone entering our homes and spitting on the floor. Similarly, the *ofuro*, or traditional tub, has hot clean water that all bathers use. So one must first enter the bathroom, wash carefully and rinse off *before* entering the tub. Time in the *ofuro* is for relaxing and soaking. Again, Westerners who lather up in the tub are committing a terrible desecration.

To many Canadians today, the word "Jap" seems like a natural abbreviation for Japanese. Certainly for newspaper headlines it would seem to make sense. So people are often shocked to see me bristle when they have used the word

Jap innocently. To Japanese-Canadians, Jap or Nip (from "*Nippon*") were epithets used generously during the pre-war and war years. They conjure up all of the hatred and bigotry of those times. While a person using the term today may be unaware of its past use, every Japanese-Canadian remembers.

The thin thread of Japanese culture that does link me to Japan was spun out of the poverty and desperation of my ancestors. My grandparents came to a Canadian province openly hostile to their strange appearance and different ways. There were severe restrictions on how much and where they could buy property. Their children, who were born and raised in Canada, couldn't vote until 1948 and encountered many barriers to professional training and property ownership. Asians, regardless of birthplace, were third-class citizens. That is the reality of the Japanese-Canadian experience and the historical cultural legacy that came down to the third and fourth generations – to me and my children.

The first Japanese immigrants came to Canada to make their fortunes so they could return to Japan as people of wealth. The vast majority was uneducated and impoverished. But in the century spanning my grandparents' births and the present, Japan has leapt from an agrarian society to a technological and economic giant.

Now, the Japanese I meet in Japan or as recent immigrants to Canada come with far different cultural roots. Present-day Japanese are highly educated, upper-middle class and proud of their heritage. In Canada they encounter respect, envy and curiosity in sharp contrast to the hostility and bigotry met by my grandparents.

Japanese immigrants to North America have names that signify the number of generations in the new land (or just as significantly, that count the generational distance *away* from Japan). My grandparents are *Issei*, meaning the first generation in Canada. Most *Issei* never learned more than a rudimentary knowledge of English. *Nisei*, like my parents, are the second generation here and the first native-born group. While growing up they first spoke Japanese in the home and then learned English from playmates and teachers. Before the Second World War, many *Issei* sent their children to be educated in Japan. When they returned to Canada, they were called *Kika-nisei* (or *Kibei* in the United States). Most have remained bilingual, but many of the younger *Nisei* now speak Japanese with difficulty because English is their native tongue. My sisters and I are *Sansei* (third generation); our children are *Yonsei*. These generations, and especially *Yonsei*, are growing up in homes where English is the only spoken language, so they are far more likely to speak school-taught French as their second language than Japanese.

Most *Sansei*, like me, do not speak Japanese. To us, the *Issei* are mysteries. They came from a cultural tradition that is a hundred years old. Unlike people in present-day Japan, the *Issei* clung tightly to the culture they remembered and froze that culture into a static museum piece like a relic of the past. Not being able to speak each other's language, *Issei* and *Sansei* were cut off from each other. My parents dutifully visited my grandparents and we children would be trotted out to be lectured at or displayed. These visits were excruciating, because we children didn't understand the old culture, and didn't have the slightest interest – we were Canadians.

My father's mother died in 1978 at the age of ninety-one. She was the last of the *Issei* in our family. The final months of her life, after a left-hemisphere stroke, were spent in that terrible twilight – crippled, still aware, but unable to communicate. She lived the terminal months of her life, comprehending but mute, in a ward with Caucasian strangers. For over thirty years I had listened to her psychologically black-mailing my father by warning him of her imminent death. Yet in the end, she hung on long after there was reason to. When she died, I was astonished at my own reaction, a great sense of sadness and regret at the cleavage of my last link with the source of my genes. I had never been able to ask what made her and others of her generation come to Canada, what they felt when they arrived, what their hopes and dreams had been, and whether it was worth it. And I wanted to thank her, to show her that I was grateful that, through them, I was born a Canadian.

Source: David Suzuki, *Metamorphosis: Stages in a Life* (1987); repr., Eva C. Karpinski and Ian Lea, eds., *Pens of Many Colours* (Toronto: Harcourt, Brace Jovanovich, 1993), 388-91.

Rosemary Brown (1930–)

Racism, Canadian Style

Rosemary Brown has been one of Canada's best-known defenders of the rights of women, visible minorities, and disadvantaged Canadians in general. Born in Jamaica to a middle-class family, Brown moved to Canada after high school. She received her Bachelor of Arts degree from McGill and later a Master of Social Work from the University of British Columbia. Her early career was as a social worker in British Columbia, and she was the ombudswoman for that province's Status of Women Council from 1970 to 1972.

A member of the New Democratic Party, Brown was elected to the British Columbia legislature in 1972; in fact, she was the first black woman to be elected to any Canadian legislature. Re-elected in 1975, 1979, and 1983, she was a leading figure in the NDP both in British Columbia and on the national stage.

In this selection from her autobiography, Brown recalls her early experiences at McGill University, which in the 1950s had very few black students. She had thought that studying in Canada would minimize problems with the kinds of racism that were associated with the

United States. As her poignant account reveals, however, racism was alive and well in Canada. Yet not all Canadians were racists. Brown recounts the profound influence on her of English professor and writer Hugh MacLennan (1907–90). She also tells how she was helped to find a summer job by a fellow McGill student who was a member of one of Canada's quintessential establishment families, the Westons.

Living in Montreal, even in the relative seclusion of Royal Victoria College, the women's residence at McGill University, brought me my first contact with racism, Canadian-style. I had been raised on a diet of poems and stories about the oppression of being Black in the United States, but always there was the rider that Canada was different. Indeed, my family thought that by sending me to university in Canada they were guaranteeing that I would not have to deal with what they referred to as the "ugliness" of prejudice while receiving a reasonably good education (not as good as I would have received in England, but certainly superior to anything offered in the United States).

I must confess that the graduates of McGill, Dalhousie and the University of Toronto I met before leaving Jamaica fed the myth of a discrimination-free Canada by never mentioning prejudice. They spoke glowingly of their Canadian friends, indulgently of their Canadian professors and lovingly of their Canadian social experience. There were many jokes about the weather, some feeble attempts to include French phrases in their conversation and great bragging about the superiority of the academic standards. The only complaint that I remember hearing concerned the shortage of Jamaican girls enrolled at the universities.

The boys felt that they had to justify dating white Canadian girls while extolling the beauty and virtue of the childhood girlfriends left in Jamaica, from whom they had extracted promises of fidelity during their absence and to whom they had pledged eternal love.

I read the brochures sent to me by Royal Victoria College and McGill University avidly. I was hungry to add to my limited knowledge of Canada, which did not go much beyond the country's expanse of snow and ice, the dependence of the world on its prairies for wheat, its brave and loyal support of England during the war (unlike the Americans) and the idiosyncrasies of Prime Minister Mackenzie King (and his mother), who seemed to retain power forever.

I conjured up in my mind's eye a community of plain, simple, gentle folk who lived uneventful lives in a cold uneventful country inhabited by very few Black people and a handful of Native Indians who resided on reserves.

I was happy with the prospect of my studying in Canada; so was Roy. We both assumed that I would not have any interest whatsoever in Canadian men, that I would not be distracted by a glittering social life; I would study, complete my four years, and return to Jamaica, probably to attend the law school that was in its infancy at the University of the West Indies. In any event it was obvious to both of us that we were destined to marry and grow old together, and the four years apart would only serve to strengthen our attachment to each other.

Canada was not what I expected. Three weeks after I had settled into a double room in Royal Victoria College, the assistant warden of women called me into her office and explained that I was being given a single room, because the College had been unable to find a roommate to share the double with me. She tried to break the news to me gently, pointing out how lucky I was to secure a single room and how much more private and quiet that would be for studying. I was moved into a single room at the same rate as the double – and two white women students were immediately moved into the double room.

I was stunned! I could not believe that not one of the other students in residence had been willing to share a room with me. Other West Indian women who had been at Royal Victoria College before me shrugged the matter off as not being surprising; having had similar experiences themselves they had known all along that no roommate would be found to share my room. Every year, West Indian women, given the option, requested the cheaper double room, moved in and were later moved into the more expensive single rooms at the lower double room rate. The bureaucracy was embarrassed by the whole procedure, but had not found a satisfactory way around it. It lived in the vain hope that one year things would change and a student would be found willing to share a

double room with a Black student, and so it persisted. Despite the fact that that particular form of racism worked in my favour economically, it made me angry and my anger was compounded by frustration. It eventually became clear that the experience would be typical of the prejudice I ran into during my years in residence – polite, denied and accepted.

The dining room behaviour was another example of the peculiar brand of racism practised in Royal Victoria College at that time. Whenever I entered the dining room at mealtime I would anxiously scan the tables, hoping to find a seat at a table with another Black student. If there was none available, I would look for a seat with one of the two or three white friends I had managed to make (I had made some, including Sue Curtis, whose father was the Attorney General of Newfoundland at the time). If that failed, I just sat anywhere, knowing that I would probably complete my entire meal without anyone speaking to me or including me in their conversation.

At first, because I am outgoing, a bit of an extrovert, I assumed that my tablemates were shy, so I used to initiate conversation with the person sitting beside me or across from me – the cold and unfriendly response to these overtures soon convinced me to stop.

I was truly grateful for the people who acted as a buffer against the hurts; although they did not transform Royal Victoria College into a home away from home, they managed to give me a glimpse of that other Canada that existed beyond prejudice and discrimination. Dr. Muriel Roscoe, Dean of Women, and her assistant Marie Madeline Mottola monitored our activities to ensure that we did not withdraw into a lonely shell of self-pity, but participated in social events on and around the campus. Mike DeFreitas, the senior custodian and an early West Indian immigrant who had retired from the railroad, took on the responsibility of surrogate father. He never hesitated to chastise us for staying out late during weeknights and made it his business to meet and to know the young men who dated us. The other Caribbean women were a special source of support, and although Dr. Roscoe encouraged us not to confine our social contact to our immediate and exclusive circle, she recognized the value and necessity of the love and nurturing that we gave and received from each other.

I was neither lonely nor unhappy during my stay at McGill. The West Indian community was large, vibrant and close-knit. My closest women friends were two other Jamaicans, Patsy Chen and Merle Darby, who had attended Wolmer's, the same private school that I had, and whom I knew well. In addition, because the ratio of male to female West Indian students was almost three to one there was never a shortage of dates. Many of the older male students were dating white Canadians but in the early 1950s interracial dating was not as acceptable as it is today and many more of the male students either refrained from doing it or did it clandestinely.

Interracial dating was absolutely taboo for West Indian women. We were all very conscious of the sexual stereotypes that we were told inhabited the fantasy world of white males, and at that time it was still very important to West Indian men that the women they married be perceived to be pure and virginal. The tragedy, of course, was that the West Indian male students internalized and accepted the white criteria of beauty and since the "only life" Black women had to live could not "be lived as a blonde," as a popular TV commercial of the time exhorted, the Black men assumed that white men saw no beauty in us, and therefore their only interest would be in our sexual availability.

Even more tragic was the fact that we Black women students (unlike our counterparts of today) shared this perception of our unattractiveness and consequently closed ourselves off from the world of white males. Tragic because the decision to do so was not based on our assessment of our worth, but on our acceptance of our male colleagues' assessment of our lack of worth.

* * *

The real excitement of my academic life at McGill was discovering Hugh MacLennan and Canadian literature. During my voracious reading years as an adolescent and teenager, I had discovered and come to love Mazo de la Roche and Lucy Maude Montgomery, and for me that was all there was to Canadian literature. I had inherited from my English high school teachers the belief that very little of value was being produced by writers in the colonies, so I had no curiosity about Canadian literature. Quite frankly I did not think that there was any.

It was with a sort of bemused inquisitiveness that in my second year I registered for the course in Canadian Literature taught jointly by Hugh MacLennan, the author, and Louis Dudek, the poet. As the works of Gabrielle Roy, Morley Callaghan, Earle Birney and Hugh MacLennan entered my life, they opened up such a rich and exciting world to me that I came to see Canada through new eyes and to develop an addiction to Canadian authors that I have never lost.

In addition, I fell in love with Hugh MacLennan. I found him a kind and inspiring teacher who found the time to talk, discuss and listen as I struggled towards a better understanding of Canadian mores, cultures, attitudes and customs. One teacher stands out in memory from my high school: Lucille Waldron (Mair), my history teacher. One teacher stands out in memory from my university years: Hugh MacLennan, my Canadian Literature professor.

* * *

The less polite face of racism remained hidden until later. Although the women who shared the residence at Royal Victoria College were content just to treat us as though we did not exist, never acknowledging our presence except when necessary and then only with the minimum of courtesy, the landladies and landlords who lived in the neighbourhoods near McGill had no such inhibitions. There was nothing subtle about the racism of the landlords and ladies of Montreal. During the summer the women's residence was closed and we were all expected to return to out respective homes or seek accommodation elsewhere. Of course, my first summer in Canada, I hastened home to Jamaica and remained there until it was time to return to school. I needed desperately to be free of prejudice and discrimination, to see my family, and to reassure myself that I was still a whole and valued human being; and to assess my feelings for Roy. But by the following year, I was in love with one of the male students and wanted to spend the vacation in Montreal to be near him.

Job hunting in Montreal that summer proved to be a nightmare. My Chinese-Jamaican friend Patsy Chen secured a job immediately as a waitress at a golf and country club. Although I applied to the same club that she did, and to others as well, I was never accepted. The employment counsellor kept recommending that I accept childcare jobs or light housework jobs, despite the fact that I explained I was not interested in doing housework or caring for children. She finally explained that although she had personally recommended me for a number of different jobs, only the people seeking domestic servants were interested in hiring me.

The older, wiser, senior West Indian women students, experienced in these matters, had never bothered to seek employment in Montreal. As soon as the academic semester ended, they headed for New York, where they were able to secure any type of work they wanted.

Discouraged by my job hunt, I reported to Gretchen Weston, the assistant warden in residence who was also the designated counsellor for foreign students, that I would be returning to Jamaica for the summer since I had been unable to find employment. Gretchen, who happened to be the daughter of one of the Westons of Weston's financial empire and was herself a student at McGill, was clearly upset by my report; she asked me to allow her to make some enquiries and report back to me in a couple of days. The following day she called to tell me to report to the Weston's plant in Longueil for work the following Monday.

Source: Rosemary Brown, *Being Brown: A Very Public Life* (Toronto: Random House, 1989), 23-33.

Dan George (1899–1981)

"I Am a Native of North America"

Dan George, or Teswahno, was a logger, longshoreman, and itinerant musician. Born on Burrard Indian Reserve No. 3, in British Columbia, he was chief of the Squamish band from 1951 to 1963. During this period, his skill as an actor and speaker was recognized. In the role of a wise, gentle Indian elder, he appeared in the CBC's "Cariboo Country" and in the play "The Ecstasy of Rita Joe" by George Ryga (1932–). George performed in eight Hollywood feature films, with his best-known roles being in *Little Big Man* in 1970 and in *Harry and Tonto* in 1974.

He was also a writer. During the Canadian centennial in 1967, George's "Lament for Confederation" helped many Canadians to take a second look at the celebration and to recognize that not everyone could rejoice on Canada's hundredth birthday. His prose poetry appeared in two books. The following selection comes from *My Spirit Soars*, published in 1982, after his death in Vancouver the previous year.

In the course of my lifetime I have lived in two distinct cultures. I was born into a culture that lived in communal houses. My grandfather's house was eighty feet long. It was called a smoke house, and it stood down by the beach along the inlet. All my grandfather's sons and their families lived in this large dwelling. Their sleeping apartments were separated by blankets made of bull rush reeds, but one open fire in the middle served the cooking needs of all. In houses like these, throughout the tribe, people learned to live with one another; learned to serve one another; learned to respect the rights of one another. And children shared the thoughts of the adult world and found themselves surrounded by aunts and uncles and cousins who loved them and did not threaten them. My father was born in such a house and learned from infancy how to love people and be at home with them.

And beyond this acceptance of one another there was a deep respect for everything in nature that surrounded them. My father loved the earth and all its creatures. The earth was his second mother. The earth and everything it contained was a gift from See-see-am . . . and the way to thank this great spirit was to use his gifts with respect.

I remember, as a little boy, fishing with him up Indian River and I can still see him as the sun rose above the mountain top in the early morning . . . I can see him standing by the water's edge with his arms raised above his head while he softly moaned . . . "Thank you, thank you." It left a deep impression on my young mind.

And I shall never forget his disappointment when once he caught me gaffing for fish "just for the fun of it." "My Son," he said, "The Great Spirit gave you those fish to be your brothers, to feed you when you are hungry. You must respect them. You must not kill them just for the fun of it."

This then was the culture I was born into and for some years the only one I really knew or tasted. This is why I find it hard to accept many of the things I see around me.

I see people living in smoke houses hundreds of times bigger than the one I knew. But the people in one apartment do not even know the people in the next and care less about them.

It is also difficult for me to understand the deep hate that exists among people. It is hard to understand a culture that justifies the killing of millions in past wars, and is at this very moment preparing bombs to kill even greater numbers. It is hard for me to understand a culture that spends more on wars and weapons to kill, than it does on education and welfare to help and develop.

It is hard for me to understand a culture that not only hates and fights his brothers but even attacks nature and abuses her. I see my white brothers going about blotting out nature from his cities. I see him strip the hills bare, leaving ugly wounds on the face of mountains. I see him tearing things from the bosom of mother earth as though she were a monster, who refused to share her treasures with him. I see him throw poison in the waters, indifferent to the life he kills there; and he chokes the air with deadly fumes.

My white brother does many things well for he is more clever than my people but I wonder if he knows how to love well. I wonder if he has ever really learned to love at all. Perhaps he only loves the things that are his own but never learned to love the things that are outside and beyond him. And this is, of course, not love at all, for man must love all creation or he will love none of it. Man must love fully or he will become the lowest of the animals. It is the power to love that makes him the greatest of them all . . . for he alone of all animals is capable of love.

Love is something you and I must have. We must have it because our spirit feeds upon it. We must have it because without it we become weak and faint. Without love our self esteem weakens. Without it our courage fails. Without love we can no longer look out confidently at the world. Instead we turn inwardly and begin to feed upon our own personalities and little by little we destroy ourselves.

You and I need the strength and joy that comes from knowing that we are loved. With it we are creative. With it we march tirelessly. With it, and with it alone, we are able to sacrifice for others.

There have been times when we all wanted so desperately to feel a re-assuring hand upon us . . . there have been lonely times when we so wanted a strong arm around us . . . I cannot tell you how deeply I miss my wife's presence when I return from a trip. Her love was my greatest joy, my strength, my greatest blessing.

I am afraid my culture has little to offer yours. But my culture did prize friendship and companionship. It did not look on privacy as a thing to be clung to, for privacy builds up walls and walls promote distrust. My culture lived in big family communities, and from infancy people learned to live with others.

My culture did not prize the hoarding of private possessions, in fact, to hoard was a shameful thing to do among my people. The Indian looked on all things in nature as belonging to him and he expected to share them with others and to take only what he needed.

Everyone likes to give as well as receive. No one wishes only to receive all the time. We have taken much from your culture . . . I wish you had taken something from our culture . . . for there were some beautiful and good things in it.

Soon it will be too late to know my culture, for integration is upon us and soon we will have no values but yours. Already many of our young people have forgotten the old ways. And many have been shamed of their Indian ways by scorn and ridicule. My culture is like a wounded deer that has crawled away into the forest to bleed and die alone.

The only thing that can truly help us is genuine love. You must truly love us, be patient with us and share with us. And we must love you – with a genuine love that forgives and forgets . . . a love that forgives the terrible sufferings your culture brought ours when it swept over us like a wave crashing along a beach . . . with a love that forgets and lifts up its heads and sees in your eyes an answering love of trust and acceptance.

This is brotherhood . . . anything less is not worthy of the name.

I have spoken.

Source: Chief Dan George, *My Heart Soars* (Surrey, B.C.: Hancock House, 1989), 36-41.

Preston Manning (1942–)

NEW CANADA

The Reform Party grew to great national significance with the federal election of 1993 and became the Official Opposition in 1997. It resembles other political movements which have burst from the grassroots of western Canada. Its national leader, Preston Manning, the son of Ernest Manning (1908–96), former Social Credit premier of Alberta, came to maturity amidst third-party, regionally based politics.

While earlier western protest parties reflected the anger of people impoverished by the policies of Ottawa and the financial power of Montreal and Toronto, Manning's party speaks for a region which resents federal regulation, taxes, and redistributive social policies. Reformers criticize multiculturalism, immigration at a time of unemployment, and "giving in to Quebec." It wants to restore what supporters describe as "family values."

Preston Manning has argued for a "New Canada" of equal provinces, free to do what they choose in social and cultural policy, and without any of the ideas and values he associates with the "Old Canada," such as the 1840s partnership of French and English. This selection, taken from a speech he delivered to a Reform Party convention at Saskatoon in April 1991, sets out the main elements of his thinking.

The Reformer's Vision of New Canada

This brings me then to the Reformer's Vision of New Canada.

First of all, let me say charitably but clearly that I do not look to Quebec or Quebec politicians to define New Canada. New Canada cannot simply be a reaction to Quebec demands and aspirations. New Canada must be open and big enough to include a New Quebec, but it must be more than viable without Quebec.

Once we get New Canada defined, the question of whether New Quebec wishes to be a part of New Canada must be addressed, but that is not our starting point. This is what distinguishes the Reform Party's vision of Canada from those of all three of the traditional federal parties.

If you want a revised definition of Canada and a revised constitution that is essentially a reaction to Quebec's latest demands, then look to the federal PCs, Liberals, or NDP because that is their starting point. That's been their starting point for the last 30 years.

If you want a definition of New Canada and a new Constitution that takes as its starting point the needs, aspirations, and common sense of the common people in the other nine provinces and two territories, with an open invitation for input from Quebec federalists, then it is the Reformer's vision of Canada that you should examine.

And when we put our ear to the political ground, and listen hard, which is the one thing a populist party ought to do best, we hear disjointed but meaningful words and phrases – which taken together add up to this 42-word definition of New Canada: "New Canada should be a balanced, democratic federation of provinces, distinguished by the conservation of its magnificent environment, the viability of its economy, the acceptance of its social responsibilities, and recognition of the equality and uniqueness of all its provinces and citizens."

Let me repeat that – or at least the key concepts and phrases – New Canada, federation, balanced federation, democratic federation, federation of provinces, environmentally sustainable, economically viable, socially responsible, recognizing equality and uniqueness of citizens, recognizing equality and uniqueness of provinces.

Let me express this definition of New Canada a second way, for those of you who are goal-oriented and respond to "mission statements."

Canada's mission in the 21st century will be to create by evolution, not revolution, a more balanced society on the northern half of the North American continent:

• A society where the economy is productive, competitive, and prosperous, but in harmony rather than conflict with the environment and social needs of its citizens.

• A society where the governmental system is truly federal and democratic, recognizing the equality and uniqueness of all the provinces and citizens.

Let me express this definition of New Canada a third way. Many Canadians (this is a national trait) are more certain of what they don't want than what they do want. So let me say what New Canada is not.

New Canada must be a federation of provinces, not a federation of founding races or ethnic groups.

New Canada must be a balanced federation, not an unbalanced, federation where one province has special status or a special deal; not an unbalanced federation where all the provinces have special status and Canada has no status; not an unbalanced federation where one generation centralizes all the power in Ottawa, and the next generation centralizes it all in the provincial capitals in the name of decentralization.

New Canada must be a balanced federation where the division of powers between the federal and provincial governments is fair, functional, and flexible, not a federation where the balance of powers is simply the product of a tug-of-war between federal and provincial politicians.

New Canada must be a truly democratic federation, not a federation where powerful interest groups on the left or the right succeed in getting their ideology entrenched in the Constitution so that the public cannot choose a different course even if they want to.

The proponents of New Canada can safely argue that the Constitution of New Canada should entrench a commitment to freedom, federalism, and democracy, but any attempt to go beyond that – to entrench the concepts of a Swedish-style welfare state (as Audrey McLaughlin suggests) or an American-style market economy (as some of us might prefer) cannot be sold to the Canadian people at this point in time.

Fourthly, let me say that of course further refinements and expansions of this definition of New Canada are required. This is one area where the Reform Party can and must open its arms wide to all Canadians for their contributions, and where you people can help me more than any other.

The Reform Party of Canada is gradually getting the policy-making resources, the research capability, the legal help required to help flesh out exactly what Canadians mean by each of these phrases in our vision of New Canada, and how to express these in terms of constitutional reforms and public policy.

But at the same time, we need to take our definition of New Canada and hammer it into concrete terms which mean something on the street. How can you explain New Canada in 30 seconds to teenagers who are going to live most of their lives in the 21st century, to working men and women who are up to their ears in raising children and paying bills, to new Canadians and aboriginals and seniors who often feel left out of such discussions altogether?

I'm not sure how this can be done, but I'm convinced that our Vision of New Canada will not become a living reality capable of commanding attention and inspiring support among the common people until we can translate:

• "New Canada" into "your future home."

• "Balanced federalism" into "federal and provincial governments that work for you without taxing you to death."

• "Democratic federalism" into "election ballots, referendum ballots, where your 'X' gives you a real say in running the country."

• "Viable economy" into "good jobs with good incomes for you and your children."

• "Social responsibility" into "affordable health care, crime-free streets, and decent pensions for the old."

• "Environmental sustainability" into "clean air, clean water in the place where you live."

If some of you could take this speech – with my conceptual definition of New Canada, imperfect and incomplete as it may be – broaden it out where it needs broadening, and deepen it where it needs deepening, and translate it into the language of the street and the neighborhood where you live – that could be one of the greatest services that you could render this party and your country in the coming year.

The Road to New Canada

This brings us at last to the Reformer's map – a map highlighting the road that leads from Old Canada to New Canada.

We cannot afford – Canada cannot afford – to be in the position of Christopher Columbus when he started out for the New World. He had no map. When he started, he didn't know where he was going; when he got there, he didn't know where he was; when he got home he didn't know where he'd been; and he was doing it all on borrowed money.

So how do we get from where we are now, to that new nation of the 21st century?

First of all, let the people and politicians of Quebec define the New Quebec. We welcome the current constitutional ferment in Quebec because one of its effects will be to crack the Canadian Constitution wide open and force the rest of Canada to address the task of developing a New Constitution, rather than attempting to patch up the old one.

Thus we view the Allaire Report, the deliberations of the Quebec Liberals, the Report of the Belanger Campeau Commission, and the deliberations of the PQ and BQ on alternative visions of Sovereignty Association – with positive interest. These reports and deliberations are useful – not for what they attempt to say about the future of Canadian federalism – but for what they say about the possible shape of a New Quebec.

At this stage there are only two simple messages that the Reform Party of Canada would like to communicate to the people of Quebec.

The one is to invite genuine Quebec federalists to contribute to our vision of a New Canada.

The other is to express the hope that all Quebecers will insist upon seeing the draft Constitution of the New Quebec before they make any final judgment as to whether it is superior to the Constitution of New Canada.

If I were a resident of Quebec, and being asked to get out of one constitutional ship and into another, I would want to see more than the brochures on the second ship.

And so we say, let Quebec define the New Quebec. But at the same time we say with even more vigor and insistence, let the rest of Canada (and federalists in Quebec if they so wish) clearly define New Canada.

Reformers believe that New Canada should be a place where the people themselves take ownership of their own Constitution rather than entrusting it to "top down" constitution makers and dice rollers such as the Meech Lake gang.

We therefore propose that the first step toward developing the Constitution of New Canada should be the organization of regional constitutional conventions – one in British Columbia, one for the Prairie Provinces, one in Ontario, and one for the Atlantic Provinces – to be followed by a national constitutional convention.

Premier Wells of Newfoundland is in a strong position to provide leadership in initiating an Atlantic Canada constitutional convention, and perhaps Premier Filmon of Manitoba could provide leadership in initiating a prairie provinces constitutional convention. If they would take the lead, others would follow.

Delegates to these conventions should be elected, and their mandate should be to produce a draft Constitution for New Canada within a limited period of time. They should have access to qualified technical committees capable of producing draft constitutional proposals. They should receive representations from ordinary citizens and interest groups. Delegates to a national constitutional convention should be chosen by delegates to the regional conventions.

The final result of the deliberations of these conventions should be presented to the provincial and federal governments for modification and adoption through a federal-provincial conference and the constitutional amendment process provided by the current Constitution unless a better process can be proposed.

The people of Canada should also be provided with an opportunity to ratify any new Constitution for New Canada through a national constitutional referendum modeled after the Australian constitutional referendum process.

Thirdly, we say, once the New Quebec and the New Canada are clearly defined – with adequate levels of public input and support – the stage will be set for a conclusive Constitutional Negotiation.

This will be the Canadian way of dealing with our secession crisis, and may be contrasted with the American approach. When the Americans faced their secession crisis in the mid-19th century, after 25 years of attempting to settle the underlying issue through political and judicial compromises, they finally settled it by force of arms through a civil war.

Surely no Canadian wants our secession crisis to come to that. Just as Canada gained its independence from Great Britain, not by an armed revolution, but by unspectacular but nevertheless effective negotiation, so should we handle our secession crisis.

The initial object of the great Canadian constitutional negotiation of the 1990s should be to see if the vision of the New Quebec can be reconciled with the vision of a New Canada within a broader constitutional framework.

Let it be clear that it is the hope of Reformers and Canadian federalists in all parties that such a reconciliation can be accomplished. We want to change the question from "Do you want to leave the Old Canada?" – the Canada of Trudeau and Chretien and Mulroney and McLaughlin – to, "Do you want to be part of the New Canada as defined by a new generation of federalists and internationalists?"

In my judgment, the more that the people of Quebec and the people of the rest of Canada are involved in the defining of the New Quebec and the New Canada, the higher will be the probability that the two visions can be reconciled. This is because rank and file people everywhere want more or less the same things for themselves and their children – a safe environment, good jobs with good incomes, high-quality education and health services, respect for their personal values and cultural heritages, and the freedom to live their lives in peace and dignity.

Conversely, the more the visions of the New Quebec and the New Canada are the pet projects of intellectual or political elites, or self-serving politicians hoping to ride either Quebec nationalism or Canadian panic to political power, the lower will be the probability that the two visions can be reconciled.

Finally, we say that if the vision of a New Quebec within a New Canada cannot be realized – if the two visions are too different or if the political judgment and will to reconcile them is not present – then the focus of the great Canadian constitutional negotiation should turn to defining mutually advantageous terms and conditions of a more separate relationship.

I believe that in fairness to the people of Quebec it should be stated that, if the negotiations take this turn, whoever is negotiating on behalf of New Canada is unlikely to be attracted to the concept of sovereignty-association as currently advanced by some Quebec politicians.

The principal object of those negotiating on behalf of New Canada will be to minimize the economic and other disbenefits to New Canada of a Quebec secession, and to enter only into those relationships with an independent Quebec which are clearly in New Canada's interest.

The objective of all of this – defining New Canada, Constitutional Conventions, the Great Constitutional Negotiation – is to get on the road to New Canada as quickly as possible, and to get to New Canada by the turn of this century.

The issue of the future relationship of Quebec to New Canada must be resolved one way or the other in the next several years. We cannot go on as we have. We cannot stagger into the 21st century still fixating on English-French relations, a house divided against itself, foolishly hoping to survive or prosper as a first rank industrial nation.

There are, of course, those who will say there is no time for this process because the timetable is in the hands of Quebec and the current federal government. I do not believe this to be the case. There is a tide in the affairs of men, and it is not governed by the whims of Robert Bourassa or Brain Mulroney.

If what Quebec is really asking for is some form of sovereignty-association, then it needs someone credible to negotiate with. The timetable of such negotiations must be agreeable to both parties or no such negotiation can take place. In addition, neither the Bourassa administration nor the Mulroney administration has any real mandate to conduct such a negotiation. Real mandates to conduct negotiations of this magnitude cannot be achieved through referenda alone; they require elections. And an agreement negotiated by the federal government or the Quebec government without such a real mandate would be as worthless as the Meech Lake accord.

In other words, I am saying that the great Canadian constitutional negotiation – the real thing, not a charade – cannot proceed in earnest until a Quebec provincial election and a federal general election have been held.

The principal issue in that Quebec provincial election will be "Who really speaks for the New Quebec, and who should be entrusted to negotiate on its behalf with the representatives of New Canada?"

The principal issue in the next federal general election will be "Who speaks for New Canada, and who should be entrusted to negotiate on its behalf with the representative of the New Quebec?"

Any political party leader who cavalierly seeks to occupy that position for purely partisan or personal reasons is a fool, for he or she will face a task even more difficult and dangerous than that which faced Macdonald in 1867.

But it is our task as Reformers, and my task as your leader, to so position and conduct ourselves in the months ahead that we will not be found wanting or deficient should Canadians ask us to shoulder a portion of that awesome responsibility.

Conclusion

In conclusion, I have no hesitancy in asking Canadians to get on the road to New Canada. A Canadian is by definition someone whose heritage includes the acceptance of the challenge to leave an Old Country for a New Country. Even our aboriginal peoples have in their legends the story of a "Long Journey" when they too came from somewhere else. None of us would be here tonight if one of our ancestors had not accepted that challenge.

Of course, there will always be those who will say, "You can't get to New Canada from Old Canada; it cannot be done."

A dozen other countries in eastern Europe may be writing new constitutions and reorganizing their economies, but someone will say it can't be done here in Canada. The Berlin Wall can be torn down, but some will say that Canadians must live forever with the walls that separate Quebec from the rest of Canada or that separate region from region. Other countries can reform their constitutions through constitutional conventions and referendums, and replace tired old political parties with new ones, but some will say, "That's not the Canadian way and it can't be done here."

The negative thinkers who take this line are the same type of people who said to Columbus, "You'll never get to the New World, you'll fall off the edge" – who said to the first French and English settlers, "You'll never survive there, you won't last the first winter."

These are the same type of people who said to Alexander Mackenzie, "You'll never get to the Pacific or the Arctic, you'll either drown or turn back" – who said to Sir John A. Macdonald, "You can't build a railway across the continent you can't get across the Shield, or through the Rockies."

These are the same type of people who said, "You can't grow grain on the Canadian Prairies, the season's too short," or "You can't get oil out of tar sand."

Every generation of Canadians has been buffeted by the cold winds of these negative voices. Old Canada was built in defiance of those who said it couldn't be done, and New Canada will be built in defiance of the same voices, no matter how loud they are or what positions they hold.

And so I ask you:

• Can we define a New Canada to replace the Old Canada that is dying?

• Can we leap the barriers of narrow vision and negativism, and for once in our lives conduct ourselves like Big Canadians worthy of this vast territory we call our home?

• Can we get on the road to New Canada by the next federal election, by electing genuine Reformers to the next Parliament?

These are the questions which I propose, with your direction and support, to ask ever last Canadian who will listen over the next two years.

And if Canadians show the resolve and enthusiasm that you have demonstrated – if enough of our fellow Canadians will not only say, "Yes, we can!" but also "Yes, we will!" – then New Canada is much closer than we imagine.

Source: Canadian Speeches, vol. 5, no. 3 (May 1991), 27-33.

Lewis Mackenzie (1940–)

"Goodbye to Sarajevo"

Major-General Lewis Mackenzie was born in Truro, Nova Scotia, joined the Queen's Own Rifles as a career officer, and served in a series of peacekeeping operations in the Middle East, Cyprus, Vietnam, and Central America. In 1992 he was appointed chief of staff of the United Nations Protection Force (UNPROFOR) between Croatia and Serbia in the former Yugoslavia. He arrived in Sarajevo to set up his headquarters, only to find a merciless war exploding around him.

Canada's tradition of international peacekeeping dates back to the Suez campaign of 1956. Lester Pearson, Canada's secretary of state for external affairs, suggested the stationing of UN troops along the Suez Canal, separating Israeli and Egyptian forces. The UN Emergency Force was created, involving Canadian troops and under the command of a Canadian officer, Lieutenant-General E.L.M. Burns (1897–1985). Pearson was awarded the Nobel Peace Prize for his efforts.

Since then Canadian peacekeeping forces have served in a variety of world trouble spots, including the Congo in 1960, Cyprus in 1964, the Golan Heights from 1974, and the former Yugoslavia and Rwanda in the 1990s. Canada has developed substantial expertise, and acquired international prestige, in the field of peacekeeping. In part, this derives from Canada's non-threatening status as a middle power, its reputation of tolerance and diversity at home, and the bilingual capability of its armed forces. For many Canadians, Canada's peacekeeping role is an important and proud element of a national identity.

In this selection, General Mackenzie looks back on his final days in Sarajevo. The account illustrates the horrors of the ethnic conflict raging in the former Yugoslavia, and it offers a matter-of-fact tribute to the courage and professionalism of Canada's soldiers in the face of very real dangers.

JULY 27–AUGUST 1 Over the next few days, Steve Gagnon and I visited the Canadian combat engineers in Sectors West and North. They were involved in everything from lifting mines and booby traps to opening vehicle routes by removing rubble. Both the Serb and Croatian armies had tremendous respect for their professionalism and, in some instances, would not move into a mined area unless they were accompanied by a Canadian soldier.

I visited one location on the afternoon of July 30 where there was a major minefield operation underway, controlled by our engineers. I crawled into the back of one of our APCS* that was being used as the command post for the operation. Sitting in front of a large map was a Canadian master corporal with two radios. I asked him, "Who are you talking to?"

He replied, "Well, sir, I have a Croatian colonel on this side and a Serbian lieutenant-colonel on the other."

"And you are controlling the operation by telling them what to do?"

"Yes, sir."

To me, that said it all about the quality of the soldiers we manage to attract and keep in the Canadian Armed Forces. Here was a young man trained on the first rung of the leadership ladder as a master corporal, and he was totally at ease and confident while controlling two foreign colonels in a complex and dangerous operation. There was certainly nothing wrong with the quality of our soldiers; we just needed more of them.

On the morning of July 31, I thanked Mike Gauthier for the visit to see his boys and congratulated him on commanding such a positive and happy unit. My old friend, Alex Morrison, Executive Director of the Canadian Institute for Strategic Studies, was supposed to fly with Steve and me to Sarajevo. Unfortunately, his plane was late arriving from Canada, and so we had to leave without him.

Steve and I stepped out of the aircraft and onto the runway in Sarajevo, and knew we were "home." Dobrinja was still the scene of sporadic fighting; mortar fire and the sound of exploding artillery rounds could be heard around the city. We were briefed that someone from the Presidency had called to say that they had intercepted a Bosnian-Serb radio message giving orders for "MacKenzie and the PTT [Post, Telegraph, Telephones] to be destroyed tonight." Hmmm, I thought, it's nice to be back.

This time I could say a legitimate goodbye to our folks working and living at the PTT building. They were under a lot of pressure following the deaths of two Ukrainian soldiers just before my arrival. The Ukrainian unit had been manning our one remaining counter-bombardment radar position overlooking Sarajevo from the north, and had come under fire. Two were dead and a number of others seriously injured. There was significant circumstantial evidence that their trench had been grenaded by TDF [Bosnian Muslim] soldiers who had illegally dug in closer than fifty metres to the UN position, in their continuing

---

* Armoured personnel carriers.

quest to shield themselves from Serbian fire. As usual, it was never possible to prove which side had actually carried out the cowardly act.

Just before dark, Steve and I went back to the airport to spend the night with Michel and the last group of his Van Doos. We had a quiet meal in the customs building, after which I spoke to most of the soldiers in "N" Company and the battalion's headquarters personnel. Approximately 300 were present, so I had a good chance to tell them all how proud I was of what they had done, and particularly the spirit they had shown while doing it.

Since a lot of firing was going on in Dobrinja, it was difficult to sleep. This was my first and last night at the airport itself, so I stood back from the window and watched the fireworks for hours, mesmerized by the beauty of it all, yet, at the same time, realizing that every explosion represented more deaths and suffering in a war that should never have started, and probably never would end until there was no one left to care.

Naturally, I had just fallen asleep when it was time to get up at 0330. After a quick breakfast, three cups of coffee and a cigarette, we mounted up in Michel's APC and drove 100 metres to the airport tarmac.

It never failed to impress me as a commanding officer how a few simple words of direction could result in complex operations being carried out so well. Michel had ordered everyone to be on the airport parking apron at 0400 ready to go. Following his order, years of training, practice, knowledge and regimental spirit kicked in, and 400-plus soldiers had

started working to a common purpose. The chain of command from major to captain to lieutenant to warrant officer to sergeant to master corporal to private all sang the same tune, while the sergeants-major kept an eye on everyone and everything. Vehicles were fuelled and maintained, weapons and ammunition checked, equipment stowed, groups within the convoy arranged with individuals designated in charge, route cards prepared, schedules issued, sleeping arrangements made, and sentries posted. And all without fuss or fanfare.

Just before the sun came up, the first convoy group headed off towards Lukavica en route to the main Belgrade-Zagreb highway some twelve hours away. I said goodbye to Michel and wished him well: "You have every reason to be proud of what your unit has done here, Michel. It rates a chapter in your regimental history. Good luck, I'll see you in Canada."

During the next hour, over 100 vehicles crawled off the runway on their way back to Croatia. A red glow from some burning buildings in Dobrinja, less than 200 metres away, complemented the taillights of the APCs as they disappeared into the darkness, creating an eerie atmosphere around the entire scene.

As the last vehicle, an APC, started to move, I stepped in front of it and shook the hands of each member of the crew and their sergeant. I thanked them for all their good work, stepped back and watched them drive off down the runway.

It was without a doubt the happiest moment of my life. They weren't safely back in Croatia yet, but over 800 Canadian soldiers had spent a month in one of the most dangerous places in the world, and they'd all left alive. Corporal Reid had lost his foot, and eighteen others had sustained injuries from shrapnel and snipers' bullets, and that was bad enough – but they were alive. All things considered, that was a pretty good outcome. I thought a small prayer of thanks – to God and our regimental system that produces such good units and soldiers.

Colonel d'Avout and Lieutenant-Colonel de Stabenrath had kindly organized a farewell breakfast for Steve and me in the terminal building. It was a very classy affair, in stark contrast to our surroundings. The media were allowed in, and d'Avout and I signed a certificate of handover of command. He said some overly nice words, and I responded in my halting French: "*Vous soldats de la France à Sarajevo, écrivez une autre chapitre de l'histoire militaire de la France. La France et la reste du monde sont fiers de vous.*"

We were scheduled to depart on a Canadian Hercules; however, following the dictum of changing your routine at the last minute for security reasons, we climbed on board an American aircraft thirty minutes after our scheduled departure time and flew to Zagreb, which would be the new location of UNPROFOR's headquarters.

As we took off from Sarajevo airport for the last time, I watched French soldiers moving into the dug-in positions left by Michel's battalion. The surrounding area was pockmarked with shell craters; the roads were blocked by burnt-out vehicles. Hardly a building was undamaged, and black smoke was rising from the centre of the city. But as we reached a few thousand feet, the city was transformed into a patchwork of red tile roofs and green parks against a blue sky. Sarajevo was beautiful again: my less than perfect eyesight was unable to see the scars of war as we gained altitude. Wouldn't it be wonderful, I thought, if it could look like that again down at street level. I glanced over at Dobrinja. Even from that distance, I could see buildings burning.

Source: Lewis Mackenzie, *Peacekeeper: The Road to Sarajevo* (Vancouver: Douglas and McIntyre, 1993), 320-3.

Elijah Harper (1942–)

"No Ordinary Hero"

To some Canadians, especially those of the First Nations, Elijah Harper is a hero; to others, especially from Quebec, he is a villain. He is known as the man who, almost singlehanded, prevented the ratification of the Meech Lake Accord in 1990. That accord was designed to complete the process begun in 1992 by bringing Quebec into the new Canadian constitution with recognition as a "distinct society."

Harper is a Canadian native (Ojibway-Cree) leader and provincial and federal politician. He was chief of the Red Sucker Lake band in Manitoba from 1978 to 1981, and from 1981 to 1992 he served in the Manitoba Legislature and as a provincial cabinet minister. In 1993 he was elected to the House of Commons, but he failed to regain his seat in the 1997 federal elections.

In June 1990 Harper, clasping an eagle feather in his hand, used procedural delays to block ratification of the Meech Lake Accord, which he felt did not adequately address the concerns of First Nation Canadians. Thus, the accord failed to get the required number of provincial endorsements, and time ran out. Indian leaders in Canada heaped praise on Harper; one of them called him "our Wayne Gretzky." In the following introduction to his book *No Ordinary Hero*, Harper eloquently explains his position.

In 1987, closed-door negotiations among Canada's provincial and territorial governments and the prime minister resulted in a proposal to amend the Canadian constitution – the Meech Lake Accord. The process that led to the accord was, as one constitutional expert describes it, "rushed, secret and elitist."

The gatherings clearly showed that little had changed since European settlers first came to our land. There was still no representation by or consultation with aboriginal peoples. Yet, the Meech Lake Accord touched on concerns critical to Canada's native people: reform of the Senate, Supreme Court of Canada appointments, future constitutional conferences, the amending formula, fisheries and immigration.

The main purpose of the accord was formally to embrace the province of Quebec. The document was based upon the valid concept of Quebec as a distinct society within Canada. Aboriginal people are not against the right of Quebec to their own distinct society. Quebec *is*

a distinct society. The people of Quebec have their own language, culture and system of law; they have their own identity, history and vision of the future. Of course they are a distinct society. So are aboriginal people.

The accord totally ignored the integrity of aboriginal peoples as distinct societies. In referring to the "two founding nations," the architects of the accord neglected to acknowledge the equally legitimate place of aboriginal people within the Canadian federation.

This was just one example of the way politics has always been used to silence aboriginal people. The old style of politics has done more to damage this country than anything else I can think of.

Just before the accord died, the prime minister offered aboriginal people several things to get me to say yes instead of no to the accord: conferences on aboriginal issues, a future commitment to constitutional recognition, a joint definition of treaty rights and a royal commission. But such promises had been made

– and broken – before. Besides, it was too little and too late.

These were days of immense pressure on me and on all legislators. It is not easy to stand apart from one's colleagues in the legislature. It is not easy to beat the consequences of a failed constitutional proposal.

But we are the First Nations of this country. We need to be recognized for the great contributions we have made. We shared our land and our resources with those who came here. We cared about these people and helped them to survive. Yet our contribution and our role as the original peoples of this land are not even recognized in the constitution. As a Canadian and an aboriginal person, I could not support an amendment to the supreme law of the country that failed to recognize the place of all the founding cultures of the federation. The suffering of native people is too great.

Aboriginal people in Canada die on average ten years younger than other Canadians. Three out of ten aboriginal families have no furnaces or heat in their homes, yet Canada has one of the highest standards of living in the world. Thirty-four per cent have no indoor plumbing; our homes are overcrowded and in poor condition. About 45 per cent of aboriginal people are on social assistance. Few of our people are in secondary schools. Only 5 per cent graduate from secondary school. In my province, Manitoba, aboriginal people comprise 7 per cent of the population, yet they make up 45 per cent of the jail population. Family income on reserves is about $10,000, less than half the national average. Alcoholism,

drunkenness and solvent abuse are epidemic on some reserves, and we suffer the negative stereotyping that naturally follows from that. Unemployment is about 66 per cent; on some reserves it is as high as 90 per cent.

Even our languages are in danger. Many have already become extinct. Our religions were forbidden for long enough that much has been forgotten.

But these are only statistics. I cannot bring to you the despair. I cannot bring to you the fifteen-year-old boy in Winnipeg who will never share a bright future because that child was so depressed by what he saw every day that he took his own belt and hanged himself.

As aboriginal people, we expect to be treated fairly. Meech Lake didn't do that, the Charlottetown Accord didn't do that, and that is why aboriginal people said no and will continue to say no until we are treated as equals in our own land. We are not interested in short-term solutions. We are fighting for our children, our culture, our heritage and what we believe in.

Some progress has been made. We have achieved much in the arts, in athletics, among our community leadership, and in business. While state action has often been misdirected or the product of dubious political will, we have also seen attempts by governments, often with good will, to make improvements.

Building the future is more than saying no to that which is wrong. It is also saying yes to that which is fair and just. It is shaping the days, years and centuries to come with our ideas and our aspirations. It is about building bonds and coalitions with others who share our conditions or seek our vision of the future.

Some things are going to have to change. First, we as aboriginal people are going to have to work together as we did before governments developed their policies of dividing and conquering. They almost worked. We have been kept weak by those tactics. We have been divided.

We must attack our problems on two levels. We must attack them as individual problems and we must work to eradicate their origins. We must change personal circumstances and the system. We must build houses for the homeless, but we must also build better communities around them. We must cure the sick, but we must also eliminate the poor water, inadequate sanitation, poor nutrition and poverty that make our people sick. If we don't solve all our problems on those two levels, we will be eternally fighting against a current over which we have no control.

Most important, we must regain control over our future. We must take back what we never gave up. We must become fully self-governing again. We must carry on the visions and dreams of our forefathers of what this country, our homeland, should be.

I have always said that it was an honour and a privilege to have been elected the first treaty Indian in the Manitoba legislature. After Meech Lake, three other aboriginal leaders in Manitoba were elected. We need many more aboriginal people elected across this country.

This is one part of the work we have ahead of us.

We must redefine our First Nations so that they reflect our traditional values in a modern context. It has been our own constitution, our principles and values that have kept us strong. We must keep our eye on the future by never losing sight of our past.

Those few weeks during Meech Lake were a difficult time for all of us. The pressures were great. I stood to represent the shame and anger felt by the majority of Canadians over the betrayal by the Canadian government of the fairness and justice on which our nation purports to be founded. Personally, I can never thank aboriginal people across the country enough for their support, for their show of solidarity. I did not act alone. Through them I found strength. I had the collective will and the prayers of my people behind me.

After enduring so many years of injustice, aboriginal people are working to redress the inequities imposed upon our nations and communities. My role in Meech Lake was one small contribution to the struggle of aboriginal people for recognition and rights. I was proud to be able to advance the cause from within the political structure.

On June 23, 1990, when hundreds of aboriginal people held candles aloft and sang a traditional Cree song of thanksgiving, they were celebrating the death of the Meech Lake Accord and a rebirth of our people. There was born a new pride and a knowledge that we can make a difference, that we can direct the future of our country.

During those days when I stood in the legislature to speak for aboriginal people, our voice was one. I could feel the strength of all our people, a generation of our people, giving strength to my voice. In unity there is strength, in unity there is power, in unity there is hope. It is a feeling I never want to lose. It is a feeling I know our people felt every day hundreds of years ago, and it is a feeling I want all aboriginal people to share again.

Source: Elijah Harper with Pauline Comeau, *No Ordinary Hero* (Vancouver: Douglas and McIntyre, 1993), 1-4.

Jean Chrétien (1934–)

On Veterans

Jean Chrétien is one of Canada's most experienced political leaders. Born in Shawinigan, Quebec, he was first elected to Parliament in 1963. He held several different Cabinet portfolios in the Liberal governments of Lester Pearson and Pierre Trudeau, and, after serving as leader of the Opposition, he became prime minister in 1993. His government was re-elected in 1997.

Chrétien is best known as a strong federalist. He played an important role in the 1980 Quebec referendum and in the repatriation of the Constitution with a Charter of Rights and Freedoms in 1982. Styling himself as an average Canadian, the "p'tit gars de Shawinigan," he often wears his patriotism on his sleeve, as in a series of speeches in which he talked passionately about "his" Rocky Mountains – despite his not being a westerner – and their beauty.

The fiftieth anniversary of the landing on Normandy was an occasion of note throughout the Western world. Canada was no exception, and a large contingent of Canadian veterans returned to Normandy to mark the event. Prime Minister Chrétien paid tribute to the heroic veterans of the Second World War, at the same time linking their efforts to the vision of a strong, tolerant, and united Canada.

We are gathered here, on this calm and peaceful day, to remember a very different day 50 years ago.

We are reunited on this calm and peaceful day to commemorate a very different day, 50 years ago, when the winds of freedom swept these beaches.

On the beach behind us, Canadians gave their lives so the world would be a better place. They gave their lives so we – all of us, Canadians and Europeans – could live free, decent lives. Free of fear and oppression.

Who were these young men? They are buried not far from here.

On their graves you will find names like McMillan and Nillson and Cormier and Freedman. Names like Cherulli and Bergeron and Osborne. Names like and Silverberg and Topolnitski. Names like Sigurdson and May and Chartrand and Stinson.

The men in these graves came from towns like Estevan and Galt and Rivière du Loup and Corner Brook and Prince George and the Rama First Nation Reserve. They came from every region. From every province.

Some were not even born in Canada. They were Canadians by choice. And they died on the beaches of the continent they had left behind, fighting for the country they adopted – the country they loved.

There are some who would say these men had nothing in common. Not geography. Not language. Not background. Not religion. Or ethnicity. Or color.

But they had one thing very much in common. They were all part of a young nation. A new kind of nation. Where the ancient hatreds of the past were no match for the promise of the future. Where people believed they should speak different languages, worship in different ways, and live in peace.

They died on the shores and in the fields of a Europe consumed by hate and terror. A Europe under the yoke of evil. A Europe in which whole races were being wiped out, where freedom and dissent were crushed.

Three hundred and fifty-nine of them died on these beaches the first day alone, 50 years ago today. In the days and weeks that followed, during the battle of Normandy, more than 5,000 of them died in the fields and country-side around us. And many more died before Europe was finally liberated.

They did not die as anglophones or franco-phones, as Easterners or Westerners, as Christians or Jews, as immigrants or natives. They died as Canadians.

Today we honor these men and what they died for. And we thank their comrades – the thousands who fought and triumphed and lived. The veterans who were here on the Longest Day 50 years ago. And who are with us today.

The men who cradled and comforted their fallen comrades. Who buried them. And who fought on. With courage and determination.

Today you are showing a new courage. Many of you are retracing your steps of 50 years ago. Reliving the great adventure and the great horror.

This is *your* day. And on behalf of the people of Canada, I say *thank you*.

Thank you for your sacrifices half a century ago. And thank you for your greatest achievement of all – your legacy.

Your efforts here on these beaches, along with your comrades from the other allied countries, helped turn the tide of war.

You liberated the people of this region. You helped them rebuild their lives and their communities. And you began the liberation of this continent after a long and brutal nightmare.

You helped secure not just an historic victory, but – even more important – a lasting, solid peace.

Your other accomplishment was just as remarkable. You gave birth to the modern Canada.

A small nation of 12 million people, our country took on challenges and responsibilities out of all proportion with our small size. One million men and women served in uniform. Millions more served at home – in industry, at home, on farms. Canada became a major fighting force and an important arsenal of democracy.

And here on Juno Beach, we began the liberation of Europe not under an imperial flag, not commanded by foreign officers – but as Canadians.

In this, the greatest invasion the world has ever known, Canada was a full partner with our allies the United States and Great Britain.

Not one of 30 nations, not one of 20 nations, but one of three.

So that day 50 years ago was not only a turning point in the war. It was a turning point in our development as a proud, independent nation. It was our coming of age.

Canada entered the war as a young nation, barely out of its infancy. We emerged from the war as an adult nation – a major industrial power and a force for peace in the world.

Today, we recall a valiant victory. We join the people of Normandy and France in celebrating the triumph of justice over injustice, of freedom over its foes. We pay tribute to the brave efforts of all our allies and our friends.

We also thank the people of Normandy for their warmth and their generosity over the years to the thousands of our veterans and their families who have returned. Your hospitality now recalls the smiles and the support our soldiers saw on that day long ago.

Half a century of peace and security. A modern, robust nation that is the envy of people all over the world. *This* is the debt we owe to the Canadians who came ashore 50 years ago.

Of course, it is a debt we can never completely repay. But it is one we must remember every day of our lives.

We have the obligation to strive for tolerance, understanding and generosity at home. We can never become complacent about democracy and freedom.

That is the best monument we could build to the heroes of D-Day. A society that lives up to the ideals and values that they fought and died for.

To those of you who fought here 50 years ago, to your comrades who died in battle and the ones who are no longer with us, *you* won a great and lasting peace.

It is our solemn pledge to you that as Canadians – at home and abroad – we will continue to *earn* that peace.

Source: Speech delivered in Courseulles, France, June 6, 1944; reprinted in *Canadian Speeches: Issues of the Day*, vol. 8, no. 4 (July 1994), 40-1.

Denise Chong

"BEING CANADIAN"

Denise Chong is a Canadian-born economist who worked for Prime Minister Pierre Elliott Trudeau in the 1970s. In her book *The Concubine's Children* (1994), she told how she rediscovered the courageous and tragic story of what her Chinese forebears had done so that she would be born and grow up Canadian.

It was the kind of story others – perhaps even she – would be told to suppress or to glorify, but, as Denise Chong argues here, only truth can add real nobility to our roots. Her speech, delivered during Citizenship Week, 1995, is a stirring appeal to honesty and courage – and to pride in the country all our varied ancestors helped to create.

I ask myself what it means to be a Canadian. I was lucky enough to be born in Canada. So I look back at the price paid by those who made the choice that brought me such luck.

South China at the turn of the century became the spout of the tea pot that was China. It poured out middle class peasants like my grandfather, who couldn't earn a living at home. He left behind a wife and child. My grandfather was 36 when exclusion came. Lonely and living a penurious existence, he worked at a sawmill on the mud flats of the Fraser River, where the Chinese were third on the pay scale behind "Whites" and "Hindus." With the door to Chinese immigration slammed shut, men like him didn't dare even go home for a visit, for fear Canada might bar their re-entry. With neither savings enough to go home for good, nor the means once in China to put rice in the mouths of his wife and child there, my grandfather wondered when, if

ever, be could return to the bosom of a family. He decided to purchase a concubine, a second wife, to join him in Canada.

The concubine, at age 17, got into Canada on a lie. She got around the exclusion law in the only way possible: she presented the authorities with a Canadian birth certificate. It had belonged to a woman born in Ladner, British Columbia, and a middleman sold it to my grandfather at many times the price of the old head tax. Some years later, the concubine and my grandfather went back to China with their two Vancouver-born daughters. They lived for a time under the same roof as my grandfather's first wife. The concubine became pregnant. Eight months into her pregnancy, she decided to brave the long sea voyage back so that her third child could be born in Canada. His false Canadian birth certificate would get her in. Accompanied by only my grandfather, she left China. Three days after the boat docked, on the second-floor of a tenement on a back alley in Vancouver's Chinatown, she gave birth to my mother.

Canada remained inhospitable. Yet my grandparents *chose* to keep Canada in their future. Both gambled a heritage and family ties to take what they thought were better odds in the lottery of life. The gratitude owed them can perhaps best be expressed by my mother's brother in China – the son of my grandfather and his first wife. In the late 1980s, my mother and I found the family left behind. My uncle pressed a letter into my mother's hand on the last night of our visit. It read, in part, "As parents, who would not be concerned about the future of his or her children? I hope to get my children out of China to take root in Canada. Then, the roots of the tree will grow downwards and the leaves will be luxuriant. We will be fortunate, the children will be fortunate and our children's children will be fortunate. The family will be glorious and future generations will have a good foundation . . ."

My own sense, four generations on, of being Canadian is one of belonging. I belong to a family. I belong to a community of values. I didn't get to choose my ancestors, but I can try to leave the world a better place for the generations that follow. The life I lead begins before and lingers after my time.

The past holds some moral authority over us. Rather than forget it, we must acknowledge that we have one, and learn the lessons of it. We have to be vigilant about looking past the stereotypes and seeing the contrasting truths. It means understanding that someone's grandfather didn't change the family name from French to English to forsake his heritage, but to make it easier to find a job. It means lifting the charge against the early Chinese of having no family values by seeing how the laws and history cleaved their families in two. It means going to the Legion and looking at a Sikh and seeing the veteran as well as the turban.

If we don't, we won't see that the layers of injustice cut deep. It happened in my own family. My grandfather couldn't afford a concubine. To repay the cost of my grandmother's false papers and passage to Canada, he indentured her as a tea house waitress. In the bachelor societies of the Chinatowns of their day, a *kay toi neu* was seen as one and the same as a prostitute – both were there to woo men to spend money. My grandmother would spend the rest of her lifetime trying to climb up from that bottom rung of society. I, too, condemned my *Popo*, until I learned what she had been fighting against all her life.

Despite the luck of my mother's birth, discrimination continued to cast a long shadow over her growing-up years. Her parents separated. In neither of their lifetimes would either find work outside Chinatown. My mother knew too well the path to the pawn shop where she accompanied her mother to translate as she bargained her jewelry to pay her gambling debts. The wall on my mother's side of the bed at the rooming house was wallpapered with academic certificates. My mother wanted to become a doctor. She didn't know that it would be years after her time before the faculty of medicine at the University of British Columbia would admit its first Chinese student. Despite the narrow confines of her life, the opportunity of education gave my mother a chance to dream.

Eventually, exclusion against Chinese immigration was lifted and other barriers of discrimination began to fall. My mother's generation was the last to grow up in Chinatown. Gradually, the Chinese became part of the larger society. In 1947, my mother no longer had to call herself Chinese. With exclusion lifted, and the new citizenship act that Canada brought in that same year, for the first time in her life my mother could call herself Canadian.

My parents walked out from the shadow of the past. They were determined to raise their five children as Canadians. In our own growing-up years in Prince George, my mother wanted us to be as robust as our playmates; she enriched the milk in our glasses with extra cream. My parents wanted us to take to heart the Canadian pastimes. They bought us skis to share among us. Every winter they bought us new used skates. There was a piano upstairs on which we learned to play *O Canada* for school assemblies. There was a hockey net in the basement so my brothers could practice for the pond.

My parents wanted us to understand that we were part of Canada's future. They instilled the importance of an education. They encouraged us to believe that individuals could make a difference. I remember when Mr. and Mrs. Diefenbaker came to Prince George. I remember when a dashing Pierre Trudeau made his first visit. My parents made sure we were turned out to greet every visiting dignitary. My grandparents, in their time, were barred from government jobs. I, their granddaughter, would come to work as senior economic advisor to Prime Minister Pierre Trudeau.

I am now the mother of two young children. I want to pass on a sense of what it means to be a Canadian. But what worries me as a parent, and as a Canadian, is whether we can fashion an enduring concept of citizenship that will be the glue that holds us together as a society.

Curiously, Canadian citizenship elicits the most heartfelt response outside Canada. Any Canadian who has lived or travelled abroad quickly discovers that Canadian citizenship is a coveted possession. In the eyes of the rest of the world, it stands for an enlightened and gentle society.

Can we find a strong concept of citizenship that could be shared by all Canadians when we stand on our own soil? Some would say it is unrealistic to expect a symbol to rise out of a rather pragmatic past. We spilled no revolutionary blood, as did France – where the word *citoyen* was brought into popular usage – or America. Some lament the absence of a founding myth; we don't have the equivalent of a Boston Tea Party. Others long for Canadian versions of heroes to compete with the likes of American images that occupy our living rooms and our playgrounds.

The one Canadian symbol with universal recognition is the flag. But where does the maple leaf strike a chord? Outside Canada. On the back packs of Canadian travellers. Of late, in Great Britain and Ireland, flying from the masts of boats and local fishermen as a show of support for Canada in its turbot dispute with Spain.

Some say Canadian citizenship is devalued because it is too easy to come here. But what sets Canadian society apart from others is that ours is an inclusive society. Canada's citizenship act remains more progressive than many countries. Canadians by immigration have equal status with Canadians by birth. In contrast, in western Europe, guest workers, even if they descended from those who originally came, can be sent "home" any time. In Japan, Koreans and Filipinos have no claim to the citizenship of their birth. The plight of the Palestinians in Kuwait after the Gulf War gave the lie to a "free Kuwait."

Canadian citizenship recognizes differences. It praises diversity. It is what we as Canadians *choose* to have in common with each other. It is a bridge between those who left something to make a new home here and those born here. What keeps the bridge strong is tolerance, fairness, understanding, and compassion. Citizenship has rights and responsibilities. I believe one responsibility of citizenship is to use that tolerance, fairness, understanding and compassion to leaf through the Canadian family album together.

My family story is about one family living on two sides of the globe, in a village in China and in the Chinatowns of the west coast of Canada. I knew I had to understand my grandparents' difficult and tangled decision to leave China for an unknown land. I had to understand the cultural baggage they brought, in order to see what they shed along the way and what they preserved. I had to see what they created anew as they acquired western sensibilities.

I also had to open the windows on the old Chinatowns in Canada. I had first to chip away at the layers of paint that stuck them shut, so intent had the former inhabitants been on shutting out inquiry. Some wondered why I'd want to write the story of my grandfather, who came a peasant and lived out his days alone in a rooming house. And why my grandmother, who lived by the wages and wits that came with being a *kay toi neu?* I see no honor lost in laying down the truth of their lives. It re-visits the once harsh verdict I myself had.

The same holds true for other leaves of the Canadian album. Often, the only ones whose memory is preserved are those who either prayed or worked hard, or both. But others are just as real, if not more so, with their strengths and weaknesses, triumphs and foibles. My story happens to take place in dingy rooming houses, alleyways and mah jong parlors in decaying Chinatowns. The backdrop of others may be the church basement, the union hall, school or hockey rink, or even the front porch. These stories, like mine, serve to illuminate Canada's social history.

How we tell our stories is the work of citizenship. The motive of the storyteller should be to put the story first. To speak with authenticity and veracity is to choose narrative over commentary. It is not to glorify or sentimentalize the past. It is not to sanitize our differences. Nor to rail against or to seek compensation today for injustices of bygone times. In my opinion, to try to rewrite history leads to a sense of victimization. It marginalizes Canadians. It backs away from equality in our society, for which we have worked hard to find expression.

I believe our stories ultimately tell the story of Canada itself. In all our pasts are an immigrant beginning, a settler's accomplishments and setbacks, and the confidence of a common future. We all know the struggle for victory, the dreams and the lost hopes, the pride and the shame. When we tell our stories, we look in the mirror. I believe what we will see is that Canada is not lacking in heroes. Rather, the heroes are to be found within.

The work of citizenship is not something just for the week that we celebrate citizenship every year. It is part of every breath we take. It is the work of our lifetimes.

The world is changing, and changing fast. People's lives are on the move. We travel more. We move to take new jobs, to find a bigger house, to live next to the schools we want our children to go to, to find a smaller house when they've grown up and left home. Families are far-flung, even to different continents. Children may have more than one home, a parent in each. Few of us as adults live in or can even re-visit our childhood home. Some of us cannot even return to the neighborhoods of our childhood and find the landscape familiar.

There are political pressures that could redefine Canada as we know it. Canadians continue to debate the future of the federation and question whether the country is governable. A growing regionalism could fracture the national interest. On a global scale, the trend is integration, economically and culturally. The availability and dominance of American culture crowds our ability as Canadians to find the time and space to preserve our own culture and to share it with each other. Clicking the remote control and finding the television show of our choice is a display of our consumerism, not our Canadianism. Somehow, in this rapidly changing, busy world, we have to satisfy the emotional longing for roots, for understanding who we are, and what we are.

If we do some of this work of citizenship, we will stand on firmer ground. Sharing experience will help build strength of character. It will explain our differences, yet make them less divisive. We will yell at each other less, and understand each other more. We will find a sense of identity and a common purpose. We will have something to hand down to the next generation.

My grandfather's act of immigration to the new world and the determination of my grandmother, the girl who first came here as a *kay toi neu*, to chance the journey from China back to Canada so that my mother could be born here, will stand as a gift to all future generations of my family. Knowing they came hoping for a better life makes it easy to love both them and this country.

In the late 1980s, I would find myself in China, on a two-year stint living in Peking and working as a writer. In a letter to my mother in Prince George, I confessed that, despite the predictions of friends back in Canada, I was finding it difficult to feel any "Chineseness." My mother wrote back: "You're Canadian, not Chinese. Stop trying to feel anything." She was right. I stopped such contrivances. I was Canadian; it was that which embodied the values of my life.

Source: Denise Chong, "Being Canadian," in *Canadian Speeches: Issues of the Day*, vol. 9, no. 2 (May 1995), 17-22.